Discover
New Zealand

Experience the best
of New Zealand

This edition written and researched by

Charles Rawlings-Way,
Brett Atkinson, Sarah Bennett,
Peter Dragicevich, Lee Slater

Auckland p51

Rotorua & the Centre p95

Marlborough & Nelson p189

p149

Wellington & Lower North Island

p225

Christchurch & Central South

p267

Queenstown & the South

Contents

Discover

Contents

On the Road

This Is New Zealand

New Zealand is a ludicrously photogenic place. Across the country, gorgeous vistas and lush panoramas open up like scenes from a wilderness documentary. Drag your eyes away from the view and you'll discover rich Maori culture, fabulous museums, a hyperactive sports scene (bungy jumping, skiing, skydiving, white-water rafting...) and the nation's overriding passion for rugby.

To fuel your adventures, stop by a local organic farmers market and stock up on goodies. You'll also find Maori faves such as paua (abalone) and kina (sea urchin) on many restaurant menus. Thirsty? NZ sauvignon blanc has been collecting trophies for decades, the craft-beer scene is booming and coffee culture is firmly entrenched.

After you're fed and watered, it's time to head outside. Sublime forests, mountains, lakes, beaches and fiords await – an accessible, remarkable web of wilderness that has made NZ one of the best hiking (locals call it 'tramping') destinations on earth. Spending a few dreamy hours wandering through the wilds will cure what ails you.

Rugby fans will know all about NZ's deified national team, the All Blacks. World Cup winners in 2011 and favourites to go back-to-back in 2015, the 'ABs' would never have become world-beaters without their awesome Maori players. But rugby is just one example of how Maori culture impresses itself on contemporary Kiwi life. Across NZ you can join in a *hangi* (Maori feast), visit a *marae* (meeting house) or catch a cultural performance, usually involving a blood-curdling *haka* (war dance).

Also for your consideration is the fact that NZ is a remarkably easy place to visit. On-the-road frustrations are rare: buses and trains are punctual, roads are in good nick, ATMs proliferate and pickpockets are practically nonexistent. This decent nation is a place where you can relax and enjoy (rather than endure) your holiday.

Skiing at Treble Cone (p281), near Wanaka
KIERAN SCOTT/GETTY IMAGES ©

> Sublime forests, mountains, lakes, beaches and fiords await

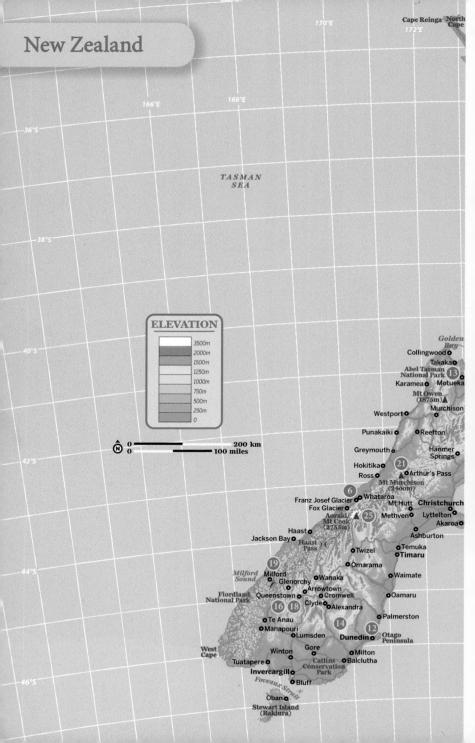

Map labels (North Island and upper South Island):

Great Exhibition Bay
174°E · 176°E · 178°E
Bay of Islands
Kaitaia ⑨
Russell
Kaikohe
Opononi
Northland
Whangarei
Dargaville
Great Barrier Island
Kaipara Harbour
Wellsford
Hauraki Gulf
Helensville
Whitianga
① ② Auckland ㉔
Pukekohe Drury Coromandel Peninsula
Thames
Ngaruawahia Huntly Tauranga Te Kaha Te Araroa
Raglan Hamilton Bay of Plenty
㉒ Cambridge Ruatoria
Kawhia Waikato Whakatane Opotiki
Waitomo Caves Rotorua Tokomaru Bay
⑦ Te Kuiti ③ ⑪ Tolaga Bay
Taupo Gisborne
New Plymouth Whanganui National Park Turangi Wairoa
Mt Taranaki (Mt Egmont) ⑧ Tongariro National Park Hawke Bay
(2518m) ▲ Stratford Mt Ruapehu (2797m) ⑰ Napier
Opunake Ohakune Hastings
Hawera
Whanganui
Waipukurau
⑩ Dannevirke
Palmerston North Woodville
Marlborough Sounds Levin
Tasman Bay Upper Hutt
Lower Hutt Masterton
Nelson Picton
⑮ ★ WELLINGTON
Blenheim ④ ㉓
Cook Strait Cape Palliser
⑤ Kaikoura
Pegasus Bay
⑳ Banks Peninsula
SOUTH PACIFIC OCEAN

25
Top Highlights

25 New Zealand's Top Highlights

Auckland Harbour & Hauraki Gulf

A yachty's paradise, the island-studded Hauraki Gulf is Auckland's aquatic playground, providing ample excuse for the City of Sails' pleasure fleet to breeze into action. Despite the busy maritime traffic, the gulf has its own resident pods of whales and dolphins. Rangitoto Island is an icon of the city, its near-perfect volcanic cone providing the backdrop for many a tourist snapshot. Yet it's Waiheke Island (p82), with its beautiful beaches, acclaimed wineries and upmarket eateries, that is Auckland's most popular island escape. Vineyards and olive trees, Waiheke Island

1

2

IAN TROWER/GETTY IMAGES ©

Urban Auckland

Embraced by two harbours and liberally sprinkled with extinct volcanoes, Auckland (p60) isn't your average metropolis. It's regularly rated one of the world's most liveable cities, and it's blessed with good beaches, is flanked by wine regions and sustains thriving dining, drinking and live-music scenes. Cultural festivals are celebrated with gusto in this ethnically diverse city, which has the distinction of having the world's largest Pacific Islander population.

Geothermal Rotorua

The first thing you'll notice about Rotorua (p104) is the sulphur smell – this geothermal hot spot whiffs like old socks! But as the locals point out, volcanic by-products are what everyone is here to see: geysers, bubbling mud and boiling pools of mineral-rich water. Rotorua is unique: a fact exploited by some fairly commercial local businesses. But you don't have to spend a fortune – there are plenty of affordable (and free) volcanic encounters to be had in parks, Maori villages or just along the roadside.

Champagne Pool, Wai-O-Tapu Thermal Wonderland (p111)

The Best...
Geothermal Hot Springs

HOT WATER BEACH
Dig your own spa pool in the Coromandel sand. (p92)

POLYNESIAN SPA
Rotorua's long-running bathhouse has lake-edge hot pools. (p107)

HANMER SPRINGS
Let it all hang out at this subalpine hot spot. (p248)

SPA PARK HOT SPRING
Free-and-easy swimming at Taupo's thermal swimming hole. (p125)

PHOTOGRAPHER RUSM/GETTY IMAGES ©

The Best...
City Life

LIVE MUSIC IN DUNEDIN
Reggae, garage, dub,
hip-hop... Dunedin rocks.
(p301)

**WELLINGTON'S
CAFFEINE SCENE**
Wide-awake Wellington
cranks out serious coffee.
(p166)

SHOPPING IN AUCKLAND
Buy-up big brands, rum-
mage for retro or browse
the bookshelves. (p79)

PARTY IN QUEENSTOWN
Cuddle-up with après-ski
drinkers. (p284)

**CHRISTCHURCH ON THE
REBOUND**
Resourceful and inspira-
tional, 'Chch' continues to
reinvent itself postquake.
(p237)

Wellington

4

Named the 'coolest little capital in the world' in Lonely Planet's *Best in Travel,* windy Wellington (p158) lives up to the mantle by keeping things fresh and dynamic. It's been long famed for a vibrant arts and music scene and fuelled by excellent espresso and more restaurants per head than New York, but now a host of craft-beer bars have elbowed-in on the action. Edgy yet sociable, colourful yet often dressed in black, Wellington is big on the unexpected and unconventional. Erratic weather only adds to the excitement.

Kaikoura

5

First settled by Maori with their keen nose for seafood, Kaikoura (p205; meaning 'to eat crayfish') is now New Zealand's best spot for both consuming and communing with marine life. Crayfish is still king, but on fishing tours you can hook into other edible wonders of the deep. Whales are definitely off the menu, but you're almost guaranteed a good gander at Moby's mates on a whale-watching tour, or there's swimming with seals and dolphins.

Franz Josef & Fox Glaciers

These spectacular glaciers (p260 and p264) are remarkable for many reasons, including their rates of accumulation and descent. Short walks meander towards the glaciers' fractured faces, or you can tramp on the ice with a guide. The ultimate encounter is on a scenic flight, which provides grandstand views of Aoraki/Mt Cook, Westland forest and a seemingly endless ocean.

Walkers on Franz Josef Glacier

DAVID WALL PHOTO/GETTY IMAGES ©

OLIVER STREWE/GETTY IMAGES ©

Waitomo Caves

Waitomo (p145) is a must-see: an astonishing maze of subterranean caves, canyons and rivers perforating the northern King Country limestone. Black-water rafting is the big lure here (like white-water rafting but through a dark cave), plus glowworm grottoes, underground abseiling and more stalactites and stalagmites than you'll ever see in one place again. Above ground, Waitomo township is a quaint collaboration of businesses: a craft brewery, a cafe, a holiday park and some decent B&Bs. But don't linger in the sunlight – it's party time downstairs!

Tongariro Alpine Crossing

At the centre of the North Island, Tongariro National Park presents an alien landscape of alpine desert punctuated by three smoking, smouldering volcanoes. This track (p134) offers the perfect taste of what the park has to offer, skirting the base of two of the mountains and providing views of craters, brightly coloured lakes and the vast Central Plateau stretching out beyond. It's for these reasons that it's often rated as one of the world's best single-day wilderness walks.

Emerald Lakes

⑧

The Best...
Tramping

ABEL TASMAN COAST TRACK
Tramp through Abel Tasman National Park. Three to five days, 51km. (p219)

TONGARIRO ALPINE CROSSING
Volcanic vents, alpine vegetation and lush forest. One day, 18km. (p134)

MILFORD TRACK
Rainforest and towering mountains at Milford Sound. Five days, 53.5km. (p310)

QUEEN CHARLOTTE TRACK
Hike or bike through the scenic Marlborough Sounds. Three to five days, 71km. (p201)

BANKS PENINSULA TRACK
Rolling hills and picturesque bays. Four days, 35km. (p246)

The Best...
Maori Experiences

WHAKAREWAREWA THERMAL VILLAGE
Weaving, carving and cultural performances in Rotorua. (p105)

ONE TREE HILL (MAUNGAKIEKIE)
This volcanic cone (one of the many in Auckland) is an important historic site. (p65)

TE PAPA
Maori *marae* (meeting house), galleries and guided tours at NZ's national museum in Wellington. (p162)

RAGLAN BONE CARVING STUDIO
One of many hands-on bone-carving studios around NZ. (p140)

Bay of Islands

Turquoise waters lapping in pretty bays, dolphins frolicking at the bows of boats, pods of orcas gliding gracefully by: chances are these are the kinds of images that drew you to NZ in the first place, and these are exactly the kinds of experiences that the Bay of Islands (p316) delivers so well. Whether you're a hardened sea dog or a confirmed landlubber, there are myriad options to tempt you out on the water to explore the 150-odd islands that dot this beautiful bay. Bottlenose dolpins, Bay of Islands

STEVE CLANCY/GETTY IMAGES ©

Rugby

10

Rugby Union is NZ's national game and governing preoccupation. If your timing's good you might catch the revered national team, the All Blacks, in action. The 'ABs' are resident gods: mention Richie McCaw or Dan Carter in any conversation and you'll win friends for life. Visit the New Zealand Rugby Museum (p177) in Palmerston North, watch some kids running around a suburban field on a Saturday morning, or yell along with the locals in a small-town pub as the big men collide on the big screen.

Maori Culture

11

NZ's indigenous Maori culture is accessible and engaging: join in a *haka* (war dance); chow down at a traditional *hangi* (Maori feast cooked in the ground); carve a pendant from bone or *pounamu* (jade); learn some Maori language; or check out a cultural performance with song, dance, legends, arts and crafts. Big-city and regional museums around NZ are crammed with Maori artefacts and historical items, but this is also a living culture: vibrant, potent and contemporary. Rotorua (p112) is a top spot to experience Maori culture, with a fab regional museum and cultural performances aplenty. *Haka* performance

NEW ZEALAND'S TOP 25 HIGHLIGHTS ● ● ● 19

Otago Peninsula

The Otago Peninsula (p302) is proof there's more to the South Island's outdoor thrills than heart-stopping alpine scenery. Against a backdrop of rugged, hidden beaches and an expansive South Pacific horizon, it's very easy to come face to face with penguins, seals and sea lions. Beyond the rare yellow-eyed penguin (hoiho), other fascinating avian residents include the royal albatross. Otago Peninsula's Taiaroa Head is the world's only mainland royal albatross colony: visit in January or February for the best views of these magnificent ocean-spanning birds. Sea lions, Sandfly Bay

Abel Tasman National Park

Here's nature at its most seductive: lush green hills fringed with sandy coves, slipping gently into warm shallows before meeting a crystal-clear sea. Abel Tasman National Park (p219) is the quintessential postcard paradise, where you can put yourself in the picture assuming an endless number of poses: tramping, kayaking, swimming, or even makin' whoopee in the woods. This sweet-as corner of NZ raises the bar and keeps it there. Sea kayaking

Central Otago

Here's your chance to balance virtue and vice, all with a background of some of NZ's most starkly beautiful landscapes in Central Otago (p305). Take to two wheels to negotiate the easygoing Otago Central Rail Trail, cycling into heritage South Island towns such as Clyde and Naseby. Tuck into well-earned beers in laid-back country pubs, or linger for a classy lunch in the vineyard restaurants of Bannockburn. Other foodie diversions include Cromwell's weekly farmers market, and the summer stone-fruit harvest of the country's best orchards. Cyclists, Central Otago

14

The Best...
Foodie Experiences

EATING OUT IN AUCKLAND
Fine dining, cafes, delicatessens and food trucks. (p71)

BAY OF PLENTY KIWIFRUIT
A dozen fuzzy, ripe kiwifruit from a roadside stall costs around $1. (p120)

HOKITIKA WILDFOODS FESTIVAL
Eating insects is fun! (www.wildfoods.co.nz)

CENTRAL OTAGO
Eye-popping scenery and the best of NZ food and wine. (p305)

WEST COAST WHITEBAIT
Have a patty and a pint at a country pub. (p258)

The Best...
Wine Regions

MARLBOROUGH
NZ's biggest and best.
Don't be picky, just drink
some sauvignon blanc.
(p206)

MARTINBOROUGH
A small-but-sweet wine
region a day trip from
Wellington: easy-drinking
pinot noir. (p177)

HAWKE'S BAY
Rolling acres of chardon-
nay vines encircle Napier
and Hastings. (p185)

GIBBSTON VALLEY
A valley with a meandering
river (of wine?) in Central
Otago, near Queenstown.
(p284)

WAIPARA VALLEY
A short hop north of
Christchurch, produc-
ing spectacular riesling.
(p237)

15

Marlborough Wine Region

It's hard to avoid Marlborough sauvignon blanc in the world's liquor stores these days – crisp, zesty and drinkable, it's a global smash hit. Whether on a minibus, a bicycle or the back seat of someone's car, touring the cellar doors of the Marlborough Wine Region (p206) near Blenheim is a decadent delight. And it's not just sav blanc on offer: there's also plenty of cool-climate pinot noir, chardonnay, riesling and pinot gris to swill around the back of your palate. Left: Vineyard near Renwick; Above: Winetasting in the Marlborough Wine Region

ABOVE: PETE SEAWARD/LONELY PLANET © /LEFT: PICTUREGARDEN/GETTY IMAGES ©

Skiing & Snowboarding

16

NZ is studded with massive mountains: you'll find decent snow right through the winter season (June to October). Most of the famous slopes are on the South Island: hip Queenstown (p276) and hippie Wanaka (p289) have iconic ski runs such as Coronet Peak, the Remarkables and Treble Cone close at hand. There's also brilliant snowboarding and cross-country (Nordic) skiing here. And on the North Island, Mt Ruapehu offers the chance to ski down a volcano!

Skiing, Coronet Peak

WILL SALTER/GETTY IMAGES ©

Napier Art Deco

17

Like a cross between a film set and a 1930s time capsule, Napier (p183) was levelled by an earthquake in 1931, and was then rebuilt in high art-deco style. Must-sees include the National Tobacco Company and Daily Telegraph buildings, the sculpted live-music shell and the suburb Marewa. There are some great places to eat and drink here too: wine and welcome are right on time, even if the architecture is firmly rooted in the past.

NATIONAL TOBACCO COMPANY LTD

AMOS CHAPPLE/GETTY IMAGES ©

Queenstown

Queenstown (p276) may be renowned as the birthplace of bungy jumping, but there's more to NZ's adventure hub than leaping off a bridge attached to a giant rubber band. Against the backdrop of the jagged indigo profile of the Remarkables mountain range, travellers can spend days skiing, tramping or mountain biking, before dining in cosmopolitan restaurants or partying in some of NZ's best bars. Next-day options include hang gliding, kayaking or river rafting, or easing into your NZ holiday with sleepier detours to Arrowtown or Glenorchy. Rafting on the Shotover River

18

The Best...
Extreme Activities

BUNGY JUMPING
Hurl yourself off a perfectly good bridge/canyon/high-wire in Queenstown. (p277)

SKYDIVING
Taupo – the skydiving capital of the world. (p125)

SKIING
Hit the perfect powder on South Island slopes. (p281)

RAFTING, ABSEILING & ROCK-CLIMBING
Waitomo Caves offers black-water rafting, abseiling and rock-climbing. (p146)

MOUNTAIN BIKING
There are 100km of NZ's best mountain-bike tracks at Redwoods Whakarewarewa Forest. (p113)

EXTREME AUCKLAND
SkyWalk, SkyJump and the adventurous EcoZip Adventures. (p67)

Milford Sound

The Best...
Markets

OTAGO FARMERS MARKET
Organic fruit and veg,
Green Man beer, robust
coffee and homemade
pies. (p299)

OTARA MARKET
Auckland's multicultural
Otara Market brims with
buskers, arts and crafts,
fashions and food. (p79)

ROTORUA NIGHT MARKET
Gourmet night-bites,
buskers and local crafts on
Thursday night. (p111)

HARBOURSIDE MARKET
Wellington's obligatory
fruit-and-veg pit stop.
(p166)

Milford Sound

19

Fingers crossed you'll be
lucky enough to see Milford
Sound (p312) on a clear, sunny day. That's definitely when
the world-beating collage of
waterfalls, verdant cliffs and
peaks, and dark cobalt waters
is at its best. More likely
though is the classic Fiordland combination of mist and
drizzle, with the iconic profile
of Mitre Peak revealed slowly
through shimmering sheets
of precipitation. Either way,
keep your eyes peeled for
seals and dolphins, especially
if you're exploring NZ's most
famous fiord by kayak.

STEVE BLY/GETTY IMAGES ©

20 Akaroa & Banks Peninsula

Infused with a healthy dash of Gallic ambience, French-themed Akaroa (p245) bends languidly around one of the prettiest harbours on Banks Peninsula. Sleek dolphins and plump penguins inhabit clear waters perfect for sailing and exploring. Elsewhere on the peninsula, the spidery Summit Rd prescribes the rim of an ancient volcano, while winding roads descend to hidden bays and coves. Spend your days tramping and kayaking amid the improbable landscape and seascape, while relaxing at night in chic bistros or cosy B&B accommodation.

Akaroa

RICHARD CUMMINS/GETTY IMAGES ©

TranzAlpine

A classic scenic train journey, the *TranzAlpine* (p260) cuts clear across the country from the Pacific Ocean to the Tasman Sea in less than five hours. Yes, there's an enormous mountain range in the way – that's where the scenic part comes in. A cavalcade of tunnels and viaducts takes you up through the Southern Alps to Arthur's Pass, where the 8.5km Otira tunnel burrows right through the bedrock of NZ's alpine spine. Then it's all downhill (but only literally) to sleepy Greymouth.

Raglan Surf Safari

Laid-back, hippified and surprisingly multicultural, little Raglan (p139) is the mythical surf village you always knew was there but could never find. A few kilometres south of town are some of the best point breaks on the planet: join the hordes of floating rubber people at Manu Bay (p142) and Whale Bay (p142). We can't guarantee the perfect wave, but when a southwesterly swell is running, you'll be in line for some seriously *looong* rides. Surfing, Manu Bay

Te Papa

Dominating the Wellington waterfront, Te Papa (p162) is NZ's national museum. It's an inspiring, high-tech, interactive repository of historical and cultural remnants. And best of all, it's free! Expect plenty of Maori artefacts and culture (including a *marae*), engaging tours (a great way to see a lot in a short time), plenty of kid-friendly exhibits and a slew of innovative displays celebrating all things Kiwi. Don't miss the earthquake simulator, and the national art collection.

The Best...
Museums

TE PAPA
Interactive Kiwi culture, history and performance, plus Maori artefacts and a *marae* (meeting house). (p162)

CANTERBURY MUSEUM
Brilliant collection of Kiwi artefacts. (p234)

AUCKLAND MUSEUM
This shiny Greek temple is a great introduction to Maori culture. (p66)

OTAGO MUSEUM
Otago culture and landscapes: dinosaurs, geology, wildlife and Maori heritage. (p295)

ROTORUA MUSEUM
An amazing old building with a wing dedicated to local Maori culture. (p108)

Hot Water Beach

Get yourself into hot water on the Coromandel Peninsula at the legendary Hot Water Beach (p92), where warm geothermal springs bubble up through the sand. If you time your arrival to within a couple of hours either side of low tide, with some creative digging you can kick back in your custom-made spa pool and watch the surf lap along the beach. If you don't carry a shovel around with you in your luggage, you can hire one from the local cafe.

The Best...
Beaches

GREG BALFOUR EVANS / ALAMY ©

PATRICK MINUTA/ IA PHOTOGRAPHY/GETTY IMAGES ©

25

Aoraki/Mt Cook

At a cloud-piercing 3724m, Aoraki (p254) is NZ's crowning peak. Unless you're a professional mountaineer, it's unlikely you'll be scaling the summit, but there are plenty of other ways to experience this massive mount: take a walk around the rumbling glaciers and moody lakes dappling its flanks, carve up the snow on a ski trip, or get closer to the top on an eye-popping scenic flight. Afterwards, retreat to your accommodation and warm up by an open fire. View of Aoraki/Mt Cook from the Hooker Valley Track (p255)

New Zealand's Top Itineraries

Auckland to the Bay of Islands

5 DAYS

City to the Sea

If you're on a tight, five-day schedule with jetlag bending your mind, focus on Auckland's must-see sights, eat and drink your way around town, ferry across Auckland Harbour to Waiheke Island, then maybe take an overnight trip north to the Bay of Islands.

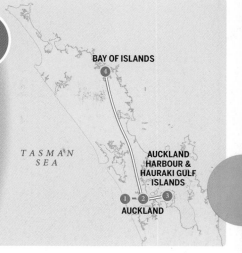

1 Central Auckland (p60)

One of the world's great nautical cities, Auckland offers islands, beaches and ocean access, plus stellar bars and restaurants. Don't miss the Maori and South Pacific Islander exhibits at Auckland Museum, a stroll across the Domain to K Rd for lunch, a visit to the grand Auckland Art Gallery and the iconic Sky Tower.

CENTRAL AUCKLAND ➔ PONSONBY

🚗 **10 minutes** Via Pitt St to Ponsonby Rd. 🚌 **15 minutes** Inner Link bus Queen St to Ponsonby Rd.

2 Ponsonby (p69)

Auckland is a city of enclaves, each with its own flavour. Parnell fosters an affluent 'village' vibe; Newmarket is festooned with boutiques; Devonport resembles a 19th-century maritime village...but Ponsonby wins on the foodie front. Head straight for Ponsonby Rd: Thai, Japanese and Italian, plus cafes and wine bars.

PONSONBY ➔ WAIHEKE ISLAND

🚌 **15 minutes** Inner Link bus Ponsonby Rd to central Auckland, then ⚓ **50 minutes** From Quay St to Waiheke Island.

3 Auckland Harbour & Hauraki Gulf Islands (p82)

Steeped in ocean-going credibility, Auckland Harbour is awash with yachts and ferries. Take the ferry over to Rangitoto Island, then chug into Devonport for a meal: check out Cheltenham Beach while you're in the 'hood. Afterwards, ferry-hop to Waiheke Island for some fabulous wineries and beaches.

WAIHEKE ISLAND ➔ BAY OF ISLANDS

⚓ **50 minutes** Waiheke Island to Quay St, then 🚗 or 🚌 **Three hours** From Auckland to Bay of Islands via SH1 and SH11.

4 Bay of Islands (p316)

A few hours' drive north of Auckland (make it an overnighter) is the utterly photogenic Bay of Islands. Like a tourism brochure in 3D, the area is a yachting, snorkelling and beach-bumming paradise. Swim with dolphins or set sail for an uninhabited island (take your pick from 150 of them!).

Waitemata Harbour, Auckland (p60)
JOHN W BANAGAN/GETTY IMAGES ©

Queenstown to Kaikoura
Winter Wanderer

Yes, we know a whole bunch of you are here for one thing only: snow! Hit Queenstown on the South Island for perfect powder and great bars and restaurants. Further north, Kaikoura's winter days are crisp: the whales are wallowing and the crowds are absent.

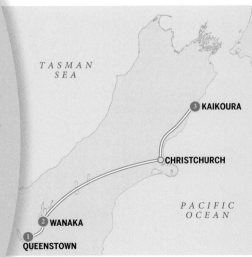

TASMAN SEA

❸ KAIKOURA

CHRISTCHURCH

PACIFIC OCEAN

❷ WANAKA

❶ QUEENSTOWN

① Queenstown (p276)

Take a direct flight into the rather international Queenstown and get ready for some seriously snowy fun, with access to world-class skiing and restaurants, plus a kickin' nocturnal scene. If you're here in late June or early July, the Queenstown Winter Festival goes berserk, with live music, comedy, parades and lots of family fun. On the ski front, Coronet Peak is the region's oldest ski field, with a multimillion dollar snow-making system, treeless slopes, consistent gradient and excellent skiing for all levels. It's great for snowboarders too. The visually remarkable Remarkables are more family-friendly – look for the big sweeping run called 'Homeward Bound'.

When you've had your fill of snowy slopes, the extreme activities on offer in Queenstown will keep the winter chills at bay: try kayaking, bungy jumping, paragliding, jetboating, white-water rafting, skydiving or mountain biking.

QUEENSTOWN ❂ WANAKA

🚗 or 🚌 **One hour** From Queenstown to Wanaka along Cardrona Valley Rd.

② Wanaka (p289)

As an alternative to Queenstown, head to Wanaka. It's like Queenstown's little brother – with all the benefits but little of the hype. Ski fields near here include Treble Cone, with steep intermediate and advanced slopes, plus snowboarding half-pipes and a terrain park; Cardrona, with high-capacity chairlifts, beginners' tows and extreme snowboarding terrain; and Snow Farm New Zealand, the country's only commercial Nordic (cross-country) ski area. Want something a little wilder? Take an overnight trip to Westland Tai Poutini National Park on the West Coast to check out Franz Josef and Fox Glaciers.

WANAKA ❂ KAIKOURA

 One hour From Wanaka to Christchurch, then 🚗 **2½ hours** or 🚌 **Three hours** From Christchurch to Kaikoura.

③ Kaikoura (p205)

From Wanaka, fly north to Christchurch, a city rebuilding and reinventing itself after the 2011 earthquakes – peek out the aeroplane window as you pass massive, brooding Aoraki/Mt Cook. From Christchurch, drive for a few hours north to Kaikoura, a photogenic little town on the South Island's northwest coast. In winter (especially), migrating humpback and sperm whales come close to the shore. Check them out up close on a whale-watching tour while the summer crowds are a million miles (or at least a few months) away.

Snowboarding, Coronet Peak (p281)
KYLE SPARKS /GETTY IMAGES ©

10 DAYS

Auckland to Queenstown
Kiwi Classics

Classy cities, geothermal eruptions, fantastic wine, Maori culture, glaciers, extreme activities, isolated beaches and forests. These are just a few of our favourite NZ things, and what you'll want to see if you're a first-time, short-trip visitor. It's the best of the country, north and south.

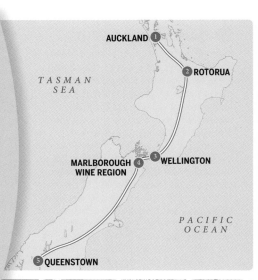

TASMAN SEA

AUCKLAND ①

② ROTORUA

③ WELLINGTON

MARLBOROUGH WINE REGION ④

PACIFIC OCEAN

⑤ QUEENSTOWN

① Auckland & Around (p60)

The 'City of Sails', Auckland is a South Pacific melting pot – spend a few days shopping, eating, drinking and experiencing NZ at its most cosmopolitan. Need a night out of town? Truck north to the winterless Bay of Islands for sailing, surfing, kayaking and scuba diving, or scoot southeast to explore the forests and beaches of the Coromandel Peninsula.

AUCKLAND ○ ROTORUA

🚗 or 🚌 **Three hours** From Auckland to Rotorua via SH1. ✈ **40 minutes** From Auckland to Rotorua.

② Rotorua (p104)

Further south is Rotorua, a real geothermal hot spot: giggle at volcanic mud bubbles, gasp as geothermal geysers blast boiling water into the sky, and get a nose full of rotten-egg gas. Rotorua is also a great place to experience Maori culture via a *haka* (war dance), *hangi* (feast) or legend-loaded cultural performance.

ROTORUA ○ WELLINGTON

🚗 **Six hours** From Rotorua to Wellington via SH1. ✈ **1¼ hours** From Rotorua to Wellington.

③ Wellington (p158)

Way down in Wellington, the coffee's hot, the beer's cold and wind from the politicians generates its own low-pressure system. Clinging to the hillsides like a mini San Francisco, NZ's capital city is the place for serious arts, live music and hip street culture. Don't miss the boutiques, bars and cafes on Cuba St.

WELLINGTON ○ MARLBOROUGH WINE REGION

🚢 **3¼ hours** From Wellington to Picton, then 🚗 or 🚌 **25 minutes** From Picton to Blenheim.

④ Marlborough Wine Region (p206)

Swan over to the South Island for a few days (even the ferry trip is scenic) and experience the best the bottom half of NZ has to offer. Start with a tour through the Marlborough Wine Region – the sauvignon blanc they produce in this cool microclimate is world class. The mirror-perfect inlets and tree-cloaked headlands of the Marlborough Sounds make a great day trip from here.

MARLBOROUGH WINE REGION ○ QUEENSTOWN

🚌 **Five hours** From Blenheim to Christchurch, then 🚗 **Six hours** From Christchurch to Queenstown. ✈ **Three hours** From Blenheim to Queenstown via Christchurch. 🚗 **11 hours** From Marlborough Wine Region to Queenstown via SH6.

⑤ Queenstown (p276)

Further south is Christchurch: the South Island's biggest city is being born again after the 2011 earthquakes. From here you can meander southwest to bungy- and ski-obsessed party town Queenstown, a must-visit for adrenaline junkies. Hop on a flight directly back to Auckland to round-out your classic Kiwi adventure.

Havana Coffee Works (p167), Wellington
PETE SEAWARD /LONELY PLANET ©

10 DAYS

Auckland to Auckland
Northern Exposure

Three-quarters of New Zealanders live on the North Island – time to find out why! Auckland is the obvious launch pad, but beyond the big smoke you'll discover ancient forests, erupting geothermal geysers, art-deco architecture, astonishing caves, islands and salubrious wine regions.

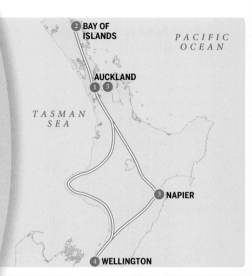

Auckland (p60)

Begin in Auckland, NZ's biggest city. There's not much you can't see, eat or buy here (prime your credit card). Eat streets abound: our faves are Ponsonby Rd in Ponsonby, K Rd in Newton and New North Rd in Kingsland. Hike up One Tree Hill (Maungakiekie) to burn off resultant calories, and don't miss Auckland Art Gallery and Auckland Museum.

AUCKLAND ⭕ BAY OF ISLANDS

🚗 or 🚌 **Three hours** From Auckland to Bay of Islands via SH1 and SH11.

 Bay of Islands (p316)

Heading north, you'll reach the magnificent Bay of Islands: spend a day bobbing around on a yacht, snorkelling or dolphin-swimming. Adventurous, road-eager types might want to continue to the rugged northern tip of NZ: Cape Reinga is shrouded in solitude and Maori lore.

BAY OF ISLANDS ⭕ NAPIER

🚗 **8½ hours** From Bay of Islands to Napier via Rotorua, Mt Maunganui or the Coromandel Peninsula. ✈ **Three hours** From Whangarei to Napier via Auckland.

③ Napier (p179)

It's a long haul from the Bay of Islands to Napier on the East Coast: break up the journey with a night in geothermal Rotorua, surfie Mt Maunganui in the Bay of Plenty, or one of the laid-back beach towns on the Coromandel Peninsula. Once you roll into Napier, check out the amazing art-deco architecture and the surrounding chardonnay vineyards of the Hawke's Bay Wine Region.

NAPIER ⭕ WELLINGTON

🚗 or 🚌 **4½ hours** From Napier to Wellington via SH2. ✈ **One hour** From Napier to Wellington.

 Wellington (p158)

Boot it south into the sheepy/winey Wairarapa region (try the superb pinot noir produced around Martinborough), before soaring over the cloud-wrapped Rimutaka Range into hipper-than-hip Wellington. Don't miss Te Papa, NZ's national museum, and a night on the tiles along Cuba St or Courtenay Pl.

WELLINGTON ⭕ AUCKLAND

🚗 **10 hours** From Wellington to Auckland via Mt Taranaki, Raglan, Hamilton or Waitomo Caves. ✈ **One hour** From Wellington to Auckland.

⑤ Auckland (p60)

Take the northwesterly route back to Auckland slow and easy, passing the epic volcanic cone of Mt Taranaki en route. Hit the point breaks near Raglan if you're into surfing, or go underground at Waitomo Caves for glorious glowworms and black-water rafting. Hamilton, NZ's fourth-biggest town, has a happening nocturnal scene if you're craving some city-sized action.

Cape Reinga Lighthouse, Bay of Islands (p316)
COLIN MCKIE /GETTY IMAGES ©

2 WEEKS

Auckland to Christchurch
Icons & Beyond

Check some big-ticket attractions off your list on this trip, with some kayaking, caving and tramping breaking up the road trip. With a couple of weeks at your disposal, you'll really be able to switch to holiday mode, embrace nature and savour the flavours of dual-island travel.

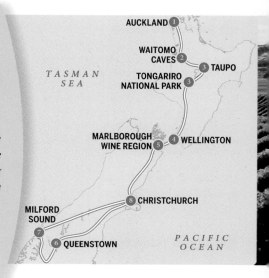

1 Auckland (p60)

Cruise the hip, inner-city streets of Auckland: hike up One Tree Hill (Maungakiekie), ride a bike along Tamaki Dr then take your pick of myriad lunch spots along K Rd or in Kingsland. Dinner in Ponsonby will attune your taste buds to NZ's brand of 'Pacific fusion' cooking. Afterwards, hit the bars around Viaduct Harbour or Vulcan Lane.

AUCKLAND ➔ WAITOMO CAVES

🚗 or 🚌 **Three hours** From Auckland to Waitomo Caves via SH1 and SH39.

2 Waitomo Caves (p145)

The amazing Waitomo Caves are an underground labyrinth of glowworm-filled caverns. Don a wetsuit and headlamp and dive in for black-water rafting, abseiling or floating along on an inner-tube in the inky darkness. There are a couple of good eateries here for refuelling afterwards.

WAITOMO CAVES ➔ TAUPO

🚗 **Two hours** From Waitomo Caves to Taupo via SH30.

3 Taupo & Tongariro National Park (p123 & p130)

From Waitomo, hook southeast to progressive Taupo and try skydiving (you know you want to) or go tramping around the triple-peaked, volcanic wilderness of Tongariro National Park. The Tongariro Alpine Crossing is one of the best day walks in NZ.

TAUPO ➔ WELLINGTON

🚗 or 🚌 **Five hours** From Taupo to Wellington via SH1.

4 Wellington (p158)

Watch the nocturnal freak show pass by in late-night, caffeinated Wellington – a great place to prop up the bar and try some NZ craft beers. Spend a few hours wandering through NZ's national museum, Te Papa, then roll onto the ferry for the trip across Cook Strait to the South Island.

WELLINGTON ➔ MARLBOROUGH WINE REGION

⛴ **3¼ hours** From Wellington to Picton, then
🚗 or 🚌 **25 minutes** From Picton to Blenheim.

Vineyards, Marlborough Wine Region (p206)
PETE SEAWARD/LONELY PLANET ©

and spend a night at either the iconic Franz Josef Glacier or the impressive Fox Glacier. Hike around the icy valleys, or take a helicopter up onto the glaciers themselves: a sure-fire way to develop feelings of insignificance. Drive up over Haast Pass to adrenaline-addled Queenstown for a night or two of partying Kiwi-style.

QUEENSTOWN ○ MILFORD SOUND

🚗 **3½ hours** From Queenstown to Milford Sound via Te Anau.

⑦ Milford Sound (p312)

Mix and match highways to Te Anau for the beguiling side-road to Milford Sound – you might want to do a bit of kayaking here, or take a boat trip around the craggy inlets and mirror-topped waterways. This is NZ at its most pure, pristine and perfect.

MILFORD SOUND ○ CHRISTCHURCH

🚗 **3½ hours** From Milford Sound to Queenstown, then ✈ **One hour** From Queenstown to Christchurch.

⑧ Christchurch & Around (p234)

Veer back east to Queenstown and hop a flight to the southern capital of Christchurch, a city bursting with creative energy as it rebuilds from the 2011 earthquakes. While away a day or two exploring, shopping and gallery-hopping. Take an afternoon to explore the quirky harbour town of Lyttelton or the amazing Banks Peninsula south of the city, with its French-influenced village of Akaroa.

⑤ Marlborough Wine Region (p206)

Track west from pretty Picton and disappear into the leafy vine-rows and welcoming cellar-door tasting rooms of the Marlborough Wine Region. If you have an extra day, explore the waterways and woodlands of the Marlborough Sounds, or continue west to the golden-sand bays of Abel Tasman National Park.

MARLBOROUGH WINE REGION ○ QUEENSTOWN

🚌 **Five hours** From Blenheim to Christchurch, then 🚗 **Six hours** From Christchurch to Queenstown. ✈ **Three hours** From Blenheim to Queenstown via Christchurch. 🚗 **11 hours** From Marlborough Wine Region to Queenstown via SH6.

⑥ Queenstown (p276)

Time to get your skates on: track down the rain-swept, lonesome West Coast

New Zealand Month by Month

 ## January

 ### Festival of Lights

New Plymouth's Pukekura Park sparkles during this festival (www.festivaloflights.co.nz). It's a magical scene: pathways glow and trees are impressively lit with thousands of lights. Live music, dance and kids' performances, too.

 ### World Buskers Festival

Christchurch hosts a gaggle of jugglers, musos, tricksters, puppeteers, mime artists and dancers, performing throughout this 10-day summertime festival (www.worldbuskersfestival.com).

 ## February

 ### Waitangi Day

On 6 February 1840 the Treaty of Waitangi (www.nzhistory.net.nz) was first signed between Maori and the British Crown. The day is a public holiday across New Zealand, but in Waitangi there are guided tours, concerts, markets and family fun.

Marlborough Wine & Food Festival

NZ's biggest and best wine festival (www.wine-marlborough-festival.co.nz) features tastings from about 50 Marlborough wineries, plus fine food and entertainment. The mandatory over-indulgence usually happens on a Saturday early in the month.

New Zealand Festival

Feeling artsy? This month-long spectacular (www.festival.co.nz) happens in Wellington from February to March every even-numbered

Top Events

 **World Buskers Festival**, January

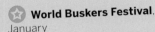 **Marlborough Wine & Food Festival**, February

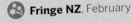 **Fringe NZ**, February

Wellington Sevens, February

World of WearableArt Award Show, September

(left) January Festival of Lights

year. NZ's cultural capital exudes artistic enthusiasm with theatre, dance, music, writing and visual arts.

 Fringe NZ

Music, theatre, comedy, dance, visual arts...but not the mainstream stuff that makes it into the New Zealand Festival. These are the fringe-dwelling, unusual, emerging, controversial, low-budget and/ or downright weird acts that don't seem to fit in anywhere else (www.fringe.co.nz).

 Splore

Explore Splore (www.splore.net), a cutting-edge, three-day outdoor summer fest in Tapapakanga Regional Park on the Coromandel Peninsula. There's contemporary live music, performance, visual arts, safe swimming, pohutukawa trees.

 Wellington Sevens

Yeah, we know, it's not rugby season, but February sees the world's top seven-a-side rugby teams crack heads (www.sevens.co.nz) as part of the HSBC Sevens World Series: everyone from stalwarts like Australia, NZ and South Africa to minnows like the Cook Islands, Kenya and Canada.

 # March

 **Te Matatini National Kapa Haka Festival**

This engrossing Maori *haka* (war dance) competition (www.tematatini.co.nz) happens in early March in odd-numbered years: much gesticulation, eye-bulging and tongue extension. Venues vary: 2015 will be Christchurch. And it's not just the *haka:* expect traditional song, dance, storytelling and other performing arts.

 BikeFest Lake Taupo

Feeling fit? Try racing a bicycle 160km around Lake Taupo and then come and talk to us... In the week prior to the big race, BikeFest (www.bikefest.co.nz) celebrates all things bicycular: BMX, mountain bike, unicycle and tandem.

 WOMAD

Local and international music, arts and dance performances fill New Plymouth's Bowl of Brooklands to overflowing (www.womad.co.nz). An evolution of the original world-music festival dreamed-up by Peter Gabriel. Perfect for families.

 Pasifika Festival

With upwards of 140,000 Maori and notable communities of Tongans, Samoans, Cook Islanders, Niueans, Fijians and other South Pacific Islanders, Auckland has the largest Polynesian community in the world. These vibrant island cultures come together at this annual fiesta (www.aucklandcouncil.govt.nz).

 # April

 National Jazz Festival

Every Easter, Tauranga hosts the longest-running jazz fest (www.jazz.org.nz) in the southern hemisphere. The line up is invariably impressive (Kurt Elling, Keb Mo), and there's plenty of fine NZ food and wine to accompany the finger-snappin' za-bah-de-dah sonics.

 # May

 New Zealand International Comedy Festival

Three-week laugh-fest (www.comedy-festival.co.nz) with venues across Auckland, Wellington and various regional centres: Whangarei to Invercargill with all the midsized cities in between. International gag-merchants (Arj Barker, Danny Bhoy) line up next to home-grown talent.

August

 Taranaki International Arts Festival

Beneath the snowy slopes of Mt Taranaki, August used to be a time of quiet repose and reconstitution. Not anymore: this whizz-bang arts festival (www.taft.co.nz/artsfest) now shakes the winter from the city (New Plymouth) with music, theatre, dance, visual arts and parades.

 Bay of Islands Jazz & Blues Festival

You might think that the Bay of Islands is all about sunning yourself on a yacht, but in the depths of winter, this jazzy little festival (www.jazz-blues.co.nz) will give you something else to do.

September

 World of WearableArt Award Show

A bizarre (in the best possible way) two-week Wellington event (www.worldof wearableart.com) featuring amazing hand-crafted garments. Entries from the show are displayed at the World of Wear-ableArt & Classic Cars Museum (p214) in Nelson after the event (Cadillacs and corsetry?).

 Auckland Boat Show

Auckland Harbour blooms with sails and churns with outboard motors (www.auckland-boatshow.com).

June

 Matariki

Maori New Year is heralded by the rise of Matariki (aka Pleiades star cluster) in May and the sighting of the new moon in June. Three days of remembrance, education, music, film, community days and tree planting take place, mainly around Auckland and Northland (www.teara.govt.nz/en/matariki-maori-new-year).

July

 Queenstown Winter Festival

This southern snow-fest (www.winterfestival.co.nz) has been running since 1975, and now attracts around 45,000 snow bunnies. It's a 10-day party, studded with fireworks, jazz, street parades, comedy, a Mardi Gras, a masquerade ball and lots of snow-centric activities on the mountain slopes.

October

 Nelson Arts Festival

Sure, Nelson is distractingly sunny, but that doesn't mean

the artsy good stuff isn't happening inside and out. Get a taste of the local output over two weeks in October (www.nelson-festivals.co.nz).

Kaikoura Seafest

Kaikoura is a town built on crayfish. Well, not literally, but there sure are plenty of crustaceans in the sea here, many of which find themselves on plates during Seafest (www.seafest.co.nz). Also a great excuse to drink a lot and dance around.

November

Toast Martinborough

Bound for a day of boozy indulgence, wine-swilling Wellingtonians head over Rimutaka Hill and roll into upmarket Martinborough (www.toastmartinborough.co.nz). The Wairarapa Wine Country produces some seriously good pinot noir: don't go home without trying some (...as if you'd be so silly).

Pohutukawa Festival

A week of markets, picnics, live music, kite-flying, cruises, snorkelling and poetry on the Coromandel Peninsula. It's all very clean-living and above-board, but not everything has to be about drinking, dancing and decadence. And just look at those pohutukawa trees (www.pohutukawa-festival.co.nz). Sometimes strays into early December.

December

Rhythm & Vines

Wine, music and song (all the good things) in sunny east-coast Gisborne on New Year's Eve (www.rhythmandvines.co.nz). Top DJs, hip-hop acts, bands and singer-songwriters compete for your attention. Or maybe you'd rather just drink some chardonnay and kiss someone on the beach.

Far left: June Kites flying at Auckland's Matariki festival **Left: February** Waitangi Day celebrations

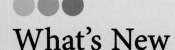

What's New

For this new edition of Discover New Zealand, our authors hunted down the fresh, the transformed, the hot and the happening. Here are a few of our favourites. For up-to-the-minute recommendations, see lonelyplanet.com/new-zealand.

1 GAP FILLER, CHRISTCHURCH
Thanks to this eccentric project, new things are constantly springing up on Christchurch's flattened blocks – and many of them are delightfully oddball. Check the website to see what's new. (p235)

2 ROTORUA CANOPY TOURS
A new network of flying foxes, zip lines and rope bridges, 22m high in a canopy of native New Zealand forest outside Rotorua. (p105)

3 NGA TOI/ARTS TE PAPA, WELLINGTON
This new and improved multigallery space within the national museum shows frequently changing art exhibitions from its own collection and beyond. (p162)

4 TRANSITIONAL CATHEDRAL, CHRISTCHURCH
Called the Cardboard Cathedral by practically everyone, Christchurch's pop-up architectural showcase is endeavouring to fill the big shoes left by its wounded stone sister. (www.christchurchcathedral.co.nz; 234 Hereford St; suggested donation $5; ⊗9am-5pm)

5 QUAKE CITY, CHRISTCHURCH
The tragic story of Christchurch's earthquakes is succinctly told in this affecting new museum in the heart of the devastated city centre. (p235)

6 WHAKATANE DISTRICT MUSEUM
On the Whakatane waterfront, this beaut new regional museum and gallery delivers the historic low-down on NZ's sunniest town. (p121)

7 WEST COAST WILDERNESS TRAIL
Crossing a spectacular landscape at the foot of the Southern Alps, this 120km cycle trail offers easy day rides through to a four-day journey from Greymouth to Hokitika. (www.westcoastwildernesstrail.co.nz)

8 MTG HAWKE'S BAY, NAPIER
Napier's sparkling new waterfront Museum Theatre Gallery complex is a sure-fire winner, the many millions spent on renovations rewarding visitors with accessible film, theatre, museum and art experiences. (p180)

9 SILO PARK MARKETS, AUCKLAND
From December to March, Auckland's Wynyard Quarter hosts weekly markets with local arts and crafts and a tasty selection of food trucks. On Friday nights, classic movies are shown outdoors. (www.silopark.co.nz; Wynyard Quarter)

10 GOOD GEORGE BREWING, HAMILTON
Make the short trek from central Hamilton to this excellent craft brewery in a renovated church. Acoustic music sessions in the garden bar make for a perfect Sunday afternoon. (p138)

11 HAIRY FEET, PIOPIO
The newest addition to NZ's array of Hobbit-themed movie locations is in the rugged Mangaotaki Valley in the King Country. Here's your chance to visit Trollshaw Forest. (☏07-877 8003; www.hairyfeetwaitomo.co.nz; 1411 Mangaotaki Rd, PioPio; adult/child $50/25; ⊗10am & 1pm)

Get Inspired

Books

o **The Luminaries** (Eleanor Catton, 2013) New Zealand goldfield epic set in the 1860s. Man Booker Prize winner.

o **Mister Pip** (Lloyd Jones, 2007) Reflections of *Great Expectations* in an isolated Bougainville community. Man Booker Prize shortlisted.

o **The 10pm Question** (Kate De Goldi, 2009) Frankie is 12 and has many questions; Sydney has some difficult answers.

o **In My Father's Den** (Maurice Gee, 1972) A harrowing homecoming; made into a film in 2004.

Films

o **The Piano** (1993, director Jane Campion) Betrayal and passion on an 1850s NZ frontier.

o **The Lord of the Rings trilogy** (2001–03, director Peter Jackson) *The Fellowship of the Ring, The Two Towers* and the Oscar-winning *The Return of the King.* Then came *The Hobbit*...

o **Whale Rider** (2002, director Niki Caro) Maori

on the East Coast are torn between tradition and today's world.

o **Boy** (2010, director Taika Waititi) Coming-of-age poignancy and self-deprecation. The highest-grossing NZ-made film of all time!

Music

o **Royals** (Lorde, 2013) Schoolyard chant-evoking, worldwide hit from 16-year-old Ella Yelich-O'Connor.

o **Slice of Heaven** (David Dobbyn with Herbs, 1986) South Pacific smash from veteran Dave.

o **Not Many** (Scribe, 2003) Hot Kiwi hip-hop.

o **Home Again** (Shihad, 1997) Riff-driven power from NZ's guitar-rock kings.

o **Somebody That I Used To Know** (Gotye, 2011) He's from Melbourne, but co-vocalist Kimbra is a Hamilton gal.

Websites

o **Department of Conservation** (www.doc.govt.nz) Parks, camping and conservation info.

o **DineOut** (www.dineout.co.nz) Restaurant reviews across NZ.

o **Te Ara** (www.teara.govt.nz) Online encyclopedia of NZ.

o **Muzic.net** (www.muzic.net.nz) Gigs, reviews, band bios and charts.

Short on time?

This list will give you an instant insight into NZ.

Read *The Bone People* (Keri Hulme, 1984) Maori legends, isolation and violence: Man Booker Prize winner, exploring traumatic family interactions.

Watch *Once Were Warriors* (1994, director Lee Tamahori) Brutal, tragic, gritty: Jake 'the Muss' Heke in urban Auckland.

Listen *Don't Dream it's Over* (Crowded House, 1986) Neil Finn catches a deluge in a paper cup – timeless melancholia.

Log on *100% Pure New Zealand* (www.newzealand.com) Comprehensive tourist info.

Lord of the Rings film set
MATT MUNRO/LONELY PLANET ©

Need to Know

Currency
New Zealand dollars ($)

Language
English, Maori and New Zealand Sign Language

Visas
Citizens of Australia, the UK and 56 other countries don't need visas for NZ (the length-of-stay varies). Other countries do. See www.immigration.govt.nz.

Money
ATMs are widely available in cities and larger towns. Credit cards are accepted in most hotels and restaurants.

Mobile Phones
European phones will work on NZ's network, but most American or Japanese phones will not. Use global roaming or a local SIM card and prepaid account.

Wi-Fi
Often available in hotels, hostels, libraries, cafes and pubs.

Internet Access
Internet cafes in most cities and large towns, plus public libraries; around $6 per hour.

Tipping
Not expected, but tip 5% to 10% for good restaurant service.

When to Go

Auckland
GO Feb–Apr

Rotorua
GO Oct–Dec

Wellington
GO Dec–Feb

Christchurch
GO Jan–Mar

Queenstown
GO Jun–Aug

High Season
(Dec–Feb)
- Summertime: local holidays, busy beaches, festivals and sporting events.
- Pay up to 25% more for city hotels.
- High season in the ski towns (Queenstown, Wanaka) is winter (June to August).

Shoulder Season
(Mar & Apr, Sep–Nov)
- Prime travelling time: fine weather, short queues and warm(ish) ocean.
- Long evenings supping Kiwi wines and craft beers.

Low Season
(May–Aug)
- Head for the Southern Alps for brilliant skiing.
- No crowds, good accommodation deals and a seat in any restaurant.
- Warm-weather beach towns might be half asleep.

Advance Planning

- **Three months before** Read a Kiwi novel: Eleanor Catton, Keri Hulme, Lloyd Jones, Janet Frame, Maurice Gee...
- **One month before** Book accommodation and regional flights, trains, ferries etc.
- **One week before** Book a bungy jump, surf lesson, cave tour or Maori cultural experience.
- **One day before** Reserve a table at a top Auckland/Wellington restaurant and make sure you've packed your tramping boots.

Daily Costs

Budget Less than $130

○ Dorm beds or campsites: per night $25–35

○ Main course in a budget eatery: less than $15

○ Explore NZ with a Naked Bus or InterCity bus pass: five trips from $151

Midrange $130–$250

○ Double room in a midrange hotel/motel: $100–200

○ Main course in a midrange restaurant: $15–32

○ Hire car: from $30 per day

Top End More than $250

○ Double room in a top-end hotel: from $200

○ Three-course meal in a classy restaurant: $80

○ Domestic flight from Auckland to Christchurch: from $100

Exchange Rates		
Australia	A$1	NZ$1.07
Canada	C$1	NZ$1.04
China	¥10	NZ$1.83
Euro zone	€1	NZ$1.60
Japan	¥100	NZ$1.14
Singapore	S$1	NZ$0.91
UK	UK£1	NZ$1.92
US	US$1	NZ$1.16

For current exchange rates see www.xe.com

What to Bring

○ **Driver's licence** The best way to see NZ is under your own steam.

○ **Insect repellent** Kiwi sandfly bites just keep on giving.

○ **Power-plug adaptor** Keep all your gadgets charged.

○ **Travel insurance** Ensure you're covered for 'high-risk' activities (skiing, white-water rafting, surfing etc).

○ **Rain jacket** Perfect one minute, raining the next...

Arriving in New Zealand

○ **Auckland International Airport** (p80) Airbus Express buses run into the city every 10 to 30 minutes, 24 hours. Door-to-door shuttle buses run 24 hours. A taxi into the city costs around $70 (45 minutes).

○ **Wellington Airport** (p171) Airport Flyer buses run into the city every 10 to 20 minutes from 6.30am to 9.30pm. Door-to-door shuttle buses run 24 hours. A taxi into the city costs around $30 (20 minutes).

○ **Christchurch Airport** (p243) Christchurch Metro Red Buses 3 and 29 run into the city regularly from 6.30am to 11pm. Door-to-door shuttle buses run 24 hours. A taxi into the city costs around $50 (20 minutes).

Getting Around

○ **Bus** Well-organised, regular links between most towns.

○ **Car** Car hire from major cities and airports. Drive on the left.

○ **Ferry** Daily between North and South Islands.

○ **Plane** Domestic carriers fly between cities.

○ **Train** Scenic railways cross the Southern Alps and link some major cities.

Sleeping

○ **B&Bs** Bed (and breakfast) down in a locally run cabin/house/mansion (DB&B means dinner too!).

○ **Farmstays** Work on a farm, eat with the family.

○ **Hostels** Spartan and decent or beery and oversexed.

○ **Hotels** From cheap pub rooms to five-star hotels.

○ **Motels** Cookie-cutter sameness, but reliable.

Be Forewarned

○ **Summertime blues** December to February: crowds and steep accommodation prices.

○ **Winter** Beaches are empty but mountains are full: ski season runs June to August (and beyond).

○ **Take the long way home** Getting from A to B takes time: many roads are wiggly, two-lane affairs.

Auckland

Paris may be the city of love, but Auckland is the city of many lovers according to its Maori name, Tamaki Makaurau. Those lovers so desired this place that they fought over it for centuries.

It's hard to imagine a more geographically blessed city. Its two harbours frame a narrow isthmus punctuated by volcanic cones and surrounded by fertile farmland. From any of its numerous vantage points, you'll be astounded at how close the Tasman Sea and Pacific Ocean come to kissing and forming a new island.

As a result, water is never far away – whether it's the ruggedly beautiful west-coast surf beaches or the glistening Hauraki Gulf with its myriad islands.

And within 90 minutes' drive from the high-rise heart of the city, there are the forests, beaches and gold-mining towns of the Coromandel Peninsula. Don't miss a trip to Hot Water Beach, offering a hint of New Zealand's famed geothermal hubbub.

View across Waitemata Harbour to Auckland city
DAVID WALL/GETTY IMAGES ©

Auckland

Onewa Rd

NORTHCOTE

Engine Room

Little Shoal Bay

Harbour Bridge

Auckland Bridge Climb & Bungy

Curran St

Westhaven Marina

Wynyard Wharf

Freemans Bay

St Mary's Bay

Northern Mwy

Northern Mwy

Britomart

Waitemata Harbour

See City Centre Map (p62)

Jellicoe Wharf

Fergusson Wharf

MECHANICS BAY

STANLEY BAY

Kawakawa Bay

Whitford

Maraetai

Orapiu

COWES

Onetangi Bay

Waiheke Island

PALM BEACH

Hauraki Gulf

Moutapu Island

Rangitoto Island

Takapuna

Auckland

Southern Mwy

Howick

Waiheke Island

0   10 km
0   5 miles

Calliope Road Cafe

Victoria Rd

DEVONPORT

Patuone Ave

Ngataringa Park

Albert Rd

Vauxhall Rd

Mt Victoria Reserve

Devonport Sea Cottage

Kerr St

Parituhu

Devonport Motel

Devonport Beach

Devonport Wharf

CHELTENHAM

Mt Victoria

Devonport Domain

Navy Museum

North Head

Cheltenham Beach

Duders Beach

King Edward Pde

Coastal Walk

Waitemata Golf Club

Seabreeze Rd

BELMONT

Lake Rd

Takapuna Head

Rangitoto Channel

Waiheke Island (see inset)

0   1 km
0   0.5 mile

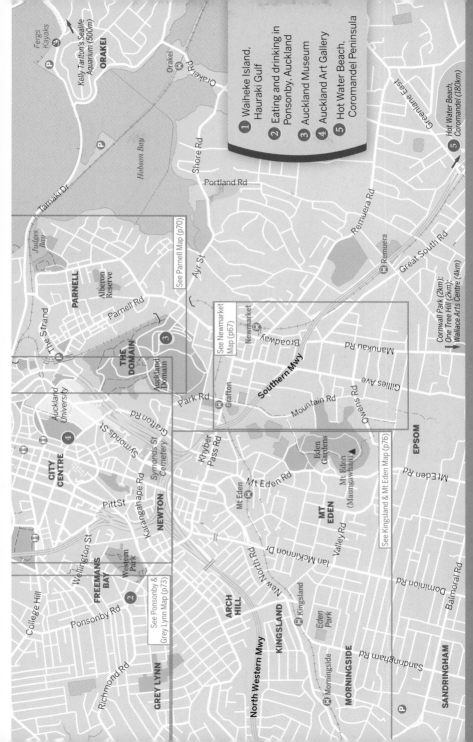

Auckland Highlights

Waiheke Island

Just a short ferry ride from the centre of Auckland, Waiheke Island (p82) may well be the highlight of your entire trip to NZ. You can arrive from Sydney or Los Angeles at breakfast time and then be on Waiheke for a vineyard-restaurant lunch with eye-popping views. Finish off with a swim on an uncrowded beach. Stonyridge winery (p83)

OLIVER STREWE/GETTY IMAGES ©

Restaurants, Cafes & Bars

Charismatic, multicultural eating and drinking opportunities abound across Auckland. Ponsonby (p72) is the pick of the bunch, with myriad wine bars and sassy restaurants. Elsewhere, dress up for the classy restaurants and bars around Viaduct Harbour, order some fast sushi in the city centre, or swing by the kickin' cafes in Parnell and Newmarket. Vulcan Lane and K Rd are also prime drinking hot spots. Vulcan Lane cafes

ANDREW WATSON/GETTY IMAGES ©

Auckland Museum

If you have the slightest interest in Maori and Pacific Islander culture, your first stop should be the Auckland Museum (p66). The Maori galleries are loaded with artefacts from around the country, and there are cultural performances daily – see why NZ's All Blacks rugby team uses the *haka* (war dance) to put the fear of God into their opposition. There's plenty of natural history, war history and kids stuff, too.

JOHN ELK/GETTY IMAGES ©

GUY WILKINSON/GETTY IMAGES ©

Auckland Art Gallery

Renovated in fine style, Auckland Art Gallery (p65) provides a hushed, cultured escape from the streets. The Main Gallery and the New Gallery (predictably) focus on the old and the new respectively: look for European masters and early colonial works in the former, and contemporary Kiwi creations and temporary exhibitions in the latter.

DAVID WALL PHOTO/GETTY IMAGES ©

Hot Water Beach

Pack your swimsuit and get up early for a day trip to the legendary geothermal springs of Hot Water Beach (p92) on the Coromandel Peninsula, or book a B&B and stay overnight. En route from Auckland, explore the heritage streetscapes of Thames and Coromandel Town. Hot Water Beach is near Hahei, and there are some gorgeous stretches of sand around Whitianga.

Auckland's Best...

Points of View

○ **Mt Eden** (Maungawhau) Killer views from Auckland's highest (196m) volcanic cone. (p75)

○ **Sky Tower** The southern hemisphere's tallest structure. (p60)

○ **One Tree Hill** (Maungakiekie) Historic volcanic cone: 182m tall with a 360-degree outlook. (p65)

○ **On the water** Take a ferry out onto the harbour and see Auckland from the water. (p69)

Fresh-Air Factories

○ **Auckland Domain** Eighty city-centre hectares of recreational greenery and themed gardens. (p61)

○ **Tamaki Drive** Tree-lined runway for joggers and the generically good-looking. (p61)

○ **Eden Garden** Burgeoning blooms on the slopes of Mt Eden. (p68)

○ **Albert Park** A formal Victorian-era garden full of canoodling students. (p60)

Eat Streets & Drinking Dens

○ **Ponsonby Rd, Ponsonby** Auckland's hippest strip. (p69)

○ **Karangahape Rd (K Rd), Newton** Edgy strip of restaurants and bars. (p73)

○ **New North Rd, Kingsland** Emerging eat street with great Thai and French. (p74)

○ **Viaduct Harbour, Central Auckland** Upmarket waterfront eating and drinking – dress up! (p72)

○ **Vulcan Lane, Central Auckland** Photogenic city-centre collation of cafes and bars. (p75)

Need to Know

Festivals

○ **Devonport Food & Wine Festival** (www.devonportwinefestival.co.nz) Sassy two-day sip-fest in mid-February.

○ **Auckland Arts Festival** (www.aucklandfestival.co.nz) Auckland's biggest arts party: three weeks in March, odd-numbered years.

○ **Pasifika Festival** (www.aucklandcouncil.govt.nz) Giant Polynesian party in March: performances, food, and arts and crafts.

○ **New Zealand International Film Festival** (www.nzff.co.nz) Beat a retreat from the cold July streets for art-house treats.

ADVANCE PLANNING

○ **One month before** Book your city beds (and on the Coromandel Peninsula if it's summer), plus transport, accommodation and activities on the Hauraki Gulf Islands.

○ **Two weeks before** Book tickets for concerts, the rugby and a Cathedral Cove sea-kayak tour on the Coromandel.

○ **One week before** Book harbour-cruise tickets and dinner at a top Auckland restaurant: try **Grove** (p72) or the **French Cafe** (p74).

RESOURCES

○ **Auckland NZ** (www.aucklandnz.com) The city's official tourist site.

○ **Destination Coromandel** (www.thecoromandel.com) Tourist info for the Coromandel.

○ **Auckland i-SITEs** (www.aucklandnz.com) Central tourist info; located at the SkyCity complex and the Princes Wharf ferries on Quay St.

○ **MAXX Regional Transport** (www.maxx.co.nz) Public transport details: bus, train and ferry.

GETTING AROUND

○ **Walk** Around Central Auckland and along the waterfront.

○ **Ferry** To the Hauraki Gulf Islands (Waiheke, Rangitoto) and Devonport on the North Shore.

○ **Bus** All around the city.

○ **Car** The Coromandel Peninsula is 90 minutes away.

○ **Airbus Express** Buses pinball between Auckland airport and the city.

○ **Train** To access the southwestern suburbs.

BE FOREWARNED

○ **Crowds** Summer (December to February) is the busy season: expect queues at Auckland's big-ticket sights, lots of beach-bums on the Coromandel Peninsula and elevated accommodation prices.

Left: Performers at the Pasifika Festival (p43); **Above:** Albert Park (p60)

Auckland Walking Tour

Auckland's CBD can feel a little scrappy and disorienting: this walk aims to shed some light by taking you through the best bits, with a few hidden nooks and architectural treats thrown in for good measure.

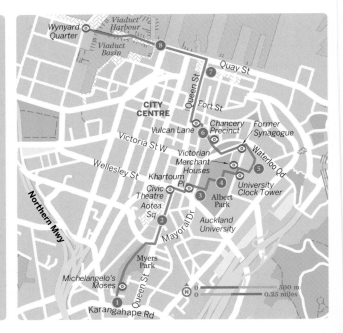

WALK FACTS
- **Start** St Kevin's Arcade
- **Finish** Wynyard Quarter
- **Distance** 4.5km
- **Duration** Three hours

1 St Kevin's Arcade

Start among the secondhand boutiques of St Kevin's Arcade on Karangahape Rd, then take the stairs down to Myers Park: look out for the reproduction of Michelangelo's Moses at the bottom of the stairs. Continue through the park, taking the stairs on the right just before the overpass to head up to street level.

2 Auckland Town Hall

Heading down Queen St, you'll pass the noble Auckland Town Hall (p79) – host to everyone from the NZ Symphony Orchestra to big-ticket touring rock bands – and sprawling, paved Aotea Square, the civic heart of the city. On the next corner is the wonderfully art deco Civic Theatre (p60), built in 1929 and reopened in 2000 after a major overhaul. Don't miss the amazing Indian-inspired lobby.

3 Auckland Art Gallery

Turn right on Wellesley St and then left onto Lorne St. Immediately to your right is Khartoum Pl, a pretty little square with tiling celebrating the suffragettes; NZ women were the first in the world to win the vote. Head up the stairs to the fabulously renovated Auckland Art Gallery (p65), home to priceless pieces by international (Picasso, Matisse) and local (Goldie, McCahon) artists. Free tours kick-off at 11.30am and 1.30pm daily.

4 Albert Park

Behind the gallery is Albert Park (p60), a Victorian formal garden. Cross through it and turn left onto Princes St, where a row of Victorian merchant houses faces the intricately styled University Clock Tower.

5 Old Government House

Cut around behind the clock tower to the restrained grandeur of Old Government House (p60), and then follow the diagonal path back to Princes St. The good-looking building on the corner of Princes St and Bowen Ave was once the city's main synagogue.

6 High Street

Head down Bowen Ave and cut through the park to the Chancery Precinct, an upmarket area of designer shops and cafes. A small square connects it to High St, Auckland's main fashion strip. Take a left onto Vulcan Lane, lined with historical pubs and cool cafes.

7 Britomart Train Station

Turn right onto Queen St and follow it down to the Britomart Train Station (p81), housed in the former Central Post Office. You're now standing on reclaimed land – the original shoreline was at Fort St, about 200m behind you (to the south).

8 Viaduct Harbour

Turn left on Quay St and head to Viaduct Harbour (p61), bustling with bars, cafes and lunching types, and then continue over the bridge to the rejuvenated Wynyard Quarter. Cool off with a cocktail at Conservatory (p77) while you're here.

Auckland In...

TWO DAYS

Acquaint yourself with inner Auckland: take our walking tour from **St Kevin's Arcade** on Karangahape Rd (K Rd) to the **Wynyard Quarter** (p61). Catch a ferry to **Devonport** (p64), head up **North Head** (p64) and cool down at **Cheltenham Beach** (p82) before heading back for dinner in Newton.

On day two, climb **One Tree Hill** (p65), then visit the **Auckland Museum** (p66) and **Auckland Domain** (p61). Cruise along **Tamaki Drive** (p61) for harbour views in the afternoon and then spend the evening dining and drinking in **Ponsonby** (p69).

FOUR DAYS

On the third day catch the ferry to **Waiheke Island** (p82), where beaches and wineries await.

On the final day, head west for breakfast in **Titirangi** (p86) before exploring **Piha** (p86) and **Karekar** (p87). Back in the city, it's time for a big night out on **K Road** (p77) or **Britomart** (p77).

One Tree Hill (p65)
ANDERS BLOMQVIST/GETTY IMAGES ©

Discover Auckland

At a Glance

○ **Central Auckland** (p60) High-rise hub: waterfront eating and drinking, Queen St shopping and K Rd nightlife.

○ **Ponsonby & Grey Lynn** (p69) Alternative foodie haunts and bars.

○ **Parnell & Newmarket** (p61) Old-money 'hoods: pricey restaurants and boutiques.

○ **Hauraki Gulf Islands** (p82) Catch the ferry: offshore wineries and beaches.

○ **Coromandel Peninsula** (p87) Holiday towns, forests and beaches.

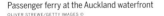
Passenger ferry at the Auckland waterfront

◉ Sights

CITY CENTRE

Albert Park   Park

(Map p62) On the city's eastern flank, Albert Park is a Victorian formal garden bordering the campus of **Auckland University**, and incorporates a row of stately Victorian merchant houses (Princes St) and **Old Government House** (Map p62; Waterloo Quadrant). The latter was the colony's seat of power from 1856 until 1865, when Wellington became the capital. The stately University Clock Tower (1926) has influences from art nouveau (the incorporation of NZ flora and fauna into the decoration), and the Chicago School.

Sky Tower   Landmark

(Map p62; www.skycityauckland.co.nz; cnr Federal & Victoria Sts; adult/child $28/11; ⊙8.30am-10.30pm) ⌀ The impossible-to-miss Sky Tower looks like a giant hypodermic giving a fix to the heavens. Spectacular lighting renders it space-age at night and the colours change for special events. At 328m it is the southern hemisphere's tallest structure. A lift takes you up to the observation decks in 40 stomach-lurching seconds; look down through the glass floor panels if you're after an extra kick. Visit at sunset and have a drink in the Sky Lounge Cafe & Bar.

The Sky Tower is also home to the SkyWalk (p67) and SkyJump (p67).

Civic Theatre   Architecture

(Map p62; www.civictheatre.co.nz; cnr Queen & Wellesley Sts) The 'mighty Civic' (1929) is one of seven 'atmospheric theatres' remaining in the world and a fine survivor from cinema's Golden Age. The auditorium has lavish Moorish decoration, and the starlit southern-hemisphere sky in the ceiling (complete with cloud projections) gives the illusion of being under a night sky. It's mainly used for touring musicals, international concerts and film-festival screenings.

St Patrick's Cathedral   Church

(Map p62; www.stpatricks.org.nz; 43 Wyndham St; ⏰7am-7pm) Auckland's Catholic cathedral (1907) is one of the city's loveliest buildings. Polished wood and Belgian stained glass lend warmth to the interior of the majestic Gothic Revival church. There's a historical display in the old confessional on the left-hand side.

BRITOMART, VIADUCT HARBOUR & WYNYARD QUARTER

Stretching for only a small grid of blocks above the train station, Britomart is a compact enclave of historic buildings and new developments that has been transformed into one of the city's best eating, drinking and shopping precincts.

Once a busy commercial port, the **Viaduct Harbour** (Map p62; www.waterfrontauckland.co.nz) was given a major makeover for the 1999/2000 and 2003 America's Cup yachting events. It's now a fancy dining and boozing precinct, and guaranteed to have at least a slight buzz any night of the week.

Connected to the Viaduct by a raiseable bridge, Wynyard Quarter opened in advance of another sporting tournament, 2011's Rugby World Cup. With its public plazas, waterfront cafes, events centre, fish market and children's playground, it has quickly become Auckland's favourite new place to promenade.

Voyager – New Zealand Maritime Museum   Museum

(Map p62; ☎09-373 0800; www.maritimemuseum.co.nz; 149-159 Quay St; admission adult/child $17/8.50, with harbour cruise $29/14.50; ⏰9am-5pm, free guided tours 10.30am & 1pm) This museum traces NZ's seafaring history, from Maori voyaging canoes to the America's Cup. Re-creations include a tilting 19th-century steerage-class cabin and a 1950s beach store and bach (holiday home). *Blue Water Black Magic* is a tribute to Sir Peter Blake, the Whitbread-Round-the-World– and America's Cup–winning yachtsman who was murdered in 2001 on an environmental monitoring trip in the Amazon. There are also optional one-hour harbour cruises on the *Ted Ashby,* a ketch-rigged sailing scow.

PARNELL & NEWMARKET

Auckland Domain   Park

(Map p70; ⏰24hr) Covering about 80 hectares, this green swathe contains sports fields, interesting sculpture, formal gardens, wild corners and the **Wintergarden** (Map p70; www.wintergardenpavilion.co.nz; ⏰9am-5.30pm Mon-Sat, 9am-7.30pm Sun Nov-Mar, 9am-4.30pm Apr-Oct) **FREE**, with its fernery, tropical house, cool house, cute cat statue, coffee kiosk and neighbouring cafe. The mound in the centre of the park is all that remains of Pukekaroa, one of Auckland's volcanoes.

TAMAKI DRIVE

This scenic, pohutukawa-lined road heads east from the city, hugging the waterfront. In summer it's a jogging/cycling/rollerblading blur.

A succession of child-friendly, peaceful swimming beaches starts at Ohaku Bay. Around the headland is Mission Bay, a popular beach with an iconic art-deco fountain, historic mission house, restaurants and bars. Safe swimming beaches Kohimarama and St Heliers follow. Further east along Cliff Rd, the Achilles Point lookout offers panoramic views. At its base is Ladies Bay, popular with nudists.

Buses 745 to 769 from Britomart follow this route.

Kelly Tarlton's Sealife Aquarium   Aquarium

(☎09-531 5065; www.kellytarltons.co.nz; 23 Tamaki Dr; adult/child $36/20; ⏰9.30am-5pm) 🐟 Sharks and stingrays swim over and around you in transparent tunnels that

City Centre

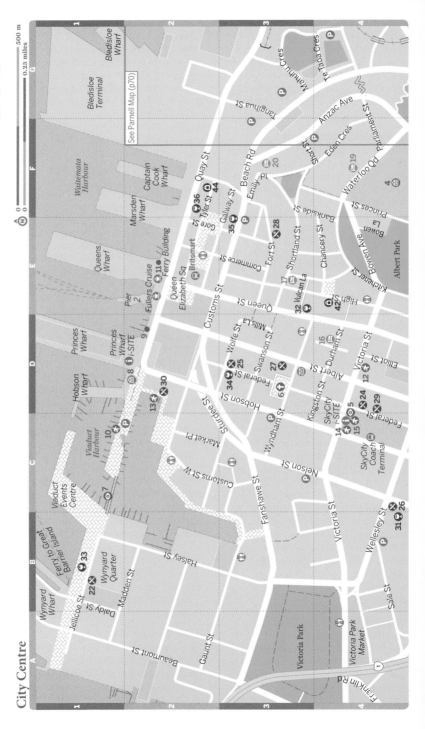

See Parnell Map (p70)

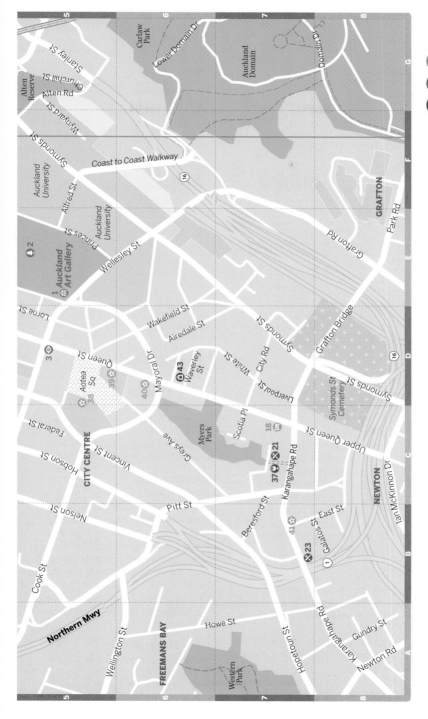

CITY CENTRE

FREEMANS BAY

NEWTON

GRAFTON

Northern Mwy

Cook St
Wellington St
Nelson St
Hobson St
Federal St
Lorne St
Queen St
Symonds St
Stanley St

Alten Reserve
Alten Rd
Wynyard St
Churchill St
Symonds St
Auckland University
Alfred St
Princes St
Auckland University
Wellesley St

Carlaw Park
Lower Domain Dr
Auckland Domain
Domain Dr

Coast to Coast Walkway

Auckland Art Gallery

Aotea Sq

Wakefield St
Airedale St
Mayoral Dr
Waverley St
White St
City Rd
Symonds St
Grafton Bridge
Grafton Rd
Park Rd

Vincent St
Greys Ave
Myers Park
Scotia Pl
Liverpool St
Upper Queen St
Symonds St Cemetery
Symonds St

Pitt St
Howe St
Hopetoun St
Beresford St
Galatos St
East St
Karangahape Rd
Karangahape Rd
Gundry St
Newton Rd
Ian McKinnon Dr

Western Park

1
2
3
38
39
40
43
18
37
21
41
23

63

City Centre

were once stormwater tanks. You can also enter the tanks in a shark cage with snorkel ($95), or dive into the tanks ($165). Other attractions include the Penguin Discovery tour (daily 10am, $199 per person) where just four visitors per day can get up close with Antarctic penguins. For all experiences, book online for a 10% to 20% discount and to check times.

A free shark-shaped shuttle bus departs from 172 Quay St (opposite the ferry terminal) on the half-hour from 9.30am to 3.30pm.

DEVONPORT

With well-preserved Victorian and Edwardian buildings and loads of cafes, Devonport is a short ferry trip from the city.

For a self-guided tour of historic buildings, pick up the *Old Devonport Walk* pamphlet from the i-SITE.

Ferries to Devonport (adult/child return $11/5.80, 12 minutes) depart from the Auckland Ferry Building every 30 minutes (hourly after 8pm) from 6.15am to 11.15pm (until 1am Friday and Saturday), and from 7.15am to 10pm on Sunday and public holidays. Some Waiheke Island and Rangitoto ferries also stop here.

Mt Victoria & North Head   Volcano
Mt Victoria (Takarunga; Victoria Rd) and **North Head** (Maungauika; Takarunga Rd; ☺6am-10pm) were Maori *pa* (fortified villages) and they remain fortresses of sorts, with the navy maintaining a presence. Both have gun embankments and North Head is riddled with tunnels, dug at the end of the 19th century in response to the Russian threat, and extended during WWI and WWII.

Navy Museum   Museum
(www.navymuseum.mil.nz; Torpedo Bay; ☺10am-5pm) FREE The navy has been in Devonport since the earliest days of the colony. Its history is on display at

OLIVER STREWE/GETTY IMAGES ©

 ## Don't Miss
Auckland Art Gallery

Following a significant 2011 refurbishment, Auckland's premier art repository now has a stunning glass-and-wood atrium grafted onto its 1887 French-chateau frame. Along with important works by Pieter Bruegel the Younger, Guido Reni, Picasso, Cézanne, Gauguin and Matisse, it also showcases the best of NZ art. Highlights include the intimate 19th-century portraits of tattooed Maori subjects by Charles Goldie, and the starkly dramatic text-scrawled canvasses of Colin McCahon. Free tours depart from the main entrance daily at 11.30am and 1.30pm.

NEED TO KNOW

Map p62; www.aucklandartgallery.com; cnr Kitchener & Wellesley Sts; admission for special exhibitions varies; ⊙10am-5pm

this well-presented and often moving museum, focusing on the stories of the sailors themselves.

WESTERN SPRINGS

Auckland Zoo   Zoo

(Map p76; www.aucklandzoo.co.nz; Motions Rd; adult/child $25/10; ⊙9.30am-5pm, last entry 4.15pm) 🖉 At this modern, spacious zoo, the big foreigners tend to steal the attention from the timid natives, but if you can wrestle the kids away from the tigers and orang-utans, there's a well-presented NZ section. Called *Te Wao Nui,* it's divided into six ecological zones: Coast (seals,

penguins), Islands (mainly lizards, including NZ's pint-sized dinosaur, the tuatara), Wetlands (ducks, herons, eels), Night (kiwi, naturally, along with frogs, native owls and weta), Forest (birds) and High Country (cheekier birds and lizards).

OTHER AREAS

One Tree Hill   Park

(Maungakiekie; www.cornwallpark.co.nz) This volcanic cone was the isthmus' key *pa* and the greatest fortress in the country, and from the top (182m) there are 360-degree views. At the summit is the

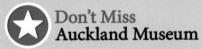

Don't Miss
Auckland Museum

Dominating the Auckland Domain is this imposing neoclassical temple (1929) capped with an impressive copper-and-glass dome (2007). The displays of Pacific Island and Maori artefacts on the ground floor are essential viewing. Highlights include a 25m war canoe and an extant carved meeting house (remove your shoes before entering). There's also a fascinating display on Auckland's volcanic field, including an eruption simulation, and the upper floors showcase military displays, fulfilling the building's dual role as a war memorial.

Hour-long museum highlights tours (included with admission) depart at 10.45am, 12.45pm and 2.15pm. Admission options incorporating Maori culture and performances are also available.

NEED TO KNOW

Map p70; ☑09-309 0443; www.aucklandmuseum.com; Auckland Domain; adult/child $25/10; ⊙10am-5pm

grave of John Logan Campbell, who gifted the land to the city in 1901 and requested that a memorial be built to the Maori people on the summit. Nearby is the stump of the last 'one tree'.

To get to One Tree Hill from the the city take a train to Greenlane and walk 1km along Green Lane West. By car, take the Greenlane exit of the Southern Motorway and turn right into Green Lane West.

Wallace Arts Centre Gallery

(www.tsbbankwallaceartscentre.org.nz; Pah Homestead, 72 Hillsborough Rd, Hillsborough; ⊙10am-3pm Tue-Fri, to 5pm Sat & Sun) FREE
Housed in a gorgeous 1879 mansion with views to One Tree Hill and the Manakau Harbour, the Wallace Arts Centre is endowed with contemporary NZ art from an extensive private collection, which is changed every four to six weeks.

Have lunch on the verandah and wander among the magnificent trees in the surrounding park.

Bus 299 (Lynfield) departs every 15 minutes from Wellesley St in the city (near the Civic Theatre) and heads to Hillsborough Rd ($4.50, about 40 minutes).

Rainbow's End   Amusement Park
(www.rainbowsend.co.nz; 2 Clist Cres; Superpass unlimited rides adult/child $52/42; ☺10am-5pm) It's a bit dull by international standards but Rainbow's End has enough rides (including a corkscrew rollercoaster) to keep the kids happy all day.

🏃 Activities

Visitors centres and public libraries stock the city council's *Auckland City's Walkways* pamphlet, which has a good selection of urban walks, including information on the Coast to Coast Walkway (p68).

Sail NZ   Sailing
(Map p62; ☎0800 397 567; www.explorenz. co.nz; Viaduct Harbour) Shoot the breeze on a genuine America's Cup yacht (adult/child $160/115) or head out on a Whale & Dolphin Safari (adult/child $160/105); dolphins are spotted 90% of the time and whales 75%. The *Pride of Auckland* fleet of glamorous large yachts offers 90-minute Harbour Sailing Cruises (adult/child $75/55), 2½-hour Dinner Cruises ($120/85) and full-day Sailing Adventures (adult/child $165/125).

SkyWalk   Extreme Sports
(Map p62; ☎0800 759 925; www.skywalk.co.nz; Sky Tower, cnr Federal & Victoria Sts; adult/child $145/115; ☺10am-4.30pm) SkyWalk involves circling the 192m-high, 1.2m-wide outside halo of the Sky Tower without rails or a balcony. Don't worry, they're not completely crazy – there is a safety harness.

SkyJump   Extreme Sports
(Map p62; ☎0800 759 586; www.skyjump.co.nz; Sky Tower, cnr Federal & Victoria Sts; adult/child $225/175; ☺10am-5pm) This thrilling 11-second, 85km/h base wire leap from

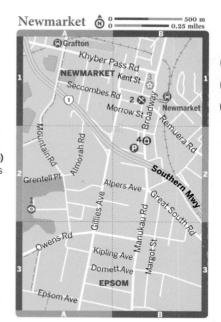

Newmarket ⊙ | 0   500 m
              | 0   0.25 miles

Newmarket

⊙ **Sights**
1 Eden Garden............................A2

❶ **Eating**
2 Teed St Larder B1

⊙ **Entertainment**
3 Rialto... B1

⊙ **Shopping**
4 Texan Art Schools Newmarket..........B2

the observation deck of the Sky Tower is more like a parachute jump than a bungy. Combine it with the SkyWalk in the Look & Leap package ($290).

Fergs Kayaks   Kayaking
(☎09-529 2230; www.fergskayaks.co.nz; 12 Tamaki Dr, Okahu Bay; ☺9am-6pm) Hires kayaks and paddle boards (per hour/day from $20/50), bikes (per hour/day $20/120) and inline skates (per hour/day $15/30). Day and night guided kayak trips are available to Devonport ($95, three hours, 8km) or Rangitoto Island ($120, six hours, 13km).

If You Like...
Parks & Gardens

If you like wandering through Albert Park (p60), you'll enjoy these other Auckland green zones.

1 AUCKLAND BOTANIC GARDENS
(www.aucklandbotanicgardens.co.nz; 102 Hill Rd, Manurewa; ⏰8am-6pm mid-Mar–mid-Oct, to 8pm mid-Oct–mid-Mar) This 64-hectare park has more than 10,000 plants (including threatened species), dozens of themed gardens and an infestation of wedding parties.

2 EDEN GARDEN
(Map p67; www.edengarden.co.nz; 24 Omana Ave; adult/child $8/6; ⏰9am-4pm) On Mt Eden's eastern slopes, and noted for its camellias, rhododendrons and azaleas.

3 PARNELL ROSE GARDENS
(Map p70; 85-87 Gladstone Rd; ⏰7am-7pm) These formal gardens are blooming excellent from November to March.

4 BASTION POINT
(Hapimana St) Politics, harbour views and lush lawns combine on this pretty headland with a chequered history.

5 WESTERN SPRINGS
(Map p76; Great North Rd) Parents bring their children to this picturesque park for the popular adventure playground.

Parnell Baths   Swimming
(Map p70; www.parnellbaths.co.nz; Judges Bay Rd; adult/child $6.30/free; ⏰6am-8pm Mon-Fri, 8am-8pm Sat & Sun) Outdoor saltwater pools with an awesome 1950s mural.

Balloon Expeditions   Ballooning
(☎09-416 8590; www.balloonexpeditions.co.nz; flight $340) Hour-long flights in a hot-air balloon at sunrise, including breakfast and bubbles.

Coast to Coast Walkway   Tramping
(www.aucklandcity.govt.nz) Right across the country from the Tasman to the Pacific (actually, only 16km), this walk encompasses One Tree Hill, Mt Eden, the Domain and the University, keeping mainly to reserves rather than city streets.
Do it in either direction: starting from the Viaduct Basin and heading south, it's marked by yellow markers and milestones; heading north from Onehunga there are blue markers. Our recommendation? Catch the train to Onehunga and finish up at the Viaduct's bars.
From Onehunga Station, take Onehunga Mall up to Princes St, turn left and pick up the track at the inauspicious park by the motorway.

 Tours

Potiki Adventures   Cultural Tour
(☎021 422 773; www.potikiadventures.co.nz; adult/child from $150/80) Tours to Waiheke Island and explorations of Auckland from a Maori cultural perspective.

Tamaki Hikoi   Cultural Tour
(☎0800 282 552; www.tamakihikoi.co.nz; 1-/3hr $40/95) Guides from the Ngati Whatua *iwi* (tribe) lead various Maori cultural tours, often including walking and a cultural performance.

NZ Winepro   Wine Tasting
(☎09-575 1958; www.nzwinepro.co.nz; tours $85-275) Explores Auckland's wine regions, combining tastings with sightseeing.

Explorer Bus   Bus Tour
(☎0800 439 756; www.explorerbus.co.nz; adult/child $40/20) 🚌 This hop-on, hop-off service departs from the Ferry Building every hour from 10am to 3pm (more frequently in summer), heading to 14 tourist sites around the central city.

Auckland Ghost Tours   Walking Tour
(☎09-630 5721; www.aucklandghosttours.com; adult/child $50/25) Stories of Auckland's

scary side on a two-hour walking tour of the central city.

Fullers — Cruise
(Map p62; ☎09-367 9111; www.fullers.co.nz; Ferry Bldg, 99 Quay St; adult/child $40/20; ⏱10.30am & 1.30pm) Daily 1½-hour harbour cruises including Rangitoto and a free return ticket to Devonport.

Sleeping

CITY CENTRE

Kiwi International Hotel — Hotel $
(Map p62; ☎09-379 6487; www.kiwihotel. co.nz; 411 Queen St; r $59-109, apt $169; P☎) Rooms – most with en suite bathrooms – definitely are compact, but they're clean and well kept, and the location bordering Queen St and Karangahape Rd is very convenient.

Waldorf Celestion — Apartment $$
(Map p62; ☎09-280 2200; www.celestion-waldorf.co.nz; 19-23 Anzac Ave; apt $170-277) ✐ A rash of Waldorfs have opened in recent years, all presenting similar symptoms: affordable, modern apartments in city-fringe locations. We prefer this one for its stylish red, black and grey colour palate.

CityLife — Hotel $$
(Map p62; ☎09-379 9222; www.heritagehotels. co.nz/citylife-auckland; Durham St; apt $179-339; P@☎⚲) ✐ A worthy tower-block hotel offering numerous apartments over dozens of floors, ranging from studios to three-bedroom suites. Facilities include a heated lap pool, gym, valet parking and a babysitting service.

Hotel de Brett — Boutique Hotel $$$
(Map p62; ☎09-925 9000; www.hoteldebrett. com; 2 High St; r $300-600; @☎) This hip, refurbished historic hotel has been zooshed up with stripy carpets and clever designer touches in every nook of the extremely comfortable rooms. Prices include breakfast, free broadband and a predinner drink.

Quadrant — Hotel $$$
(Map p62; ☎09-984 6000; www.thequadrant. com; 10 Waterloo Quadrant; apt $250-380; ☎) ✐ Slick, central and full of all the whiz-bang gadgets, this apartment-style complex is an excellent option. The only catch is that the units are tiny and the bathrooms beyond small.

PONSONBY & GREY LYNN

Abaco on Jervois — Motel $$
(Map p73; ☎09-360 6850; www.abaco.co.nz; 57 Jervois Rd; r $135-155, ste $194-215; P) A contemporary, neutral-toned motel including stainless-steel kitchenettes (with dish drawers and ovens) and fluffy white towels for use in the spa. The darker rooms downstairs are priced accordingly.

Great Ponsonby Arthotel — B&B $$$
(Map p73; ☎09-376 5989; www.greatpons.co.nz; 30 Ponsonby Tce; r $265-400; P@) ✐ In a

---

Auckland Volcanic Field

Some cities think they're tough just by living in the shadow of a volcano. Auckland's built on 50 of them, and no, they're not all extinct. The last one to erupt was Rangitoto about 600 years ago and no one can predict when the next eruption will occur. Auckland's quite literally a hot spot – with a reservoir of magma 100km below, waiting to bubble to the surface. But relax: this has only happened 19 times in the last 20,000 years.

Some of Auckland's volcanoes are cones, some are filled with water and some have been completely quarried away. The most interesting to explore are Mt Eden (p75), One Tree Hill (p65) and Rangitoto (p82).

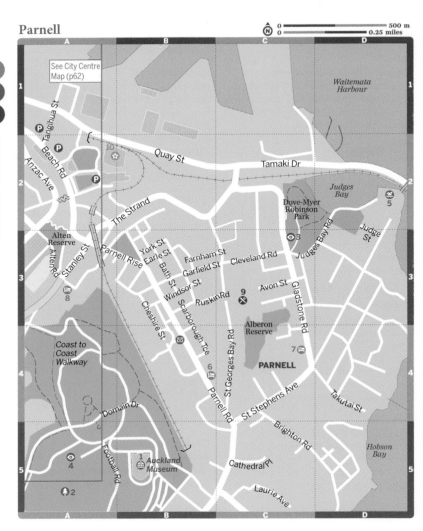

quiet cul-de-sac near Ponsonby Rd, this deceptively spacious Victorian villa has gregarious hosts, impressive sustainability practices and great breakfasts. Studio apartments open onto an attractive rear courtyard.

MT EDEN

Bavaria   Guesthouse $$
(Map p76; ✆09-638 9641; www.bavariabandb-hotel.co.nz; 83 Valley Rd; s $95-130, d $150-180; P@🛜) This spacious villa offers large,

airy rooms and a buffet breakfast. The communal TV lounge, dining room and deck all encourage mixing and mingling.

Eden Park B&B   B&B $$$
(Map p76; ✆09-630 5721; www.bedandbreakfastnz.com; 20 Bellwood Ave; s $135-150, d $235-250; 🛜) ✔ The hallowed turf of Auckland's legendary Eden Park rugby ground is only a block away and, while the rooms aren't overly large, they mirror the Edwardian elegance of this fine wooden villa.

Parnell

PARNELL & NEWMARKET

Quest Carlaw Park   Apartment **$$**
(Map p70; ☎09-304 0521; www.questcarlawpark.co.nz; 15 Nicholls Lane; apt $170-335; P@⊚) ⬤ It's in an odd spot but this set of smart, modern apartments is handy for Parnell, the city and the Domain, and if you've got a car you're practically on the motorway.

Parnell Inn   Motel **$$**
(Map p70; ☎09-358 0642; www.parnellinn.co.nz; 320 Parnell Rd; r $105-130; P@⊚) You'll get a chipper welcome from the friendly folks at this good-looking, revamped motel. Rooms 3 and 4 have great harbour views and some rooms have kitchenettes.

Quality Hotel Parnell   Hotel **$$**
(Map p70; ☎09-303 3789; www.theparnell.co.nz; 20 Gladstone Rd; r $150-310; P⊚) More than 100 motel rooms and units are available in this recently renovated complex. The newer north wing has great harbour views.

DEVONPORT

Devonport Motel   Motel **$$**
(☎09-445 1010; www.devonportmotel.co.nz; 11 Buchanan St; r $150; ⊚) This minimotel has two units in the tidy back garden. They're modern, clean, self-contained and in a quiet location close to Devonport's attractions.

Parituhu   B&B **$$**
(☎09-445 6559; www.parituhu.co.nz; 3 King Edward Pde; r $125-155; ⊚) There's only one double bedroom (with its own adjoining bathroom) available in this relaxing and welcoming Edwardian waterfront bungalow.

Devonport Sea Cottage   Cottage **$$**
(☎09-445 7117; www.devonportseacottagenz.com; 3a Cambridge Tce; d $130-150; ⊚) Head up the garden path to your own cute and cosy self-contained cottage.

OTHER AREAS

Jet Park   Hotel **$$**
(☎09-275 4100; www.jetpark.co.nz; 63 Westney Rd, Mangere; r $120-150; @⊚⊠) ⬤ Comfortable rooms and a decent vibe; with departure screens in the lobby and free airport shuttles there's no excuse for missing your flight.

Eating

CITY CENTRE

Food Truck Garage   Cafe **$**
(Map p62; www.foodtruckgarage.co.nz; 90 Wellesley St, City Works Depot; mains $10-14; ⊙11am-10pm, limited menu 3-5pm; ⬤) ⬤ In the funky new City Works Depot, the Food Truck Garage serves up healthy versions of fast food classics like burgers, tacos and wraps. Across the menu there's definitely no trade-off of taste for well-being.

Depot   Modern NZ **$$**
(Map p62; www.eatatdepot.co.nz; 86 Federal St; dishes $17-32; ⊙7am-late) TV chef Al Brown's first Auckland eatery offers first-rate Kiwi comfort food in informal surrounds (communal tables, butcher tiles and a constant buzz). Dishes are designed to be shared, and a pair of clever shuckers serve up the city's freshest clams and oysters.

Ima   Middle Eastern **$$**
(Map p62; ☎09-300 7252; www.imacuisine.co.nz; 57 Fort St; breakfast $11-20, lunch $16-24, dinner shared dishes $18-30; ⊙7am-2.30pm Mon-Fri, 5.30-10.30pm Tue-Sat) Named after the Hebrew word for mother, the menu

blends Israeli, Palestinian, Yemeni and Lebanese dishes. Try the *shakshuka* (baked eggs in a spicy tomato sauce) for breakfast or lunch, or rustle up a group for Ima's excellent shared dinners.

Federal & Wolfe — Cafe $$

(Map p62; 10 Federal St; mains $12-21; ⏰7am-3pm Mon-Sat; 🛜) 🍴 Packing crates and mismatched chairs lend an air of recycled chic to this corner cafe. Look forward to first-rate coffee and delicious food, much of it organic and free range.

Grove — Modern NZ $$$

(Map p62; 📞09-368 4129; www.thegroverestaurant.co.nz; St Patrick's Sq, Wyndham St; mains $45, tasting menu with/without wine pairing $240/145; ⏰noon-3pm Thu-Fri, 6pm-late Mon-Sat) Romantic fine dining at its best: the room is cosy and moodily lit, the menu encourages sensual experimentation and the service is effortless. If you can't find anything to break the ice from the extensive wine list, give it up mate – it's never going to happen.

Masu — Japanese $$$

(Map p62; www.skycityauckland.co.nz; 90 Federal St, SKYCITY Grand Hotel; mains $30-45, tasting menu $88; ⏰noon-3pm & 5.30pm-late) Superb Japanese food – especially from the sushi bar and the robata grill – and the added attraction of refreshing cocktails made from *shochu* (Japanese liquor).

BRITOMART, VIADUCT HARBOUR & WYNYARD QUARTER

Baduzzi — Italian $$

(Map p62; 📞09-309 9339; www.baduzzi.co.nz; cnr Jellicoe St & Fish Lane; small plates $10-20, mains $22-32; ⏰11.30am-late) This smart and sassy eatery does sophisticated spins on meatballs – try the crayfish (lobster) ones – and other robust but elegant Italian dishes. Cosy up in the intimate booths, grab a seat at the bar, or soak up some Auckland sunshine outside.

Soul Bar — Modern NZ $$$

(Map p62; 📞09-356 7249; www.soulbar.co.nz; Viaduct Harbour; mains $22-42; ⏰11am-late)

Eating seafood by the water is a must in Auckland and this modernist gastrodome also boasts an unbeatable see-and-be-seen location.

PONSONBY & GREY LYNN

Little Bird — Cafe $

(Map p73; www.littlebirdorganics.co.nz; 1a Summer St; mains $9-16; ⏰7am-4pm; 🍴) 🍴 Welcome to an 'unbakery', where virtually everything on the menu is prepared uncooked, but still very tasty and healthy. Tuck into dishes studded with açai berries, quinoa and organic fruit, and there are even bagels, pad thai and tacos. Also great are the juices, smoothies and cakes.

Blue Breeze Inn — Chinese $$

(Map p73; 📞09-360 0303; www.thebluebreezeinn.co.nz; 146 Ponsonby Rd, Ponsonby Central; small plates $10-18, larger plates $26-38; ⏰5pm-late) Regional Chinese flavours combine with a funky retro Pacific ambience. The waitstaff are sassy, the rum cocktails are deliciously strong, and menu standouts include steamed buns with Peking pork belly and pickled cucumber, and cumin-spiced lamb.

Mekong Baby — Asian $$

(Map p73; www.mekongbaby.com; 262 Ponsonby Rd; mains $24-32; ⏰noon-late Tue-Sun) Stylish and buzzing restaurant and bar offering excellent Southeast Asian flavours, mainly from Vietnam, Cambodia and Laos. Try the goat curry.

Ponsonby Central — Cafes, Restaurants $$

(Map p73; www.ponsonbycentral.co.nz; 136-138 Ponsonby Rd; mains $15-35; ⏰11.30am-10.30pm Sun-Wed, to midnight Thu-Sat) From Auckland's best pizza to Uruguayan, Argentinean, Thai and Japanese, loads of flavour-filled restaurants and cafes fill this upmarket laneway collection of eateries and gourmet food shops.

Ponsonby Road Bistro — International $$

(Map p73; 📞09-360 1611; www.ponsonbyroadbistro.co.nz; 165 Ponsonby Rd; mains $25-36; ⏰noon-3pm Mon-Fri, 5.30pm-late Mon-Sat) Portions are large at this modern,

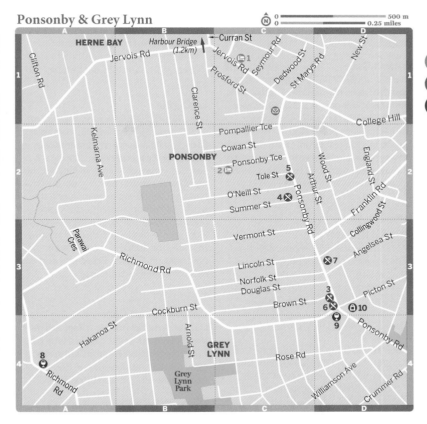

Ponsonby & Grey Lynn

upmarket restaurant with Italian and French sensibilities and first-rate service. Imported cheese and wine are a highlight, and the crispy-based pizzas make a delicious shared snack.

NEWTON

Alleluya
Cafe **$**

(Map p62; St Kevin's Arcade, Karangahape Rd; mains $10-19; ⊙9am-5.30pm Mon-Sat, to 3pm Sun; 🛜✏) To the bohemian denizens of K Rd, Alleluya means good coffee, moreish cakes and lots of vegetarian options. It's situated at the end of the city's hippest arcade, with windows offering a wonderful snapshot of the city skyline.

Coco's Cantina
Italian **$$**

(Map p62; www.cocoscantina.co.nz; 376 Karangahape Rd; mains $25-32; ⊙5pm-late Tue-Sat) Rub shoulders with Auckland's hipsters and foodsters at this bustling cantina where the wait for a table is part of the experience. Propping up the bar is hardly a hardship: the ambience and drinks

73

list see to that. The rustic menu is narrowly focused, seasonal and invariably delicious.

French Cafe
French $$$

(Map p76; ☎09-377 1911; www.thefrenchcafe. co.nz; 210 Symonds St; mains $46, tasting menu with/without wine pairings $220/140; ☺noon-3pm Fri, 6pm-late Tue-Sat) The legendary French Cafe has been rated as one of Auckland's top restaurants for more than 20 years now and it still continues to excel. The cuisine is nominally French-influenced, but chef Simon Wright sneaks in lots of tasty Asian and Pacific Rim touches.

KINGSLAND

Atomic Roastery
Cafe $

(Map p76; www.atomiccoffee.co.nz; 420c New North Rd; snacks $9-10; ☺8am-3pm Mon-Sat, 9am-2pm Sun) Java hounds should follow their noses to this, one of the country's best-known coffee roasters. Tasty accompaniments include pies served in minifrypans, bagels, salads and cakes.

Sake Bar 601
Japanese $$

(Map p76; ☎09-849 7268; www.601newnorth road.co.nz; 601 New North Rd; mains $20-35; ☺11.30am-1.30pm & 6-9.30pm Tue-Sat) Order a frosty Sapporo beer and watch the friendly Japanese surf-crazy owners prepare some of the best sushi and sashimi in town. Other standouts are the tempura prawns and terikayi chicken. The compact restaurant is very popular so book ahead.

MT EDEN

Merediths
Modern NZ $$$

(Map p76; ☎09-623 3140; www.merediths.co.nz; 365 Dominion Rd; 6-9 course degustation $90-140; ☺noon-3pm Fri, 6pm-late Tue-Sat) Dining at Merediths is the culinary equivalent of black-water rafting – tastes surprise you at every turn, you never know what's coming next and you're left with a sense of breathless exhilaration.

PARNELL & NEWMARKET

Teed St Larder
Cafe $

(Map p67; www.teedstreetlarder.co.nz; 7 Teed St; ☺8am-4pm) Polished concrete floors, beer crate tables and colourful oversized lampshades set the scene at Newmarket's best cafe. There are plenty of enticing cooked items on the menu, but it's hard to go past the delicious sandwiches and tarts.

La Cigale
French $$

(Map p70; ☎09-366 9361; www.lacigale.co.nz; 69 St Georges Bay Rd; cafe $8-18, bistro mains $34; ☺cafe 9am-4pm Mon-Fri, bistro dinner Wed-Fri from 6pm, market 9am-1.30pm Sat & Sun) Catering to Francophile foodies, this warehouse stocks French imports and has a patisserie-laden cafe. During the weekend farmers markets, this *cigale* (cicada) really chirps; stalls are laden with local artisan produce. From Wednesday to Friday the space is converted into a quirky evening bistro. Booking ahead is recommended.

DEVONPORT

Calliope Road Cafe
Cafe $

(33 Calliope Rd; mains $9-18; ☺8am-3pm Wed-Mon) Devonport's best cafe is a little back from the main tourist strip, and serves a tasty mix of cafe classics and Southeast Asian dishes to locals in the know.

OTHER AREAS

St Heliers Bay Bistro
Modern NZ $$

(www.stheliersbaybistro.co.nz; 387 Tamaki Dr; mains $14-26; ☺7am-11pm) Catch the bus along pretty Tamaki Dr to this classy eatery with harbour views. No bookings are taken, but the switched-on crew soon find space for diners. Look forward to dishes infused with mainly Mediterranean and Middle Eastern flavours.

Engine Room
Modern NZ $$$

(☎09-480 9502; www.engineroom.net.nz; 115 Queen St, Northcote; mains $34-36; ☺6pm-late Tue-Sat, noon-2.30pm Fri) One of Auckland's best restaurants, this informal eatery serves up lighter-than-air goats cheese soufflés, inventive mains and oh-my-God chocolate truffles. It's worth booking ahead and catching the ferry to Northcote wharf; the restaurant is a further 1km walk away.

AMOS CHAPPLE/GETTY IMAGES ©

 ## Don't Miss
Mt Eden

From the top of Auckland's highest volcanic cone (196m), the entire isthmus and both harbours are laid bare. The symmetrical crater (50m deep) is known as Te Ipu Kai a Mataaho (the Food Bowl of Mataaho, the god of things hidden in the ground) and is highly *tapu* (sacred). Do not enter it, but feel free to explore the remainder of the mountain. The remains of *pa* (fortified village) terraces and food storage pits are clearly visible.

Drive to the top or join the fitness freaks jogging or trudging up. Tour buses are banned from the summit, but shuttles will transport infirm passengers to the top from the car park on the lower slopes.

NEED TO KNOW
Maungawhau; Map p76; ⏲road access 7am-11pm

Drinking & Nightlife

CITY CENTRE

Brothers Beer　　　　Craft Beer
(Map p62; www.brothersbeer.co.nz; 90 Wellesley St, City Works Depot; ⏲noon-10pm Wed-Sat, noon-8pm Tue & Sun, closed Mon) Our favourite Auckland bar combines industrial decor with 18 taps crammed with Brothers' own brews and guest beers from NZ and further afield.

Mo's　　　　Bar
(Map p62; www.mosbar.co.nz; cnr Wolfe & Federal Sts; ⏲4pm-3am Mon-Fri, 6pm-3am Sat) There's something about this tiny corner bar that makes you want to invent problems just so the barperson can solve them with soothing words and an expertly poured martini.

Cassette Nine　　　　Club
(Map p62; www.cassettenine.com; 9 Vulcan Lane; ⏲noon-late Tue-Sat) Hipsters gravitate to

75

Kingsland & Mt Eden

Map labels

GRAFTON

NEWTON

EDEN TERRACE

MT EDEN

ARCH HILL

GREY LYNN

KINGSLAND

WESTERN SPRINGS

MORNINGSIDE

SANDRINGHAM

MT ALBERT

Mt Eden

Eden Park

Kingsland

Morningside

Great North Rd
Bullock Track
Old Mill Rd
Surrey Cres
Cumminner Rd
Great North Rd
Newton Rd
Ian McKinnon Dr
New North Rd
North Western Mwy
Bond St
Central Rd
Kingsland Ave
School Rd
New North Rd
Western Springs Rd
St Lukes Rd
Linwood Ave
Baldwin Ave
Asquith Ave
Morningside Dr
Sainsbury Rd
Sandringham Rd
Reiners Ave
Bellwood Ave
Walters Rd
Onslow Rd
View Rd
Bellevue Rd
Dominion Rd
Valley Rd
King Edward Pde
Prospect Tce
Horoeka Ave
Wynyard St
Pentland Ave
Woodford Rd
Sherbourne St
Esplanade Rd
Bellevue Rd
Mt Eden Rd
Clive Rd
Normanby Rd
Boston Rd
Nugent Rd
Khyber Pass Rd
Grafton Rd
Symonds St
France St
Enfield St
Edwin St
Valley Rd
Oaklands Rd
Stokes Rd

1
2
3
4
5
6
7
8
9
10
11
12
13
14
15
16

Scale: 0 500 m / 0 0.25 miles

Kingsland & Mt Eden

this eccentric bar-club for music ranging from live indie to international DJ sets.

BRITOMART, VIADUCT HARBOUR & WYNYARD QUARTER

Tyler Street Garage   Bar

(Map p62; www.tylerstreetgarage.co.nz; 120 Quay St; ⊙11.30am-late) Just in case you were in any doubt that this was actually a garage, they have left the parking lines painted on the concrete floor. A compact roof terrace looks over the wharves.

Orleans   Bar, Live Music

(Map p62; www.orleans.co.nz; 48 Customs St; ⊙11.30am-midnight Sun-Thu, to 4am Fri & Sat) This South Pacific gumbo spin on a southern US jazz bar has wicked cocktails, and live jazz and blues every night. Bar snacks include po' boy sandwiches.

Conservatory   Bar

(Map p62; www.theconservatory.co.nz; North Wharf, 1-17 Jellicoe St; ⊙11am-late Mon-Fri, 10.30am-late Sat & Sun) The coolest of the new Wynyard Quarter hang-outs is this

liquored up greenhouse sprouting a living wall of greenery and a profusion of cocktails.

PONSONBY & GREY LYNN

Golden Dawn   Bar

(Map p73; www.goldendawn.co.nz; 134b Ponsonby Rd, cnr Ponsonby & Richmond Rds; ⊙4pm-late Tue-Thu, from 3pm Fri-Sun) Occupying an old shopfront and an inviting stables yard, this hip late-night drinking den regularly hosts happenings including DJs and live bands. Entrance is via the unmarked door just around the corner on Richmond Rd.

Freida Margolis   Bar

(Map p73; www.facebook.com/FreidaMargolis; 440 Richmond Rd, West Lynn; ⊙4pm-late) Formerly a butcher – look out for the West Lynn Organic Meats sign – this corner location is now a great little neighbourhood bar with a backstreets of Bogota ambience.

NEWTON

Wine Cellar & Whammy Bar   Bar, Live Music

(Map p62; www.facebook.com/thewhammybar; St Kevin's Arcade, Karangahape Rd; ⊙5pm-midnight Mon-Thu, 5.30pm-2am Fri & Sat) Secreted downstairs in an arcade, this bar is dark, grungy and very cool, with regular live music in the neighbouring Whammy Bar from Thursday to Saturday.

Galbraith's Alehouse   Brewery, Pub

(Map p76; www.alehouse.co.nz; 2 Mt Eden Rd; ⊙noon-11pm) Brewing real ales and lagers on-site, this cosy English-style pub offers bliss on tap. There are always more craft beers on the guest taps, and the food's also very good.

Kings Arms Tavern   Live Music, Pub

(Map p76; www.kingsarms.co.nz; 59 France St) Auckland's leading small venue for local and up-and-coming international bands.

MT EDEN

Liquid Molten   Wine Bar, Tapas

(Map p76; www.molten.co.nz; 42 Mt Eden Rd; ⊙4pm-late Mon-Sat) Grab a spot in the cosy leather banquettes or venture out to the al fresco garden. Either way enjoy a grown up but relaxed ambience, a great wine and beer list, and innovative bar food.

KINGSLAND

Neighbourhood
Bar

(Map p76; www.neighbourhood.co.nz; 498 New North Rd; ⏰11am-late; 📶) With picture windows overlooking Eden Park and a front terrace that's pick-up central after dark, this upmarket pub is the place to be either side of rugby fixtures. DJs play on weekends.

Portland Public House
Bar, Live Music

(Map p76; 463 New North Rd; ⏰noon-late Tue-Sun) With mismatched furniture, cartoon-themed art, and lots of hidden nooks and crannies, the Portland Public House is like spending a few lazy hours at a good mate's place. It's also an excellent location for live music.

⭐ Entertainment

For listings, check the *NZ Herald's Time Out* magazine on Thursday and again in its Saturday edition. Visit www.kroad.co.nz for Karangahape Rd bars and clubs.

LIVE MUSIC

Power Station
Live Music

(Map p76; www.powerstation.net.nz; 33 Mt Eden Rd) Midrange venue popular with up-and-coming overseas acts and established Kiwi bands.

Vector Arena
Stadium

(Map p70; 📞09-358 1250; www.vectorarena.co.nz; Mahuhu Cres; ⏰9am-2pm) Auckland's top indoor venue for major touring acts.

CINEMA

Rialto
Cinema

(Map p67; 📞09-369 2417; www.rialto.co.nz; 167 Broadway, Newmarket; adult/child $16.50/10) Mainly art-house and international films, plus better mainstream fare and regular specialist film festivals.

NZ Film Archives
Cinema

(Map p62; 📞09-379 0688; www.filmarchive.org.nz; 300 Karangahape Rd, Newton; ⏰11am-5pm Mon-Fri) Around 2000 Kiwi feature films, documentaries and TV shows, which you can watch for free on a computer monitor.

Auckland Ferry Building (p82)

THEATRE, CLASSICAL MUSIC & COMEDY

Auckland's main arts and entertainment complex is grouped around Aotea Sq. Branded **The Edge** (☎09-357 3355; www.the-edge.co.nz), it comprises the Town Hall, Civic Theatre (p60) and Aotea Centre.

Auckland Town Hall
Classical Music

(Map p62; 305 Queen St) This elegant Edwardian venue (1911) hosts the NZ Symphony Orchestra (www.nzso.co.nz) and Auckland Philharmonia (www.apo.co.nz). Also used by international rock bands.

Aotea Centre
Theatre

(Map p62; 50 Mayoral Dr; ⊙9am-5.30pm Mon-Fri, 10am-4pm Sat & Sun) Theatre, dance, ballet and opera. NZ Opera (www.nzopera.com) regularly performs here.

Classic Comedy Club
Comedy

(Map p62; ☎09-373 4321; www.comedy.co.nz; 321 Queen St; tickets $5-27) Performances on Mondays and Wednesdays to Saturdays.

 Shopping

Followers of fashion should head to the Britomart Precinct, Newmarket's Teed and Nuffield Sts, and Ponsonby Rd. For vintage clothing and secondhand boutiques try K Rd or Ponsonby Rd.

CITY CENTRE

Real Groovy
Music

(Map p62; www.realgroovy.co.nz; 438 Queen St; ⊙9am-7pm Sat-Wed, to 9pm Thu & Fri) Masses of new, secondhand and rare releases in vinyl and CD format, as well as concert tickets, giant posters, DVDs, books, magazines and clothes.

Pauanesia
Gifts

(Map p62; www.pauanesia.co.nz; 35 High St; ⊙9.30am-6.30pm Mon-Fri, 10am-4.30pm Sat & Sun) Homewares and gifts with a Polynesian and Kiwiana influence.

Zambesi
Clothing

(Map p62; www.zambesi.co.nz; 56 Tyler St; ⊙10am-6pm) Iconic NZ label much sought after by local and international celebs.

Auckland for Children

All of the east coast beaches (St Heliers, Kohimarama, Mission Bay, Okahu Bay, Cheltenham, Narrow Neck, Takapuna, Milford, Long Bay) are safe for supervised kids, while sights such as Rainbow's End, Kelly Tarlton's (p61), Auckland Museum (p66) and Auckland Zoo (p65) are all firm favourites. Parnell Baths (p68) has a children's pool, but on wintry days, head to the thermal pools at Parakai or Waiwera.

PONSONBY & GREY LYNN

Texan Art Schools
Art & Crafts

(Map p73; www.texanartschools.co.nz; 95 Ponsonby Rd; ⊙9.30am-5.30pm) A collective of 200 local artists sell their wares here. Also in **Newmarket** (Map p67; 366 Broadway).

KINGSLAND

Royal Jewellery Studio
Jewellery

(Map p76; www.royaljewellerystudio.com; 486 New North Rd; ⊙10am-5pm) Work by local artisans, including beautiful Maori designs and authentic *pounamu* (greenstone) jewellery.

OTHER AREAS

Otara Market
Market

(Newbury St; ⊙6am-noon Sat) Held in the car park between the Manukau Polytech and the Otara town centre, this market has a palpable Polynesian atmosphere and is good for South Pacific food, music and fashions. Take bus 497 from Britomart ($6.80, 50 minutes).

❶ Information

Medical Services

Auckland City Hospital (☎09-367 0000; www.adhb.govt.nz; Park Rd, Grafton; ⊙24hr) The city's main hospital has a dedicated accident and emergency (A&E) service.

Auckland Metro Doctors & Travelcare (☎09-373 4621; www.aucklandmetrodoctors.co.nz; 17

If You Like…
Extreme Action

If you like SkyWalk (p67) and SkyJump (p67), check out these other Auckland adrenaline rushes.

1 AUCKLAND BRIDGE CLIMB & BUNGY
(☎09-360 7748; www.bungy.co.nz; Curran St, Herne Bay; adult/child climb $120/80, bungy $150/120) Climb up or jump off the Auckland Harbour Bridge.

2 NZ SKYDIVE
(☎09-373 5778; www.nzskydive.co.nz; 12,000ft $330) Tandem skydives from Mercer airfield, 55km south of Auckland. A free shuttle for overseas visitors is available from Auckland.

3 G-MAX REVERSE BUNGY
(Map p62; ☎09-377 1328; cnr Albert & Victoria Sts; ride $40; ☺9am-10pm Sun-Thu, 10am-2am Fri & Sat) Imagine a giant slingshot with yourself as the projectile as you're reverse-bungyed 60m into the air.

4 AUCKLAND JET BOAT TOURS
(Map p62; ☎050 825 5382; www.aucklandjetboattours.co.nz; floating pavilion, 220 Quay St; adult/child incl museum $85/45) Take a 35-minute blast around the harbour.

Emily Pl; ☺9am-5.30pm Mon-Fri, 10am-2pm Sat) Health care for travellers, including vaccinations and travel consultations.

Tourist Information

Auckland Domestic Airport i-SITE (☎09-256 8480; ☺7am-9pm) Located in the Air New Zealand terminal.

Auckland International Airport i-SITE (☎09-275 6467; ☺24hr) On your left as you exit the customs hall.

Princes Wharf i-SITE (Map p62; ☎09-307 0612; www.aucklandnz.com; 137 Quay St; ☺9am-5.30pm)

SkyCity i-SITE (Map p62; ☎09-363 7182; www.aucklandnz.com; SkyCity Atrium, cnr Victoria & Federal Sts; ☺8am-8pm)

ⓘ Getting There & Away

Air

Auckland is the main international gateway to NZ, and a hub for domestic flights. **Auckland International Airport** (AKL; ☎09-275 0789; www.aucklandairport.co.nz; Ray Emery Dr, Mangere) is 21km south of the city centre. It has separate international and domestic terminals, each with a tourist information centre. A free shuttle service operates every 15 minutes (5am to 10.30pm) between the terminals and there's also a signposted footpath (about a 10-minute walk).

Air New Zealand (☎09-357 3000; www.airnewzealand.co.nz) Flies to Kaitaia, Kerikeri, Whangarei, Hamilton, Tauranga, Whakatane, Gisborne, Rotorua, Taupo, New Plymouth, Napier, Whanganui, Palmerston North, Masterton, Wellington, Nelson, Blenheim, Christchurch, Queenstown and Dunedin.

Jetstar (☎0800 800 995; www.jetstar.com) To Wellington, Christchurch, Queenstown and Dunedin.

Bus

Coaches depart from 172 Quay St, opposite the Ferry Building, except for InterCity services, which depart from **SkyCity Coach Terminal** (Map p62; ☎09-913 6220; 102 Hobson St).

Go Kiwi (☎07-866 0336; www.go-kiwi.co.nz) Daily Auckland City–International Airport–Thames–Tairua–Whitianga shuttles.

InterCity (www.intercity.co.nz)

Naked Bus (☎0900 62533; www.nakedbus.com) Naked Buses travel along SH1 as far north as Kerikeri (four hours) and as far south as Wellington (12 hours), as well as heading to Tauranga (3½ hours) and Napier (12 hours).

Car & Campervan

Hire

Apex Car Rentals (☎09-307 1063; www.apexrentals.co.nz; 156 Beach Rd; ☺8am-5pm)

Budget (☎09-976 2270; www.budget.co.nz; 163 Beach Rd; ☺7am-6pm Mon-Fri, 8am-5pm Sat & Sun)

Britz, Kea & Maui (☎09-255 3910; www.maui.co.nz; 36 Richard Pearse Dr, Mangere; ☺8am-6pm)

Go Rentals (📞09-257 5142; www.gorentals.
co.nz; George Bolt Memoral Dr, Bay 2-10, Cargo
Central; ⏰6am-10pm)

Omega (📞09-377 5573; www.omegarentals.
com; 75 Beach Rd; ⏰8am-5pm)

Thrifty (📞09-309 0111; www.thrifty.co.nz; 150
Khyber Pass Rd; ⏰8am-5pm)

Train

Northern Explorer (📞0800 872 467; www.
kiwirailscenic.co.nz) trains leave from Britomart
station (Queen St) at 7.50am on Monday,
Thursday and Saturday and arrive in Wellington
at 6.25pm. Standard fares to Wellington range
from $119 to $186, but some discounted seats are
available at $99 (first in, first served).

ℹ️ Getting Around

To & From the Airport

A taxi between the airport and the city usually
costs between $65 and $85, more if you strike
traffic snarls.

Airbus Express (📞09-366 6400; www.airbus.
co.nz; 1 way/return adult $16/28, child $6/12)
Runs between the terminals and the city, every
10 to 15 minutes from 7am to 7pm and at least
hourly through the night. Reservations are
not required; buy a ticket from the driver or online.
The trip usually takes less than an hour (longer
during peak times).

Super Shuttle (📞0800 748 885; www.
supershuttle.co.nz) This convenient
door-to-door shuttle charges $29
for one person heading between
the airport and a city hotel; the
price increases for outlying
suburbs.

Public Transport

The Maxx (📞09-366
6400; www.maxx.co.nz)
information service covers
buses, trains and ferries
and has an excellent
trip-planning feature. A
Discovery Pass provides
a day's transport on most
trains and buses and on

North Shore ferries ($16); buy it on the bus or
train or at Fullers offices.

Bus

Bus routes spread their tentacles throughout
the city and you can purchase a ticket from
the driver. Single-ride fares in the inner city are
$1 for an adult and $0.60 for a child. If you're
travelling further afield there are fare stages from
$1.90/1.10 (adult/child) to $10.30/6.10.

The most useful services are the
environmentally friendly Link Buses that loop in
both directions around three routes (taking in
many of the major sights) from 7am to 11pm:

- City Link (adult/child $0.50/0.30, free for AT
  HOP cardholders, every seven to 10 minutes) –
  Britomart, Queen St, Karangahape Rd, with
  some buses connecting to Wynyard Quarter.

- Inner Link ($1.90, every 10 to 15 minutes) –
  Queen St, SkyCity, Victoria Park, Ponsonby Rd,
  Karangahape Rd, Museum, Newmarket, Parnell
  and Britomart.

- Outer Link (maximum $3.40, every 15
  minutes) – Art Gallery, Ponsonby, Herne Bay,
  Westmere, MOTAT 2, Pt Chevalier, Mt Albert,
  St Lukes Mall, Mt Eden, Newmarket, Museum,
  Parnell, University.

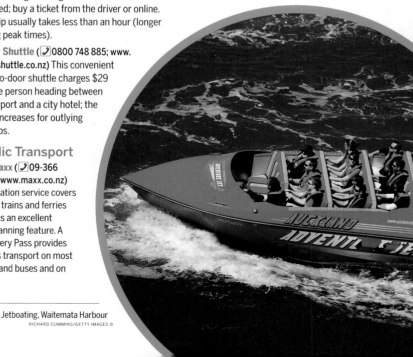

Jetboating, Waitemata Harbour
RICHARD CUMMINS/GETTY IMAGES ©

Detour:
North Shore Beaches

Fine swimming beaches stretch from North Head to Long Bay. The gulf islands shelter them from strong surf, making them safe for supervised children. Aim for high tide unless you fancy a lengthy walk to waist-deep water.

Cheltenham Beach is a short walk from Devonport. **Takapuna Beach**, closest to the Harbour Bridge, is Auckland's answer to Bondi and the most built up. Nearby **St Leonards Beach**, popular with gay men, requires clambering over rocks at high tide.

Ferry

Auckland's Edwardian baroque **Ferry Building (Map p62; Quay St)** sits grandly at the end of Queen St. Fullers (p69) ferries (to Bayswater, Birkenhead, Devonport, Great Barrier Island, Half Moon Bay, Northcote, Motutapu, Rangitoto and Waiheke) leave directly behind the building, while **360 Discovery (Map p62; ☎0800 360 3472; www.360discovery.co.nz; Pier 4, 139 Quay St; cruise adult/child $27/17, three-day pass $35/21; ⏱10am, noon & 2.30pm)** ferries (to Coromandel, Gulf Harbour, Motuihe, Rotoroa and Tiritiri Matangi) leave from adjacent piers.

Train

There are just four train routes: west to Waitakere, south to Onehunga, and two run south to Pukekohe. Services are at least hourly from around 6am to 8pm (later on the weekends). Buy a ticket from machines or ticket offices at train stations. All trains have wheelchair ramps.

Taxi

Auckland Co-op Taxis (☎09-300 3000; www.3003000.co.nz) is one of the biggest companies. There's a surcharge for transport to and from the airport and cruise ships, and for phone orders.

HAURAKI GULF ISLANDS

The Hauraki Gulf, stretching between Auckland and the Coromandel Peninsula, is dotted with *motu* (islands) and gives the Bay of Islands stiff competition in the beauty stakes. Some islands are only minutes from the city and make excellent day trips. Wine-soaked Waiheke and volcanic Rangitoto really shouldn't be missed.

Rangitoto Island

Sloping elegantly from the waters of the gulf, 259m **Rangitoto (www.rangitoto.org)**, the largest and youngest of Auckland's volcanic cones, provides a picturesque backdrop to all of the city's activities. As recently as 600 years ago it erupted from the sea and was probably active for several years before settling down.

Rangitoto makes for a great day trip. Its harsh scoria slopes hold a surprising amount of flora (including the world's largest pohutukawa forest) and there are excellent walks, but you'll need sturdy shoes and plenty of water. Although it looks steep, up close it's shaped more like an egg sizzling in a pan. The walk to the summit only takes an hour and is rewarded with sublime views.

ⓘ Getting There & Around

Fullers (☎09-367 9111; www.fullers.co.nz; Ferry Bldg, 99 Quay St; adult/child return Auckland or Devonport $29/14.50) has ferry services to Rangitoto from Auckland's Ferry Building (20 minutes, three daily on weekdays, four on weekends) and Devonport (two daily). It also offers the **Volcanic Explorer (adult/child incl ferry $60/30; ⏱departs 9.15am & 12.15pm)**, a guided tour around the island in a canopied 'road train'.

Waiheke Island

Waiheke is 93 sq km of island bliss a 35-minute ferry ride from central Auckland. Once they could hardly give land away here; nowadays multimillionaires rub shoulders with the old-time hippies and bohemian artists who gave the island its green repute. While beaches are the big drawcard, wine is a close second.

⊚ Sights

Waiheke's two best beaches are **Onetangi**, a long stretch of white sand at the centre of the island, and **Palm Beach**, a pretty little horseshoe bay between Oneroa and Onetangi. Both have nudist sections; head west just past some rocks in both cases. **Oneroa** and neighbouring **Little Oneroa** are also excellent, but you'll be sharing the waters with moored yachts in summer. The *Waiheke Art Map* brochure, free from the i-SITE, lists galleries and craft stores.

Goldie Vineyard   Winery
(www.goldiewines.co.nz; 18 Causeway Rd; tastings $10, refundable with purchase; ⊙tasting room noon-4pm daily, cafe noon-4pm Sat & Sun & daily late Dec–mid-Jan) Founded as Goldwater Estate in 1978, this is Waiheke's pioneering vineyard. The tasting room sells well-stocked baskets for a picnic among the vines ($60 for two people).

Stonyridge   Winery
(☑09-372 8822; www.stonyridge.com; 80 Onetangi Rd; tastings per wine $3-15; ⊙11.30am-5pm) ⊘ Famous organic reds, an atmospheric cafe, tours ($10, 35 minutes, 11.30am Saturday and Sunday) and the occasional dance party.

Artworks Complex   Arts Centre
(2 Korora Rd; ☎) The Artworks complex houses a **community theatre** (☑09-372 2941; www.artworkstheatre.org.nz); an **art-house cinema** (☑09-372 4240; www.waihekecinema.net; adult/child $14/7); an attention-grabbing **art gallery** (☑09-372 9907; www.waihekeartgallery.org.nz; admission free; ⊙10am-4pm); and **Whittaker's Musical Museum** (☑09-372 5573; www.musical-museum.org; ⊙1-4pm, live shows 1.30pm Sat) **FREE**, a collection of antique concert

instruments. This is also the place for free internet access, either on a terminal at the **library** (⊙9am-5.30pm Mon-Fri, 10am-4pm Sat; ☎) or on the complex's wi-fi network.

Stony Batter
Historic Reserve
Historic Site

(www.fortstonybatter.org; Stony Batter Rd; adult/child $8/5; ⏰9am-5pm) At the eastern end of the island, Stony Batter has WWII tunnels and gun emplacements that were built in 1941 to defend Auckland's harbour. The 20-minute walk from the carpark leads through private farmland and derives its name from the boulder-strewn fields. Bring a torch and cash.

Connells Bay
Gardens

(📞09-372 8957; www.connellsbay.co.nz; Cowes Bay Rd; adult/child $30/15; ⏰by appointment, late Oct-late Mar) A pricey but excellent private sculpture park featuring a stellar roster of NZ artists. Admission is by way of a two-hour guided tour; book ahead.

Activities

Ask at the i-SITE about the island's beautiful coastal walks (ranging from one to three hours) and the 3km Cross Island Walkway (from Onetangi to Rocky Bay).

Hike Bike Ako
Walking, Cycling

(📞021 465 373; www.hikebikeako.co.nz; walking adult/child $99/79, cycling & combination $139) Explore the island on a guided walking (three hours) or cycling (five hours) tour, or a combination (five hours) of both. Tours all include pick up from the ferry, lunch at a cafe or vineyard, and Maori legends, history and culture.

Ross Adventures
Kayaking

(📞09-372 5550; www.kayakwaiheke.co.nz; Matiatia Beach; half-/full-day trips $85/145, per hour hire from $25) It's the fervently held opinion of Ross that Waiheke offers kayaking every bit as good as the legendary Abel Tasman National Park.

EcoZip Adventures
Ziplining

(📞0800 246 947; www.ecozipadventures.co.nz; Trig Hill Rd; adult/child $99/69) With vineyard, native bush and ocean views, three separate 200m stretches make for an exciting ride, and there's a gentle 1.5km walk back up through the bush after the thrills.

Waiheke Bike Hire
Bicycle Rental

(📞09-372 7937; www.waihekebikehire.co.nz; Matiatia Wharf) Hires mountain bikes (half-/full day $25/35) from its base near the wharf and at the Oneroa i-SITE.

Tours

Ananda Tours
Food & Wine

(📞09-372 7530; www.ananda.co.nz) Gourmet wine and food tours ($120), and a wine connoisseurs' tour ($230). Small-group, informal tours can be customised, including visits to artists' studios.

Fullers
Food & Wine

(📞09-367 9111; www.fullers.co.nz) Runs a Wine on Waiheke tour (adult $119, 4½ hours, departs Auckland 1pm) visiting three of the island's top wineries and includes a platter of nibbles; and a Taste of Waiheke tour (adult $129, 5½ hours, departs Auckland 11am) which includes three wineries plus an olive grove and light lunch. There's also a 1½-hour Explorer tour (adult/child $52/26, departs Auckland 10am, 11am and noon). All prices include the ferry and an all-day local bus pass.

🍴 Eating

Dragonfired
Pizzeria $

(Little Oneroa Beach; mains $8-16; ⏰10.30am-8.30pm; 🍴) Specialising in 'artisan woodfired food', this caravan by the beach serves the three Ps: pizza, polenta plates and pocket bread. It's easily Waiheke's best place for cheap eats.

Wai Kitchen
Cafe $$

(www.waikitchen.co.nz; 1/149 Ocean View Rd, Oneroa; mains $17-23; ⏰9am-4pm, extended hours summer) Why? Well firstly there's the lively menu that abounds with Mediterranean and Asian flavours. Then there's the charming service and the breezy ambience of this glassed-in wedge, facing the *wai* (water).

Oyster Inn
Seafood, Modern NZ $$

(📞09-372 2222; www.theoysterinn.co.nz; 124 Ocean View Rd; mains $23-36; ⏰11am-late) The Oyster Inn is a popular destination for Auckland's smart set. They're attracted by the excellent seafood-skewed bistro menu, oysters and champagne, and a buzzy but relaxed vibe that's part bar and part restaurant. Brunch from 11am on the verandah is a great way to ease another Waiheke day.

Te Whau
Winery **$$$**

(☏09-372 7191; www.tewhau.com; 218 Te Whau Dr; mains $37-42; ⏱11am-5pm Wed-Mon, 6.30pm-late Sat Nov-Easter, reduced hours winter) ◢ Perched on the end of Te Whau peninsula, this winery restaurant has exceptional views, food and service, and one of the finest wine lists you'll see in the country. Try its own impressive Bordeaux blends, merlot, chardonnay and rosé for $3 per taste (11am to 5pm).

ℹ Information

Waiheke Island i-SITE (☏09-372 1234; www.waihekenz.com; 118 Ocean View Rd; ⏱9am-5pm) As well as the very helpful main office, there's a (usually unstaffed) counter in the ferry terminal at Matiatia Wharf.

ℹ Getting There & Away

Fullers (☏09-367 9111; www.fullers.co.nz; return adult/child $36/18; ⏱5.20am-11.45pm Mon-Fri, 6.25am-11.45pm Sat, 7am-9.30pm Sun) Frequent passenger ferries from Auckland's Ferry Building to Matiatia Wharf (on the hour from 9am to 5pm), some via Devonport.

Sealink (☏09-300 5900; www.sealink.co.nz; adult/child/car/motorcycle return $36.50/20/152/58; ⏱4.30am-6.30pm Mon-Thu, 4.30am-8pm Fri, 6am-6.30pm Sat & Sun) Runs car ferries to Kennedy Point, mainly from Half Moon Bay (east Auckland) but some leave from Wynyard Wharf in the city. The ferry runs at least every two hours and takes 45 minutes (bookings essential).

ℹ Getting Around

Bus

The island has regular bus services, starting from Matiatia Wharf and heading through Oneroa (adult/child $1.60/80c, five minutes) on their way to all the main settlements, as far west as Onetangi (adult/child $4.40/2.40, 30 minutes); see MAXX (☏09-366 6400; www.maxx.co.nz) for timetables. A day pass (adult/child $9/5.50) is available from the Fullers counter at Matiatia Wharf.

Waiheke Vineyard Hopper (☏09-367 9111; www.waihekevineyardhopper.co.nz; per person $20; ⏱Dec 26-early Feb) Handy option with dedicated shuttles travelling around eight different Waiheke vineyards every 40 minutes during summer. A $54 pass also includes ferry tickets and local Waiheke buses.

Car, Motorbike & Scooter

Waiheke Auto Rentals (☏09-372 8998; www.waihekerentals.co.nz; Matiatia Wharf; per day car/scooter from $69/79)

Taxi

Waiheke Independent Taxis (☏0800 300 372)

Oneroa Bay, Waiheke Island
DAVID WALL/GETTY IMAGES ©

WEST AUCKLAND

West Auckland epitomises rugged: wild black-sand beaches, bush-shrouded ranges, and mullet-haired, black-T-shirt-wearing 'Westies'. The latter is just one of several stereotypes of the area's denizens. Others include the back-to-nature hippie, the eccentric bohemian artist and the dope-smoking surfer dude, all attracted to a simple life at the edge of the bush.

Titirangi

This little village marks the end of Auckland's suburban sprawl and is a good place to spot all of the area's stereotypes over a coffee, wine or cold beer. Once home to NZ's greatest modern painter, Colin McCahon, there remains an artsy feel to the place.

It's a mark of the esteem in which McCahon is held that the house he lived and painted in during the 1950s has been opened to the public as **McCahon House** (www.mccahonhouse.org.nz; 67 Otitori Bay Rd; admission $5; ⊙10am-3pm Wed, Sat & Sun), a minimuseum.

Cathedral Cove (p93), Coromandel Peninsula

Piha

If you notice an Auckland surfer dude with a faraway look, chances are they're daydreaming about Piha...or just stoned. This beautifully rugged, iron-sand beach has long been a favourite for refugees from the city's stresses – whether for day trips, weekend teenage parties or family holidays.

Although Piha is popular, it's also incredibly dangerous, with wild surf and strong undercurrents; so much so that it's spawned its own popular reality TV show, *Piha Rescue*.

Sights & Activities

Perched on its haunches near the centre of the beach is **Lion Rock** (101m), whose 'mane' glows golden in the evening light.

For surfboard hire, head to Piha Store.

Eating

Piha Store   Bakery $
(Seaview Rd; snacks $2-10; ⊙7.30am-5.30pm)
Call in for pies and other baked goods, groceries and ice creams. The attached

DAVID WALL/GETTY IMAGES ©

Detour:
Karekare

Few stretches of sand have more personality than Karekare. Wild and gorgeously undeveloped, this famous beach has been the setting for onscreen moments both high- and lowbrow, from Oscar-winner *The Piano* to *Xena, Warrior Princess*.

Karekare rates as one of the most dangerous beaches in the country, with strong surf and ever-present rips, so don't even think about swimming unless the beach is being patrolled by lifeguards (usually only in summer). Pearl Jam singer Eddie Vedder nearly drowned here while visiting Neil Finn's Karekare pad.

To get here take Scenic Dr and Piha Rd until you reach the well-signposted turn-off to Karekare Rd.

Lion Rock Surf Shop rents surfboards (two hours/half-day/day $20/30/40) and body boards ($10/20/30).

ⓘ Getting There & Away

There's no public transport to Piha, but **NZ Surf 'n' Snow Tours** (☏09-828 0426; www.newzealandsurftours.com; one way $25, return trip incl surfing gear $99) provides shuttles when the surf's up. **Go Hitch** (☏0800 467 442; www.gohitch.co.nz; per person $40; ⏰departs Sat-Sun 8.30am & 10.30am) also operates a Piha shuttle from central Auckland and Ponsonby on weekends.

COROMANDEL PENINSULA

Thames

Dinky wooden buildings from the 19th-century gold rush still dominate Thames, but grizzly prospectors have long been replaced by alternative lifestylers. It's a good base for tramping or canyoning in the nearby Kauaeranga Valley.

◉ Sights

Goldmine Experience　　Mine
(www.goldmine-experience.co.nz; cnr Moanataiari Rd & Pollen St; adult/child $15/5; ⏰10am-4pm daily Jan-Mar, to 1pm Apr, May & Sep-Dec) Walk through a mine tunnel, watch a stamper

battery crush rock, learn about the history of the Cornish miners and try your hand at panning for gold ($2 extra).

School of Mines & Mineralogical Museum　　Museum
(www.historicplaces.org.nz; 101 Cochrane St; adult/child $5/free; ⏰11am-3pm Wed-Sun Mar-Dec, daily Jan-Feb) The Historic Places Trust runs tours of these buildings, which house an extensive collection of NZ rocks, minerals and fossils. The oldest section (1868) was part of a Methodist Sunday school, situated on a Maori burial ground. The Trust has a free self-tour pamphlet taking in Thames' significant buildings.

Historical Museum　　Museum
(cnr Cochrane & Pollen Sts; adult/child $5/2; ⏰1-4pm) Pioneer relics, rocks and old photographs of the town.

🤸 Activities

Canyonz　　Canyoning
(☏0800 422 696; www.canyonz.co.nz; trips $360) 🍃 All-day canyoning trips to the Sleeping God Canyon in the Kauaeranga Valley. Expect a vertical descent of over 300m, requiring abseiling, water-sliding and jumping. Trips leave from Thames at 8.30am, and 7am pickups from Hamilton are also available. Note that Thames is only 90 minutes' drive from central Auckland, so with your own transport a day trip from Auckland is possible.

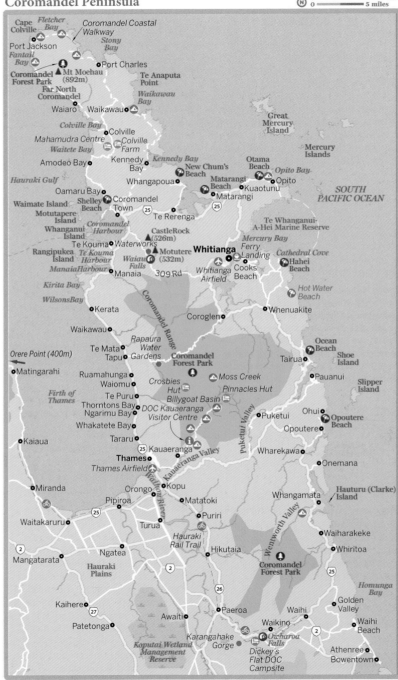

Eyez Open
Cycling

(📞07-868 9018; www.eyezopen.co.nz) Rents out bikes ($30 per day) and organises small-group cycling tours of the Coromandel Peninsula (one- to three-day tours from $150 to $660).

Eating

Cafe Melbourne
Cafe $

(www.facebook.com/CafeMelbourneGrahams-Town; 715 Pollen St; mains $12-19; ⏰8am-5pm Mon-Thu, 8am-9pm Fri, 9am-4pm Sat & Sun) Stylish and spacious, this cafe definitely channels the cosmopolitan vibe of a certain Australian city. Chic industrial furniture and shared tables promote a convivial ambience, and the menu travels from brunchy ricotta pancakes to beef sliders and fish curry for lunch.

Wharf Coffee House & Bar
Cafe, Bar $

(www.facebook.com/TheWharfCoffeehouseand-Bar; Queen St, Shortland Wharf; snacks & mains $10-18; ⏰9am-3pm Mon, to 8pm Tue, Wed & Sun, to 9pm Thu-Sat) Perched beside the water, this rustic wood-lined pavilion does great fish and chips. Grab a table outside with a beer or a wine to understand why the Wharf is a firm local favourite.

ℹ️ Information

Thames i-SITE (📞07-868 7284; www.thamesinfo.co.nz; 206 Pollen St; ⏰9am-5pm)

ℹ️ Getting There & Around

InterCity (📞09-583 5780; www.intercity.co.nz), Tairua Bus Company (📞07-808 0748; www.tairuabus.co.nz) and Go Kiwi (📞0800 446 549; www.go-kiwi.co.nz) all run bus services to Thames.

. . . .

Coromandel Town

Crammed with heritage buildings, Coromandel Town is a thoroughly quaint little place. Its natty cafes, interesting art stores, excellent sleeping options and delicious smoked mussels could keep you here longer than you expected.

Note that Coromandel Town is just one part of the entire Coromandel Peninsula, and its location on the peninsula's west coast means means it is not a good base for visiting Cathedral Cove and Hot Water Beach on the peninsula's east coast.

◎ Sights

Coromandel Goldfield Centre & Stamper Battery
Historic Building

(📞021 0232 8262; www.coromandelstamper-battery.weebly.com; 360 Buffalo Rd; adult/child $10/5; ⏰10am-4pm, tours hourly 10am-3pm) The rock-crushing machine clatters into life during the informative tours of this 1899 plant. You can also try panning for gold ($5). Outside of tours stop to see NZ's largest working waterwheel.

Coromandel Mining & Historic Museum
Museum

(841 Rings Rd; adult/child $5/free; ⏰10am-1pm Sat & Sun Feb–mid-Dec, 10am-4pm daily mid-Dec–Jan) Small museum with glimpses of pioneer life.

🏃 Activities

Driving Creek Railway & Potteries
Railway

(📞07-866 8703; www.drivingcreekrailway.co.nz; 380 Driving Creek Rd; adult/child $25/10; ⏰10.15am & 2pm) 🖊 A lifelong labour of love for its conservationist owner, this unique train runs up steep grades, across four trestle bridges, along two spirals and a double switchback, and through two tunnels, finishing at the 'Eye-full Tower'. The hour-long trip passes artworks and regenerating native forest – more than 17,000 natives have been planted, including 9000 kauri. It's worth lingering for the video about the extraordinary guy behind it all, well-known potter Barry Brickell. Booking ahead is recommended in summer.

Coromandel Kayak Adventures
Kayaking

(📞07-866 7466; www.kayakadventures.co.nz) Paddle-powered tours including half-day ecotours (from $150) and fishing trips (half-/full day $200/340).

Tours

Tri Sail Charters Sailing
(☎ 0800 024 874; www.trisailcharters.co.nz; half-/full day $55/110) Cruise the Coromandel Harbour with your mates (minimum of four) on an 11.2m trimaran.

Coromandel Adventures Driving Tour
(☎ 07-866 7014; www.coromandeladventures. co.nz; adult/child $25/15) Various trips including a hop-on, hop-off service around Coromandel Town and transfers to Whangapoua Beach.

Sleeping

Hush Boutique Accommodation Studios $$
(☎ 07-866 7771; www.hushaccommodation. co.nz; 425 Driving Creek Rd; campervan $35, cabin & studio $120-199) Rustic but stylish studios are scattered throughout a stand of native bush at this easygoing spot. Lots of honey-coloured natural wood creates a warm ambience, and the shared Hush Alfresco area with kitchen facilities and a barbecue is a top spot to catch up with fellow travellers.

Jacaranda Lodge B&B $$
(☎ 07-866 8002; www.jacarandalodge.co.nz; 3195 Tiki Rd; s $85, d $140-170; 🛜) 🌿 Located among six hectares of farmland and rose gardens, this two-storey cottage is a relaxing retreat. Look forward to excellent breakfasts from the friendly owner, often using produce – plums, almonds, macadamia nuts and citrus fruit – from the property's spray-free orchard. Some rooms share bathrooms.

Driving Creek Villas Cottages $$$
(☎ 07-866 7755; www.drivingcreekvillas.com; 21a Colville Rd; villa $325; 🛜) This is the posh, grown-up's choice – three spacious, self-contained, modern, wooden villas with plenty of privacy. The Polynesian-influenced interior design is slick and the bush setting, complete with bubbling creek, sublime.

Eating

Chai Tea House Cafe $
(www.facebook.com/ChaiTeaHouse; 24 Wharf Rd; snacks $6-12; ⊙10am-5pm Tue-Sun; 🍴)
🌿 Welcoming cafe with a bohemian New Age bent serving up lots of organic, vegan and vegetarian goodies. The outdoor garden is a very relaxing space, and is also used for occasional live-music gigs.

Mussel Kitchen Seafood $$
(www.musselkitchen.co.nz; cnr SH25 & 309 Rd; mains $9-18; ⊙9am-3.30pm & 6-10pm Jan & Feb) This cool cafe-bar sits among fields 3km south of town. Mussels are served either with Thai- and Mediterranean-tinged sauces, or grilled on the half-shell. In summer, the garden bar is perfect for a mussel-fritter burger and a frosty beer. Smoked and chilli mussels are available for takeaway.

Pepper Tree Modern NZ $$
(☎ 07-866 8211; www.peppertreerestaurant. co.nz; 31 Kapanga Rd; lunch $18-26, dinner $26-36; ⊙10am-9pm; 🛜) Coromandel Town's most upmarket option dishes out generously proportioned meals with an emphasis on local seafood. On a summer's evening, the courtyard tables under the shady tree are the place to be.

ℹ Information

Coromandel Town Information Centre
(☎ 07-866 8598; www.coromandeltown.co.nz; 85 Kapanga Rd; ⊙10am-4pm)

ℹ Getting There & Away

The best way to Coromandel Town from Auckland is on a 360 Discovery (☎ 0800 360 3472; www.360discovery.co.nz) ferry. The town is also serviced by InterCity (☎ 09-583 5780; www. intercity.co.nz), Tairua Bus Company (☎ 07-808 0748; www.tairuabus.com; advance fares from $1) and Go Kiwi (☎ 0800 446 549; www.go-kiwi. co.nz) buses.

Whitianga

Whitianga's big attractions are the sandy beaches of Mercury Bay and the diving, boating and kayaking opportunities afforded by the craggy coast and nearby Te Whanganui-A-Hei Marine Reserve. The pretty harbour is a renowned base for game-fishing (especially marlin and tuna, particularly between January and March).

Sights & Activities

Buffalo Beach stretches along Mercury Bay, north of Whitianga Harbour. A five-minute passenger ferry ride (p93) will take you across the harbour to **Ferry Landing**. From here you can walk to local sights like Whitianga Rock Scenic & Historical Reserve, a park with great views over the ocean, and the **Shakespeare Cliff Lookout**.

Mercury Bay Museum — Museum
(www.mercurybaymuseum.co.nz; 11a The Esplanade; adult/child $5/50¢; ⊙10am-4pm) A small but interesting museum focusing on local history – especially Whitianga's most famous visitors, Kupe and Cook.

Lost Spring — Spa
(www.thelostspring.co.nz; 121a Cook Dr; per hour/day $35/60; ⊙11am-6pm Sun-Fri, to 8pm Sat) This expensive but intriguing Disney-meets-Rotorua thermal complex comprises a series of hot pools in a lush junglelike setting, complete with an erupting volcano. Children under 14 aren't permitted, leaving the grown-ups to marinate themselves in tropical tranquility, cocktail in hand.

Tours

There are a baffling number of tours to **Te**

Whanganui-A-Hei Marine Reserve, where you'll see interesting rock formations and, if you're lucky, dolphins, fur seals, penguins and orcas.

Banana Boat — Cruise
(☎07-866 5617; www.whitianga.co.nz; rides $10-35; ⊙Dec 26-Jan 31) Monkey around in Mercury Bay on the bright-yellow motorised Banana Boat – or split to Cathedral Cove.

Cave Cruzer — Cruise
(☎07-866 0611; www.cavecruzer.co.nz) A rigid-hull inflatable offering a one-hour (adult/child $50/30) or two-hour (adult/child $75/40) tour.

Eating

Cafe Nina — Cafe $
(20 Victoria St; mains $8-20; ⊙8am-3pm) Barbecue for breakfast? Why the hell not. Too cool to be constricted to four walls, the kitchen grills bacon and eggs on an outdoor hotplate while the punters spill out onto tables in the park. Other dishes

Driving Creek Railway (p89), Coromandel Town
DAVID WALL/GETTY IMAGES ©

DAVID WALL PHOTO/GETTY IMAGES ©

★ Don't Miss
Hot Water Beach

Justifiably famous, **Hot Water Beach** is quite extraordinary. For two hours either side of low tide, you can access an area of sand in front of a rocky outcrop at the middle of the beach where hot water oozes up from beneath the surface. Bring a spade, dig a hole and, voila, you've got a personal spa pool. Surfers stop off before the main beach to access some decent breaks.

Spades ($5) can be hired from the **Hot Water Beach Store** (Pye Pl; ⊙9am-5pm), which also has **Hottie's Cafe** attached.

Spend the night at **Hot Water Beach B&B** (☑07-866 3991; www.hotwaterbedand breakfast.co.nz; 48 Pye Pl; r $260), a hillside pad with priceless views, a spa bath on the deck, and attractive living quarters.

The Hahei bus services **Tairua Bus Company** (TBC; ☑07-864 7194; www.tairuabus. co.nz) and Cathedral Cove Shuttle stop here, but usually only on prebooked requests.

include robust Greek salads and tasty quesadillas.

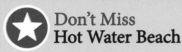

Squids
Seafood **$$**
(☑07-867 1710; www.squids.co.nz; 15/1 Blacksmith Lane; mains $15-29; ⊙11am-2.30pm & 5.30pm-late) On a corner facing the harbour, this informal restaurant offers good-value seafood meals in a prime location. Steamed mussels, smoked seafood platters and chowder combine with occasional Asian touches, and the steaks are also good.

ℹ Information

Whitianga i-SITE (☑07-866 5555; www. whitianga.co.nz; 66 Albert St; ⊙9am-5pm Mon-Fri, to 4pm Sat & Sun) Information and internet access. Hours are extended in summer.

ℹ Getting There & Around

Sunair (☑0800 786 247; www.sunair.co.nz) operates flights linking Whitianga to Auckland, Great Barrier Island and Tauranga. Bus services are offered by InterCity (www.intercity.co.nz),

Tairua Bus Company (☎07-864 7770; www.tairuabus.co.nz) and Go Kiwi (☎07-866 0336; www.go-kiwi.co.nz).

The **passenger ferry** (☎07-866 5472; www.whitiangaferry.co.nz; adult/child/bicycle $3/1.50/1.50; ⏰7.30am-6.30pm Easter–late Oct, to 10.30pm late-Oct–Easter) links Buffalo Beach with Ferry Landing.

Hahei

A legendary Kiwi beach town, little Hahei balloons to bursting in summer but is nearly abandoned otherwise – apart from the busloads of tourists doing the obligatory stop-off at Cathedral Cove.

Sights

Cathedral Cove   Beach
Beautiful Cathedral Cove, with its famous gigantic stone arch and natural waterfall shower, is best enjoyed early or late in the day – avoiding the worst of the hordes.

From the car park, a kilometre north of Hahei, it's a rolling walk of around 30 to 40 minutes. The walk from Hahei Beach to Cathedral Cove takes about 70 minutes. Another option is a 10-minute ride in a water taxi.

Hahei Beach   Beach
Long, lovely Hahei Beach is made more magical by the view to the craggy islands in the distance.

 Activities

Cathedral Cove Sea Kayaking   Kayaking
(☎07-866 3877; www.seakayaktours.co.nz; 88 Hahei Beach Rd; half-/full day $95/160; ⏰9am & 2pm) This outfit runs guided kayaking trips around the rock arches, caves and islands in the Cathedral Cove and Mercury Bay area. The Remote Coast Tour heads the other way when conditions permit, visiting caves, blowholes and a long tunnel.

Tours

Hahei Explorer   Boat Tour
(☎07-866 3910; www.haheiexplorer.co.nz; adult/child $70/40) Hour-long jetboat rides touring the coast.

Sleeping

Purangi Garden Accommodation   Cottages $$
(☎07-866 4038; www.purangigarden.co.nz; Lees Rd; d $170-190) On a quiet cove on the Purangi River, this relaxing spot has accommodation ranging from comfortable chalets through to larger houses and a spacious, self-contained yurt. Well-established gardens and rolling lawns lead to the water – perfect for swimming and kayaking – and don't be surprised if the friendly owners drop off some organic fruit or freshly baked bread.

Hahei and Hot Water Beach are both a short drive away.

Church   Cottages $$
(☎07-866 3533; www.thechurchhahei.co.nz; 87 Hahei Beach Rd; cottage $130-250; @🛜)
🍽 Set within a subtropical garden, these beautifully kitted-out, rustic timber cottages have plenty of character. The ultra-charming wooden church at the top of the drive is Hahei's swankiest **eatery** with excellent Mediterranean- and Asian-inspired dishes made to be shared, and a stellar, if pricey, selection of Kiwi craft beers.

ℹ Getting There & Around

Tairua Bus Company (TBC; ☎07-864 7770; www.tairuabus.co.nz) has bus connections to Hahei. In the height of summer the council runs a bus service from the Cooks Beach side of the ferry landing to Hot Water Beach, stopping at Hahei (adult/child $3/2). Another option on the same route is the **Cathedral Cove Shuttle** (☎027 422 5899; www.cathedralcoveshuttles.co.nz; up to 5 passengers $30).

Cathedral Cove Water Taxi (☎027 919 0563; www.cathedralcovewatertaxi.co.nz; return/1 way adult $25/15, child $15/10; ⏰every 30min) Water taxis from Hahei to Cathedral Cove.

Rotorua & the Centre

Volcanic activity defines this region, and nowhere is this subterranean sexiness more obvious than in Rotorua. Here the daily business of life goes on among steaming hot springs, explosive geysers, bubbling mud pools and the billows of sulphurous gas responsible for the town's 'unique' eggy smell.

Rotorua is also a stronghold of Maori tradition: check out a power-packed concert performance, chow down at a *hangi* (feast) or learn the techniques behind Maori arts and crafts.

To the south of Auckland, verdant fields fold down into New Zealand's mightiest river, the Waikato, which lends its name to the region. Adrenaline junkies are drawn to the wild surf of Raglan and rough-and-tumble underground pursuits in the extraordinary Waitomo Caves. And the thrills don't stop there. The area around Taupo and Tongariro National Park now rivals Rotorua for daredevil escapades: jetboating, bungy jumping, skydiving, skiing or just soaking in a thermal pool.

Champagne Pool, Wai-O-Tapu Thermal Wonderland (p111) **95**

Mt Tarawera

Rotorua & the Centre

1 Waitomo Caves
2 Geothermal sights and activities, Rotorua
3 Maori culture, Rotorua
4 Surfing, Raglan
5 Tongariro Alpine Crossing

0 ───── 50 km
0 ───── 25 miles

Whakaari (White Island)

Bay of Plenty

Opotiki
Whakatane
Mt Maunganui
Tauranga

Kaimai Range

Te Urewera National Park

Maungapohatu
Aniwaniwa
Tuai

Lake Waikaremoana

Hawke Bay

Tarawera
Te Haroto
Te Pohue

Tutira
Tangoio
Eskdale

Waimangu
Waiotapu
Parekarangi
Tahorakuri
Wairakei

Rotorua
Upper Atiamuri
Atiamuri

Tokoroa

Cambridge
Hamilton
Huntly
Rangiaowhia

Kaimai Range

Mt Tihiraupenga
Mt Pureora
Pureora Forest Park

Kinloch
Acacia Bay
Lake Taupo
Taupo

Kuratau Junction
Turangi
Rangipo

Kaimanawa Forest Park

Desert Rd

Tongariro National Park

Pureora Forest Park
Mt Hauhungaroa

Hauhungaroa Range

National Park
Whakapapa Village
Mt Ruapehu

Owhango
Horopito

Pureora Forest Park

Rangataua Ranges

Otorohanga
Waitomo Caves
Te Kuiti
Eight Mile Junction
Kopaki
Mapiu
Moeatoa

Raglan
Ocean Beach
Ruapuke Beach
Kawhia

Taumarunui
Okahukura
Taumarunui
Awakino

Whanganui National Park

Whangamomona

TASMAN SEA

New Plymouth

Mt Taranaki (Mt Egmont)
Egmont National Park

Stratford

N

Rotorua & the Centre Highlights

Waitomo Caves

Luring tourists for more than 100 years, Waitomo (p145) is an amazing place to explore, above ground or below. Hundreds of caves perforate the region's limestone landscape, and there are plenty of opportunities to delve underground: stay dry on an underground walking tour with glowworms and a boat ride, or get wet on an adrenaline-charged, subterranean rafting and abseiling adventure.

1

2 ## Go Geothermal!

It seems wherever you go in this region there's a bubbling pool of mud, a steaming hot spring, an erupting geyser or a plume of sulphurous gas egging its way into your nostrils. Much of it is stand-and-watch-type stuff (too hot to handle!), but don't miss the chance to immerse yourself in some hot springs. In Rotorua, try the Polynesian Spa (p107) for starters. Geyser, Rotorua

Maori Rotorua

Rotorua is a great (and very organised) place to engage with Maori culture. Wander around a traditional Maori community at Whakarewarewa Thermal Village (p105; don't miss the geothermally cooked corn!) and catch a cultural performance while you're there. Other established concert-and-*hangi* faves include Tamaki Maori Village (p112) and Mitai Maori Village (p112).

ADINA TOVY/GETTY IMAGES ©

MERTEN SNIJDER/GETTY IMAGES ©

STUART BLACK/GETTY IMAGES ©

Surfing in Raglan

The sensational surf breaks peeling into the shore just south of Raglan (p139) – at Manu Bay and Whale Bay – have been luring stoned-looking hippie surfers here for decades. But your adventures in the waves are just part of the Raglan experience. Also here is a rambling old pub plus some beaut accommodation, cafes and eateries: stay a few days and you'll never want to leave. Surfing, Ngarunui Beach (p141)

Tongariro Alpine Crossing

Want some alpine time? Make a beeline for Tongariro, NZ's oldest national park. Crowned by three snowy volcanic peaks, the park is home to the country's best day walk, the Tongariro Alpine Crossing (p134), and the North Island's best skiing at Whakapapa and Turoa. If you have a bit more time up your sleeve (or in your boots), tackle the longer Tongariro Northern Circuit (p131), which is dotted with volcanic craters and lakes.

Rotorua & the Centre's Best...

Extreme Action

o **Black-water rafting**
Get fast, wet, dark, claustrophobic and subterranean in Waitomo. (p146)

o **Skydiving** Cross it off your bucket list in Taupo. (p125)

o **Zorbing** Rolling downhill inside a plastic bubble with a bucket of water thrown in...how fabulously illogical! (p105)

o **Snowboarding** Strap a plank to your ankles and careen down Mt Ruapehu. (p130)

Swim Spots

o **Ngarunui Beach**
Lifesaver-patrolled, kid-sized surf just south of Raglan. (p141)

o **Waikite Valley Thermal Pools** Take a scenic drive south of Rotorua for a soothing geothermal soak. (p111)

o **Lake Taupo** A 'refreshing' freshwater dip will banish even the sternest of hangovers. (p123)

o **Tauranga** Jump into the ocean and splash around with dolphins off Tauranga. (p115)

Eat Streets

o **The Strand, Tauranga**
Harbour-side eats, drinks and people-watching. (p117)

o **Victoria St, Hamilton**
Central Hamilton's hip foodie strip – with the Hood St bars around the corner. (p137)

o **Maunganui Rd, Mt Maunganui** While away a sunny afternoon in the Mount's cafes and bars. (p120)

o **Tutanekai St, Rotorua**
Undercover cafes and restaurants line 'Eat Streat'. (p109)

Need to Know

Small Towns

- **Raglan** Multicultural surfie nirvana on the wave-washed Waikato coast. (p139)

- **Mt Maunganui** Solid surf and a cafe-strewn main street in the shadow of Mauao. (p119)

- **Waitomo** It's not just about caves and glowworms: Waitomo township is a wee winner! (p145)

- **Cambridge** Anglo eccentricities abound in this horse-happy town. (p143)

ADVANCE PLANNING

- **One month before** Organise internal flights, car hire, and seats on the *Northern Explorer* train through the North Island's heartland.

- **Two weeks before** Book accommodation across the region and a surf lesson in Raglan (if it's summer) or a ski lesson on Mt Ruapehu (if it's winter).

- **One week before** Book a Maori cultural performance in Rotorua, an underground adventure in Waitomo Caves and a skydive in Taupo.

RESOURCES

- **Rotorua i-SITE** (www. rotoruanz.com) Info on accommodation, Maori culture, activities and family stuff.

- **Tauranga i-SITE** (www. bayofplenty.co.nz) The Bay of Plenty's greatest hits.

- **Hamilton i-SITE** (www. hamiltonwaikato.com) The low-down on NZ's fourth-biggest town.

- **Great Lake Taupo** (www.greatlaketaupo. com) Deals and info on accommodation, events and things to do around the big lake.

- **Visit Ruapehu** (www. visitruapehu.com) Shine a light into NZ's moody, mountainous heart.

GETTING AROUND

- **Car** For the freedom to explore.

- **Bus** Between the larger towns.

- **Walk** Around the Mauao Base Track in Mt Maunganui.

- **Boat** Across Lakes Rotorua and Taupo.

- **Train** The *Northern Explorer* tracks between Auckland and Wellington via Hamilton, Waitomo Caves and Tongariro National Park.

BE FOREWARNED

- **Surf safety** The beaches around the Bay of Plenty and Raglan on the Waikato coast are fab for surfing, but go easy if you're not strapped to a board: rips and undertows take as much water away from the beach as the waves bring in.

Rotorua & the Centre Itineraries

Go for a roam around the middle of the North Island. Between Auckland and Wellington you'll discover hip cities, hippie surf towns, brilliant museums and an overload of heart-starting activities.

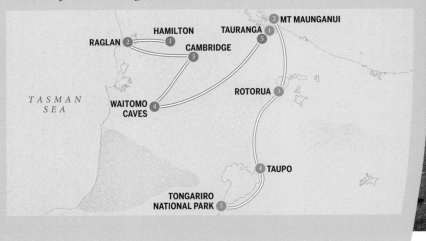

HAMILTON TO TAURANGA
3 DAYS
WAIKATO WANDERINGS

On the banks of the slow-rolling Waikato River, ❶ **Hamilton** (p135) doesn't score heavily with scenery or big-ticket attractions, but it's a vibrant little city with great eateries, a beaut museum and an effervescent nocturnal scene. Trundle over the hills to ❷ **Raglan** (p139), NZ's quintessential surf town, with a string of brilliant breaks to the south (and a great pub too!). Alternatively, over in ❸ **Cambridge** (p143) you can express your equine enthusiasms on a horse-stud tour, or swan around the main street in your riding boots and jodhpurs.

Heading south, the amazing ❹ **Waitomo Caves** (p145) are a must-see (or, perhaps, a must-do). Here's your chance to don a wetsuit and a helmet with a torch strapped to the top, and hurl yourself into an underground limestone chasm. Brilliant! Or, if adrenaline addiction is less of a motivator, take a tour of a dazzling glowworm cave or just hang with the locals at the cafe or pub above ground.

To round out your tour, track north to the Bay of Plenty: ❺ **Tauranga** (p115) is a sophisticated city and NZ's biggest port. And like any port town, the incoming tide keeps things worldly and progressive. Cool down with dinner and drinks on the Strand.

5 DAYS

TAURANGA TO TONGARIRO NATIONAL PARK
SEA TO SUMMIT

Seaside ❶ **Tauranga** (p115) is lovely, but the locals insist ❷ **Mt Maunganui** (p119) is lovelier (and we tend to agree). This sandy little town is home to fab surf, cool cafes and bars. Circumnavigate the base of the photogenic 'Mount' itself ('Mauao' in Maori), dappled with red pohutukawa blooms in summer, or head for the summit.

Track south to ❸ **Rotorua** (p104), a true Kiwi highlight: ogle the astonishing geothermal attractions (geysers, mud pools, mineral pools); catch an authentic Maori cultural performance and *hangi;* or blow away the jetlag with extreme sports (skydiving, zorbing, jetboating, white-water

rafting...). Don't miss the excellent Rotorua Museum.

Further south, ❹ **Taupo** (p123) sits on the shores of NZ's biggest lake. Drop a line in the water, or try kayaking, jetboating or skydiving – Taupo bills itself the Skydiving Capital of the World. There are some hip places to eat and drink here too.

Next stop is ❺ **Tongariro National Park** (p130), NZ's oldest national park, and home to awesome tramping tracks and winter skiing on Mt Ruapehu.

Tongariro National Park (p130)
AVID EPPERSON/GETTY IMAGES ©

Discover Rotorua & the Centre

Lake Rotorua
ANTHONY KO/GETTY IMAGES ©

ROTORUA

Catch a whiff of Rotorua's sulphur-rich, asthmatic airs and you've already got a taste of New Zealand's most dynamic thermal area, home to spurting geysers, steaming hot springs and exploding mud pools. The Maori revered this place, naming one of the most spectacular springs Wai-O-Tapu (Sacred Waters). Today 35% of the population is Maori, with their cultural performances and traditional *hangi* as big an attraction as the landscape itself.

◉ Sights

Te Puia   Geyser, Cultural Tour
(Map p114; ☏07-348 9047, 0800 837 842; www.tepuia.com; Hemo Rd; tours adult/child $48.50/24.50, daytime tour & performance combo $60.50/30.50, evening tour, performance & hangi combo $150/75; ⏲8am-6pm Nov-Apr, to 5pm May-Oct) Rotorua's main drawcard is Te Whakarewarewa (pronounced 'fa-ka-re-wa-re-wa'), a thermal reserve 3km south of the city centre. There are more than 500 springs here, the most famous of which is **Pohutu** ('Big Splash' or 'Explosion'), a geyser which erupts up to 20 times a day, spurting hot water up to 30m skyward. You'll know when it's about to blow because the adjacent **Prince of Wales' Feathers** geyser will start up shortly before. Both these geysers form part of Te Puia, the most polished of NZ's Maori cultural attractions.

Tours take 1½ hours and depart hourly from 9am (the last tour an hour before closing). Daytime 45-minute cultural performances start at 10.15am, 12.15pm and 3.15pm; nightly three-hour Te Po indigenous concerts and *hangi* feasts start at 6pm (following on from a 4.30pm tour in a combo package).

Whakarewarewa Thermal Village
Village

(Map p114; ☎07-349 3463; www.whakarewarewa. com; 17 Tyron St; tour & cultural performance adult/child $35/15; ⏰8.30am-5pm) Whakarewarewa Thermal Village is a living village where *tangata whenua* (the locals) still reside, as they have for centuries. The villagers show you around and tell you the stories of their way of life and the significance of the steamy bubbling pools, silica terraces and the geysers that, although inaccessible from the village, are easily viewed from vantage points (the view of Pohutu is just as good from here as it is from Te Puia, and considerably cheaper).

There are cultural performances at 11.15am and 2pm, and guided tours at 9am, 10am, 11am, noon, 1pm, 3pm and 4pm.

Lake Rotorua
Lake

Lake Rotorua is the largest of the district's 16 lakes and is − underneath all that water − a spent volcano. The lake can be explored by boat, with several operators situated at the lakefront.

Government Gardens
Gardens

(Map p106; Hinemaru St) The manicured English-style Government Gardens surrounding the Rotorua Museum are pretty as a picture, with roses aplenty, steaming thermal pools dotted about and civilised amenities such as croquet lawns and bowling greens.

 ## Activities

EXTREME SPORTS

Rotorua Canopy Tours
Extreme Sports

(Map p114; ☎07-343 1001, 0800 226 679; www. canopytours.co.nz; 173 Old Taupo Rd; 3hr tour per adult/child/family $129/85/399; ⏰8am-8pm Oct-Apr, 8am-6pm May-Sep) Explore a 1.2km web of bridges, flying foxes, ziplines and platforms, 22m high in a lush native forest canopy 10 minutes out of town (...they say that rimu tree is 1000 years old!).

Plenty of native birds to keep you company. Free pick-ups available.

Agroventures
Extreme Sports

(Map p114; ☎07-357 4747, 0800 949 888; www.agroventures.co.nz; Western Rd, off Paradise Valley Rd, Ngongotaha; 1/2/4/8 rides $49/75/99/179; ⏰9am-5pm) Agroventures is a hive of action, 9km north of Rotorua on SH5 (shuttles available). Start off with the 43m **bungy** and the **Swoop**, a 130km/h swing that can be enjoyed alone or with friends. If that's not enough, try **Freefall Xtreme**, which simulates skydiving by blasting you 3m into the air on a column of wind. Also here is the **Shweeb**, a monorail velodrome from which you hang in a clear capsule and pedal yourself along recumbently at speeds of up to 60km/h. Alongside is the **Agrojet**, allegedly NZ's fastest jetboat, splashing around a 1km course.

Zorb
Extreme Sports

(Map p114; ☎07-357 5100, 0800 227 474; www. zorb.com; cnr Western Rd & SH5, Ngongotaha; 1/2/3 rides $45/70/90; ⏰9am-5pm, to 7pm Dec-Mar) The Zorb is 9km north of Rotorua on SH5 − look for the grassy hillside with large, clear, people-filled spheres rolling down it. Your eyes do not deceive you! There are three courses: 150m straight, 180m zigzag or 250m 'Drop'. Do your zorb strapped in and dry, or freestyle with water thrown in.

Skyline Rotorua
Extreme Sports

(Map p114; ☎07-347 0027; www.skyline.co.nz; Fairy Springs Rd; adult/child gondola $25/12.50, luge 3 rides $42/32, sky swing $63/53; ⏰9am-11pm) This gondola cruises up Mt Ngongotaha, about 3km northwest of town, from where you can take in panoramic lake views or ride a speedy luge back down on three different tracks. For even speedier antics, try the Sky Swing, a screaming swoosh through the air at speeds of up to 160km/h.

MOUNTAIN BIKING

On the edge of town is the Redwoods Whakarewarewa Forest (p113), home to some of the best mountain-bike trails in

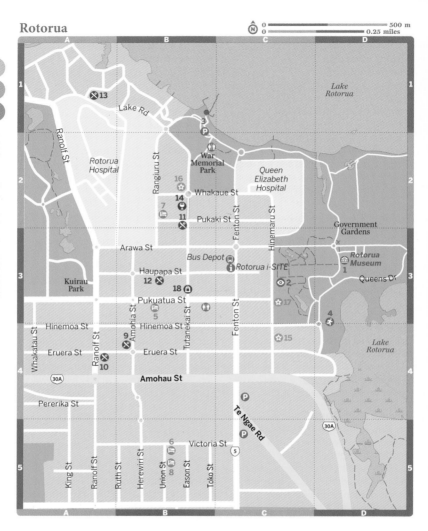

the country. There are close to 100km of tracks to keep bikers of all skill levels happy for days on end. Pick up a trail map at the forest visitor centre.

Mountain Bike Rotorua
Bicycle Rental

(Map p114; ☏0800 682 768; www.mtbrotorua. co.nz; Waipa State Mill Rd; mountain bikes per 2hr/day from $35/45, guided half-/full-day rides from $130/275; ◔9am-5pm) This outfit hires out bikes at the Waipa Mill car park entrance to the Redwoods Whakarewarewa

Forest, the starting point for the bike trails. There's also a satellite bike depot across the forest at the visitor centre, so you can ride through the trees one-way then catch a shuttle back.

WHITE-WATER RAFTING & KAYAKING

There's plenty of kayaking and white-water action around Rotorua with the chance to take on the Grade V **Kaituna River**, complete with a startling 7m drop at Okere Falls. Most of these trips take a day. Some companies head further out to the **Rangitaiki River** (Grade III–VI) and **Wairoa River** (Grade V), raftable only when the dam is opened every second Sunday.

River Rats
Rafting, Kayaking

(🕿07-345 6543, 0800 333 900; www.riverrats. co.nz) Takes on the Wairoa ($129), Kaituna ($105) and Rangitaiki ($139), and runs a scenic trip on the lower Rangitaiki (Grade II) that is good for youngsters (adult/child $139/110). Kayaking options include freedom hire ($40/60 per half-/full day) and guided four-hour Lake Rotoiti trips ($110).

Wet 'n' Wild
Rafting

(🕿07-348 3191, 0800 462 7238; www.wetnwil-drafting.co.nz; 2-5-day trip $650-1095) Runs trips on the Kaituna ($99), Wairoa ($110) and Mokau ($160), as well as easy-going Rangitaiki trips (adult/child $130/110) and longer trips to remote parts of the Motu and Mohaka.

Kaituna Cascades
Rafting, Kayaking

(🕿07-345 4199, 0800 524 8862; www. kaitunacascades.co.nz) Rafting on the Kaituna ($84), Rangitaiki ($118) and Wairoa ($108), plus kayaking options and combos.

Go Wild Adventures
Kayaking

(🕿07-533 2926; www.adventurekayaking.co.nz; per 2hr/half-day/full day from $80/95/130)

Takes trips on Lakes Rotorua, Rotoiti, Tarawera and Okataina. Also offers freedom hire (from $50 per day).

THERMAL POOLS & MASSAGE

Polynesian Spa
Spa, Massage

(Map p106; 🕿07-348 1328; www.polyne-sianspa.co.nz; 1000 Hinemoa St; adults-only pools $25, private pools per 30min adult/child from $18/6.50, family pool adult/child/family $14.50/6.50/36, spa therapies from $85; ⊙8am-11pm, spa therapies 10am-7pm) A bathhouse opened at these Government Gardens springs in 1882, and people have been swearing by the waters ever since. There is mineral bathing (36°C to 42°C) in several picturesque pools at the lake's edge, marble-lined terraced pools and a larger, main pool. Also here are luxury therapies (massage, mud and beauty treatments) and a cafe.

Tours

Happy Ewe Tours
Cycling

(🕿022 622 9252; www.happyewetours.com; per person $35; ⊙10am & 2pm) Saddle-up for a three-hour, small-group bike tour of Rotorua, wheeling past 20 sights around the city. It's all flat and slow-paced, so you don't need to at your physical peak (you're on holiday after all).

Geyser Link Shuttle
Tour

(🕿03-477 9083, 0800 304 333; www.travelhead-first.com/local-legends/geyser-link-shuttle)

WILFRIED KRECICHWOST/GETTY IMAGES ©

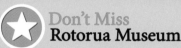

Don't Miss
Rotorua Museum

This outstanding museum occupies a grand Tudor-style edifice. It was originally an elegant spa retreat called the Bath House (1908): displays in the former shower rooms give a fascinating insight into some of the eccentric therapies once administered here, including 'electric baths' and the Bergonie Chair.

A gripping 20-minute film on the history of Rotorua, including the Tarawera eruption, runs every 20 minutes from 9am (not for small kids – the eruption noises are authentic!). The fabulous **Don Stafford Wing** houses eight object-rich galleries dedicated to Rotorua's Te Arawa people, featuring woodcarving, flax weaving, jade, interactive audiovisual displays and the stories of the revered WWII 28 Maori Battalion. Also here are two **art galleries** (with air swabbed clean of hydrogen sulphide), and a cool cafe with garden views (although the best view in town can be had from the **viewing platform** on the roof).

NEED TO KNOW

Map p106; ☎07-351 8055; www.rotoruamuseum.co.nz; Queens Dr, Government Gardens; adult/child $20/8; ⊗9am-5pm, to 6pm Dec-Feb, tours hourly 10am-4pm, plus 5pm Dec-Feb

Tours of some of the major sights, including Wai-O-Tapu (half-day adult/child $70/35) or Waimangu (half-day adult/child $70/35), or both (full day $120/60).

Rotorua Duck Tours Tour
(☎07-345 6522; adult/child/family $68/38/175; ⊗tours 11am, 1pm & 3.30pm

Oct-Apr, 11am & 2.15pm May-Sep) Ninety-minute trips in an amphibious biofuelled vehicle taking in the major sites around town and heading out onto three lakes (Rotorua, Okareka and Tikitapu/Blue). Longer Lake Tarawera trips are also available.

Mana Adventures
Cruise, Kayaking

(Map p106; ☏07-348 4186, 0800 333 660; www.manaadventures.co.nz; Lakefront; ◷9am-5pm) Down at the lake, Mana Adventures offers (weather permitting) rental pedal boats ($9/6 per adult/child per 20 minutes) and kayaks ($50/75 per hour/half-day). It also runs low-key, one-hour lake cruises ($55/39 per adult/child), trout-fishing charters and three-hour tours to Man-upirua Hot Pools on nearby Lake Rotoiti ($95/75 per adult/child).

Volcanic Air Safaris
Scenic Flights

(Map p106; ☏0800 800 848, 07-348 9984; www.volcanicair.co.nz; Lakefront; trips $95-915) A variety of floatplane and helicopter flights taking in Mt Tarawera and surrounding geothermal sites including Hell's Gate, the Buried Village and Waimangu Volcanic Valley. A 3¼-hour Whakaari (White Island)/Mt Tarawera trip tops the price list.

Sleeping

Funky Green Voyager
Hostel $

(Map p106; ☏07-346 1754; www.funkygreen-voyager.co.nz; 4 Union St; dm from $25, d with/without bathroom $68/59; @ 🛜) ⌕ Green on the outside and the inside – due to several cans of paint and a dedicated environmental policy – the shoe-free Funky GV features laid-back tunes and plenty of sociable chat among a spunky bunch of guests and worldly-wise owners, who know what you want when you travel. The best doubles have bathrooms; dorms are roomy with quality mattresses and solid timber beds.

Astray
Motel, Hostel $

(Map p106; ☏0800 481 200, 07-348 1200; www.astray.co.nz; 1202 Pukuatua St; dm/s/d from $24/40/60, f $95-150; @ 🛜) Even if you are 6ft3, Astray – a 'micro motel' that would probably be more at home in Tokyo than Rotorua – is a decent bet. Clean, tidy, quiet, friendly and central: just don't expect acres of space. Free wi-fi a bonus.

Tuscany Villas
Motel $$

(Map p114; ☏0800 802 050, 07-348 3500; www.tuscanyvillasrotorua.co.nz; 280 Fenton St; d from $145; 🛜) With its Italian-inspired architecture and pointy conifers, this family-owned eye-catcher is the pick of the Fenton St motels. It pitches itself at both corporate and leisure travellers, all of whom appreciate the plush furnishings, multiple TVs, DVD players and deep spa baths. Free wi-fi.

Six on Union
Motel $$

(Map p106; ☏0800 100 062, 07-347 8062; www.sixonunion.co.nz; 6 Union St; d/f from $105/145; 🛜🏊) Hanging baskets ahoy! This modest place is an affordable bonanza with pool and spa, and small kitchenettes in all units. Rooms are functional, and the new owners (from Yorkshire) keep the swimming-pool area in good nick. It's away from traffic noise, but still an easy walk into town.

Regent of Rotorua
Boutique Hotel $$$

(Map p106; ☏0508 734 368, 07-348 4079; www.regentrotorua.co.nz; 1191 Pukaki St; d/ste from $169/239; 🛜🏊) Wow! It's about time Rotorua showed some slumbering style, and the Regent (a renovated 1960s motel) delivers. 'The '60s was a glamorous time to travel,' say the owners: the decor follows suit, with hip black-and-white tones, funky mirrors, retro wallpaper and colourful splashes. There's a pool and restaurant, the Tutanekai St eateries are an amble away, and there's a whole new wing of rooms next door. Terrific value.

Eating

Third Place Cafe
Cafe $$

(Map p106; ☏07-349 4852; www.thirdplacecafe.co.nz; 36 Lake Rd; mains $12-18; ◷8am-4pm Mon-Fri, 8am-3pm Sat) A really interesting cafe away from the hubbub, Third Place has leapfrogged into first by our reckoning. All-day breakfast/brunch sidesteps neatly between chicken jambalaya, fish and chips, and an awesome 'mumble jumble' of crushed kumara (sweet potato), green tomatoes and spicy chorizo topped with bacon, poached egg and hollandaise sauce. Hangover? What hangover?

Abracadabra Cafe Bar
Middle Eastern, Cafe **$$**

(Map p106; 07-348 3883; www.abracadab-racafe.com; 1363 Amohia St; mains $19-30; 8.30am-11pm Tue-Fri, 9am-11pm Sat, 9am-3pm Sun) Wedged somewhere between Mexico and Morocco, Abracabara is a magical cave of spicy delights, from beef-and-apricot *tagine* to king-prawn fajitas and Tijuana pork chilli. Conjure up your own 'Day of the Dead' (tomorrow) with a tour though the dedicated tequila menu. Beaut beer terrace out the back.

Sabroso
Latin American **$$**

(Map p106; 07-349 0591; www.sabroso.co.nz; 1184 Haupapa St; mains $18-29; 5-9pm Thu-Mon) What a surprise! This modest Latin American cantina – adorned with sombreros, guitars, hessian tablecloths and salt-and-pepper shakers made from Corona bottles – serves adventurous south-of-the-border fare to spice up bland Kiwi palates. The black-bean chilli is a knock-out (as are the margaritas).

Leonardo's
Italian **$$**

(Map p106; 07-347 7084; www.leonar-dospureitalian.nznic.biz; 1176 Pukaki St; mains $22-32.50; 5-10pm Mon-Thu, 11.30am-2pm & 5-10pm Fri-Sun) Not far from the lake in an unpretentious shopfront, Leonardo's goes heavy on the hokey 'just like mama used to make' marketing, but what comes out of the kitchen is far from kitsch. Try the simple but perfect gnocchi with tomato, mozzarella and pesto, or the angel-hair pasta with mussels and anchovies.

Bistro 1284
Modern NZ **$$$**

(Map p106; 07-346 1284; www.bistro1284.co.nz; 1284 Eruera St; mains $35-39; 5pm-late) A fine-dining hot spot on an unremarkable stretch of Eruera St, this intimate place (all chocolate and mushroom colours) serves stylish NZ cuisine with an Asian influence. The lamb is always good, but be sure to leave room for the delectable desserts.

Drinking & Nightlife

Brew
Bar, Beer Hall

(Map p106; www.brewpub.co.nz; 1103 Tutanekai St; 4pm-late Mon-Thu, noon-late Fri, 11am-late

A Maori woodcarver at work

Sat & Sun) Run by the lads from Croucher Brewing Co, Rotorua's best microbrewers, Brew sits in a sunny spot on Rotorua's main eat-street. Sip down a pint of fruity pale ale, aromatic drunken hop bitter or malty pilsner and wonder how you'll manage a sleep-in tomorrow morning.

 Shopping

**Rotorua
Night Market**   Market
(Map p106; www.rotoruanightmarket.co.nz; Tutanekai St; ⏱5pm-late Thu) Tutanekai St is closed off on Thursday nights between Haupapa and Pukuatua Sts to allow the Rotorua Night Market to spread its wings. Expect local arts and crafts, souvenirs, cheesy buskers, coffee, wine and plenty of deli-style food stalls for dinner.

ℹ Information

Rotorua Hospital (📞07-348 1199; www.lakesdhb.govt.nz; Arawa St; ⏱24hr) Round-the-clock medical care.

Rotorua i-SITE (Map p106; 📞0800 768 678, 07-348 5179; www.rotoruanz.com; 1167 Fenton St; ⏱7.30am-7pm Sep-May, reduced hours winter) The hub for travel information and bookings, including Department of Conservation (DOC) walks. Also has an exchange bureau, a cafe, showers and lockers.

ℹ Getting There & Away

Air

Air New Zealand (📞07-343 1100; www.airnewzealand.co.nz; 1267 Tutanekai St; ⏱9am-5pm Mon-Fri) Has direct flights between Rotorua and Auckland, Wellington and Christchurch, plus Sydney (every Tuesday and Saturday).

Bus

All the major bus companies stop outside the Rotorua i-SITE, from where you can arrange bookings.

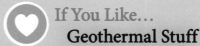

If You Like...
Geothermal Stuff

If you like Te Puia (p104), we think you'll also like these other Rotorua hot spots.

1 HELLS GATE & WAI ORA SPA
(Map p114; 📞07-345 3151; www.hellsgate.co.nz; SH30, Tikitere; admission adult/child/family $35/17.50/85, mud bath & spa $75/35/185, massage per 30/60min $85/130; ⏱8.30am-8.30pm) Hells Gate is an impressive geothermal reserve 16km northeast of Rotorua. The reserve covers 10 hectares, with a 2.5km walking track to the various attractions, including a hot thermal waterfall. The reserve also houses Wai Ora Spa, where you can get muddy with a variety of treatments.

2 WAIMANGU VOLCANIC VALLEY
(Map p114; 📞07-366 6137; www.waimangu.com; 587 Waimangu Rd; adult/child walking tour $34.50/11, boat cruise $42.50/11; ⏱8.30am-5pm daily, to 6pm Jan, last admission 3.30pm, 4.30pm Jan) The easy downhill stroll through the valley passes spectacular thermal and volcanic features, including Inferno Crater Lake and Frying Pan Lake, the largest hot spring in the world. Waimangu is 20 minutes south of Rotorua.

3 WAI-O-TAPU THERMAL WONDERLAND
(Map p114; 📞07-366 6333; www.waiotapu.co.nz; 201 Waiotapu Loop Rd, off SH5; adult/child/family $32.50/11/80; ⏱8.30am-5pm, last admission 3.45pm) A lot of interesting geothermal features packed into a small area, including the multihued Champagne Pool, bubbling mud pool, stunning mineral terraces and Lady Knox Geyser, which spouts off (with a little prompting from an organic soap) punctually at 10.15am. Wai-O-Tapu is 27km south of Rotorua along SH5.

4 WAIKITE VALLEY THERMAL POOLS
(Map p114; 📞07-333 1861; www.hotpools.co.nz; 648 Waikite Valley Rd; public pools adult/child/family $15/8/38, private pools 40min per person $18; ⏱10am-9pm) Around 35km south of Rotorua are these excellent open-air pools, formalised in the 1970s but utilised for centuries before then.

Don't Miss
Maori Concerts & Hangi

Maori culture is a big-ticket item in Rotorua and, although it is commercialised, it's a great opportunity to learn about the indigenous culture of NZ. The two big activities are concerts and *hangi* (Maori feasts), often packaged together in an evening's entertainment featuring the famous *hongi* (Maori greeting; the pressing of foreheads and noses, and sharing of life breath) and *haka* and *poi* dances.

An established favourite, **Tamaki Maori Village** (Map p106; ☎07-349 2999; www.maoriculture.co.nz; booking office 1220 Hinemaru St; adult $110, child $20-60, family $250; ☻tours depart 5pm, 6.15pm & 7.30pm Nov-Apr, 6.15pm May-Oct) does an excellent twilight tour to a *marae* (meeting house) and Maori village 15km south of Rotorua. The experience is very hands-on, taking you on an interactive journey through Maori history, arts, traditions and customs from pre-European times to the present day. The concert is followed by an impressive *hangi*.

The family-run **Mitai Maori Village** (Map p114; ☎07-343 9132; www.mitai.co.nz; 196 Fairy Springs Rd; adult $111, child $21.50-55, family $290; ☻6.30pm), a few kilometers north of town, offers a popular three-hour evening event with a concert, *hangi* and glowworm bush walk. Pick-ups available.

Te Puia (p104) and Whakarewarewa Thermal Village (p105) also put on shows, and many of the big hotels offer mainstream Maori concerts and *hangi*, including the: **Copthorne Hotel Rotorua** (Map p114; ☎07-348 0199; www.millenniumhotels.co.nz; 328 Fenton St; concert adult/child $25/15, incl hangi $55/25.25), **Holiday Inn Rotorua** (Map p114; ☎0800 476 488, 07-348 1189; www.holidayinnrotorua.co.nz/cultural-show.php; cnr Froude & Tryon Sts; concert & hangi adult/child $69/34.50) and **Millennium Hotel Rotorua** (Map p106; ☎07-347 1234; www.millenniumrotorua.co.nz; cnr Eruera & Hinemaru Sts; concert adult/child $30/15, incl hangi $70/35).

InterCity (www.intercity.co.nz) destinations include the following:

DESTINATION	PRICE	DURATION (HR)	FREQUENCY (DAILY)
Auckland	$55	3½	7
Gisborne	$64	4½	1
Hamilton	$40	1½	5
Napier	$60	4	1
Taupo	$32	1	4
Tauranga	$25	1½	2
Wellington	$65	7	5
Whakatane	$35	1½	1

Naked Bus (www.nakedbus.com) services include the following:

DESTINATION	PRICE	DURATION (HR)	FREQUENCY (DAILY)
Auckland	$15	4	3
Gisborne	$19	4¾	1
Hamilton	$10	1½	3
Napier	$18	3	3
Taupo	$10	1	3
Tauranga	$10	1½	3
Wellington	$19	8	1
Whakatane	$14	1½	1

Twin City Express (www.baybus.co.nz) buses run twice daily Monday to Friday between Rotorua and Tauranga/Mt Maunganui via Te Puke ($11.60, 1½ hours).

ℹ Getting Around

To/From the Airport

Rotorua Airport (Map p114; ☎07-345 8800; www.rotorua-airport.co.nz; SH30; 🛜) is 10km northeast of town. A taxi to/from the city centre costs about $25.

Baybus (☎0800 422 928; www.baybus.co.nz) Runs a daily airport bus service ($2.30).

Super Shuttle (☎0800 748 885, 09-522 5100; www.supershuttle.co.nz) Offers a door-to-door airport service for $21 for the first person then $5 per additional passenger.

Taxi

Rotorua Taxis (☎07-348 1111; www.rotoruataxis.co.nz)

AROUND ROTORUA

North of Rotorua

About 3km north of central Rotorua, **Rainbow Springs** (Map p114; ☎0800 724 626; www.rainbowsprings.co.nz; 192 Fairy Springs Rd; 24hr pass adult/child/family $40/20/99; ⏰8.30am-late) is a family-friendly winner. The natural springs here are home to wild trout and eels, which you can peer at through an underwater viewer. There are interpretive walkways, a new 'Big Splash' water ride, and plenty of animals, including tuatara (a native lizard) and native birds (kea, kaka and pukeko).

A highlight is the Kiwi Encounter, offering a rare peek into the lives of these endangered birds: excellent 30-minute tours (an extra $10 per person) have you tiptoeing through incubator and hatchery areas.

Southeast of Rotorua

◎ Sights & Activities

Redwoods Whakarewarewa Forest   Forest
(Map p114; www.redwoods.co.nz; Long Mile Rd, off Tarawera Rd; ⏰5.30am-8.30pm) FREE This magical forest park is 3km southeast of Rotorua on Tarawera Rd. It was originally home to over 170 tree species (a few less now), planted from 1899 to see which could be grown successfully for timber. Radiata pine proved a hit (as evident throughout NZ), but it's the mighty Californian redwoods that give the park its grandeur today.

Most walks start from the **Redwoods Gift Shop & Visitor Centre** (Map p114; ☎07-350 0110; www.redwoods.co.nz; Long Mile Rd, off Tarawera Rd; ⏰8.30am-5.30pm Mon-Fri, 10am-5pm Sat & Sun Oct-Mar, 8.30am-4.30pm Mon-Fri, 10am-4pm Sat & Sun Apr-Sep), where you can get maps and view displays about the forest. Aside from walking, the park is great for picnics, and is acclaimed for its accessible **mountain biking**. Mountain

Around Rotorua

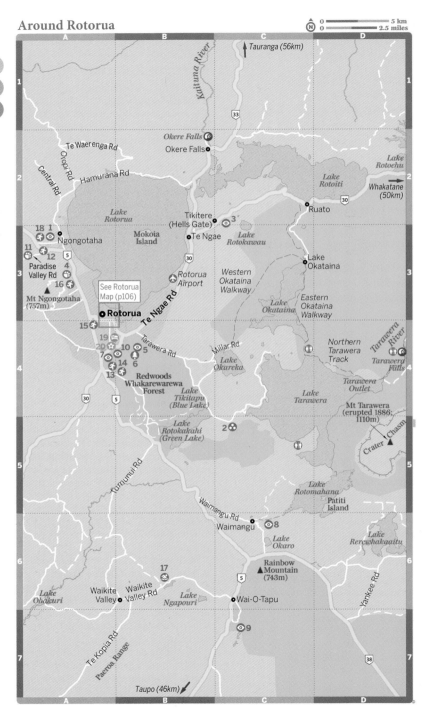

Around Rotorua

Bike Rotorua (p106) and **Planet Bike (Map p114;** ☎027 280 2817; www.planetbike.co.nz; Waipa Bypass Rd; mountain bikes per 2hr/day $35/60) offer bike hire, across the park off Waipa State Mill Rd.

Buried Village   Archaeological Site, Museum
(Map p114; ☎07-362 8287; www.buriedvillage. co.nz; 1180 Tarawera Rd; adult/child/family $35/10/66; ⊙9am-5pm Nov-Mar, to 4.30pm Apr-Oct) Fifteen kilometres from Rotorua on Tarawera Rd, beyond the pretty Blue and Green Lakes, is the buried village of Te Wairoa, interred by the eruption of Mt Tarawera in 1886. Te Wairoa was the staging post for travellers coming to see the Pink and White Terraces. Today a museum houses objects dug from the ruins, and guides in period costume escort groups through the excavated sites.

BAY OF PLENTY

The Bay of Plenty stretches along the pohutukawa-studded coast from Waihi Beach to Opotiki and inland as far as the Kaimai Range. This is where New Zealanders have come on holiday for generations, lapping up salt-licked activities and lashings of sunshine.

Tauranga

Tauranga (pronounced 'Toe-rung-ah') has been booming since the 1990s and remains one of NZ's fastest-growing cities. It's also NZ's busiest port – with petrol refineries and mountains of coal and lumber – but it's beach-seeking holidaymakers who have seen the old workhorse reborn as a show pony.

◎ Sights

Tauranga Art Gallery   Gallery
(☎07-578 7933; www.artgallery.org.nz; cnr Wharf & Willow Sts; ⊙10am-4.30pm) **FREE** The Tauranga Art Gallery presents historic and contemporary art, and houses a permanent collection along with frequently changing local and visiting exhibitions. The building itself is a former bank, although you'd hardly know it – it's an altogether excellent space with no obvious compromise (cue: applause). Touring the ground-floor and mezzanine galleries will take an hour or so.

Elms Mission House   Historic Building
(www.theelms.org.nz; 15 Mission St; house adult/ child $5/50c, gardens free; ⊙house 2-4pm Wed, Sat & Sun, gardens 9am-5pm daily) Built in 1847, Elms Mission House is the oldest building in the Bay of Plenty. Furnished in period style, it sits among other well-preserved mission buildings in leafy gardens.

🌀 Activities

Adventure Bay of Plenty   Kayaking, Mountain Biking
(☎0800 238 267; www.adventurebop.co.nz; 2hr/ half-day/full-day tours from $95/125/180) Offers an enticing array of adventure tours

If You Like...
Animal Encounters

If you like Rainbow Springs (p113), we think you'll like these other animal encounters.

1 WINGSPAN NATIONAL BIRD OF PREY CENTRE
(Map p114; 07-357 4469; www.wingspan.co.nz; 1164 Paradise Valley Rd, Ngongotaha; adult/child $25/8; 9am-3pm) About 10km north of Rotorua, Wingspan is dedicated to conserving three threatened NZ birds: the falcon, the hawk and the owl. Don't miss the 2pm flying display.

2 PARADISE VALLEY SPRINGS
(07-348 9667; www.paradisevalleysprings. co.nz; 467 Paradise Valley Rd; adult/child $30/15; 8am-dusk) In Paradise Valley at the foot of Mt Ngongotaha, 8km from Rotorua, is Paradise Valley Springs, a 6-hectare park with trout springs, big slippery eels and various land-dwelling animals such as deer, alpacas, possums and a pride of lions (which are fed at 2.30pm).

3 HAMILTON ZOO
(07-838 6720; www.hamiltonzoo.co.nz; 183 Brymer Rd; adult/child/family $19/9/56, tours extra; 9am-5pm, last entry 3.30pm) Hamilton Zoo houses 500-plus species including wily and curious chimpanzees. Guided-tour options include Eye2Eye and Face2Face opportunities to go behind the scenes to meet various animals, plus daily 'Meet the Keeper' talks from the critters' caregivers. The zoo is 8km northwest of Hamilton city centre.

4 AGRODOME
(Map p114; 07-357 1050; www.agrodome. co.nz; 141 Western Rd, Ngongotaha; 1hr tour adult/child/family $41/20/84.50, 1hr show $31/15.50/79.50, tour & show $51/25.50/118.5; 8.30am-5pm, shows 9.30am, 11am & 2.30pm, tours 10.40am, 12.10pm, 1.30pm & 3.40pm) Learn everything you need to know about sheep at the educational Agrodome, 10km north of Rotorua.

by kayak, mountain bike and horse. Half-day paddles around Mt Maunganui with a stop on Matakana Island cost $150/125 per adult/child. A two- to three-hour cycle around Tauranga costs $95.

Adrenalin Forest   Extreme Sports
(07-929 8724; www.adrenalin-forest.co.nz; Upper Pyes Pa Rd, TECT All Terrain Park; adult/child $42/27; 10am-2.30pm daily, closed Mon & Tue Jun-Aug) About 26km from Tauranga en route to Rotorua is this heart-starter: a series of high-wires, flying foxes, platforms and rope bridges strung through a grove of tall conifers.

Waimarino Adventure Park   Kayaking, Water Sports
(0800 456 996, 07-576 4233; www. waimarino.com; 36 Taniwha Pl; kayak tours from $65, kayak hire per hr/day $26/55, park day-pass adult/child $40/32; 10am-6pm Sep-Apr, 10am-5pm May-Aug) On the banks of the Wairoa River 8km west of town, Waimarino offers freedom kayak hire, self-guided kayak tours, sea kayaking trips and a magical Glowworm Tour ($120 per person) at McLaren Falls Park. The adventure park here has all kinds of watery distractions: a kayak slide, diving board, ropes course, water-walking zorbs, warm pools, and a human catapult called 'The Blob' – intense!

Tours

Dolphin Blue   Wildlife Tour
(027 666 8047; www.dolphinblue.co.nz; day trips adult/child $150/100; departs 8.30am) Unhurried, small-group (15 people maximum) day trips across Tauranga harbour and out onto the Bay of Plenty in pursuit of pods of dolphins. When you find them, you can jump in and splash around with them.

Sleeping

Roselands Motel   Motel $$
(07-578 2294, 0800 363 093; www.roselands. co.nz; 21 Brown St; d/ste from $110/135;) Tarted up with splashes of orange paint

and new linen, this sweet, old-style motel is in a quiet but central location. Expect spacious units (all with kitchenettes), friendly first-name-basis hosts and new TVs. Nice one.

Harbour City Motor Inn   Motel $$
(☏07-571 1435, 0800 253 525; www.tauranga-harbourcity.co.nz; 50 Wharf St; d/1 bedroom from $150/170; ☎) With a winning location right in the middle of town (and with plenty of parking), this newish, lemon-yellow motor inn has all the mod cons. There are spa baths in each room, and friendly staff who can offer sound advice on your itinerary.

Hotel on Devonport   Hotel $$$
(☏07-578 2668; www.hotelondevonport.net.nz; 72 Devonport Rd; d/ste from $165/205; @☎) City-centre Devonport is top of the town, with bay-view rooms, noise-reducing glass, slick interiors and sassy staff, all of which appeals to business travellers and upmarket weekenders. Help yourself to the bowl of apples in the lobby.

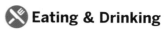

🍴 Eating & Drinking

Grindz Café   Cafe $
(☏07-579 0017; 50 First Ave; meals $5-15; ⏰7am-4pm Mon-Fri, 8am-3.30pm Sat, 8am-3pm Sun; ☎🍴) The undisputed highlight of wide-open First Ave is Grindz, a hip cafe with scattered footpath tables. Inside it's a roomy, split-level affair, with funky wallpaper, antiques and retro relics. Bagels, veggie stacks, muffins, cakes and salads are the order of the day, plus creative coffee (try 'The Trough' if you're sleepy: a four-shot soup bowl of caffeine heaven).

Elizabeth Cafe & Larder   Modern NZ, Bar $$
(☏07-579 0950; www.elizabethcafe.co.nz; 247 Cameron Rd; mains breakfast & lunch $10-20, dinner $24-34; ⏰7am-4pm Mon & Tue, 7am-5pm Wed, 7am-9pm Thu & Fri, 8am-9pm Sat, 8am-4pm Sun) 'Eat, drink, enjoy' at Elizabeth, a hip new cafe-bar on the ground floor of a four-storey city office block. Predictably, many of the customers drift down from upstairs, but you don't need a suit to enjoy a knock-out Moroccan

New Zealand falcon (kārearea), Wingspan National Bird of Prey Centre

AMOS CHAPPLE/GETTY IMAGES ©

lamb salad with a glass of Central Otago pinot gris.

Harbourside
Modern NZ $$$

(📞07-571 0520; www.harbourside.co.nz; Railway Bridge, The Strand; mains $26-38; ⏱11.30am-2.30pm & 5.30pm-late) In a marvellously atmospheric 100-year-old boathouse at the end of The Strand, Harbourside is the place for a romantic dinner, with lapping waves and the overhead railway bridge arching out over the harbour. The roast duck with Chinese cabbage, lime and chilli is hard to beat, or you can just swing by for a moody predinner drink.

Brew
Pub

(www.brewpub.co.nz; 107 The Strand; ⏱4pm-late Mon-Thu, 11am-late Wed-Sun) The long concrete bar here has room for plenty of elbows, and plenty of glasses of Croucher's crafty seasonal ales, pilsners and stouts (pray the Ethiopian coffee stout is on-tap). The vibe is social, with communal tables and plates of bar food designed to share ($8 to $28). And no TV! Winner.

ℹ Information

Tauranga Hospital (📞07-579 8000; www.bopdhb.govt.nz; 375 Cameron Rd; ⏱24hr) A couple of kilometres south of town.

Tauranga i-SITE (📞07-578 8103; www.bayofplentynz.com; 8 Wharf St; ⏱8.30am-5.30pm, reduced hours winter; 📶) Local tourist information, bookings, InterCity bus tickets and DOC maps.

ℹ Getting There & Away

Air

Air New Zealand (📞07-577 7300; www.airnewzealand.co.nz; cnr Devonport Rd & Elizabeth St; ⏱9am-5pm Mon-Fri, 10am-1pm Sat) Has daily direct flights to Auckland, Wellington and Christchurch.

Bus

Twin City Express (📞0800 422 928; www.baybus.co.nz) buses run twice daily Monday to Friday between Tauranga/Mt Maunganui and Rotorua via Te Puke ($11.60, 1½ hours).

InterCity (www.intercity.co.nz) tickets and timetables are available at the i-SITE. Destinations including the following:

Boats at Mt Maunganui

WILLIAMS-ELLIS/GETTY IMAGES ©

DESTINATION	PRICE	DURATION (HR)	FREQUENCY (DAILY)
Auckland	$46	4	3
Hamilton	$33	2	2
Rotorua	$32	1½	2
Taupo	$52	3	2
Wellington	$55	9	1

Naked Bus (www.nakedbus.com) offers substantial fare savings when you book in advance. Destinations include the following:

DESTINATION	PRICE	DURATION (HR)	FREQUENCY (DAILY)
Auckland	$16	3¼	3
Hamilton	$10	3	2
Napier	$35	5	2
Rotorua	$10	1	3
Taupo	$15	3	2
Wellington	$23	9	1
Whakatane	$18	3	1

Mt Maunganui

Named after the hulking 232m hill that punctuates the sandy peninsula occupied by the township, up-tempo Mt Maunganui is often just called 'the Mount', or Mauao, which translates into 'caught by the light of day'. Sun-seekers flock to the Mount in summer, supplied by an increasing number of 10-storey apartment towers studding the spit.

◎ Sights & Activities

The Mount lays claim to being NZ's premier **surfing** city (they teach surfing at high school!). You can carve up the waves at **Mount Beach**, which has lovely beach breaks and a 100m artificial surf reef not far offshore. Learn-to-surf operators include **Hibiscus** (☎027 279 9687, 07-575 3792; www.surfschool.co.nz; 2hr/2-day lesson $85/165), **Discovery Surf School** (☎027 632 7873; www.discoverysurf.co.nz; 2hr lesson $90, 4 lessons $320) and **Mount Surfshop** (☎07-575 9133; www.mountsurfshop.co.nz; 96 Maunganui Rd; rental per hr wetsuit/bodyboard/surfboard/paddleboard from $5/5/10/20, 2hr lesson $80; ◷9am-5pm Mon-Sat, 10am-5pm Sun).

Mauao — Mountain, Lookout

Explore Mauao (Mt Maunganui) itself on the walking trails winding around it and leading up to the summit. The steep **summit walk** takes about an hour return (with a rest at the top!). You can also clamber around the rocks on **Moturiki Island**, which adjoins the peninsula. The island and the base of Mauao comprise the **Mauao Base Track** (3.5km, 45 minutes), wandering through magical groves of pohutukawa trees that bloom between November and January. Pick up the *Mauao* map from the info desk at Beachside Holiday Park.

Mount Hot Pools — Swimming

(www.tcal.co.nz; 9 Adams Ave; adult/child/family $11/8/31; ◷6am-10pm Mon-Sat, 8am-10pm Sun) If you've worked up a sweat walking up and down Mauao, take a long relaxing soak at these hotwater pools at the foot of the hill.

Canoe & Kayak — Kayaking

(☎07-574 7415; www.canoeandkayak.co.nz; 3/5 MacDonald St; tours per person from $99) Canoe & Kayak runs 2½-hour kayaking trips around Mauao checking out seals and rock formations and hearing local legends, plus three-hour nocturnal glow-worm paddles in nearby McLarens Falls Park.

🛏 Sleeping

Seagulls Guesthouse B&B — B&B, Hostel $

(☎07-574 2099; www.seagullsguesthouse.co.nz; 12 Hinau St; dm/s/d/f from $30/65/85/110; @ ⑦) Can't face another crowded, alcohol-soaked hostel? On a quiet street not far from town, Seagulls is a gem: an immaculate, upmarket backpackers where the emphasis is on peaceful enjoyment of one's surrounds rather than wallowing in the excesses of youth (...not that there's anything wrong with that). The best rooms have bathrooms and TVs. Free wi-fi.

Mission Belle Motel — Motel $$

(☎0800 202 434, 07-575 2578; www.missionbellemotel.co.nz; cnr Victoria Rd & Pacific

Hot Fuzz: Kiwifruit

The humble kiwifruit earns NZ more than a billion dollars every year, and with the Bay of Plenty in the thick of the action, it's no wonder the locals are fond of them.

The fruit's origins are in China, where it was called the monkey peach (they were considered ripe when the monkeys munched them). As they migrated to NZ, they were renamed the Chinese gooseberry – they were a lot smaller then, but canny Kiwis engineered them to more generous sizes and began exporting them in the 1950s. The fruit was then sexily rebranded as the Zespri. Today the Zesprians grow two types of kiwifruit: the common fuzzy-covered green fruit, and the gold fruit with its smooth complexion. To learn more about the kiwifruit, visit **Kiwi360** (☏0800 549 4360, 07-573 6340; www.kiwi360.com; 35 Young Rd, off SH2; admission free, tour adult/child/family $20/6/46; ⏱9am-5pm) near Te Puke.

Ave; d/f from $130/190; ☎) With a distinctly Tex-Mex exterior (like something out of an old Clint Eastwood movie), this family-run motel goes all modern inside, with especially good two-storey family rooms with large bathtubs, plus sheltered barbecue and courtyard areas.

Eating & Drinking

Providores Urban Food Store
Cafe, Delicatessen **$**

(☏07-572 1300; 19a Pacific Ave; meals $5-22; ⏱7.30am-5pm, closed Mon & Tue Apr-Oct; 🖥) Mexican rugs and comfy couches set the mood here as your eyes peruse fresh-baked breads, buttery croissants, home-smoked meats and cheeses, organic jams and free-range eggs – perfect ingredients for a bang-up breakfast or a hamper-filling picnic on the beach. Superb.

Drawing Room
Modern NZ, French **$$$**

(☏07-575 0096; www.thedrawingroom-nz.tumblr.com; 107 Maunganui Rd; mains $34; ⏱6pm-late Mon-Sat, 3pm-late daily Nov-Mar) This outstanding new Frenchy food room fills a niche: upmarket but totally unpretentious, with a commitment to local produce and local art (the window mural changes monthly). Designwise it's leather banquettes and timber floorboards; boozewise it's NZ craft beers, single malts and an inspired selection of Kiwi and French wines. Order the pan-fried scallops, and leave room for a secret dessert!

Major Tom's
Bar

(www.majortomsbar.com; 297 Maunganui Rd; ⏱4-11pm Sun-Tue, 5-11pm Wed & Thu, 4pm-1am Fri & Sat; ☎) A funky little bar set back from the main drag in what looks like Major Tom's spaceship. Inside it's all kooky antiques, vintage couches, dangling inverted desk lamps and prints of Elvis, the *Mona Lisa* and (of course) David Bowie. Fabulous streetside terrace, cool tunes, free wi-fi and occasional live acts. Everybody sing: 'Planet Earth is blue, and there's nothing I can do...'

ℹ Information

The reception desk at Beachside Holiday Park (1 Adams Ave) doubles as an informal info centre for the Mount, open 8.30am to 7pm.

ℹ Getting There & Away

InterCity and Naked Bus services visiting Tauranga also stop at Mt Maunganui, with Rotorua and Auckland fares similar to those to/from Tauranga. Buses stop on Salisbury Ave.

Whakatane

A true pohutukawa paradise, Whakatane (pronounced 'Fokka-*tar*-nay') sits on a natural harbour at the mouth of the river of the same name. It's the hub of the Rangitaiki agricultural district, but there's much more to Whakatane than farming – blissful beaches, a sunny main-street vibe and volcanic Whakaari (White Island) for starters.

Sights

Te Manuka Tutahi Marae — Marae

(☏07-308 4271; www.mataatua.com; 105 Muriwai Dr; ⊙9am-4pm Dec-Feb, reduced hours Mar-Nov) **FREE** The centrepiece of this recently opened Ati-Awa *marae* (meeting house) isn't new: **Mataatua Wharenui** (The House That Came Home) is a fantastically carved 1875 meeting house. In 1879 it was dismantled and shipped to Sydney, before spending 71 years in the Otago Museum from 1925. It was returned to the Ati-Awa in 1996. You can check out Mataatua Wharenui from the outside for free (behave respectfully), or book an excellent 90-minute cultural tour (adult/child $49/15).

Whakatane District Museum — Museum, Gallery

(☏07-306 0509; www.whakatanemuseum.org.nz; Esplanade Mall, Kakahoroa Dr; admission by donation; ⊙9am-5pm Mon-Fri, 10am-2pm Sat & Sun) This impressive new museum/gallery in the library building has artfully presented displays on early Maori and European settlement in the area: Maori *taonga* (treasures) trace a lineage back to the *Mataatua* canoe. Other displays focus on Whakaari (White Island) and Motuhora (Whale

Island). The gallery section presents a varied program of NZ and international exhibitions.

 Activities

The **Kohi Point Walkway** is highly recommended: a bushy four-hour, 5.5km track with panoramic cliff-top views and a genuine 'gasp' moment when you set eyes on Otarawairere Bay. Ask the i-SITE for a walk map.

Diveworks Dolphin & Seal Encounters — Diving, Wildlife Tour

(☏0800 354 7737, 07-308 2001; www.whaleislandtours.com; 96 The Strand; dolphin & seal swimming adult/child $160/130, diving incl gear from $215) This dive/ecotour company runs dolphin- and seal-swimming trips from Whakatane (cheaper if you're just watching from the boat), plus guided tours of Motuhora (Whale Island; adult child $120/85) and diving at Whakaari (White Island; two dives including gear $275).

Kiwifruit orchard
BILL BIRTWHISTLE/GETTY IMAGES ©

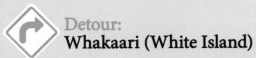

Detour:
Whakaari (White Island)

New Zealand's most active volcano, which last erupted in 2013, lies 49km off the Whakatane coast. The island is dramatic, with hot water hissing and steaming from vents over most of the crater floor. Temperatures of 600°C to 800°C have been recorded.

Fixed-wing air operators run flyover tours only, while boat and helicopter tours will usually include a walking tour around the island including a visit to the ruins of the sulphur-mining factory – an interesting story in itself.

The only official boat trip to Whakaari (on board the good ship *Pee Jay*) is offered by **White Island Tours** (🕿 0800 733 529, 07-308 9588; www.whiteisland.co.nz; 15 The Strand, Whakatane; 6hr tour adult/child $199/130; ⊙ departures btwn 7am & 12.30pm), with dolphin-spotting en route and a two-hour tour of the island.

Full-day snorkelling and diving trips, with lunch and gear provided, can be arranged with **Dive White Island** (🕿 0800 348 394, 07-307 0714; www.divewhite.co.nz; 186 The Strand, Whakatane; snorkelling per person $225, 2hr dive with gear $395). Expect underwater volcanic terrain and lots of fish to look at.

Frontier Helicopters (🕿 0800 804 354, 07-308 4188; www.vulcanheli.co.nz; Whakatane Airport; flights per person from $650) can take you on a two-hour trip to Whakaari (departing from Whakatane) that includes a one-hour guided walk on the volcano.

For fixed-wing scenic flights over Whakaari, with lots of photo opportunities, try **White Island Flights** (🕿 0800 944 834; www.whiteislandflights.co.nz; Whakatane Airport; flights per person $249).

Sleeping

Captain's Cabin
Apartment $$

(🕿 07-308 5719; www.captainscabin.co.nz; 23 Muriwai Dr; d from $125, extra person $25) On the serene side of town with sparkling water views, this homely self-contained unit is perfect if you're hanging round for a few days (cheaper for two nights or more). A cosy living area cleverly combines bedroom, lounge, kitchen and dining, with a second smaller room and bijou bathroom – all sweetly decorated along nautical lines. Sleeps three.

White Island Rendezvous
Hotel, B&B $$

(🕿 0800 733 529, 07-308 9500; www.whiteisland.co.nz; 15 The Strand E; d $100-160, apt from $200, B&B $190; 🛜) An immaculate 28-room complex run by the on-the-ball White Island Tours people (cheaper rates for tour-goers). Lots of balcony and deck space for inhaling the sea air, while interiors are decked out with timber floors for a nautical vibe. Deluxe rooms come with spas; disabled-access facilities available. The B&B next door includes cooked breakfast.

Eating

L'Epicerie
Cafe $

(🕿 07-308 5981; www.lepicerie.co.nz; 73 The Strand; mains $10-16; ⊙ 7.30am-3.30pm Mon-Fri, 8am-4pm Sat, 8.30am-2.30pm Sun) *Ooh-la-la!* This classic French cafe in central Whakatane is a real surprise, serving terrific omelettes, croissants, crepes and *croque monsieurs* at communal tables. Fabulous coffee and deli shelves crammed with preserves, breads, mustards and deliciously stinky French cheeses complete a very Franco scene.

Roquette Modern NZ $$$
(☎ 07-307 0722; www.roquette-restaurant.
co.nz; 23 Quay St; mains lunch $20-34, dinner
$30-36; ☼10am-late Mon-Sat) A modern
waterside restaurant on the ground
floor of one of the town's big new apart-
ment buildings, ritzy Roquette serves
up refreshing Mediterranean-influenced
fare with lots of summery salads, risotto
and fish dishes. Laid-back tunes, lots
of glass and mosaics, good coffee and
sexy staff to boot. Try the char-grilled
lamb salad.

ℹ Information

Whakatane i-SITE (☎0800 924 528, 07-306
2030; www.whakatane.com; cnr Quay St &
Kakahoroa Dr; ☼8am-5pm Mon-Fri, 10am-4pm
Sat & Sun; 🛜) Free internet access (including
24-hour wi-fi on the terrace outside the
building), tour bookings, accommodation and
general DOC enquiries.

ℹ Getting There & Around

Air

Air New Zealand (☎0800 737 000, 07-308 8397;
www.airnewzealand.com) has daily flights linking
Whakatane to Auckland.

Bus

InterCity (www.intercity.co.nz) buses stop
outside the i-SITE and connect Whakatane with
Rotorua ($20, 1½ hours, one daily), Tauranga
($30, eight hours, one daily via Rotorua) and
Gisborne ($46, three hours, one daily via Opotiki),
with onward connections.

Naked Bus (www.nakedbus.com) destinations
include the following:

DESTINATION	PRICE	DURATION (HR)	FREQUENCY (DAILY)
Auckland	$35	6	1
Gisborne	$20	3¼	1
Hamilton	$25	2½	1
Rotorua	$19	1½	1
Tauranga	$18	4	1
Wellington	$65	10	1

LAKE TAUPO REGION

NZ's largest lake, Lake Taupo, sits in the
caldera of a volcano that began erupting
about 300,000 years ago.

Today the 622-sq-km lake and its
surrounding waterways are serene
enough to attract fishing enthusiasts
from all around the world. Well positioned
by the lake, both Taupo and Turangi are
popular tourist centres.

Taupo

With a postcard-perfect setting on the
northeastern shores of the lake, Taupo
now rivals Rotorua as the North Island's
premier resort town. There's an abun-
dance of adrenaline-pumping activities
on offer but for those with no appetite
for white knuckles and churned stom-
achs, there's plenty of enjoyment to
be had simply strolling by the lake and
enjoying the views, which on clear days
encompass the snowy peaks of Tongariro
National Park.

◎ Sights

Taupo Museum Museum
(Map p125; www.taupo.govt.nz/museum; Story
Pl; adult/child $5/free; ☼10am-4.30pm) With
an excellent Maori gallery and quirky dis-
plays, which include a 1960s caravan set
up as if the occupants have just popped
down to the lake, this little museum
makes an interesting rainy-day diversion.
The centrepiece is an elaborately carved
Maori meeting house, Te Aroha o Rongo-
heikume. Historical displays cover local
industries, a mock-up of a 19th-century
shop and a moa skeleton, and there's
also a gallery devoted to local and visiting
exhibitions.

Maori Rock Carvings Carvings
Accessible only by boat, these 10m-
high carvings were etched into the cliffs
near Mine Bay by master carver Matahi
Whakataka-Brightwell in the late 1970s.
They depict Ngatoro-i-rangi, the vision-
ary Maori navigator who guided the

Tuwharetoa and Te Arawa tribes to the Taupo area a thousand years ago.

Huka Falls
Waterfall

(Huka Falls Rd) **FREE** Clearly signposted and with a car park and kiosk alongside, these falls mark the spot where NZ's longest river, the Waikato is slammed into a narrow chasm, making a dramatic 10m drop into a surging pool. You can also take a few short walks around the area or pick up the Huka Falls Walkway back to town, or the Aratiatia Rapids Walking/Cycling Track to the rapids.

Volcanic Activity Centre
Museum

(www.volcanoes.co.nz; Karetoto Rd; adult/child $10/6; ⊙9am-5pm Mon-Fri, 10am-4pm Sat & Sun) What's with all the geothermal activity around Taupo? This centre has the answers, with excellent, if text-heavy, displays on the region's geothermal and volcanic activity, including a live seismograph keeping a watch on what's currently going on. A favourite exhibit with kids is the Earthquake Simulator, a little booth complete with teeth-chattering shudders and jarring wobbles.

Craters of the Moon
Thermal Area

(www.cratersofthemoon.co.nz; Karapiti Rd; adult/child $8/4; ⊙8.30am-5.30pm) This lesser-known geothermal area sprang to life as a result of the hydroelectric tinkering that created the power station. The perimeter loop walk takes about 45 minutes and affords great views down to the lake and mountains beyond. It's signposted from SH1, about 5km north of Taupo.

Wairakei Terraces & Thermal Health Spa
Hot Pools

(☎07-378 0913; www.wairakeiterraces.co.nz; Wairakei Rd; thermal walk adult/child $18/9, pools $25, massage from $80; ⊙8.30am-7pm) At our pick of the region's hot pools, mineral-laden waters from the nearby Wairakei geothermal steamfield cascade over silica terraces into pools (open to those 14 years and over) nestled in serene native gardens. Take a therapeutic soak and a self-guided tour on the **Terraces Walkway**. On this you'll find a recreated Maori village, carvings depicting the history of NZ, Maori and local *iwi* (tribe) Ngati Tuwahretoa, and artificially made geysers and silica terraces, that re-create, on a smaller scale, the famous Pink and White Terraces, which were destroyed by the Tarawera eruption in 1886. The night-time **Maori Cultural Experience** – which includes a traditional challenge, welcome, concert, tour and *hangi* meal – gives an insight into Maori life in the geothermal areas (adult/child $98/49).

Huka Falls
DANITA DELIMONT/GETTY IMAGES ©

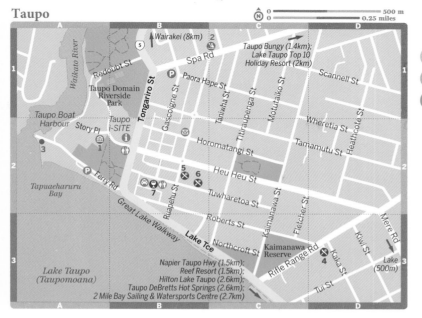

Taupo

🏃 Activities

Taupo Tandem Skydiving
Skydiving

(☎07-377 0428, 0800 826 336; www.
taupotandemskydiving.com; Anzac Memorial Dr;
12,000ft/15,000ft $249/339) Various packages that include DVDs, photos, T-shirts etc ($388 to $679); bungy combo available.

Huka Falls Walkway
Walking, Cycling

Starting from the Spa Park car park at the end of County Ave (off Spa Rd), this scenic, easy walk takes just over an hour to reach the falls, following the eastern bank of the Waikato River. Continuing on from the falls is the 7km **Huka Falls to Aratiatia Rapids Walking Track** (another two-plus hours). The Taupo–Huka Falls–Ariatiatia loop bike ride will take around four hours in total.

Spa Park Hot Spring
Hot Pools

(Spa Park) FREE The hot thermal waters of the Otumuheke Stream meet the bracing Waikato River at this pleasant and well-worn spot under a bridge, creating a free natural spa bath. It's near the beginning of the Huka Falls Walkway, about 20 minutes from the centre of town.

Taupo DeBretts Hot Springs
Hot Pools

(☎07-377 6502; www.taupodebretts.com; 76 Napier Taupo Hwy; adult/child $20/10; ⊙8.30am-9.30pm) 🅿 A variety of mineral-rich indoor and outdoor thermal pools are on offer. The kids will love the giant dragon waterslide, while the adults can enjoy a wide

Below: Bungy jumping over the Waikato River; **Right:** Jet boating, near Huka Falls on the Waikato River

(BELOW) ANDERS BLOMQVIST/GETTY IMAGES ©: (RIGHT) ROBIN BUSH/GETTY IMAGES ©

choice of treatments, such as massage and body scrubs.

Canoe & Kayak
Canoeing, Kayaking

(Map p125; ☏07-378 1003, 0800 529 256; www.kayaktoursnz.co.nz; 54 Spa Rd; ⏰9am-5pm Mon-Sat) Instruction and boat hire, as well as guided tours, including a two-hour trip on the Waikato River ($49) or a half-day to the Maori carvings (p123) for $95.

Hukafalls Jet
Jetboating

(☏07-374 8572, 0800 485 253; www.hukafalls-jet.com; 200 Karetoto Rd; adult/child $109/65) 🌊 This 30-minute thrill ride takes you up the river to the spray-filled foot of the Huka Falls and down to the Aratiatia Dam, all the while dodging daringly and doing acrobatic 360-degree turns. Trips run all day (prices include shuttle transport from Taupo).

Rapid Sensations & Kayaking Kiwi
Kayaking

(☏07-374 8117, 0800 35 34 35; www.rapids.co.nz; 413 Huka Falls Rd) Offers kayak trips to the Maori carvings ($98, four hours), a gentle paddle along the Waikato ($48, two hours), white-water rafting on the Tongariro River ($88 to $115), guided mountain-bike rides ($90) and bike hire (half-/full day $45/60).

2 Mile Bay Sailing & Watersports Centre
Sailing, Kayaking

(☏0274 967 350 0275 886 588; www.sailingcentre.co.nz; Lake Tce; ⏰9am-10pm) Has a lakeside cafe-bar and hires out paddle boards ($30), kayaks (from $30), canoes (from $30), windsurfers (from $55), sailboats ($75) and catamarans (from $65); rates are per hour.

Taupo Bungy
Bungy Jumping

(☏07-377 1135, 0800 888 408; www.taupobungy.co.nz; 202 Spa Rd; solo/tandem

$169/338; ⏱9am-5pm, extended hours summer)
On a cliff high above the Waikato River,
this picturesque bungy site is the North
Island's most popular, with plenty of
vantage points for the chickens. The cou-
rageous will be led onto a platform jutting
20m out over the cliff, where they can
throw themselves off the edge for a heart-
stopping 47m plunge. Tandem leaps are
available, as they are for the Cliffhanger
giant swing (solo/tandem $119/238).

Tours

Chris Jolly
Outdoors   Boat Tour, Fishing
(Map p125; ☎07-378 0623, 0800 252 628; www.
chrisjolly.co.nz; Taupo Boat Harbour, Ferry Rd;
⏱adult/child $44/16) Operates the *Cruise
Cat,* a large, modern launch that offers
fishing trips and daily cruises to the
Maori carvings (10.30am, 1.30pm and
5pm). Sunday brunch trips (adult/child
$62/34) are also worthwhile. Charters,
and guided tramping and mountain-
biking trips also available.

Helipro   Helicopter
(☎07-377 8805, 0800 435 4776; www.helipro.
co.nz; Anzac Memorial Dr; flights $99-1250)
Specialises in heli-tours, which include
alpine and White Island landings, as well
as shorter scenic flights over the town,
lake and volcanoes.

Paradise Tours   Bus Tour
(☎07-378 9955; www.paradisetours.co.nz;
adult/child $99/45) Three-hour tours to the
Aratiatia Rapids, Craters of the Moon
and Huka Falls. Also offers day tours to
Tongariro National Park, Orakei Korako,
Rotorua, Hawke's Bay and Waitomo
Caves.

Sleeping

Lake Taupo Top 10
Holiday Resort   Holiday Park $
(☎07-378 6860, 0800 332 121; www.taupotop10.
co.nz; 41 Centennial Dr; campsites from $48, units
$97-306; @🛈🐾) ✐ This slick 20-acre
park about 2.5km from the i-SITE has all
mod-cons, including heated swimming

pool, tennis courts and an on-site shop. Manicured grounds, swish new accommodation options and spotless facilities help make it a contender for camp of the year.

Reef Resort
Apartments $$

(📞0800 733 378, 07-378 5115; www.accommodationtaupo.com; 219 Lake Tce; d $150-250; 🛜🏊) This smart complex stands out among Taupo's waterfront apartment complexes for its classy, well-priced one-to three-bedroom apartments, centred upon an appealing pool patio.

Lake
Motel $$

(📞07-378 4222; www.thelakeonline.co.nz; 63 Mere Rd; d $130-200; @🛜) A reminder that 1960s and '70s design wasn't all Austin Powers–style groovaliciousness, this distinctive boutique motel is crammed with furniture from the era's signature designers. The four one-bedroom units all have kitchenettes and dining/living areas, and everyone has use of the pleasant garden out back.

Hilton Lake Taupo
Hotel $$$

(📞07-378 7080; www.hilton.com/laketaupo; 80-100 Napier Rd; from $220; @🛜🏊) Occupying the historic Terraces Hotel (1889) and a modern extension, this large complex offers the expected Hilton standard of luxury including swish suites, an outdoor heated pool, and Bistro Lago, the decent in-house restaurant. It's a little out of town but is handy for the DeBretts thermal complex.

🍴 Eating & Drinking

L'Arté
Cafe $

(www.larte.co.nz; 255 Mapara Rd, Acacia Bay; snacks $4-9, mains $10-19; ⏰9am-4pm Wed-Sun, daily Jan) Lots of mouth-watering treats are made from scratch at this fantastically artful cafe on the hill that backs Acacia Bay. Brunch in the sunshine, then check out the sculpture garden and gallery.

Piccolo
Cafe $$

(Map p125; www.taupocafe.co.nz; 41 Ruapehu St; mains $12-24; ⏰7am-4pm; 🛜📶) This sharp, modern cafe is well tuned, offering a cabinet-load of pastries, sandwiches and salads, with great-value wines by the glass should you feel inclined. Excellent coffee, and sublime home-baked sweets.

Plateau
Pub $$

(Map p125; www.plateautaupo.co.nz; 64 Tuwharetoa St; mains $20-35; ⏰11.30am-late; 🛜) An ambient place for a handle or two of the Monteith's range, popular Plateau delivers in the food department, too. Its menu of modern pub classics features the likes of smoked salmon salad with corn cakes, and an artful steak sandwich.

Brantry
Modern NZ $$$

(Map p125; 📞07-378 0484; www.thebrantry. co.nz; 45 Rifle Range Rd; mains $30, 2-/3-course set menu $45/55; ⏰dinner) Operating out of an unobtrusive 1950s house, the Brantry continues its reign as one of the best in the region for its well-executed, good-value offerings centred on meaty mains turned out in classical style. Bookending with entrée and dessert is highly recommended.

Vine Eatery & Bar
Tapas, Wine Bar

(Map p125; www.vineeatery.co.nz; 37 Tuwharetoa St; tapas $9-20; ⏰9am-late) The clue's in the name at this wine bar sharing its barnlike home with the Scenic Cellars wine store. Share traditional tapas alongside larger divisible dishes, accompanied by your choice of an expansive array of wines at keen prices. This is Taupo's best bet for a sophisticated nibble and natter among the town's well-heeled.

ℹ Information

Taupo i-SITE (Map p125; 📞07-376 0027, 0800 525 382; www.greatlaketaupo.com; Tongariro St; ⏰8.30am-5pm) Handles bookings for accommodation, transport and activities; dispenses cheerful advice; and stocks DOC maps and town maps.

ℹ Getting There & Away

Taupo Airport (📞07-378 7771; www. taupoairport.co.nz; Anzac Memorial Dr) is 8km south of town. InterCity and **Naked Bus** (www.

nakedbus.com) services stop outside the i-SITE, where bookings can be made.

Getting Around

There are plenty of shuttle services operating year-round to Turangi and Tongariro National Park. Ask at the i-SITE who will best suit your needs as services vary according to season (ski or hike).

Busit! (☎0800 4287 5463; www.busit.co.nz) Local buses are run by Busit!, including the Taupo North service running as far as Huka Falls and Wairakei, twice daily Monday to Friday.

Hotbus (☎0508 468 287; www.alpinehotbus. co.nz) A hop-on, hop-off minibus service around the town's key attractions.

Taxi

Expect to pay about $25 for a cab from the airport to the centre of town.

Taupo Taxi (☎07-378 5100; www.taupotaxi. co.nz)

Top Cabs (Map p125; ☎07-378 9250; 23 Tuwharetoa St)

....

Turangi & Around

Once a service town for the nearby hydroelectric power station, sleepy Turangi's claim to fame nowadays is as the 'Trout Fishing Capital of the World' and as one of the country's premier white-water-rafting destinations. Set on the Tongariro River, the town is a shortish hop for snow-bunnies from the ski fields and walking tracks of Tongariro National Park.

Sights & Activities

Tongariro National Trout Centre   Aquarium
(www.troutcentre.com; SH1; adult/child $10/ free; ☉10am-3pm) The DOC-managed trout hatchery has polished educational displays, a collection of rods and reels dating back to the 1880s and freshwater aquariums displaying river life, both nasty and nice. A gentle stroll along the landscaped walkway leads to the hatchery, keeping ponds, an underwater viewing chamber, the Tongariro River and a picnic area.

Tongariro River Trail   Walking, Cycling
(www.tongarirorivertrail.co.nz) Should you have at least half a day to spare around Turangi, the must-do is the picturesque Tongariro River Trail, a 16km dual-use walking and cycling loop track starting from town and heading upriver to the Red Hut suspension bridge, taking in the National Trout Centre along the way. It takes around four hours to walk the entire loop, and around two hours to bike on easy terrain; hire bikes from Tongariro River Rafting (p130) who offer a $35 bike-hire and Trout Centre entry package.

Red Hut suspension bridge, Tongariro River Trail
KYLE GEORGE/GETTY IMAGES ©

Tongariro River Rafting
Rafting

(07-386 6409, 0800 101 024; www.trr.co.nz; Atirau Rd) Test the white waters with a Gentle Family Float (adult/child $75/65), splash straight into the Grade III rapids (adult/child $115/105), or try a more physical kayaking trip ($129).

Tokaanu Thermal Pools
Hot Pools

(www.tokaanuthermalpools.co.nz; Mangaroa St, Tokaanu; adult/child $6/4, private pools per 20min $10/6; 10am-9pm) Soak in thermally heated water at this unpretentious, family-orientated facility, 5km northwest of Turangi.

Sleeping

Creel Lodge
Lodge $$

(07-386 8081, 0800 273 355; www.creel. co.nz; 183 Taupahi Rd; units $130-150;) Set in green and peaceful grounds, this heavenly hideaway backs onto a fine stretch of the Tongariro River. Spacious units have separate lounges, kitchens, soothing patios for sundowners and free use of barbecues. **Creel Tackle House & Cafe** (07-386 7929; www.creeltackle.com; 183 Taupahi Rd) on-site.

Judges Pool Motel
Motel $$

(07-386 7892, 0800 583 439; www.judgespoolmotel.co.nz; 92 Taupahi Rd; d $110; @) This older motel has tidy, spacious rooms with kitchenettes. All one-bedroom units have outdoor decks for relaxing beers, although the barbecue area is the best place to talk about the one that got away. Free-range eggs from the owners' chooks sold cheap.

Oreti Village
Apartments $$$

(07-386 7070; www.oretivillage.com; Mission House Dr, Pukawa; apt $220-280;) This enclave of smart self-contained apartments sits high over the lake surrounded by bird-filled native bush and landscaped with colourful rhododendrons. Gaze at blissful lake views from the balcony, undertaking a spot of tennis or taking a dip in the indoor pool. Take SH41 for 15km, heading northwest of Turangi, and turn right into Pukawa Rd.

Eating

Licorice
Cafe $

(57 SH1, Motuoapa; mains $9-17; 8am-4pm Mon-Sat, 9am-3pm Sun) Look for the giant licorice allsort on the roof of this roadside cafe, 8km north of Turangi. It's better than any of the cafes in the town itself, with fine coffee and baking.

Lakeland House
International $$

(07-386 6442; 88 Waihi Rd, Waihi; brunch $16-25, dinner $23-42; 10am-3pm & 6pm-late) Destination dining at the southern end of Lake Taupo, with generous pastas, salads and chowder dominating the daytime menu. Come evening, meatlovers can salivate over a rack of lamb with tamarillo and plum compote, rounded off with a toothsome passionfruit meringue gateau. Six kilometres from Turangi, just off SH41.

Information

Turangi i-SITE (07-386 8999, 0800 288 726; www.greatlaketaupo.com; Ngawaka Pl; 8.30am-5pm;) A good stop for information on Tongariro National Park, Kaimanawa Forest Park, trout fishing, and snow and road conditions.

Getting There & Away

Both InterCity and **Naked Bus** (www.nakedbus. com) coaches stop outside the i-SITE.

THE CENTRAL PLATEAU

Tongariro National Park

Tongariro National Park (797 sq km) lies in the heart of the North Island. Its major landmarks are three active volcanoes – Ruapehu, Ngauruhoe and Tongariro.

Mt Ruapehu (www.mtruapehu.com), at 2797m, is the highest mountain in the North Island. It is also one of the world's most active volcanoes.

Ongoing rumbles are reminders that these volcanoes in the area are very much in the land of the living. The last major event was in 2012 when **Mt Tongariro** – the northernmost and lowest peak in the park (1967m) – gave a couple of good blasts from its northern craters, causing a nine-month partial closure of the famous Alpine Crossing track.

Northeast of Ruapehu is **Mt Ngauruhoe**, at 2287m, the youngest of the three volcanoes. In contrast to the others, which have multiple vents, Ngauruhoe is a conical, single-vent volcano with perfectly symmetrical slopes – which is the reason that it was chosen to star as Mt Doom in Peter Jackson's *Lord of the Rings*.

Tongariro was NZ's first national park, established in 1887. Today the park is the most popular in NZ, receiving around 200,000 visitors per annum. Many visitors come to ski – Ruapehu's snowfields being the only legitimate ski area north of Wellington – but more people arrive each summer to tramp up, down and around the mountains.

Activities

The DOC and i-SITE visitor centres at Whakapapa (p135), **Ohakune** (☎06-385 8427; www.visitruapehu.com; 54 Clyde St; ☉9am-5pm) and Turangi have maps and information on walks in the park, as well as current track and weather conditions.

Tongariro Northern Circuit   Tramping

Circumnavigating Ngauruhoe, this four-day, 50km track is a Great Walk for a number of good reasons.

The Northern Circuit passes plenty of the spectacular and colourful volcanic features that have earned the park its Unesco World Heritage Area status. Highlights include craters, including the South Crater, Central Crater and Red Crater; brilliantly colourful lakes, including the Emerald Lakes, Blue Lake and the Upper and Lower Tama Lakes; the cold Soda Springs; and various other formations, including cones, lava flows and glacial valleys.

The traditional place to start and finish the tramp is Whakapapa Village,

Mt Ruapehu

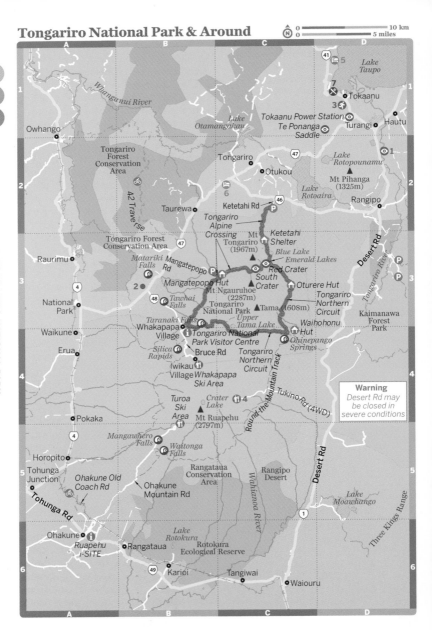

the site of the park's visitor information centre. However, many trampers begin at Mangatepopo Rd to ensure they have good weather for the tramp's most dramatic day. This reduces it to a three-day tramp, with stays at Oturere and Waihohonu Huts, ending at Whakapapa village.

Whakapapa & Turoa

Ski Areas   Skiing, Snowboarding

(Turoa 06-385 8456, Whakapapa 07-892 4000; www.mtruapehu.com; day pass adult/child $97/58) These linked resorts straddle either side of Mt Ruapehu and are NZ's two largest ski areas. Each offers similar skiing at an analogous altitude (around 2300m), with areas to suit each level of experience – from beginners' slopes to black-diamond runs for the pros. The same lift passes cover both ski areas.

Tukino

Ski Area   Skiing, Snowboarding

(☏06-387 6294, 0800 885 466; www.tukino.co.nz; day pass adult/child $50/30) Club-operated Tukino is on Mt Ruapehu's east, 46km from Turangi. It's quite remote, 14km down a gravel road from the sealed Desert Rd (SH1), and you need a 4WD vehicle to get in. It offers uncrowded, backcountry runs, mostly beginner and intermediate.

🜚 Tours

Mountain Air   Scenic Flights

(☏0800 922 812; www.mountainair.co.nz; cnr SH47 & SH48; flights $120, 25min $185, 35min $225) Offers scenic flights from its base halfway between Whakapapa Village and National Park village. Turangi and Taupo departures also available.

Whakapapa Village

Located within the bounds of Tongariro National Park on the lower slopes of Mt Ruapehu, Whakapapa Village (pronounced 'fa-ka-pa-pa'; altitude: 1140m) is the gateway to the park, home of the park's visitor centre, and the starting point for numerous walking tracks.

Activities

Whakapapa Nature Walk   Walking

Suitable for wheelchairs, this 15-minute loop track begins about 250m above the visitor centre, passing through beech forest and gardens typical of the park's vegetation zones.

Ridge Track   Tramping

A 30-minute return walk from the village that climbs through beech forest to alpine-shrub areas for views of Ruapehu and Ngauruhoe.

Taranaki Falls Track   Tramping

A two-hour, 6km loop track heads from the village to Taranaki Falls which plunge 20m over an old lava flow into a boulder-ringed pool.

Silica Rapids Track   Tramping

From Whakapapa Village this 2½-hour, 7km loop track leads to the Silica Rapids, named for the silica mineral deposits formed there by rapids on the Waikare Stream.

Sleeping

Whakapapa Village has limited accommodation, and during ski season prices hit their peak. A greater range of options can be found in National Park village and Ohakune, with the latter offering the most in the way of eating and shopping.

Tongariro Family
Holiday Park   Holiday Park $

(☏07-386 8062; www.thp.co.nz; SH47; campsites per person unpowered/powered $18/20, cabin $60-90, unit from $130; 🛜) Conveniently situated for Alpine Crossing trampers,

DAVID EPPERSON/GETTY IMAGES ©

Don't Miss
Tongariro Alpine Crossing

This legendary crossing is often lauded as NZ's finest one-day walk. It's certainly the most popular, with 60,000 to 70,000 trampers completing it every year. It's no wonder. Very few day walks offer such thrilling scenery. Among its highlights are steaming vents and springs, crazy rock formations and peculiar moonscape basins, impossible scree slopes and vast views in almost every direction. Along the way it passes diverse vegetation zones from alpine scrub and tussock to higher zones with no plant life at all.

This is an alpine crossing, and it needs to be treated with respect. You need not only a reasonable level of fitness, you should also be prepared for all types of weather.

The most crowded times on the track are the first nice days after Christmas and Easter, when there can easily be more than 1000 people strung out between the two road ends. The upside of this popularity is excellent shuttle connections, with plenty of operators offering return-trip transport.

It takes takes seven to eight hours to make the 19.4km journey, although this will vary significantly if you decide to take side-trips up to the summits of Ngauruhoe or Tongariro – both worthwhile and taking around two and three hours respectively.

NEED TO KNOW
www.doc.govt.nz

halfway along the highway between the start and finish points, this wee gem is in the middle of nowhere and everywhere at the same time. It's a welcoming camp – simple, sunny, and surrounded by forest, with plenty of grass, trees, and a playground. It's 24km to both Whakapapa Village and Turangi.

Bayview Chateau Tongariro Hotel $$$
(📞07-892 3809, 0800 242 832; www.chateau.co.nz; Whakapapa Village; d $155-355; @🛜🏊) With its sublime setting and manor house grandeur, this iconic hotel promises as much as it did when it opened its doors in 1929. Step inside, however, and you will see that its many charms are somewhat faded. But the Chateau remains one of NZ's most romantic hotels, complete with high tea in the library, aperitifs in the elegant foyer bar, and evening dining in the grand **Ruapehu Room** (mains $32-38; ⏱dinner). Other facilities include two cafes, indoor pool, cinema and nine-hole golf course.

ℹ️ Information

Tongariro National Park Visitor Centre (📞07-892 3729; www.doc.govt.nz; Whakapapa Village; ⏱8am-5pm) Has maps and info on all corners of the park, including walks, huts, and current skiing, track and weather conditions. Its exhibits on the geological and human history of the area should keep you busy for a couple of hours on a rainy day.

ℹ️ Getting There & Around

Bus

Tongariro National Park is well serviced by shuttle operators, which service Whakapapa Village, National Park village, Ohakune, Taupo and Turangi, as well as popular trailheads. In summer tramping trips are their focus, but in winter most offer ski-field shuttles. Book your bus in advance to avoid unexpected strandings.

Many shuttle bus operators are offshoots or affiliates of accommodation providers so ask about transport when you book your stay. Otherwise, try Taupo-based **Tongariro Expeditions** (📞0800 828 763; www.tongariroexpeditions.com), Turangi-based **Turangi Alpine Shuttles** (📞0272 322 135, 07-386 8226; www.turangirentals.co.nz), and Whakapapa Village–based **Roam** (📞021 588 734, 0800 762 612; www.roam.net.nz).

WAIKATO

....

Hamilton

Landlocked cities in an island nation are never going to have the glamorous appeal of their coastal cousins. Rotorua compensates with boiling mud and Taupo has its lake, but Hamilton, despite the majestic Waikato River, is more prosaic.

However the city definitely has appeal. The main street has vibrant bars around Hood St and Victoria St, and factor in excellent restaurants and cafes, and you're guaranteed to eat really well in the city after visiting highlights like the Hamilton Gardens.

◎ Sights

Hamilton Gardens Gardens
(www.hamiltongardens.co.nz; Cobham Dr; ⏱enclosed sector 7.30am-5pm, info centre 9am-5pm) **FREE** Hamilton Gardens, spread over 50 hectares, incorporates a large park, cafe, restaurant and extravagant themed enclosed gardens. There are separate Italian Renaissance, Chinese, Japanese, English, American and Indian gardens complete with colonnades, pagodas and a mini Taj Mahal.

Waikato Museum Museum
(www.waikatomuseum.co.nz; 1 Grantham St; free-$6.50; ⏱10am-4.30pm) The excellent Waikato Museum has five main areas: an art gallery; interactive science galleries; Tainui galleries housing Maori treasures, including the magnificently carved *waka taua* (war canoe), *Te Winikawaka;* a Hamilton history exhibition entitled 'Never a Dull Moment'; and a Waikato River exhibition.

Riff Raff Monument
(www.riffraffstatue.org; Victoria St; 🛜) One of Hamilton's more unusual public artworks is a life-size statue of *Rocky Horror Picture Show* writer Richard O'Brien aka Riff Raff, the time-warping alien from the planet Transsexual. It looks over a small

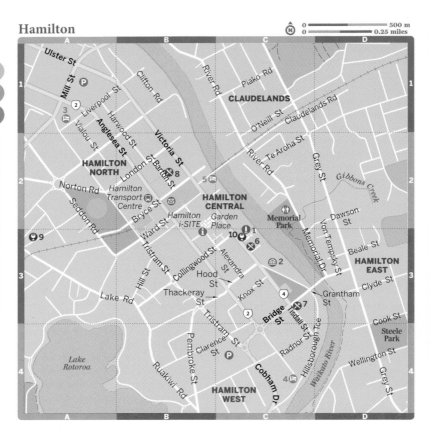

Hamilton

⊚ Sights
1 Riff Raff	C3
2 Waikato Museum	C3

⊜ Sleeping
3 Anglesea Motel	A1
4 City Centre B&B	C4
5 Ibis Hotel	B2

⊗ Eating
6 Banh Mi Caphe	C3
7 Chim Choo Ree	C3
8 Rocket Coffee	B2

⊖ Drinking & Nightlife
9 Good George Brewing	A3
10 Wonderhorse	C3

park on the site of the former Embassy
Theatre where O'Brien worked as a hair-
dresser, though it's hard to imagine 1960s
Hamilton inspired the tale of bisexual
alien decadence.

🏃 Activities

Kiwi Balloon Company Ballooning
(☎021 912 679, 07-843 8538; www.kiwibal-
looncompany.co.nz; per person $350) Floating
above lush Waikato countryside, the
whole experience takes about four hours
and includes a champagne breakfast and
an hour's flying time.

👉 Tours

Waikato River Explorer Cruise
(☎0800 139 756; www.waikatoexplorer.co.nz;
Hamilton Gardens jetty; adult/child $26/13;
⏱Thu-Sun) Scenic 90-minute cruises
along the Waikato River depart from the
Hamilton Gardens jetty. On Sunday after-
noons, three-hour wine-tasting cruises
(adult/child $55/24) operate.

Sleeping

City Centre B&B
B&B $$

(📞07-838 1671; www.citycentrebnb.co.nz; 3 Anglesea St; r $90-165; @ 🛜 🏊) At the quiet riverside end of a central city street (five minutes' walk to the Victoria/Hood St action), this sparkling self-contained apartment opens onto a swimming pool. There's also a bedroom available in a wing of the main house. Self-catering breakfast is provided.

Anglesea Motel
Motel $$

(📞0800 426 453, 07-834 0010; www.angle-seamotel.co.nz; 36 Liverpool St; units $140-300; @ 🛜 🏊) Getting great feedback from travellers and a preferred option to anything on Ulster St's 'motel row', the Anglesea has plenty of space, friendly managers, a pool and squash and tennis courts, and not un-stylish decor.

Ibis Hotel
Hotel $$

(📞07-859 9200; www.ibis.com/hamilton; 18 Alma St; r $100-130; 🛜) The rooms are compact, but they're clean and well-designed, and the riverfront Ibis is a good option if you're looking for quiet, centrally located digs just a short walk from the best of Hamilton's bars and restaurants. The shared public areas – complete with a restaurant for a good-value breakfast buffet ($20) – are spacious and colourful.

Eating

Rocket Coffee
Cafe $

(www.rocketcoffee.co.nz; 302 Barton St; coffee from $4; 🕗8am-4pm Mon-Fri) Duck down a lane off Barton St for what some locals reckon is Hamilton's hippest cafe. Rocket Coffee is a warehouselike bean barn, roasting on-site and enticing caffeine fiends to the communal table strewn with newspapers. Staff spin old-school vinyl (and take requests) in between playing barista and packaging up sacks of beans for shipment.

Banh Mi Caphe
Vietnamese $

(www.facebook.com/banhmicaphe; 198/2 Victoria St; snacks & mains $7-14; 🕚11am-4pm Tue, Wed, Sat & Sun, 11am-late Thu & Fri) Fresh spring rolls, Vietnamese *banh mi* sandwiches, and steaming bowls of *pho* (noodle soup) all feature at this hip spot channelling the backstreets of Hanoi. In

Hamilton Gardens (p135)

WADE EAKLE/GETTY IMAGES ©

the immediate vicinity there are plenty more tasty opportunities for ethnic dining, with Indian, Thai, Chinese, Mexican and Japanese restaurants also lining Victoria St and nearby Hood St.

Chim Choo Ree   Modern NZ $$$

(☑07-839 4329; www.chimchooree.co.nz; 14 Bridge St; mains $30-34; ☉11.30am-2pm & 5pm-late Mon-Sat) In an airy heritage building beside the river, Chim Choo Ree focuses on shared plates like tuna tartare, smoked potato ravioli and Sichuan pork belly, and larger, equally inventive mains using duck, lamb, venison and snapper. Local foodies wash it all down with a great wine list and flavourful New Zealand craft beers.

Drinking & Nightlife

Wonderhorse   Cocktail Bar

(www.facebook.com/wonderhorsebar; 232 Victoria St; ☉5pm-3am Wed-Sat) Look for the subtle spraypainted Wonderhorse logo on the footpath and follow the white arrow to this cool cocktail bar that also regularly features craft beers from tiny local brewers like Shunters Yard, Brewaucracy and 666. Vintage vinyl is often spinning on the turntable, and $5 cheeseburger sliders and killer cocktails complete the picture at Hamilton's best bar.

Good George Brewing   Brewery

(☑07-847 3223; www.goodgeorge.co.nz; 32a Somerset St, Frankton; tours incl beer & food $15; ☉11am-late, tours from 5.30pm Mon-Thu) Channelling a cool industrial vibe, the former Church of St George is now a shrine to craft beer. Order a tasting flight of six beers ($19), and partner the hoppy heaven with wood-fired pizzas ($20 to $23), platters ($12 to $16), and larger main meals ($20 to $34). Our favourites are the zesty White Ale and the zingy Drop Hop cider. Tours must be booked ahead.

ℹ Information

Hamilton i-SITE (☑0800 242 645, 07-958 5960; www.visithamilton.co.nz; cnr Caro & Alexandra Sts; ☉9am-5pm Mon-Fri, 9.30am-3.30pm Sat & Sun; 🛜) Accommodation, activities and transport bookings, plus free wi-fi right across Garden Pl.

Waikato Hospital (☑07-839 8899; www.waikatodhb.govt.nz; Pembroke St; ☉24hr)

Raglan Harbour

ℹ️ Getting There & Away

Air

Air New Zealand (📞0800 737 000; www.airnewzealand.co.nz) Regular direct flights from Hamilton to Auckland, Christchurch, Palmerston North and Wellington.

Bus

All buses arrive and depart from the **Hamilton Transport Centre** (📞07-834 3457; www.hamilton.co.nz; cnr Anglesea & Bryce Sts; 🛜).

Waikato Regional Council's Busit! coaches serve the region, including Ngaruawahia ($3.20, 25 minutes), Cambridge ($6.70, 40 minutes), Te Awamutu ($6.70, 50 minutes) and Raglan ($8.50, one hour).

InterCity (📞09-583 5780; www.intercity.co.nz) services numerous destinations:

DESTINATION	PRICE	DURATION	FREQUENCY (DAILY)
Auckland	$12-35	2hr	11
Cambridge	$10-20	25min	9
Matamata	$10-25	50min	4
Ngaruawahia	$10-21	20min	9
Rotorua	$14-35	1½hr	5
Te Aroha	$10	1hr	2
Te Awamutu	$10-22	35min	3
Wellington	$27-70	5hr	3

Naked Bus (📞0900 625 33; www.nakedbus.com) services run to the following destinations (among many others):

DESTINATION	PRICE	DURATION	FREQUENCY (DAILY)
Auckland	$17-19	2hr	5
Cambridge	$15	30min	5-7
Matamata	$20	1hr	1
Ngaruawahia	$15	30min	5
Rotorua	$10	1½hr	4-5
Wellington	$20-30	9½hr	1-2

Shuttle Buses

Minibus Express (📞0800 646 428, 07-856 3191; www.minibus.co.nz) Shuttles between Hamilton and Auckland airport (one way $75).

Raglan Scenic Tours (📞021 0274 7014, 07-825 0507; www.raglanscenictours.co.nz) Shuttle linking Hamilton with Raglan (one way $35). Auckland airport service also available.

Train

Hamilton is on the **Northern Explorer** (📞0800 872 467; www.kiwiscenic.co.nz) route between Auckland ($48, 2½ hours) and Wellington ($186, 9½ hours) via Otorohanga ($48, 45 minutes).

ℹ️ Getting Around

To/From Airport

Hamilton International Airport (HIA; 📞07-848 9027; www.hamiltonairport.co.nz; Airport Rd) is 12km south of the city. The **Super Shuttle** (📞0800 748 885, 07-843 7778; www.supershuttle.co.nz; one way $26) offers a door-to-door service into the city. A taxi costs around $50.

Bus

Hamilton's **Busit!** (📞0800 4287 5463; www.busit.co.nz; city routes adult/child $3.30/2.20) network services the city centre and suburbs daily from around 7am to 7.30pm (later on Friday). All buses pass through Hamilton Transport Centre.

Taxi

Hamilton Taxis (📞0800 477 477, 07-8477 477; www.hamiltontaxis.co.nz)

Raglan

Laid-back Raglan may well be NZ's perfect surfing town. It's small enough to have escaped mass development, but it's big enough to exhibit signs of life including good eateries and a bar that attracts big-name bands in summer. Along with the famous surf spots to the south – Manu Bay and Whale Bay – the harbour just begs to be kayaked upon. There's also an excellent arts scene, with several galleries and shops worthy of perusal.

◎ Sights & Activities

Old School Arts Centre
Arts Centre, Gallery

(www.raglanartscentre.co.nz; Stewart St; 🕐10am-2pm Mon & Wed, exhibition hours vary) **FREE** A community hub, the Old School Arts Centre has changing exhibitions and workshops, including weaving, carving, yoga and storytelling. Movies screen here regularly through summer ($11): grab a curry and a beer to complete the experience. The hippie/artsy **Raglan Creative Market** happens out the front on the second Sunday of the month (9am to 2pm).

Raglan Surf School Surfing

(07-825 7873; www.raglansurfingschool.co.nz; 5b Whaanga Rd; 3hr lesson incl transport from Raglan $89) Raglan Surf School prides itself on getting 95% of first-timers standing during their first lesson. Rental gear includes surfboards (from $20 per hour), body boards ($5 per hour) and wetsuits ($5 per hour). It's based at Karioi Lodge in Whale Bay.

Raglan Kayak Kayaking

(☎07-825 8862; www.raglaneco.co.nz; Raglan Wharf) Raglan Harbour is great for kayaking. This outfit runs three-hour guided harbour paddles (per person $75) and rents out single/double kayaks (per half-day $40/60). Learn the basics on the gentle Opotoru River, or paddle out to investigate the nooks and crannies of the pancake rocks on the harbour's northern edge. Stand up paddle boards are also available (one hour/half-day $20/40).

Raglan Bone Carving Studio Carving

(☎021 0223 7233; raglanbonecarvingstudio@hotmail.com; workshops $69) Carve your own bone pendant with Rangi Wills, a reformed 'troubled teenager' who found out he was actually really good at carving things. Workshops run for four hours and Rangi can provide transport from Raglan township to his studio. Bookings essential.

🎯 Tours

Raglan Scenic Tours Guided Tour

(☎07-825 0507; www.raglanscenictours.co.nz; 5a Bankart St) Sightseeing tours, including 2½ hours around the Raglan area (adult/child $55/20) and four hours around Mount Karioi including Bridal Veil Falls and Te Toto Gorge ($90/40). Various tramps and paddle boarding instruction can be arranged, and kayaks, mountain bikes and paddle boards can be hired.

Cruise Raglan Cruise

(☎07-825 7873; www.raglanboatcharters.co.nz; adult/child $40/29) Two-hour sunset cruises around Raglan Harbour on the *Wahine Moe*, with fish and chips and a few drinks. Ninety-minute morning harbour cruises ($30/15 per adult/child) are also available.

🛏 Sleeping

Raglan Backpackers Hostel $

(☎07-825 0515; www.raglanbackpackers.co.nz; 6 Wi Neera St; dm $27-29, s $58, tw & d $72-82;) This laid-back hostel is right on the water, with sea views from some rooms. Other rooms are arranged around a garden courtyard or in a

Surfing lesson, Raglan

separate building. There are free bikes and kayaks, and surfboards for hire, or take a yoga class, strum a guitar, or drip in the sauna. No wi-fi – it 'ruins the vibe'.

Bow St Studios
Apartments $$

(☎07-825 0551; www.bowstreet.co.nz; 1 Bow St; studio $145-225, cottage $205; 🛜) With a waterfront location right in town, Bow St has self-contained studios and a historic cottage. The property is surrounded by a subtropical garden and shaded by well-established pohutukawa trees, and the cool and chic decor is stylish and relaxing.

Raglan Sunset Motel
Motel $$

(☎07-825 0050; www.raglansunsetmotel.co.nz; 7 Bankart St; d from $150; 🛜) A block from Bow St's shops and restaurants with spacious and modern units. The owners also have self-contained apartments (doubles from $160) and beachhouses (four people $300) available. Bike and kayak hire is available (per half-day $30 and $45 respectively).

✖️ Eating & Drinking

Juantanameras
Latin American $

(Electric Ave, off 5 Wainui Rd; snacks $3-7; ⏰9am-5pm) Hunt down this summer-only food caravan for tasty Venezuelan *arepas* (corn cakes) or Mexican quesadillas and tacos. Get there early for *churros* (Mexican doughnuts), perfect for a local Raglan coffee just next door. It's only open Friday to Sunday in winter, and even then it can be subject to surf conditions. Welcome to laid-back Raglan.

The Shack
Cafe, International $$

(www.theshackraglan.com; 19 Bow St; tapas $6-14, mains $12-27; ⏰8am-5pm Sun-Thu, 8am-late Fri & Sat; 🛜✍️) Brunch classics – try the chickpea-and-corn fritters – and interesting shared-plate mains like tempura squid and star-anise chicken feature at the best cafe in town. A longboard strapped to the wall, wobbly old floorboards, up-tempo tunes and international staff serving Kiwi wines and craft beers complete the picture.

Banteay Srey
Cambodian $$

(☎07-825 0952; www.raglancambodian.weebly.net; 23 Bow St; mains $18-24; ⏰8.30am-9pm) The menu also strays into Western flavours, but the authentic Cambodian dishes are the ones to go for. Our pick is the Char Kreoung chicken or beef with lemongrass and lime, or the delicate Amok steamed and curried fish. On Tuesdays from 6.30pm, the restaurant hosts a buffet (per person $28). Booking ahead is recommended.

Harbour View Hotel
Pub

(14 Bow St) Classic old pub with mainstreet drinks on the shaded verandah. Decent pizza too and occasional live music on weekends and during summer.

ℹ️ Information

Raglan Information Centre (☎07-825 0556; www.raglan.org.nz; 13 Wainui Rd; ⏰9.30am-5pm Mon-Fri, 10am-5pm Sat, 10am-4pm Sun) DOC brochures plus information about accommodation and activities including kitesurfing and paddle boarding. Check out also the attached museum, especially the exhibition on the history of Raglan's surfing scene.

ℹ️ Getting There & Around

From Hamilton, Raglan is 48km west along SH23.

Waikato District Council's **Busit!** (☎0800 4287 5463; www.busit.co.nz; adult/child $8.50/5.50) heads between Hamilton and Raglan (one hour) three times daily on weekdays and twice daily on weekends.

Raglan Scenic Tours runs a Raglan–Hamilton shuttle bus (one-way $35) and direct transfers to/from Auckland International Airport.

For a cab call **Raglan Taxi** (☎07-825 0506).

South of Raglan

NGARUNUI BEACH

Less than 1km south of Ocean Beach, Ngarunui Beach is great for grommets learning to **surf**. On the cliff top is a clubhouse for the volunteer lifeguards who patrol part of the black-sand beach from late October until April. This is the

Below: Ngarunui Beach (p141);
Right: Surfers at Manu Bay
(BELOW) MAGALIE L'ABBÉ/GETTY IMAGES ©; (RIGHT) PAUL KENNEDY/GETTY IMAGES ©

only beach with lifeguards, and is the best ocean beach for **swimming**.

MANU BAY

A 2.5km journey from Ngarunui Beach will bring you to Manu Bay, a legendary **surf spot** said to have the longest left-hand break in the world. The elongated uniform waves are created by the angle at which the Tasman Sea swell meets the coastline (it works best in a southwesterly swell).

With a hill-top location fringed by native bush, **Solscape's** (07-825 8268; www.solscape.co.nz; 611 Wainui Rd; campsites from $17, caboose dm/d $30/72, teepees per person $36, cottages d $82-189;) ecofriendly accommodation includes teepees, rammed-earth domes, railway carriages, and stylish eco baches. There's room for tents and campervans, and simpler cottages are also available. Environmental impact is minimised with solar energy, and organic produce from the permaculture garden is used for guests' meals in the Conscious Kitchen cafe. Yoga, massage and surfing lessons are all available, and Solscape is also YHA-affiliated.

WHALE BAY

Whale Bay is a renowned **surf spot** 1km west of Manu Bay. It's usually less crowded than Manu Bay, but from the bottom of Calvert Rd you have to clamber 600m over the rocks to get to the break.

Deep in native bush, **Karioi Lodge** (07-825 7873; www.karioilodge.co.nz; 5b Whaanga Rd; dm/d $30/75;) offers a sauna, a flying fox, mountain bikes, bush and beach walks, sustainable gardening, tree planting and the Raglan Surf School. There are no en suites but the rooms are clean and cosy. These friendly folks also run **Sleeping Lady Lodges** (07-825 7873; www.sleepinglady.co.nz; 5b Whaanga Rd; lodges $175-260), a collection of six luxury self-contained houses nearby, all with ocean views.

Cambridge

The name says it all. Despite the rambunctious Waikato River looking nothing like the Cam, the good people of Cambridge have done all they can to assume an air of English gentility with village greens and tree-lined avenues.

Cambridge is famous for the breeding and training of thoroughbred horses.

Sights & Activities

Cambridge Museum　　Museum

(www.cambridgemuseum.org.nz; 24 Victoria St; admission by donation; ⏰10am-4pm Mon-Fri, to 2pm Sun) In a former courthouse, the quirky Cambridge Museum has plenty of pioneer relics, a military history room and a small display on the local Te Totara Pa before it was wiped out.

Boatshed Kayaks　　Kayaking

(☎07-827 8286; www.theboatshed.net.nz; 21 Amber Lane; s/d kayak for 3hr $25/50, paddle board $20; ⏰9am-5pm Wed-Sun) Located at the Boatshed Cafe with basic kayaks and paddle boards for hire. You can paddle to a couple of waterfalls in around an hour. There are also guided kayak trips at twilight (adult/child $110/40) to see a glowworm canyon up the nearby Pokewhaenua stream. Bookings are essential for these trips.

Sleeping

**Cambridge
Coach House**　　B&B, Cabin $$

(☎07-823 7922; www.cambridgecoachhouse.co.nz; 3796 Cambridge Rd, Leamington; d $150, cottage $160; 🛜❄) This farmhouse accommodation is slightly chintzy, but it's still a beaut spot to relax amid Waikato's rural splendour. There are two separate doubles and a self-contained cottage. It's a couple of kilometres south of town en route to Te Awamutu.

Cambridge Mews　　Motel $$

(☎07-827 7166; www.cambridgemews.co.nz; 20 Hamilton Rd; d $160-200; 🛜) All the spacious units in this chalet-style motel have double spa baths, decent kitchens and are immaculately maintained. It's a 10-minute walk to town.

Eating

Boatshed Cafe
Cafe $

(www.theboatshedkarapiro.co.nz; 21 Amber Lane, off Gorton Rd; mains $10-19; ⊙10am-3pm Thu-Sun) This stylish cafe on the edge of Lake Karapiro (heading south from Cambridge on SH1, turn right into Gorton Rd) is a top place for a leisurely brunch or lunch. Order the eggs Benedict, and grab an outside table for lake views and Waikato birdsong.

Red Cherry
Cafe $$

(www.redcherrycoffee.co.nz; cnr SH1 & Forrest Rd; meals $16-20; ⊙7.30am-4.30pm; 🖬) With a cherry-red espresso machine working overtime, barnlike Red Cherry offers coffee roasted on-site, delicious counter food and impressive cooked breakfasts. For lunch, the gourmet beef burger is hard to beat. Cambridge's best cafe is 4km from town en route to Hamilton.

ℹ Information

Cambridge i-SITE (☎07-823 3456; www.cambridge.co.nz; cnr Victoria & Queen Sts; ⊙9am-5pm Mon-Fri, 10am-4pm Sat & Sun; 🛜) Free Heritage & Tree Trail and town maps, and internet access.

ℹ Getting There & Away

Being on SH1, 22km southeast of Hamilton, Cambridge is well connected by bus. Environment Waikato's Busit! (☎0800 4287 5463; www.busit. co.nz) heads to Hamilton ($6.70, 40 minutes, seven daily weekdays, three daily weekends).

InterCity (☎09-583 5780; www.intercity. co.nz) services numerous destinations:

DESTINATION	PRICE	DURATION	FREQUENCY (DAILY)
Auckland	$27-45	2½hr	12
Hamilton	$10-25	30min	8
Matamata	$10-22	30min	2
Rotorua	$17-35	1¼hr	5
Wellington	$28-68	8½hr	3

Naked Bus (☎0900 625 33; www.nakedbus. com) services to the same destinations are as follows:

Abseiling into the Lost World cave (p146), Waitomo

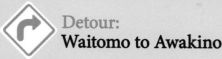

Detour:
Waitomo to Awakino

This obscure route, heading west of Waitomo on Te Anga Rd, is a slow but fascinating alternative to SH3 if Taranaki's your goal.

The **Mangapohue Natural Bridge Scenic Reserve**, 26km west of Waitomo, is a 5.5-hectare reserve with a giant natural limestone arch. It's a five-minute walk to the arch on a wheelchair-accessible pathway.

About 4km further west is **Piripiri Caves Scenic Reserve**, where a five-minute walk leads to a large cave containing fossils of giant oysters. Steps wind down into the gloom...

The impressively tiered, 30m **Marokopa Falls** are 32km west of Waitomo. A short track (15 minutes return) from the road leads to the bottom of the falls.

At **Waikawau** take the 5km detour along the unsealed road to the coast near **Ngarupupu Point**, where a 100m walk through a dank tunnel opens out on an exquisitely isolated stretch of black-sand beach.

DESTINATION	PRICE	DURATION	FREQUENCY (DAILY)
Auckland	$13-17	2½hr	6
Hamilton	$20	30min	5
Matamata	$24-25	2¼hr	1
Rotorua	$10	1¼hr	4
Wellington	$28	9½hr	1

THE KING COUNTRY

Waitomo Caves

Even if damp, dark tunnels are your idea of hell, head to Waitomo anyway. The limestone caves and glowing bugs here are one of the North Island's premier attractions.

Sights

Waitomo Caves Visitor Centre
Visitor Centre

(0800 456 922; www.waitomo.com; Waitomo Caves Rd; 9am-5pm) The big-three Waitomo Caves are all operated by the same company, based at the flash Waitomo Caves Visitor Centre (behind the Glowworm Cave), which incorporates a cafe and theatre.

Glowworm Cave
Cave

(adult/child $48/21; 45min tours every 30min 9am-5pm) The guided tour of the Glowworm Cave, which is behind the visitor centre, leads past impressive stalactites and stalagmites into a large cavern known as the Cathedral. The highlight comes at the tour's end when you board a boat and swing off onto the river. As your eyes grow accustomed to the dark you'll see a Milky Way of little lights surrounding you – these are the glowworms.

Aranui Cave
Cave

(adult/child $48/21; 1hr tours 9.30am, 11am, 1pm, 2.30pm & 4pm) Three kilometres west from the Glowworm Cave is Aranui Cave. This cave is dry (hence no glowworms) but compensates with an incredible array of limestone formations. Thousands of tiny 'straw' stalactites hang from the ceiling.

Ruakuri Cave
Cave

(0800 782 587, 07-878 6219; adult/child $67/26; 2hr tours 9am, 10am, 11.30am, 12.30pm, 1.30pm, 2.30pm & 3pm) Ruakuri Cave has an impressive 15m-high spiral staircase, bypassing a Maori burial site at the cave entrance. Tours lead through 1.6km of the 7.5km system, taking in caverns with glowworms, subterranean streams and waterfalls, and intricate limestone structures.

Activities

The Waitomo i-SITE has free pamphlets on walks in the area. The **walk** from Aranui Cave to Ruakuri Cave is an excellent short path. From the Waitomo Caves Visitor Centre, the 5km, three-hour-return **Waitomo Walkway** takes off through farmland, following Waitomo Stream to the **Ruakuri Scenic Reserve**, where a 30-minute return walk passes by a natural limestone tunnel.

Legendary Black Water Rafting Company
Caving, Adventure Tour

(📞0800 782 5874; www.waitomo.com; 585 Waitomo Caves Rd; ⊙Black Labyrinth tour 9am, 10.30am, noon, 1.30pm & 3pm; Black Abyss tour 9am & 2pm, Black Odyssey tour 10am & 2.30pm) The Black Labyrinth tour ($125, three hours) involves floating in a wetsuit on an inner tube down a river that flows through Ruakuri Cave. The highlight is leaping off a small waterfall and then floating through a long, glowworm-covered passage. The trip ends with showers, soup and bagels in the cafe. The more adventurous Black Abyss tour ($225, five hours) includes a 35m abseil into Ruakuri Cave, a flying fox and more glowworms and tubing.

Recently launched, the Black Odyssey tour ($175, four hours) is a challenging dry caving adventure including flying foxes and negotiating high wires.

Spellbound
Caving, Guided Tour

(📞0800 773 552, 07-878 7622; www.glowworm.co.nz; 10 Waitomo Caves Rd; adult/child $73/26; ⊙3hr tours 10am, 11am, 2pm & 3pm, closed Jun) Spellbound is a good option if you don't want to get wet, are more interested in glowworms than an 'action' experience, and want to avoid the big groups in the main caves. Small-group tours access parts of the heavily glowworm-dappled Mangawhitiakau cave system, 12km south of Waitomo (...and you still get to ride in a raft!).

Waitomo Adventures
Caving, Adventure Tour

(📞07-878 7788, 0800 924 866; www.waitomo.co.nz; 654 Waitomo Caves Rd) Waitomo Adventures offers various cave adventures, with discounts for combos and advance bookings. The Lost World trip ($340/490, four/seven hours) combines a 100m abseil with walking, rock-climbing, wading and swimming. Haggas Honking Holes ($260, four hours) includes three waterfall abseils, rock-climbing and a subterranean river. TumuTumu Toobing ($180, four hours) is a walking, climbing, swimming and tubing trip. St Benedict's Cavern ($180, three hours) includes abseiling and a subterranean flying fox.

Sleeping

Waitomo Top 10 Holiday Park
Holiday Park $

(📞0508 498 666, 07-878 7639; www.waitomopark.co.nz; 12 Waitomo Caves Rd; campsites from $23, cabins $70-130, units $150-180; @🖥🏊) This lovely holiday park in the heart of the village has spotless facilities, modern cabins, and plenty of outdoor distractions to keep the kids busy.

Abseil Inn
B&B $$

(📞07-878 7815; www.abseilinn.co.nz; 709 Waitomo Caves Rd; d from $150; 🖥) A *veeery* steep driveway takes you to this delightful B&B with four themed rooms, great breakfasts and witty hosts. The biggest room has a double bath and valley views.

Waitomo Caves Guest Lodge
B&B $$

(📞0800 465 762, 07-878 7641; www.waitomocavesguestlodge.co.nz; 7 Te Anga Rd; s $90, d incl breakfast $110-130; 🖥) Bag your own cosy little hillside en suite cabin at this central operation with a sweet garden setting. The top cabins have valley views. Large continental breakfast and friendly resident dog included.

✖ Eating & Drinking

Florence's Kitchen
Cafe $$

(www.facebook.com/WaitomoGeneralStore; Waitomo General Store, 15 Waitomo Caves Rd; snacks & mains $12-20; ⊙7.30am-10pm) In the Waitomo general store with a wide range of pre- and postcaving sustenance.

Huhu
Cafe, Modern NZ $$

(📞07-878 6674; www.huhucafe.co.nz; 10 Waitomo Caves Rd; small plates $11-17, mains $19-33; 🕙noon-late; 📶) Slick and modern Huhu has great views from the terrace and sublime contemporary NZ food. Sip a strong coffee or Kiwi craft beer, or graze through a seasonal tapas-style menu of delights like slow-cooked lamb, teriyaki salmon and organic Scotch fillet steak.

Morepork Cafe
Cafe, Pizzeria $$

(Kiwi Paka, Hotel Access Rd; breakfast & lunch $10-18, dinner $15-27; 🕙8am-10.30pm; 📶) At the Kiwi Paka backpackers is this cheery joint, a jack-of-all-trades eatery serving breakfast, lunch and dinner either inside or out on the deck. The 'Caveman' pizza is a definite winner.

King Country Brewing Company
Brewery

(www.facebook.com/kingcountrybrewingcompany; Waitomo General Store, 15 Waitomo Caves Rd) This craft brewery does four top drops – an IPA, a pale ale, a wheat beer and a cider – and features occasional guest beers from other smaller Kiwi breweries. Grab a tasting rack of all four for $16.

ⓘ Information

Waitomo i-SITE (📞07-878 7640, 0800 474 839; www.waitomocaves.com; 21 Waitomo Caves Rd; 🕙9am-5.30pm) Internet access, post office and booking agent.

ⓘ Getting There & Away

Naked Bus (📞0900 625 33; www.nakedbus.com) Runs once daily to Otorohanga ($20, 20 minutes), Hamilton ($25, 1¼ hours) and New Plymouth ($30, three hours).

Waitomo Shuttle (📞0800 808 279, 07-873 8279; waikiwi@ihug.co.nz; 1-way adult/child $12/7) Heads to the caves five times daily from Otorohanga (15 minutes away), coordinating with bus and train arrivals.

Waitomo Wanderer (📞03-477 9083, 0800 000 4321; www.travelheadfirst.com) Operates a daily

Waitomo Caves

RECOMMENDATIONS FROM CELINA YAPP, WAITOMO I-SITE

1 GOING UNDERGROUND
There are numerous dry caving options here, including trips into the Waitomo Glowworm, Aranui and Ruakuri caves (p145). On the way out of the Glowworm Cave you take a boat ride under the glowworms, which is a really magical experience. The 1.6km-long Ruakuri Cave is the longest dry cave walk here, with some great cave formations. Then there are around 10 different adventure caving options, many of which include black-water rafting.

2 LOCAL WALKS
The 5km **Waitomo Walkway** starts opposite the i-SITE, and winds through bush and farmland along the Waitomo Stream to the Ruakuri Scenic Reserve. Once you get there, the 1km **Ruakuri Loop Walk** is one of the best short walks in the country. It's steeped in history and has some amazing natural features: cliffs, outcrops, limestone arches...

3 LOCAL EATING
Waitomo General Store has basic provisions, and it does awesome breakfasts, sausages, pies, homemade burgers... Huhu is superb in the evening, or Morepork Cafe does a mean pizza.

4 AROUND WAITOMO
About 25km from Waitomo along Te Anga Rd, follow a track to the 17m-high **Mangapohue Natural Bridge**. A bit further on is the freely accessible **Piripiri Cave**. A further 2km walk brings you to **Marokopa Falls** – a magnificent 30m waterfall.

return services from Rotorua or Taupo, with optional caving, glowworm and tubing add-ons (packages from $133). Shuttle-only services are $99 return.

Wellington & Lower North Island

Rock into Wellington for a big-city hit: art-house cinema, designer boutiques, hip bars, live-music venues and late-night coffee shops – it's all in 'Windy Welly'. Wellington is New Zealand's capital city, but Wellingtonians also lay passionate claim to the crown of 'cultural capital'. Suited-up civil servants abound, but the city also supports a significant population of creative types who foster an admirably active and accessible arts scene.

Less than an hour away to the north, the Kapiti Coast offers more settled weather and a beachy vibe, with the Kapiti Island nature reserve a highlight. An hour from Wellington to the northeast is the Wairarapa, a burgeoning weekend-away wine region where the pinot noir grapes hang heavy on the vine. Keep trucking north and you'll bump into the glorious beaches and prosperous wine towns of the East Coast.

Max Patte's *Solace in the Wind* sculpture, Wellington harbour **149**

Cable car from the Wellington Botanic Gardens (p159)

Wellington & Lower North Island

1 Te Papa, Wellington
2 Art-deco architecture, Napier
3 Drinking & nightlife, Wellington
4 Wairarapa Wine Country
5 Kapiti Coast

100 km
50 miles

SOUTH PACIFIC OCEAN

Gisborne
Morere
Mahia
Mahia Peninsula
Wairoa
Hawke Bay
Te Haroto
Tutira
Tangoio
Te Pohue
Napier
Cape Kidnappers
Hastings
Havelock North
Hawke's Bay Wine Region
Kaimanawa Forest Park
Waipukurau
Ruahine Forest Park
Dannevirke
Taihape
Utiku
Mangaweka
Norsewood
Kaimanawa Mountains
Tongariro National Park
Mt Ruapehu
Taumatawhakatangihangakoauauotamatea-
turipukakapikimaungahoronukupokaiwhenuakitanatahu
(305m)
Tokunga Junction
Fielding
Whanganui National Park
Whanganui National Park
Castlepoint
Bulls
Mitre
Tararua Forest Park
Mt Holdsworth
Palmerston North
Masterton
Stratford
Waverley
Foxton
Shannon
Mt Hector
Carterton
Greytown
Levin
Alpha
Featherston
Whanganui
Ohau
Tararua Range
Upper Hutt
The Wairarapa
Martinborough
Egmont National Park
Hawera
South Taranaki Bight
Otaki
Kapiti Island
Paraparaumu
Kapiti Coast
Paekakariki
Porirua
Lower Hutt
Rimutaka Forest Park
Aorangi Range
Cape Palliser Lighthouse
Cape Palliser
New Plymouth
Mt Taranaki (Mt Egmont)
Opunake
Petone
WELLINGTON
Cook Strait
TASMAN SEA
D'Urville Island
Marlborough Sounds
Picton
Blenheim
Nelson
Richmond
Motueka
Takaka
Golden Bay
Collingwood
Tasman Bay
Kahurangi National Park

1 3
5

N

Wellington & Lower North Island Highlights

Te Papa

Occupying an unmissable building on the Wellington waterfront, Te Papa (p162) is NZ's national museum. 'Te Papa' translates into 'container of treasures'. And that's exactly what it is: a giant six-storey treasure box with an intense, interactive NZ focus. Maori culture is a highlight: if you're only flying through NZ on a short trip, here's your chance to visit a *marae* (meeting house) and engage with NZ's indigenous culture.

ROBIN SMITH/GETTY IMAGES ©

Napier Art Deco

Napier's 1931 earthquake (7.8 on the Richter scale) caused 261 casualties regionally – 157 in Napier. The town (p179) was subsequently rebuilt in the architectural styles fashionable at the time: art deco, Spanish Mission, Prairie... Much of this cache is beautifully preserved, and art deco has become the town's pride and joy. Take a guided tour to best interpret the town's extraordinary collection of buildings. Masonic pub, Napier

AMOS CHAPPLE/GETTY IMAGES ©

Wellington After Dark

Everyone in Wellington (p169) seems to be in a band and looks a tad de-pleted, as if they party too hard and spend their time daubing canvasses and scribbling poetry. It follows that there's a lot going on here at night! Wellington's pubs, live-music rooms and coffee shops are kickin' after dark. Go bar-hopping around Cuba St (try Matterhorn) and Cour-tenay Pl (try Malthouse) and see what kind of fun comes your way.

Wairarapa Wine Country

Over the hills (and not so far away) from Wellington is the Wairarapa district (p176). Once a sleepy enclave of farms, farmers and farmers' families, it's now a booming wine region with a boutique bent. Pinot noir is the stuff that's doing the bending: sample plenty, then bed down for the night in an upmarket B&B and swan between cafes and restaurants the next day. Lunch at Coney (p176)

Kapiti Coast

When you're travelling around from A to B, it's easy to overlook the little (and often brilliant) places in between. The Kapiti Coast (p173) definitely falls into this category: just an hour from Wellington and strewn with empty beaches and endearing coastal towns, and with Kapiti Island offshore, the area makes a great pit stop, detour or desti-nation in its own right. Pukerua Bay

Wellington & Lower North Island's Best...

Restaurants

Ortega Fish Shack The best of local submarine offerings (no, not big sandwiches). (p168)

Mt Vic Chippery Wellington fish and chips worth writing home about. (p167)

Logan Brown Classy but unpretentious eats in a converted downtown Wellington bank. (p169)

Tirohana Estate The pick of the Wairarapa's wine-and-dine options. (p179)

Mister D Napier's show-stealing new eatery will knock your socks off. (p184)

Places to Stretch Your Legs

Mt Victoria Lookout As AC/DC profess, it's a long way to the top (196m, in fact), but the views are awesome. (p159)

Wellington Botanic Gardens Catch the cable car up the slope, then wander back down through the greenery. (p159)

Queen Elizabeth Park Head for the dunes in this Kapiti Coast seaside park. (p174)

Napier art-deco walking tour Check out Napier's architectural gems on foot. (p179)

Places to Get Lost

Kapiti Island Talk with the animals (and birds) on this untrammelled offshore nature reserve. (p174)

Cape Palliser Remote seal colonies and surf breaks. (p178)

Otari-Wilton's Bush Native bushland enclave on Wellington's back doorstep. (p159)

Zealandia Disappear along forested walking trails: it's hard to believe Wellington city is just 2km away! (p159)

Need to Know

Places to Get Boozy

○ **Cuba St** Bars, backpackers, buskers... The funky, artsy heart-and-soul of the NZ capital. (p169)

○ **Wairarapa Wine Country** Day-trip or overnight in the Wairarapa's wine-soaked valleys. (p176)

○ **Hawke's Bay Wine Region** Sunny days and classy tastings around Napier. (p185)

○ **Courtenay Pl** Get down-and-dirty with Wellington's thirsty throngs. (p169)

ADVANCE PLANNING

○ **One month before** Organise domestic flights, car hire and tickets on the *Northern Explorer* train between Wellington and Auckland.

○ **Two weeks before** Book a South Island ferry crossing and accommodation across the region.

○ **One week before** Book a seat on a Hawke's Bay winery tour, a tour to Kapiti Island and a table at one of Wellington's top restaurants: try **Logan Brown** (p169) or **Ortega Fish Shack** (p168).

RESOURCES

○ **Wellington i-SITE** (www.wellingtonnz.com) The low-down on NZ's 'capital of cool'.

○ **Dominion Post** (www.dompost.co.nz) News from the nation's political heartland.

○ **Wairarapa NZ** (www.wairarapanz.com) Accommodation, wine, food and regional highlights.

○ **Napier i-SITE** (www.napiercity.co.nz) Info on the art-deco city.

○ **Hawke's Bay Tourism** (www.hawkesbaynz.com) Things to see, do, eat and drink around Hawke's Bay.

GETTING AROUND

○ **Walk** Along Courtenay Pl and up and down Cuba St.

○ **Bus** Across central Wellington.

○ **Cable car** From Lambton Quay up the hill to the Wellington Botanic Gardens.

○ **Car** From Wellington through the Wairarapa and up the East Coast.

○ **Minibus** Around the Hawke's Bay and Wairarapa wineries.

○ **Ferry** From Wellington to Picton on the South Island, and out to Kapiti Island.

○ **Train** Between Wellington and Auckland on the *Northern Explorer*.

BE FOREWARNED

○ **Windy Welly** The Crowded House song *Four Seasons In One Day* was written about Melbourne, but the same applies in Wellington: expect sun, rain and (most of all) wind at any moment.

Left: Water lily, Wellington Botanic Gardens (p159); **Above:** Fur seal, Cape Palliser (p178)

(LEFT) FELLWALKER/GETTY IMAGES ©; (ABOVE) PAUL KENNEDY /GETTY IMAGES ©

Wellington & Lower North Island Itineraries

Rub shoulders with the locals in Wellington's cafes and bars, then flush out your system with some fresh air and wilderness beyond the city's bohemian microcosm.

3 DAYS

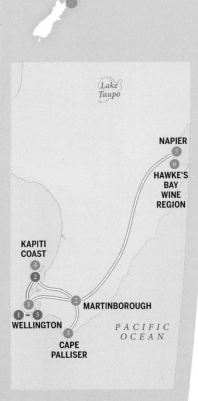

WELLINGTON TO WELLINGTON

CITY DAYS, CITY NIGHTS

Comprehend the hills, valleys and convolutions of ❶**Wellington** (p158), a far-flung San Francisco of the South: drive (or walk) up to Mt Victoria Lookout, or ride the cable car up to the Wellington Botanic Gardens. After lunch on cool Cuba St, immerse yourself in all things Kiwi at Te Papa or the excellent, locally focused Museum of Wellington City & Sea.

The next day, fuel up with coffee and eggs at Nikau in the City Gallery, then truck out to Zealandia to meet the birds and learn about NZ conservation. Alternatively, encounter some other bird-brains on a tour of Parliament House. For dinner try Ombra, then spend your evening bar-hopping along Courtenay Pl. Nocturnal entertainment could involve live music, a movie at the gloriously restored Embassy Theatre, or a midnight snack at a late-closing cafe – or all three.

Go day tripping on day three: boot it out to the ❷**Kapiti Coast** (p173) for a boat trip out to the wilds of Kapiti Island. Inspect the beaches and bird life, then head back to ❸**Wellington** for some NZ craft beer at Goldings Free Dive.

Top Left: Parliament House (p158), Wellington;
Top Right: Vineyards, Hawke's Bay (p185)

5 DAYS

WELLINGTON TO HAWKE'S BAY WINE REGION

WINE & WILDERNESS

Done central ❶**Wellington** (p158) to death? Time to hightail it over the hills for some wine tasting around classy ❷**Martinborough** (p177) in the Wairarapa Wine Country: pinot noir is the name of the game here. A bike ride through the vines is a divine way to go, or book a seat on a minibus tour. Bunk down that night in a cosy country B&B.

Recharge in the local cafes and restaurants the next morning, then track south to explore the weird wilds of ❸**Cape Palliser** (p178) with its surreal, end-of-the-world vibes: pungent seal colonies, a beach full of rusty tractors, a lonesome lighthouse...

From here you can head west to the underrated ❹**Kapiti Coast** (p173) for a night (aim for beachy Paekakariki), or get your skates on and travel north to sunny ❺**Napier** (p179) in the Hawke's Bay region. The town is home to an improbably well-preserved collection of art-deco architecture, built in the 1930s after a devastating quake. There are some cool cafes and bars here too, and encircling Napier are the vineyards and wineries of the ❻**Hawke's Bay Wine Region** (p185) – sample the brilliant chardonnay!

Discover Wellington & the Lower North Island

At a Glance

○ **Wellington** (p158) New Zealand's capital city is flush with culture, coffee and crazy nightlife.

○ **Kapiti Coast** (p173) Holiday towns, beaches and eerie Kapiti Island an hour north of Wellington.

○ **The Wairarapa** (p177) Indulgent vales full of Wellington wine weekenders.

○ **Hawke's Bay** (p185) Laid-back and sunny, with wine tasting and Napier's art-deco architecture.

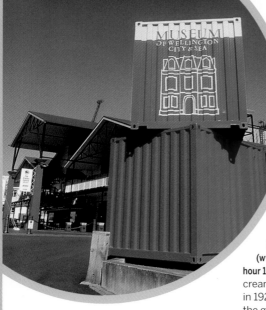

Museum of Wellington City & Sea
CLAVER CARROLL/GETTY IMAGES ©

WELLINGTON

⊙ Sights

Museum of Wellington City & Sea
Museum

(www.museumswellington.org.nz; Queens Wharf; ◷10am-5pm) **FREE** For an imaginative, interactive experience of Wellington's social and salty maritime history, swing into the Museum of Wellington. Highlights include a moving documentary about the tragedy of the *Wahine*, the interisland ferry that sank in the harbour entrance on a terrible, blustery day back in 1968, with a loss of 51 lives. Maori legends are also dramatically told using tiny hologram actors and special effects. The building itself is an old Bond Store dating from 1892.

City Gallery
Gallery

(www.citygallery.org.nz; Civic Sq, Wakefield St; charges may apply for major exhibits; ◷10am-5pm) **FREE** Housed in the monumental old library in Civic Sq, Wellington's much-loved City Gallery does a cracking job of securing acclaimed contemporary international exhibitions, as well as unearthing and supporting those at the forefront of the NZ scene. A packed events calendar and excellent Nikau Cafe (p168) enhance the experience.

Parliament House
Cultural Building

(www.parliament.nz; Bowen St; ◷tours on the hour 10am-4pm) **FREE** The austere grey-and-cream Parliament House was completed in 1922. Free one-hour tours depart from the ground-floor foyer (arrive 15 minutes prior). Next door is the 1899 neo-Gothic Parliamentary Library building, as well as the modernist **Beehive** designed by British architect Sir Basil Spence and built between 1969 and 1980.

Mt Victoria Lookout
Lookout

The city's most accessible viewpoint is on the top of 196m-high Mt Victoria, east of the city centre. You can take the Roseneath bus some of the way up, but the rite of passage is to sweat it out on the walk (ask a local for directions or just follow your nose). If you've got your own wheels, take Oriental Pde along the waterfront and then scoot up Carlton Gore Rd.

Wellington Botanic Gardens
Gardens

FREE The hilly, 25-hectare botanic gardens can be *almost* effortlessly visited via a cable-car ride (nice bit of planning, eh?), although there are several other entrances hidden in the hillsides. They boast a tract of original native forest along with varied collections including a beaut rose garden and international plant collections. Add in fountains, a cheerful playground, sculptures, duck pond, cafe, magical city views and much more, and you've got a grand outing indeed.

Cable Car
Cable Car

(www.wellingtoncablecar.co.nz; adult/child one way $4/1.50, return $7/2.50; ☉departs every 10min, 7am-10pm Mon-Fri, 8.30am-10pm Sat, 9am-9pm Sun) One of Wellington's most famous attractions is the little red cable car that clanks up the steep slope from Lambton Quay to Kelburn. At the top is the Wellington Botanic Gardens, the **Carter Observatory** (☏04-910 3140; www.carterobservatory.org; 40 Salamanca Rd; adult/child $18.50/8; ☉10am-5pm, to 9.30pm Tue & Sat) and the small-but-nifty **Cable Car Museum** (www.museumswellington.org.nz; admission free; ☉10am-5pm), which evocatively depicts the cable car's story since it was built in 1902 to open up hilly Kelburn for settlement. Take the cable car back down the hill, or ramble down through the gardens (a 20- to 60-minute walk, depending on your wend).

Zealandia
Wildlife Reserve

(☏04-920 9200; www.visitzealandia.com; Waiapu Rd; adult/child/family exhibition only $7.50/5/20, exhibition & valley $17.50/9/44; ☉10am-5pm, last entry 4pm) 🍃 This ground-breaking ecosanctuary is tucked in the hills about 2km west of town (the Karori bus passes nearby, or see the Zealandia website for the free shuttle). Living wild within the fenced valley are more than 30 native bird species, including rare takahe, saddleback, hihi and kaka, as well as tuatara and little spotted kiwi. An excellent exhibition relays NZ's natural history and world-renowned conservation story. More than 30km of tracks can be explored independently, or on regular guided tours. The night tour provides an opportunity to spot nocturnal creatures including kiwi, frogs and glowworms (adult/child $75/36). Cafe and shop on site.

Otari-Wilton's Bush
Park

(160 Wilton Rd; ☉dawn-dusk) FREE About 3km west of the city is Otari-Wilton's Bush, the only botanic gardens in NZ specialising in native flora. There are more than 1200 plant species here, including some of the city's oldest trees, as well as 11km of walking trails and delightful picnic areas. The Wilton bus from the city passes the gates.

🏃 Activities

Ferg's Kayaks
Kayaking

(www.fergskayaks.co.nz; Shed 6, Queens Wharf; ☉9am-8pm Mon-Fri, 9am-6pm Sat & Sun) Stretch your tendons with indoor rock climbing (adult/child $15/10), cruise the waterfront wearing in-line skates ($15 for two hours) or go for a paddle in a kayak or on a stand up paddle board (from $15 for one hour). There's also bike hire (one hour from $15) and guided kayaking trips.

Wild Winds
Windsurfing, Paddle Boarding

(☏04-473 3458; www.wildwinds.co.nz; 36 Customhouse Quay) With all this wind and water, Wellington was made for windsurfing, kiteboarding, and stand up paddle boarding. Take on one or all three with Wild Winds; lessons start from $110 for two hours.

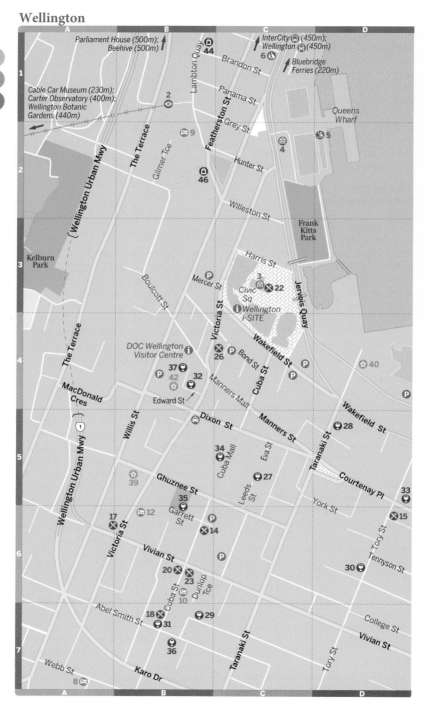

Parliament House (500m);
Beehive (500m)

Lambton Quay

Brandon St

InterCity (450m);
Wellington (450m)

Bluebridge
Ferries (220m)

Panama St

Featherston St

Grey St

Queens
Wharf

Cable Car Museum (230m);
Carter Observatory (400m);
Wellington Botanic
Gardens (440m)

Hunter St

The Terrace

Gilmer Tce

Willeston St

Frank
Kitts
Park

Kelburn
Park

Boulcott St

Harris St

Mercer St

Civic
Sq

Wellington
i-SITE

Jervois Quay

Victoria St

DOC Wellington
Visitor Centre

Wakefield St

Cuba St

Bond St

The Terrace

MacDonald
Cres

Manners Mall

Edward St

Dixon St

Manners St

Wakefield St

Willis St

Taranaki St

Courtenay Pl

Cuba Mall

Eva St

Ghuznee St

Leeds St

York St

Garrett
St

Victoria St

Vivian St

Tory St

Tennyson St

Cuba St

Dunlop
Tce

Abel Smith St

College St

Vivian St

Webb St

Karo Dr

Taranaki St

Tory St

160

Wellington

Don't Miss
Te Papa

Te Papa is the city's 'must-see' attraction, and for reasons well beyond the fact that it's NZ's national museum. Spread over six levels of galleries and interactive spaces, it's very hands-on, great fun for kids and full of surprises. You can't miss it – it's the jaunty big box on Cable St on the waterfront.

www.tepapa.govt.nz

55 Cable St

admission free

🕙10am-6pm Fri-Wed, to 9pm Thu

Galleries & Exhibits

Aptly, 'Te Papa Tongarewa' loosely translates into 'treasure box'. The riches inside include an amazing collection of Maori artefacts and the museum's own colourful *marae* (meeting house); natural history and environment exhibitions; Pacific and NZ history galleries; Ngā Toi/Arts Te Papa (the national art collection; see www.arts.tepapa.govt.nz); and hands-on 'discovery centres' for children. Expect impressive gallery spaces and plenty of high-tech twists.

Big-name, temporary exhibitions incur an admission fee, although general admission is free.

Tours & Getting Around

You could spend a day exploring Te Papa's six floors but still not see it all. To cut to the chase, head to the information desk on level two and collect a map. For exhibition highlights and to get your bearings, the one-hour Introducing Te Papa tour ($14) is a good idea; tours leave from the info desk at 10.15am, noon and 2pm daily in winter and more frequently in summer. Two cafes and two gift shops complete the Te Papa experience, one which could well take a couple of visits.

Local Knowledge

Visiting Te Papa

RECOMMENDATIONS FROM
BRIDGET MACDONALD,
SENIOR CORPORATE AFFAIRS ADVISER AT TE PAPA

1 **MAORI GALLERIES & TOURS**
On Level 4 you can see a beautiful example of a traditionally carved *marae* (meeting house), contrasting with a big contemporary *marae*. The museum also has many Maori guides, and dedicated Maori tours as well. At the Bush City exhibit you can learn about how Maori used to live and see how plants are used in modern-day life.

2 **NGĀ TOI/ARTS TE PAPA, LEVEL 5**
On Level 5 there is an exhibition called Ngā Toi: Arts Te Papa – an ever-changing art program featuring works from the national collection and elsewhere, viewable both in the galleries and online.

3 **GOLDEN DAYS, LEVEL 4**
The *Golden Days* film features nostalgic footage covering 100 years of iconic moments in NZ history. It's the good and bad of our national history: people from all over the world find a connection with it. It runs every 20 minutes.

4 **OUR SPACE, LEVEL 2**
Our Space (www.ourspace.tepapa.com) has a 14m satellite map of NZ. When you stand on it, imagery and video clips from that region light up on the wall beside you. The Wall is where people can upload their own images to our database before they arrive. Using interactive wand technology, you can look for your images and manipulate them on giant screens.

5 **AWESOME FORCES, LEVEL 2**
The Awesome Forces earthquake house here gives visitors an insight into New Zealand's geology, so that when they're travelling across the country they can understand how tectonic forces have shaped our landscapes.

Makara Peak Mountain
Bike Park Mountain Biking

(www.makarapeak.org; South Karori Rd, Karori; admission by donation) In the hills of Karori, 8km west of the city centre (on the Karori bus), this excellent 200-hectare park is laced with 60km of single-track ranging from beginner to expert. The nearby **Mud Cycles** (☎04-476 4961; www.mudcycles.co.nz; 421 Karori Rd, Karori; half-day/full day/weekend bike hire from $30/45/75) has mountain bikes for hire, and runs guided tours for riders of all abilities. Wellington is a true MTB mecca – visit tracks.org.nz for the evidence.

☞ Tours

Walk Wellington Walking Tour
(www.walkwellington.org.nz; adult/child $20/10; ⏱tours 10am daily, plus 5.30pm Mon, Wed & Fri Nov-Mar) Informative and great-value two-hour walking tours focusing on the city and waterfront, departing the i-SITE. Book online, phone or just turn up.

Zest Food Tours Guided Tour
(☎04-801 9198; www.zestfoodtours.co.nz; tours from $169) Runs three- to 5½-hour

Wellington Botanic Gardens (p159)

small-group foody tours; longer tours include lunch with matched wines at the legendary Logan Brown (p169).

John's Hop On Hop Off Bus Tour
(☎0274 535 880, 0800 246 877; www.hopon-hopoff.co.nz; per person $45) Flexible two-hour scenic loop of the city with 18 stops en route, starting at the i-SITE. Tickets are valid for 24 hours.

Movie Tours Guided Tour
(☎0274 193 077; www.adventuresafari.co.nz; tours from adult/child $45/30) Half- and full-day tours with more props, clips, and Middle-earth film locations than you can shake a staff at.

🛏 Sleeping

YHA Wellington City Hostel $
(☎04-801 7280; www.yha.co.nz; cnr Cambridge Tce & Wakefield St; dm $29-36, d with/without bathroom $120/88; @ 🛜) 🅿 Wellington's best hostel wins points for fantastic communal areas including two big kitchens and dining areas, and separate rooms for games, reading and watching movies. Sustainable initiatives (recycling, composting and energy-efficient hot water)

Wellington for Children

Let's cut to the chase: Welly's biggest hit for kids is Te Papa (p162), with the whole caboodle looking like it's curated by a team of five-year-old geniuses. It has interactive activities galore, more creepy, weird and wonderful things than you can shake a squid at, and heaps of special events for all ages. See the dedicated Kids page on the website for proof of Te Papa's prowess in this department.

Conveniently located either side of Te Papa are **Frank Kitts Park** and **Waitangi Park**, both with playgrounds and in close proximity to roller skates, ice cream, and life-saving espresso for the grown-ups.

A ride up the cable car (p159) and a lap around the Wellington Botanic Gardens (p159) will get the wee ones pumped up, and when darkness descends, head to the Carter Observatory (p159) to gaze at galaxies far, far away. On a more terrestrial bent, check out some crazy animals at the **Wellington Zoo** (www.wellingtonzoo.com; 200 Daniell St; adult/child $20/10; ⏰9.30am-5pm, last entry 4.15pm) 🐾 or Zealandia (p159).

impress, and there's a comprehensive booking service at reception, along with espresso.

Cambridge Hotel
Hostel $

(☎04-385 8829; www.cambridgehotel.co.nz; 28 Cambridge Tce; dm $25-30, with/without bathroom s $90/65, d $105/85; @ 🖥) Comfortable accommodation in a heritage hotel with a ground-floor pub. En suite rooms have Sky TV, phone and fridge (try for a room at the back if you're a light sleeper). The backpacker wing has a snug kitchen-lounge, flash bathrooms and dorms with little natural light but sky-high ceilings. Bonus $3 breakfast.

Comfort & Quality Hotels
Hotel $$

(☎0800 873 553, 04-385 2156; www.hotel-wellington.co.nz; 223 Cuba St; d $104-200; P @ 🖥 ♿) In the heart of Cuba St, the CQ has two wings: the sympathetically renovated historic 'Trekkers' building with smaller, cheaper rooms (Comfort); and the snazzier high-rise 'Quality', which adjoins five fully self-contained apartments. Shared facilities include an in-house bar and restaurant (mains $14 to $35), and parking ($25 per day).

Booklovers B&B
B&B $$

(☎04-384 2714; www.booklovers.co.nz; 123 Pirie St; s/d from $150/180; P @ 🖥) Author Jane Tolerton's gracious, book-filled B&B has three queen en suite guest rooms (one with an extra single bed). A bus service runs past the front gate to Courtenay Pl and the train station, and the city's 'green belt' begins right next door. Free wi-fi and parking.

Capital View Motor Inn
Motel $$

(☎04-385 0515, 0800 438 505; www.capitalview.co.nz; 12 Thompson St; d $125-240; P 🖥) Many of the rooms in this well-maintained, multistorey building close to Cuba St do indeed enjoy capital views – especially the large, good-value penthouse (sleeps five). All are self-contained and spruce, and there's free parking.

Victoria Court
Motel $$

(☎04-385 710, 0800 282 8502; www.victoriacourt.co.nz; 201 Victoria St; d $149-205; P 🖥) This central option continues to deliver satisfaction in the inner city through its spacious studios and apartments with kitchenettes, quality joinery and soft furnishings, and recently refreshed bathrooms. There are two disabled-access

165

units; larger units sleep up to six. Free on-site guest parking.

CityLife Wellington
Apartments $$$

(☎04-922 2800, 0800 368 888; www.heritage-hotels.co.nz; 300 Lambton Quay; d from $189; P@🛜) Luxurious serviced apartments in the city centre, ranging from studios to three-bedroom arrangements, some with full kitchen and in-room laundry facilities, and some with a harbour glimpse. Weekend rates are great bang for your buck. The vehicle entrance is from Gilmer Tce, off Boulcott St (parking $15.50 per day).

Museum Art Hotel
Hotel $$$

(☎04-802 8900, 0800 994 335; www.museum-hotel.co.nz; 90 Cable St; r & apt Mon-Thu $209-399, Fri-Sun $189-349; @🛜☒) Formerly known as 'Museum Hotel de Wheels' (to make way for Te Papa, it was rolled here from its original location 120m away), this art-filled hotel keeps the quirk-factor high. Bright-eyed staff, a very good restaurant

with flamboyant decor, and groovy tunes piped into the lobby make a refreshing change from homogenised business hotels. Tasty weekend and weekly rates.

Eating

Three excellent inner-city food markets run from dawn till around 2pm on Sundays – the seriously fruit-and-veg **Farmers Market** (cnr Victoria & Vivian Sts), and the more varied **Harbourside Market** (Wakefield St) next to Te Papa, where you'll also find artisan producers seducing foodies with their wares in the **City Market** (Chaffers Dock Bldg, 1 Herd St; ⊙8.30am-12.30pm Sun).

Aunty Mena's
Vegetarian $

(167 Cuba St; meals $10-19; ⊙11.30am-9.30pm; ✈) The lightest and healthiest of Welly's noodle houses is Aunty Mena's, a cheery cafe cranking out tasty vegie/vegan Malaysian and Chinese dishes to a diverse clientele. Easy-clean, over-lit interior.

Left: *The Mover* mural by Gabriel Heimler and Anna Proc on the Museum Art Hotel; **Below:** Havana Coffee Works

(LEFT) PETE SEAWARD/LONELY PLANET ©; (BELOW) PETE SEAWARD/LONELY PLANET ©

Fidel's   Cafe $

(www.fidelscafe.com; 234 Cuba St; snacks $4-7, mains $10-24; ⊘7.30am-10pm;) A Cuba St institution for caffeine-craving, alternative types. Eggs any-which-way, pizza and splendid salads are cranked out of the itsy kitchen, along with Welly's best milkshakes. Revolutionary memorabilia adorns the walls of the funky interior; decent outdoor areas too. A superbusy crew copes with the chaos admirably.

Mt Vic Chippery   Fish & Chips $

(www.mtvicchippery.co.nz; 5 Majoribanks St; meals $8-16; ⊘12-9pm Wed-Sun, 4-9pm Mon & Tue) Flash fish and chips by numbers. 1. Choose your fish (at least three varieties). 2. Choose your coating (beer batter, panko crumb, tempura...). 3. Choose your chips (five varieties!). 4. Add aioli, coleslaw, salad or sauce, and a quality soft drink. 5. Chow down inside or takeaway. Burgers and battered sausages will placate the piscophobes.

Havana Coffee Works   Cafe $

(www.havana.co.nz; 163 Tory St; snacks $4-7; ⊘8.30am-5pm Mon-Fri) Hitched on to the Havana headquarters and roastery, this fantastical 'First Class' coffee lounge offers a step back and forwards in time with its invented history and modern attitude towards quality service with speed. Nibbles are limited to the likes of scones and pies from the warmer.

Sweet Mother's Kitchen   American $

(www.sweetmotherskitchen.co.nz; 5 Courtenay Pl; mains $10-27; ⊘8am-10pm Sun-Thu, 8am-late Fri & Sat;) Perpetually brimming with cool cats, Sweet Mother's serves dubious but darn tasty takes on the Deep South, such as burritos, nachos, po' boys, jambalaya and key lime pie. It's cheap, cute, has craft beer and good sun.

Nikau Cafe
Cafe **$$**

(www.nikaucafe.co.nz; City Gallery, Civic Sq; lunch $14-25; ⏱7am-4pm Mon-Fri, 8am-4pm Sat; 🎵) An airy affair at the sophisticated end of the cafe scene, Nikau consistently dishes up some of the simplest but most delightful fare in town. Refreshing aperitifs, legendary kedgeree and sage eggs and divine sweets, as well as a sunny courtyard.

Tatsushi
Japanese **$$**

(99 Victoria St; dishes $4-27; ⏱11.30am-2.30pm Tue-Sat, 6-10pm Wed-Sat) A compact, Zen-like space reassuringly dominated by an open kitchen from which authentic Japanese dishes emerge such as superfresh sashimi, homemade agedashi tofu, chazuke soup, sunomono (dressed salad), and moreish Karaage chicken. Tatsushi is the real deal. Sushi and bento boxes to takeaway.

Chow
Fusion **$$**

(www.chow.co.nz; 45 Tory St; dishes $7-24; ⏱noon-midnight; 📶🎵) Well-oiled Chow is a stylish pan-Asian restaurant-cum-bar, popular with folk with a penchant for zingy food in sociable surroundings, and creative cocktails. Daily deals, free wi-fi, and the fun Library bar (p169) through the back door.

Ombra
Italian **$$**

(www.ombra.co.nz; 199 Cuba St; snacks & small plates $4-18; ⏱10am-late; 🎵) This Venetian-style *bacaro* (taverna) dishes up mouth-watering Italian fare in a lively, warm atmosphere. Admire the on-trend distressed interior while sipping an aperitif then share tasty morsels like *arancino* (fried risotto ball), *pizzette* (mini-pizza) and meatballs. Round things off with a classic dessert such as tiramisu or saffron and honey panna-cotta. *Delizioso!*

Ortega Fish Shack
Seafood **$$$**

(☎04-382 9559; www.ortega.co.nz; 16 Marjoribanks St; mains $32-39; ⏱5.30-10pm Tue-Sat) Fishing floats, salty portraits and Egyptian floor tiles set a colourful Mediterranean scene, a good hook on which to hang a seafood dinner. Fish comes many ways (roasted with Malaysian gravy, sashimi with lime dressing) while the afters head straight for France courtesy of orange crêpes and one of Welly's best cheeseboards.

Cuba Street

Logan Brown

Modern NZ $$$

(☏04-801 5114; www.loganbrown.co.nz; 192 Cuba St; mains $45-51; ☺noon-2pm Mon-Sat, 5.30pm-late Mon-Sun; 🕾) Routinely and deservedly touted as Wellington's best restaurant, Logan Brown oozes class without being pretentious or overly formal. Its 1920s banking chamber dining room is a stunner, as is the menu which features such treats as Waikanae crab cakes and venison lion with goat's curd and cherry. Bookings recommended.

Drinking & Nightlife

Goldings Free Dive

Craft Beer

(www.goldingsfreedive.co.nz; 14 Leeds St; ☺noon-11pm; 🕾) Hidden down an up-swinging back alley near Cuba St, gloriously garish Goldings is a bijou craft-beer bar with far too many merits to mention, although we'll single out ex-casino swivel chairs, a nice wine list, a ravishing Reuben sandwich plus pizza from Pomodoro, next door.

Hashigo Zake

Craft Beer

(www.hashigozake.co.nz; 25 Taranaki St; ☺noon-midnight; 🕾) This brick-walled bunker bar serves as the headquarters of a zealous importation business splicing a stimulating mix of big-flavoured international brewstars into a smartly selected NZ range.

Malthouse

Craft Beer

(www.themalthouse.co.nz; 48 Courtenay Pl; ☺3pm-late Mon & Tue, noon-1am Wed-Sun) At last count there were nearly 200 reasons to drink at this, the capital's original craft-beer bar – still boasting a high beer-geek quotient, and now housed in a low-key concrete box with leaners, comfy corner lounge, and popular alfresco area where you can watch the world go by.

Little Beer Quarter

Craft Beer

(www.littlebeerquarter.co.nz; 6 Edward St; 4pm-late Mon, noon-late Tue-Sat) Tucked away in a back lane, lovely LBQ is a lively bar

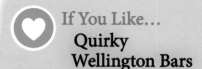

If You Like...
Quirky Wellington Bars

If you like drinking at Goldings Free Dive, we think you'll appreciate these other Wellington bars.

1 HAVANA

(www.havanabar.co.nz; 32 Wigan St; ☺11.30am-late Mon-Fri, 3pm-late Sat) Go out of your way to find Havana, a mighty fine needle in Welly's hospitality haystack, hidden down a side-street and squeezed into two adjacent heritage cottages sharing a groovy backyard. Fortify yourself with tapas and top shelf, then chinwag, smoke or flirt, or all three, before breaking out your sexy legs in the micro-disco.

2 VIVO

(www.vivowinebar.com; 19 Edward St; ☺3pm-late Mon-Fri, 5pm-late Sat) If your idea of a good time is fine wine, tapas and conversation, head to Vivo. Match wines off an epic list with any of 30 delectable small plates, and relax in the brick-lined and timbered, cellar-like dining room.

3 LIBRARY

(www.thelibrary.co.nz; 53 Courtenay Pl; ☺5pm-late) You'll find yourself in the right kind of bind at the book-filled Library, with its velveteen booths, board games and best-selling cocktails. An excellent all-round drink selection is complemented by a highly sharable menu of sweet and savoury treats including chocolate fondant and cheese.

4 HAWTHORN LOUNGE

(www.hawthornlounge.co.nz; 82 Tory St; ☺6pm-late Tue-Sat) This classy cocktail bar has a 1920s speakeasy feel, suited up in waistcoats and wide-brimmed fedoras.

5 MATTERHORN

(www.matterhorn.co.nz; 106 Cuba St; ☺3pm-late) An early riser in Welly's 21st-century bar scene, the 'Horn still hovers around the tops with its food (tapas from mid-arvo, dinner daily, brunch weekends), snappy service and live music.

handled with a lady's touch. It's warm, inviting, and soft in all the right places, but still packs a hop-headed punch with its well-curated taps and bottled selection. Good cocktails, wines, and whiskies, too, plus tasty bar food along the lines of pizza and pork scratchings.

Rogue & Vagabond Craft Beer
(www.rogueandvagabond.co.nz; 18 Garrett St) Right in the heart of Cuba fronting on to a precious pocket park, the Rogue is a lovably scruffy, colourful, kaleidoscopic craft-beer bar with heaps going on – via 18 taps; voluminous, chewy-crust pizza ($15 to $22); regular, rockin' gigs; and sifting about on the patio or slouching around on the lawn.

Southern Cross Pub
(www.thecross.co.nz; 39 Abel Smith St; ☉8am-late) Welcoming to all – from frenetic five-year-olds to Nana with her knitting – the fun, easy-going Cross rambles around a series of colourful rooms, combining a respectable restaurant, lively bar, dance floor, pool table and the best garden bar in town. There's interesting beer on tap, food to suit all budgets, and regular events including bingo, gigs, and quiz night.

Laundry Bar
(www.laundry.net.nz; 240 Cuba St; ☉10am-late Wed-Sun, 4pm-late Tue) Tumble into this junk-shop juke joint any time of the day or night for a tipple and a taco, and hang out with the hipsters in a wrinkle-free zone. Carousal is encouraged with regular gigs and deejays, lip-smacking libations, and colourful, carnivalesque decor pasted up with a very rough brush. Trailer-trash backyard complete with a caravan.

Entertainment

Circa Theatre
(☏04-801 7992; www.circa.co.nz; 1 Taranaki St; ☉Tue-Sun) Waterfront Circa houses two auditoriums in which it shows everything from edgy new works to Christmas panto. Standby tickets available an hour before the show.

BATS Theatre
(☏04-802 4175; www.bats.co.nz; 1 Kent Tce) Wildly alternative but accessible BATS presents cutting-edge and experimental NZ theatre – varied, cheap and intimate – in its freshly revamped theatre.

Light House Cinema Cinema
(☏04-385-3337; www.lighthousecuba.co.nz; 29 Wigan St; adult/child $17.50/12.50) Tucked away near the top end of Cuba St, this small, stylish and modern cinema screens a wide range of mainstream, art-house and foreign films in three small theatres. Serves high quality snacks.

Embassy Theatre Cinema
(☏04-384 7657; www.eventcinemas.co.nz; 10 Kent Tce; adult/child from $18.50/13.50) Wellywood's cinema mothership is an art-deco darling, built in the 1920s. Today she screens mainly mainstream films with state-of-the-art sound and vision. Bars and cafe on-site.

Paramount Cinema
(☏04-384 4080; www.paramount.co.nz; 25 Courtenay Pl; adult/child $15.90/10.50; ☉noon-midnight) A lovely old complex screening largely art-house, documentary and foreign flicks.

Meow Live Music, Bar
(www.welovemeow.co.nz; 9 Edward St; ☉4.30pm-late Mon, 10am-late Tue-Sun) Truly the cat's pyjamas, Meow goes out on a limb to host a diverse range of gigs and other performances, at the same time offering good-quality, inexpensive food at almost any time of day. There are treats for the sweet-tooth, and a good selection of keenly priced craft beers. Mish-mashed retro decor gives the place a speakeasy feel.

Bodega Live Music
(www.bodega.co.nz; 101 Ghuznee St; ☉4pm-late) A trailblazer of the city's modern live-music scene, the good-old Bodge' has demonstrated admirable endurance, hosting a regular and varied program of gigs – including frequent international acts – in a pleasant space with solid acoustics and a respectable dance floor.

🔒 Shopping

Vault
Arts & Crafts

(www.thevaultnz.com; 2 Plimmer Steps; ⏰9.30am-5.30pm Mon-Thu, 9.30am-7pm Fri, 10am-5pm Sat, 11am-4.30pm Sun) Jewellery, clothing, bags, ceramics, cosmetics – a bonny store with lots of NZ-made, beautiful things.

Kura
Arts & Crafts

(www.kuragallery.co.nz; 19 Allen St; ⏰10am-6pm Mon-Fri, 11am-4pm Sat & Sun) Contemporary indigenous art: painting, ceramics, jewellery and sculpture.

Kirkcaldie & Stains
Department Store

(165-177 Lambton Quay; ⏰9am-5.30pm Mon-Fri, 10am-5pm Sat & Sun) NZ's answer to Bloomingdale's or Harrods, established in 1863. Bring your travel documents with you for tax-free bargains.

ℹ️ Information

Wellington Accident & Urgent Medical Centre
(☎04-384 4944; www.wamc.co.nz; 17 Adelaide Rd, Newtown; ⏰8am-11pm) No appointment necessary; also home to the after-hours pharmacy.

Wellington Hospital (☎04-385 5999; www.ccdhb.org.nz; Riddiford St, Newtown; ⏰24hr) One kilometre south of the city centre.

Wellington i-SITE (☎04-802 4860; www.wellingtonnz.com; Civic Sq, cnr Wakefield & Victoria Sts; ⏰8.30am-5pm) Staff book almost everything, and cheerfully distribute Wellington's *Official Visitor Guide,* along with other maps and helpful pamphlets. Internet access and cafe.

ℹ️ Getting There & Away

Air
Wellington is an international gateway to NZ.
Wellington Airport (WLG; ☎04-385 5100; www.wellingtonairport.co.nz; Stewart Duff Dr, Rongotai; ⏰4am-1.30am) has touch-screen information kiosks in the luggage hall.

Air New Zealand (☎0800 737 000; www.airnewzealand.co.nz) Offers flights between Wellington and most domestic centres, including Auckland, Nelson, Christchurch, Dunedin and Queenstown. It also flies direct to Sydney, Melbourne and Brisbane.

Fidel's cafe (p167)

HAUKE DRESSLER/GETTY IMAGES ©

Jetstar (☏ 0800 800 995; www.jetstar.com) Offers economical flights from Wellington to Auckland and Christchurch, but takes no prisoners when it comes to late check-in. It also flies direct to Sydney and Melbourne.

Soundsair (☏ 03-520 3080, 0800 505 005; www.soundsair.com) Flies between Wellington and Picton up to eight times daily (from $95), Nelson (from $113) and Blenheim (from $95).

Qantas (☏ 0800 808 767; www.qantas.com.au) Flies direct between Wellington and Sydney and Melbourne.

Boat

There are two options for crossing the strait between Wellington and Picton: Bluebridge and the Interislander.

Bluebridge is based at Waterloo Quay, opposite the Wellington train station. The Interislander terminal is about 2km northeast of the city centre; a shuttle bus ($2) runs to the Interislander from platform 9 at Wellington train station (where long-distance buses also depart).

Bluebridge Ferries (☏ 04-471 6188, 0800 844 844; www.bluebridge.co.nz; 50 Waterloo Quay) Crossing takes 3½ hours; up to four sailings in each direction daily. Cars and campervans from $118; motorbikes $51; bicycles $10. Passenger fares from adult/child $51/26.

Interislander (☏ 0800 802 802, 04-498 3302; www.interislander.co.nz; Aotea Quay) Crossing takes three hours 10 minutes; up to five sailings in each direction daily. Cars are priced from $118; campervans (up to 5.5m) from $133; motorbikes from $56; bicycles $15. Passenger fares start from adult/child $55/28.

Bus

Wellington is a major bus-travel hub, with InterCity boasting the most extensive network.

InterCity (☏ 04-385 0520; www.intercity.co.nz) Services depart from platform 9 at the train station north to Auckland (11 hours) and all major towns in between and beyond such as Palmerston North (2¼ hours), Rotorua (7½ hours), and Napier (5½ hours).

Naked Bus (☏ 0900 625 33; www.nakedbus.com) Runs north from Wellington to all major North Island destinations, including Palmerston North (2½ hours), Napier (five hours), Taupo (6½ hours) and Auckland (11½ hours), with myriad stops en route. Buses depart from opposite the Amora Hotel in Wakefield St, and collect more passengers at Bunny St opposite the railway station.

Train

Wellington train station has six **ticket windows** (☏ 0800 801 700; ⊙ 6.30am-8pm Mon-Thu, to 1am Fri & Sat, to 7pm Sun), two selling tickets for KiwiRail Scenic trains, Interislander ferries and InterCity coaches; the other four ticketing local/regional **Tranz Metro** (☏ 0800 801 700; www.tranzmetro.co.nz) trains (Johnsonville, Melling, Hutt Valley, Kapiti and Wairarapa lines).

KiwiRail Scenic runs the just-hanging-in-there *Northern Explorer* service from Wellington to Auckland on Tuesday, Friday and Sunday, returning

Interislander ferry

from Auckland on Monday, Thursday, and Saturday (from $99, 12 hours).

Getting Around

Metlink (☎ 0800 801 700; www.metlink.org.nz) is the one-stop shop for Wellington's regional bus, train and harbour ferry networks.

To/From Airport

A taxi between the city centre and airport costs around $30.

Airport Flyer (☎ 0800 801 700; www.airportflyer.co.nz) The Airport Flyer bus runs between the airport, Wellington and the Hutt Valley, with a fare to downtown Wellington costing around $9. Buses run from around 6am to 8pm.

Co-op Shuttles (☎ 04-387 8787; www.co-opshuttles.co.nz; 1/2 passengers $20/26) Provides a door-to-door minibus service between the city and airport, 8km southeast of the city. Shuttles meet all arriving flights.

Bus

Frequent and efficient bus services cover the whole Wellington region and run between approximately 6am and 11.30pm. Major bus terminals are at the Wellington train station, and on Courtenay Pl near the Cambridge Tce intersection. Pick up route maps and timetables from the i-SITE and convenience stores, or online from Metlink. Fares are determined by zones: a trip across the city centre (Zone 1) costs $2, and all the way north to Masterton (Zone 14) costs $18.

Metlink also runs the **After Midnight** bus service, departing from two convenient city stops (Courtenay Pl and Cuba St) between midnight and 4.30am Saturday and Sunday, following a number of routes to the outer suburbs. Fares range from $6.50 to $13.50, depending on how far away your bed is.

Taxi

Green Cabs (☎ 0508 447 336; www.greencabs.co.nz)

Wellington Combined Taxis (☎ 04-384 4444; www.taxis.co.nz)

Train

Tranz Metro operates four train routes running through Wellington's suburbs to regional destinations. Trains run frequently from around 6am to 11pm, departing Wellington train station. The routes: Johnsonville, via Ngaio and Khandallah; Kapiti, via Porirua, Plimmerton, Paekakariki and Paraparaumu; Melling, via Petone; the Hutt Valley via Waterloo to Upper Hut; and a Wairarapa service calling at Featherston, Carterton and Masterton. Timetables are available from convenience stores, the train station, Wellington i-SITE and online. Standard fares from Wellington to the ends of the five lines range from $5 to $18.

KAPITI COAST

With wide, crowd-free beaches, the Kapiti Coast acts as a summer playground and suburban extension for Wellingtonians. The region takes its name from Kapiti Island, a wildlife sanctuary 5km offshore from Paraparaumu.

Information

The Coast's official visitor centre is **Paraparaumu i-SITE** (☎ 04-298 8195; Coastlands Mall, Rimu Rd; ☺ 9am-5pm Mon-Fri, 10am-2pm Sat & Sun), located within the Coastlands shopping centre, where you'll find all manner of other useful services such as banks, ATMs, post office and supermarkets.

Getting There & Around

Getting here from Wellington is a breeze by car: just follow SH1 for 30 minutes to Paekakariki, and around 45 to Paraparaumu. It's motorway most of the way.

Air

The recently expanded **Kapiti Coast Airport** (PPQ; www.kapitiairport.co.nz; Toru Rd, Paraparaumu Beach) in Paraparaumu is a regular destination for **Air2there** (☎ 0800 777 000; www.air2there.com), with daily flights to Blenheim and Nelson, and Air New Zealand (p171), which flies direct to Auckland.

Bus

InterCity stops at major Kapiti Coast towns on its services between Wellington (45 minutes) and northern destinations including Taupo (5½ hours) and Auckland (10 hours).

Detour:
Kapiti Island

Kapiti Island is the coastline's dominant feature, a 10km by 2km slice that since 1897 has been a protected reserve. Largely predator-free since 1998, it is home to a remarkable range and number of birds including many species that are now rare or extinct on the mainland.

The island is open to visitors, limited each day to 100 at **Rangatira**, where you can hike up to the 521m highpoint, Tuteremoana; and 60 visitors at the **northern end**, which has short, gentle walks to viewpoints and around a lagoon.

To visit the island, you must make your arrangements in advance with one of three licensed operators. All boats depart from Paraparaumu Beach, which can be reached by train. Services are provided by **Kapiti Marine Charter** (027 442 4850, 04-297 2585; www.kapitimarinecharter.co.nz; adult/child $95/55); **Kapiti Tours** (0800 527 484, 04-237 7965; www.ngatitoakapititours.co.nz; adult/child $105/65); and **Kapiti Island Nature Tours** (021 126 7525, 06-362 6606; www.kapitiislandnaturetours. co.nz; boat transport adult/child $95/55), run by the Barrett and Clark *whanau* (family), whom have a long-standing connection to the island. The latter offers day tours as well as a very special overnight stay (adult/child from $369/215), which includes an introduction to wildlife, history and Maori traditions, but also an after-dark walk in the bush to spot the cutest-ever bird, the rare little spotted kiwi. The price includes lodge accommodation in sole-occupancy rooms or bunk houses, with meals included.

More information can be found in the Department of Conservation's *Kapiti Island Nature Reserve* brochure, or in person at the **DOC Wellington Visitor Centre** (04-384 7770; www.doc.govt.nz; 18 Manners St; 9.30am-5pm Mon-Fri, 10am-3.30pm Sat).

Naked Bus (p172) also stops at major Kapiti Coast towns on its daily services.

Train

Tranz Metro (p172) commuter trains between Wellington and the coast are easier and more frequent than buses. Services run from Wellington to Paraparaumu ($12, generally half-hourly off-peak between 6am and 11pm, with more services at peak times), stopping en route in Paekakariki ($10.50).

KiwiRail Scenic (0800 872 467; www. kiwirailscenic.co.nz) has long-distance *Northern Explorer* trains connecting Wellington and Auckland stopping at Paraparaumu, while the weekday-only, peak-hour *Capital Connection*, travelling to Wellington in the morning and back to Palmerston North in the evening, stops at Paraparaumu, Waikanae and Otaki.

Paekakariki

Paekakariki is an arty little seaside village stretched along a black-sand beach, serviced by a train station and passed by the highway to Wellington, 41km to the south.

Sights

Queen Elizabeth Park   Park
(SH1; gates open 8am-8pm) **FREE** One of the last relatively unchanged areas of dune and wetland along this coast, this undulating 650-hectare beachside park offers swimming, walking, cycling and picnicking opportunities, as well as being the location of the Tramway Museum and Stables on the Park.

Tramway Museum   Museum
(www.wellingtontrams.org.nz; MacKay's Crossing entrance, Queen Elizabeth Park; admission by

donation, all-day tram rides adult/child/family $10/5/24; museum 10am-4.30pm daily, trams 11am-4.30pm Sat & Sun, daily 26 Dec-late Jan) A glimpse into historic Wellington by way of restored wooden trams and museum displays housed in a large garage, and on a 2km tram ride through Queen Elizabeth Park down to the beach.

🛏 Sleeping & Eating

Finn's
Hotel, Pub **$$**

(☎ 04-292 8081; www.finnshotel.co.nz; 2 Beach Rd; d $135-150; 📶) Finn's is the flashy beige suit of the low-key railway village, but redeems itself with spacious rooms, good-value meals (mains $17 to $29), craft beer on tap and an in-house 26-seat cinema. The hush glass keeps the highway at bay.

Beach Road Deli
Cafe **$**

(5 Beach Rd; snacks $3-8, pizza $13-22; ⏰7am-8pm Wed-Sat, 7am-4.30pm Sun) Bijou deli and wood-fired pizzeria, stocked with home-baked bread and patisserie, cheese, charcuterie and assorted imported goodies. Heaven-sent for the highway

traveller, picnicker, or those looking for a sausage to fry and a bun to put it in. Ace coffee.

Waikanae & Around

Heading north beyond Paekakariki, there's barely time to hit the speed limit before it's time to slow down for another Kapiti Coast town. The first is **Paraparaumu** (population 17,190), the region's major commercial and residential hotspot. The town has two hubs: the main town on the highway, with shopping galore, and Paraparaumu Beach with its waterside park and walkway, decent swimming and other beachy attractions, including the stunning view out to Kapiti Island.

Around 15 minutes' drive (20km) north of Paraparaumu is **Waikanae** (population 10,640), traditionally a retirees' favourite but in contemporary times a growing, go-ahead town encouraged by first-time-home-buyer flight from Wellington city.

Takahe, Kapiti Island

OLIVER STREWE/GETTY IMAGES ©

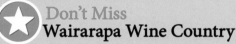

Don't Miss
Wairarapa Wine Country

Wairarapa's wineries thrive on visitors; around half of Martinborough's 25-odd wineries welcome visitors every day, with most of the rest open at the weekends. The *Wairarapa Wine Trail Map* (available from the i-SITE and many other locations) will aid your navigations. Read all about it at www.winesfrommartinborough.com.

A handy place to sample and purchase many wines, and get advice on local cellar doors is the **Martinborough Wine Centre** (www.martinboroughwinecentre.co.nz; 6 Kitchener St; ⏱10am-5pm), which also sells local olive oils, books, clothing and art.

Recommended wineries:

Ata Rangi (www.atarangi.co.nz; 14 Puruatanga Rd; ⏱1-3pm Mon-Fri, noon-4pm Sat & Sun) 🍷 One of the region's pioneering winemakers. Great drops and cute cellar door.

Coney (📞03-306 8345; www.coneywines.co.nz; Dry River Rd; ⏱11am-4pm Fri-Sun) Fingers crossed that your tasting host will be the inimitable Tim Coney, an affable character who makes a mighty syrah and may sing at random. Home to the excellent **Trio Cafe** (📞06-306 8345; snacks $12, mains $23-26; ⏱noon-3pm Sat & Sun; 🍴), too; bookings recommended.

Haythornthwaite (www.ht3wines.co.nz; 45 Omarere Rd; ⏱1-5pm) 🍷 Sustainable, hands-on winemaking producing complex drops including cherry-like pinot noir and gorgeous, aromatic Gewürztraminer whites.

Palliser (www.palliser.co.nz; Kitchener St; ⏱10.30am-4pm) 🍷 Wines so good even the Queen has some stashed away in her cellar. Slick outfit.

Poppies (www.poppiesmartinborough.co.nz; 91 Puruatanga Rd; ⏱11am-4pm) Delectable handcrafted wines served by the label's passionate winemaking and viticulturalist duo. Enjoy a well-matched platter in the stylishly simple cellar door.

Sights & Activities

Nga Manu
Nature Reserve
Wildlife Reserve

(www.ngamanu.co.nz; 281 Ngarara Rd; adult/child/family $18/8/38; ⏱10am-5pm) Waikanae's main visitor attraction, Nga Manu Nature Reserve is a 15-hectare bird sanctuary dotted with picnic areas, bush walks, aviaries and a nocturnal house with kiwi, owls and tuatara. The eels are fed at 2pm daily, and guided tours run on weekends at 2pm (Sunday only in winter).

Tuatara Brewery
Brewery

(www.tuatarabrewing.co.nz; 7 Sheffield St, Paraparaumu; ⏱11am-7pm Wed-Sun) Visit the oldest and most famous of Wellington's craft breweries at its industrial-estate premises where you can enjoy a tasting along with simple bar snacks (biersticks, pizza…) or preferably go on an enlightening tour of the brewery with Mr McInness, raconteur ($30, including tasting tray).

Sleeping & Eating

Kapiti Gateway Motel
Motel $$

(☎0800 429 360, 04-902 5876; www.kapitigateway.co.nz; 114 Main Rd, Waikanae; d $115-155; 🛜🏊) Tidy, airy motel on the highway with solar-heated pool, great hospitality and excellent local advice. Holiday hermits can make the most of the free wi-fi, kitchen facilities and Sky TV.

Long Beach
Cafe $$

(www.longbeach.net.nz; 40 Tutere St, Waikanae; meals $16-30; ⏱8.30am-10pm) Neighbourly, family-friendly Long Beach offers an extensive menu ranging from house-cured salmon and risotto, through to pizza and fish and chips. The Front Room cafe next door is also very good.

THE WAIRARAPA

The Wairarapa is the large tract of land east and northeast of Wellington, beyond the Tararua and Rimutaka Ranges. It is named after Wairarapa Moana – otherwise known as Lake Wairarapa and

Detour:
New Zealand Rugby Museum

Fans of the oval ball holler about the **New Zealand Rugby Museum** (www.rugbymuseum.co.nz; Te Manawa Complex, 326 Main St; adult/child/family $12.50/5/30; ⏱10am-5pm), an amazing space overflowing with rugby paraphernalia, from a 1905 All Blacks jumper to a scrum machine and the actual whistle used to start the first game of every Rugby World Cup. Of course, NZ won the 2011 Rugby World Cup: quiz the staff about the All Blacks' 2015 prospects.

translating as 'sea of glistening waters'. This shallow 8000-hectare lake and the surrounding wetland is the focus of much-needed ecological restoration, redressing generations of sheep farming in its ambit. Fields of fluffy sheep still bound, as do vineyards and the associated hospitality which have turned the region into a decadent weekend retreat.

Getting There & Around

From Wellington, Tranz Metro (☎0800 801 700; www.tranzmetro.co.nz) commuter trains run to Masterton ($17.50, five or six times daily on weekdays, two daily on weekends), calling at seven Wairarapa stations including Featherston and Carterton.

Martinborough

The sweetest visitor spot in the Wairarapa, Martinborough is a pretty town with a leafy town square and some charming old buildings, surrounded by a patchwork of pasture and a pinstripe of grapevines.

Detour:
Cape Palliser

The Wairarapa coast south of Martinborough around Palliser Bay and Cape Palliser is remote and sparsely populated, and a trip to its landmark lighthouse is a must-do if you can spare the time and have your own wheels. The drive to the Cape is just over an hour, but depending on stops you could take half- to a full day.

From Martinborough the road wends through picturesque farmland before hitting the coast along Cape Palliser Rd. This section of the drive is intensely scenic as it hugs the coast between the vast, wild ocean and black-sand beaches on the shoreside, and sheer cliffs on the other. Look for shadows of the South Island, visible on a clear day.

In these environs lies a significant wilderness area, **Aorangi (Haurangi) Forest Park**, which offers backcountry tramping, camping and a Department of Conservation (DOC) cottage for rent. Detailed information is available from Martinborough i-SITE. Within the park are the **Putangirua Pinnacles**, accessed through the Putangirua Scenic Reserve where there is a DOC campsite and car park. Standing like giant organ pipes, these 'hoodoos' were formed by rain washing silt and sand away and exposing the underlying bedrock. It's an easy 1½-hour walk to the lookout, or take the 3½-hour loop track past hills and coastal viewpoints.

Heading south further along the coast is the wind-worn fishing village of **Ngawi**. The first things you'll notice here are the rusty bulldozers on the beach, used to drag fishing boats ashore.

Next stop is the malodorous **seal colony**, the North Island's largest breeding area for these fellers.

Just beyond stands the **Cape Palliser Lighthouse**, where you can get a few puffs into the lungs on the 250-step climb to its foot.

🛏 Sleeping

Claremont   Motel **$$**
(☎0800 809 162, 06-306 9162; www.theclaremont.co.nz; 38 Regent St; d $130-158, 4-person apt $280; ☏) A classy accommodation enclave 15 minutes' walk to the town centre, the Claremont has two-storey, self-contained units in great nick, modern studios with spa baths, and sparkling two-bedroom apartments, all at reasonable rates (even cheaper in winter and/ or midweek). Private outlooks, attractive gardens, barbecue areas and bike hire.

Aylstone
Retreat   Boutique Hotel **$$$**
(☎06-306 9505; www.aylstone.co.nz; 19 Huangarua Rd; d incl breakfast $230-260; ☏) Set among the vines on the edge of the village, this elegant retreat is a winning spot for the romantically inclined. Six en suite rooms exude a lightly floral, French-provincial charm, and share a pretty posh reading room while the whole shebang is surrounded by micro-mansion garden sporting lawns, boxed hedges and chichi furniture.

🍴 Eating & Drinking

Café Medici   Cafe **$$**
(www.cafemedici.co.nz; 9 Kitchener St; breakfast & lunch $13-23, dinner $24-32; ☻8.30am-4pm, dinner from 6.30pm Thu-Sat) A perennial favourite among townsfolk and regular visitors, this airy cafe has Florentine flourishes and a sunny courtyard. Tasty, home-cooked food includes muffins and pies, lovely brunch dishes such as

Spanish eggs, and Med-flavoured dinner options such as Moroccan lamb tagine. Great coffee, too.

Tirohana Estate
Modern NZ **$$**

(☏06-306 9933; www.tirohanaestate.com; 42 Puruatanga Rd; lunch mains $16-33, 3-course prix fixe dinner $59; ⊙lunch noon-3pm, dinner 6pm-late Tue-Sun) A casual lunch over a glass or two will be much enjoyed on the terrace at this pretty vineyard, while evening dining in the elegant dining room is quite the occasion. The food, while 'comfort' in style (crumbed prawns, beef fillet and mash, bread and butter pudding), is amply proportioned, fresh and proficiently prepared. Impeccable service; dinner booking essential.

ℹ️ Information

The small **Martinborough i-SITE** (☏06-306 5010; www.wairarapanz.com; 18 Kitchener St; ⊙9am-5pm Mon-Fri, 10am-4pm Sat & Sun) stocks wine region maps, including one produced by the folks behind the useful site www.martinboroughnz.com.

HAWKE'S BAY

Hawke Bay, the name given to the body of water that stretches from the Mahia Peninsula to Cape Kidnappers, looks like it's been bitten out of the North Island's eastern flank. Add an apostrophe and an 's' and you've got a region that stretches south and inland to include fertile farmland, surf beaches, mountainous ranges and forests. With food, wine and architecture the prevailing obsessions, it's smugly comfortable but thoroughly appealing, and is best viewed through a rosé-tinted wineglass.

Napier

The Napier of today – a charismatic, sunny, composed city with the air of an affluent English seaside resort – is the silver lining of the dark cloud that was the deadly 1931 earthquake. Rebuilt in the popular architectural styles of the time, the city retains a unique concentration of art-deco buildings.

◎ Sights

Deco Centre
Tourist Information

(Map p182; www.artdeconapier.com; 7 Tennyson St; ⊙9am-5pm) The relocated and revamped Deco Centre is the place to start your explorations. Its one-hour guided deco walk ($17) departs the i-SITE daily at 10am; the two-hour version ($20) leaves the centre at 2pm daily. There's also a lovely little shop here, and brochures for the excellent self-guided *Art Deco Walk* ($7.50), *Art Deco Scenic Drive* ($5) and *Marewa Meander* ($3). You can also take a self-guided bike tour

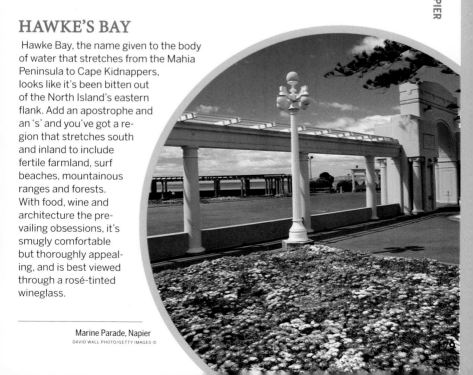

Marine Parade, Napier
DAVID WALL PHOTO/GETTY IMAGES ©

179

Hawke's Bay

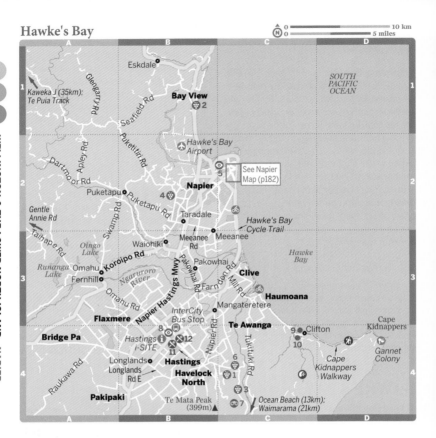

Hawke's Bay

◎ Sights
1 Black Barn Vineyards	C4
2 Crab Farm Winery	B1
3 Craggy Range	C4
4 Mission Estate	B2
5 National Tobacco Company Building	C2
6 Te Mata Estate	C4
7 Te Mata Peak Lookout	C4
8 Westerman's Building	B4

◎ Activities, Courses & Tours
9 Gannet Beach Adventures	C4
10 Gannet Safaris	C4

⊗ Eating
11 Opera Kitchen	B4
12 Taste Cornucopia	B4

($50, four hours), vintage car tour ($75, one hour), or kids' art-deco treasure hunt ($4).

Daily Telegraph Building   Architecture
(Map p182; 49 Tennyson St) The Daily Telegraph is one of the stars of Napier's art-deco show, with superb zigzags, fountain shapes and ziggurat aesthetic. If the front doors are open, nip inside and ogle at the painstakingly restored foyer.

MTG Hawke's Bay   Museum, Theatre
(Museum Theatre Gallery; Map p182; ☏06-835 7781; www.mtghawkesbay.com; 1 Tennyson St; adult/child $15/free; ☺10am-6pm) The beating cultural heart of Napier is the newly renovated MTG. It's a gleaming-white museum-theatre-gallery space by the water, bringing together live performances,

film screenings and regularly changing gallery and museum displays with touring and local exhibitions.

National Tobacco Company Building
Architecture

(Map p180; cnr Bridge & Ossian Sts, Ahuriri) Around the shore at Ahuriri, the National Tobacco Company Building is arguably the region's deco masterpiece, combining art-deco forms with the natural motifs of art nouveau. Roses, raupo (bulrushes) and grapevines frame the elegantly curved entrance. During business hours pull on the leaf-shaped brass door handles and enter the first two rooms.

National Aquarium of New Zealand
Aquarium

(Map p182; www.nationalaquarium.co.nz; 546 Marine Pde; adult/child/family $20/10/54; ⏰9am-5pm, feedings 10am & 2pm) Inside this modern complex with its stingray-inspired roof are piranhas, terrapins, eels, kiwi, tuatara and a whole lotta fish. Snorkellers can swim with sharks ($80), or sign up for a Little Penguin Close Encounter ($60).

Tours

Absolute de Tours
Bus Tour

(☎06-844 8699; www.absolutedetours.co.nz) Runs bus tours of the city, Marewa and Bluff Hill ($40) in conjunction with the Deco Centre, as well as half-day tours of Napier and Hastings ($60).

Ferg's Fantastic Tours
Guided Tours, Wine

(☎0800 428 687; www.fergstours.co.nz; tours $40-120) Tours from two to seven hours, exploring Napier and surrounding areas: wineries, Te Mata Peak, lookouts and foodie stops.

Hawke's Bay Scenic Tours
Guided Tour

(☎06-844 5693; www.hbscenictours.co.nz; tours from $50) A grape-coloured bunch of tour options including the 'Napier Whirlwind' and wineries.

Sleeping

Seaview Lodge B&B
B&B $$

(Map p182; ☎06-835 0202; www.aseaviewlodge.co.nz; 5 Seaview Tce; s $130-140, d $170; 🛜)

WELLINGTON & THE LOWER NORTH ISLAND NAPIER

National Tobacco Company Building, Napier

LATITUDESTOCK - EMMA DURNFORD/GETTY IMAGES ©

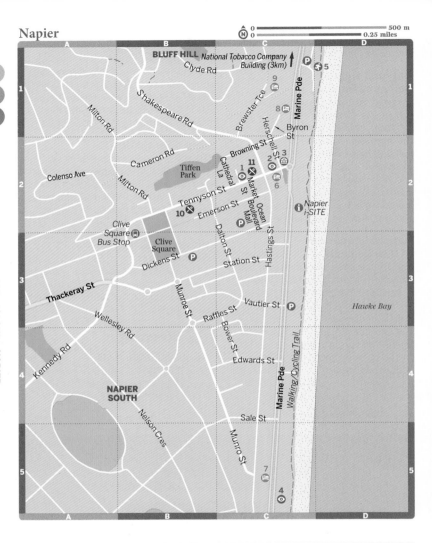

Napier

Napier

◎ Sights

1 Daily Telegraph Building	C2
2 Deco Centre	C2
3 MTG Hawke's Bay	C2
4 National Aquarium of New Zealand	C5

☉ Activities, Courses & Tours

5 Fishbike	D1

⬚ Sleeping

6 Masonic Hotel	C2
7 Pebble Beach Motor Inn	C5
8 Scenic Hotel Te Pania	C1
9 Seaview Lodge B&B	C1

☒ Eating

10 Groove Kitchen Espresso	B2
11 Mister D	C2

⬚ Drinking & Nightlife

Emporium	(see 6)

This grand Victorian villa (1890) is queen of all she surveys – which is most of the town and a fair bit of ocean. The elegant rooms have tasteful period elements and either bathroom or en suite. It's hard to resist a sunset tipple on the veranda, which opens off the relaxing guest lounge. Free wi-fi and off-street parking a bonus.

Pebble Beach Motor Inn
Motel $$

(Map p182; ☎0800 723 224, 06-835 7496; www.pebblebeach.co.nz; 445 Marine Pde; d/f from $145/165; ☎) Unlike the majority of NZ motels, this one is owner-operated (they own the building, rather than lease it from a higher power) – so maintenence and service top the list of staff priorities. There are 25 immaculate rooms over three levels, all with kitchens, spas, balconies and ocean views. Full to capacity most nights.

Masonic Hotel
Hotel $$

(Map p182; ☎06-835 8689; www.masonic.co.nz; cnr Tennyson St & Marine Pde; r $179-499; ☎) The art-deco Masonic is arguably the heart of the old town, with its accommodation, restaurants and bars taking up most of a city block. It's undergoing a gradual but much-needed refurb, and is shaping up nicely around its charming old bones. The cheaper 'original' rooms are unrefurbished, but still decent. Good online discounts and free wi-fi.

Scenic Hotel Te Pania
Hotel $$$

(Map p182; ☎06-833 7733; www.scenichotels.co.nz; 45 Marine Pde; d/1-bedroom/2-bedroom from $185/255/400; @☎) Looking like a mini UN HQ by-the-sea, the refurbished, curvilicious, six-storey Te Pania has instant retro appeal. Rooms are far from retro, however, with designer linen, leather lounges and floor-to-ceiling windows that slide open for chest-fulls of sea air.

🍴 Eating & Drinking

Groove Kitchen Espresso   Cafe $

(Map p182; www.groovekitchen.co.nz; 112 Tennyson St; meals $9-19; ⊗8am-2pm Mon-Fri, 8.30am-2pm Sat & Sun; 🎵) A sophisticated cafe squeezed into a small, groovy space where the turntable spins and the kitchen cranks out A1 brunch along with trendsetting wraps, baps, salads and killer coffee. With a bit of luck you'll be around for one of the intermittent Thursday night gigs.

Mister D   Modern NZ $$

(Map p182; ☎06-835 5022; www.misterd.co.nz; 47 Tennyson St; mains lunch $15-29, dinner $25-29; ⊗7.30am-4pm Sun-Wed, 7.30am-late Thu-Sun) This long, floor-boardy room with its green-tiled bar is the pride of the Napier foodie scene. Hip and stylish but not unaffordable, with quick-fire service delivering the likes of pulled pork with white polenta or chunky corn fritters with bacon and maple syrup. Novelty of the Year award: donuts served with syringes full of chocolate, jam or custard (DIY injecting). Super popular – bookings essential.

Emporium   Bar

(Map p182; www.emporiumbar.co.nz; Masonic Hotel, cnr Tennyson St & Marine Pde; ⊗7am-late; 🛜) Napier's most civilised bar, Emporium, with its marble-topped bar, fab art-deco details and old-fashioned relics strewn about, is super atmospheric. Brisk staff, creative cocktails, good coffee, NZ wines, bistro fare (plates $15 to $30) and prime location seal the deal.

ℹ️ Information

Napier Health Centre (☎06-878 8109; www.hawkesbay.health.nz; 76 Wellesley Rd; ⊗24hr) Round-the-clock medical assistance.

Napier i-SITE (Map p182; ☎06-834 1911; www.napiernz.co.nz; 100 Marine Pde; ⊗9am-5pm, extended hours Dec-Feb; 🛜) Handy and helpful.

ℹ️ Getting There & Away

Air

Hawke's Bay Airport (Map p180; www.hawkesbay-airport.co.nz) is 8km north of the city.

Air New Zealand (☎06-833 5400; www.airnewzealand.co.nz; cnr Hastings & Station Sts; ⊗9am-5pm Mon-Fri, 9am-noon Sat) Direct flights to/from Auckland, Wellington and Christchurch.

Sunair Aviation (www.sunair.co.nz) Has direct weekday flights between Napier, Gisborne and Hamilton.

Bus

InterCity buses can be booked online or at the i-SITE, and depart from the **Clive Square Bus Stop** (Map p182). Services run daily to Auckland ($82, 7½ hours) via Taupo ($33, two hours); Gisborne ($43, four hours) via Wairoa ($27, 2½ hours); and Wellington ($40, 5½ hours); plus four daily services to Hastings ($22, 30 minutes).

Naked Bus daily destinations include Wellington ($20, 5½ hours) via Palmerston North ($10, 2½ hours); and Auckland ($25, eight hours) via Taupo ($10, two hours).

Commemorative sign, Napier
AMOS CHAPPLE/GETTY IMAGES ©

CLAVER CARROLL/GETTY IMAGES ©

Don't Miss
Hawke's Bay Wine Region

Once upon a time, this district was most famous for its orchards. Today it's vines that have top billing, with Hawke's Bay now NZ's second-largest wine-producing region. Expect excellent Bordeaux-style reds, syrah and chardonnay. Pick up the *Hawke's Bay Winery Guide* map from the i-SITE, or download it from www.winehawkesbay.co.nz. A few of our faves:

Black Barn Vineyards (Map p180; ☎06-877 7985; www.blackbarn.com; Black Barn Rd, Havelock North; ◷9am-5pm Mon-Fri, 10am-5pm Sat & Sun) Hip, inventive winery with a bistro, gallery, Saturday farmers market (one of NZ's first) and an amphitheatre for concerts and movie screenings. Try the flagship chardonnay.

Crab Farm Winery (Map p180; ☎06-836 6678; www.crabfarmwinery.co.nz; 511 Main North Rd, Bay View; ◷10am-5pm daily, 6pm-late Fri) Decent, reasonably priced wines and a great cafe with regular live troubadours and relaxed, rustic vibes. A good stop for lunch or a glass of rosé (or both).

Mission Estate (Map p180; ☎06-845 9354; www.missionestate.co.nz; 198 Church Rd, Taradale; ◷9am-5pm Mon-Sat, 10am-4.30pm Sun) NZ's oldest winery (1851!). Follow the *looong* tree-lined drive up to the restaurant and cellar door, inside a restored seminary.

Te Mata Estate (Map p180; www.temata.co.nz; 349 Te Mata Rd, Havelock North; ◷8.30am-5pm Mon-Fri, 10am-5pm Sat) 🖉 The legendary Coleraine red at this unpretentious, old-school, family-run winery is worth the trip alone.

Craggy Range (Map p180; ☎06-873 0141; www.craggyrange.com; 253 Waimarama Rd, Havelock North; ◷10am-6pm, closed Mon & Tue Apr-Oct) Inside a cathedral-like 'wine barrel', the restaurant here, called Terroir, is one of the region's most consistent fine-dining experiences. Photogenic views of craggy Te Mata Peak.

Hastings, Havelock North & Around

Positioned at the centre of the Hawke's Bay fruit bowl, busy Hastings is the commercial hub of the region, 20km south of Napier. A few kilometres of orchards still separate it from Havelock North, with its prosperous village atmosphere and the towering backdrop of Te Mata Peak.

◉ Sights

As with Napier, Hastings was similarly devastated by the 1931 earthquake and also boasts some fine art-deco and Spanish Mission buildings, built in the aftermath. Main-street highlights include the **Westerman's Building (Map p180; cnr Russell & Heretaunga St E, Hastings),** arguably the Bay's best example of the Spanish Mission style, although there are myriad architectural gems here. The i-SITE stocks the *Art Deco Hastings* brochure ($1), detailing two self-guided walks.

Te Mata Peak   Park

(www.tematapark.co.nz) Rising melodramatically from the Heretaunga Plains 16km south of Havelock North, Te Mata Peak (399m) is part of the 98-hectare **Te Mata Trust Park**. The summit road passes sheep trails, rickety fences and vertigo-inducing stone escarpments, cowled in a bleak, lunar-meets-Scottish-Highland atmosphere. From the **Te Mata Peak Lookout (Map p180)** on a clear day, views fall away to Hawke Bay, Mahia Peninsula and distant Mt Ruapehu.

The park's trails offer walks from 30 minutes to two hours: pick up the *Te Mata Trust Park* brochure from local i-SITEs.

Cycle the Bay

The 180km network of **Hawke's Bay Trails** (www.nzcycletrail.com/hawkes-bay-trails) – part of the national Nga Haerenga, New Zealand Cycle Trails project – offers cycling opportunities from short, city scoots to hilly, single-track shenanigans. Dedicated cycle trails encircle Napier, Hastings and the coastline, with landscape, water and wine themes. Pick up the *Hawke's Bay Trails* brochure from the i-SITE or online.

Napier itself is very cycle-friendly, particularly along Marine Parade where you'll find **Fishbike** (Map p182; ☎06-833 6979; www.fishbike.co.nz; 22 Marine Pde; bike hire per half-/full day $35/50, tandems $70/90; ☺9am-5pm) renting comfortable bikes – including tandems for those willing to risk divorce.

Given the conducive climate, terrain and multitudinous tracks, it's no surprise that numerous cycle companies pedal fully geared-up tours around the Bay, with winery visits near mandatory. Operators include the following:

Bike About Tours (☎06-845 4836; www.bikeabouttours.co.nz; tours half-/full day from $35/45)

Bike D'Vine (☎06-833 6697; www.bikedevine.com; tours adult/child from $35/15)

On Yer Bike Winery Tours (☎06-650 4627; www.onyerbikehb.co.nz; full day with/without lunch $60/50)

Takaro Trails (☎06-835 9030; www.takarotrails.co.nz; day rides from $40, 3-/5-day rides incl accommodation from $479/899)

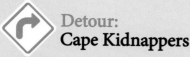

Detour:
Cape Kidnappers

From mid-September to late April, Cape Kidnappers (named when local Maori tried to kidnap James Cook's Tahitian servant boy) erupts with squawking gannets. These big birds usually nest on remote islands but here they settle for the mainland, completely unfazed by human spectators.

Early November to late February is the best time to visit. Take a tour or the walkway to the colony: it's about five hours' return from the Clifton Reserve car park ($1) at the Clifton Motor Camp. The walk is tide dependent: leave no earlier than three hours after high tide; start back no later than 1½ hours after low tide. Tour options include:

Gannet Beach Adventures (Map p180; ☏06-875 0898, 0800 426 638; www.gannets.com; 475 Clifton Rd, Clifton; adult/child $42/24) Ride along the beach on a tractor-pulled trailer before wandering out on the Cape for 90 minutes.

Gannet Safaris (Map p180; ☏06-875 0888, 0800 427 232; www.gannetsafaris.co.nz; 396 Clifton Rd, Te Awanga; adult/child $60/30) Overland 4WD trips across farmland into the gannet colony. Three-hour tours depart at 9.30am and 1.30pm.

 Tours

Long Island Guides
Guided Tour
(☏06-874 7877; www.longislandtoursnz.com; half-day from $180) Customised tours across a wide range of interests including Maori culture, bush walks, kayaking, horse riding and, inevitably, food and wine.

Prinsy's Tours
Winery Tour
(☏0800 004 237, 06-845 3703; www.prinsyexperience.co.nz; half-/full-day tours from $60/85) Affable half- or full-day wine jaunts, with layman's-lingo explanations at four or five wineries.

 Eating

Taste Cornucopia
Cafe $
(Map p180; www.tastecornucopia.co.nz; 219 Heretaunga St E, Hastings; meals $7-22; ⏱7.30am-4pm Mon-Fri, 6.30pm-late Fri; ☏) ✿ An award-winning, high-ceilinged organic cafe in central Hastings, serving filling 'abundant' breakfasts, organic coffee, smoked fish pies, curries, vegetarian lasagne and amazing 'marshmallows' that look like giant blobs of extruded toothpaste. Super NZ wine list, too. Tasty dinners Friday nights.

Opera Kitchen
Cafe $$
(Map p180; www.operakitchen.co.nz; 312 Eastbourne St E, Hastings; mains $9-25; ⏱7.30am-4pm Mon-Fri, 9am-3pm Sat & Sun; ☏) Set your rudder right with some whiskey porridge with cream and giant oats at this mod, stylish cafe abutting Hawke's Bay Opera House. For a more practical start to the day, the farmers breakfast is also a winner. Heavenly baked goods, great coffee and snappy staff. Eat in, or outside in the suntrap courtyard.

ℹ Information

Hastings i-SITE (Map p180; ☏06-873 0080; www.visithastings.co.nz; Westermans Bldg, cnr Russell St & Heretaunga St E; ⏱9am-5pm Mon-Fri, 9am-3pm Sat, 10am-2pm Sun; ☏) Internet access, free maps, trail brochures and bookings.

ℹ Getting There & Away

Napier's Hawke's Bay Airport (p184) is a 20-minute drive away. **Air New Zealand** (☏06-873 2200; www.airnewzealand.co.nz; 117 Heretaunga St W; ⏱9am-5pm Mon-Fri) has an office in central Hastings.

The **InterCity Bus Stop** (Map p180) is on Russell St. Book InterCity and Naked Bus buses online or at the i-SITE.

Marlborough & Nelson

For many travellers, Marlborough and Nelson will be their introduction to what South Islanders refer to as the 'Mainland'. Having left windy Wellington and made a white-knuckle crossing of Cook Strait, folk are often surprised to find the sun shining and temperatures up to 10 degrees warmer.

Good pals, these two neighbouring regions have much in common beyond an amenable climate: both boast renowned coastal holiday spots, particularly the Marlborough Sounds and Abel Tasman National Park. And so it follows that these two regions have an abundance of luscious produce: summer cherries for a start, but most famously the grapes that work their way into the wine glasses of the world's finest restaurants.

In high season these regions are popular and deservedly so. Plan ahead and be prepared to jostle for your gelato with Kiwi holidaymakers.

Ferry on Queen Charlotte Sound

Marlborough & Nelson

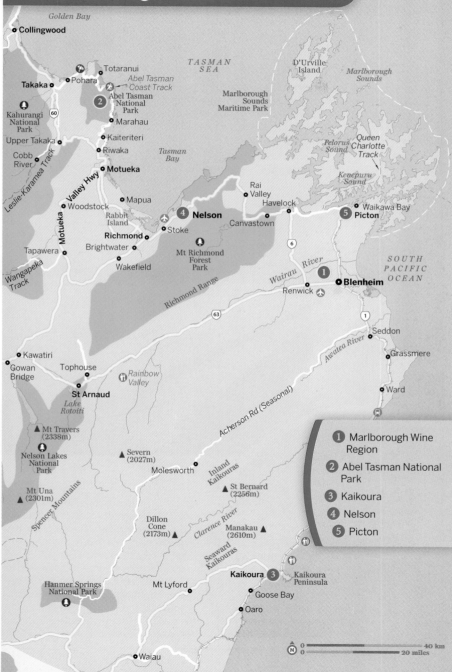

Golden Bay

Collingwood

TASMAN SEA

D'Urville Island

Marlborough Sounds

Totaranui
Takaka o Pohara
Abel Tasman Coast Track
Abel Tasman National Park
Marlborough Sounds Maritime Park

Kahurangi National Park
60
Marahau
Upper Takaka
Kaiteriteri
Cobb River
Riwaka
Tasman Bay

Queen Charlotte Track

Pelorus Sound

Motueka

Kenepuru Sound

Rai Valley
Havelock
Waikawa Bay

Woodstock
Mapua
4 **Nelson**
Picton
Rabbit Island
Stoke
Canvastown

Richmond
Brightwater
Mt Richmond Forest Park

Wairau River

1
Blenheim

SOUTH PACIFIC OCEAN

Wakefield
6
Renwick

Richmond Range

63

Seddon

Awatere River

Grassmere

Kawatiri
Gowan Bridge
Tophouse
Rainbow Valley

Ward

St Arnaud
Lake Rotoiti

Achseron Rd (Seasonal)

Mt Travers (2338m)

Nelson Lakes National Park

Severn (2027m)

Molesworth

Inland Kaikouras

Mt Una (2301m)

St Bernard (2256m)

Spencer Mountains

Dillon Cone (2173m)

Clarence River

Manakau (2610m)

Seaward Kaikouras

Hanmer Springs National Park

Mt Lyford

Kaikoura 3
Kaikoura Peninsula

Goose Bay

Oaro

Waiau

1 Marlborough Wine Region

2 Abel Tasman National Park

3 Kaikoura

4 Nelson

5 Picton

0 ———— 40 km
0 ———— 20 miles

Marlborough & Nelson Highlights

Marlborough Wine Region

Most visitors spend a couple of days sipping sauvignon blanc in the Marlborough Wine Region (p206) – the powerhouse of the New Zealand wine industry. But Marlborough is an incredibly diverse area, and there's plenty more to do here beyond the vines. Take a detour into the Marlborough Sounds for some sea kayaking, mountain biking and tramping for starters.
Marlborough vineyard

Abel Tasman National Park

Of all NZ's national parks, Abel Tasman (p219) is the most accessible, offering bush-meets-sea landscapes, beautiful golden-sand beaches and amazingly clear water. The region also lays claim to NZ's highest sunshine hours, and has very settled weather, protected on all sides by mountains. Get some sun on your skin and some miles into your calf muscles on the wonderful Abel Tasman Coast Track. Kayaking, Abel Tasman National Park

Kaikoura

3

Kaikoura (p205) is on the main migratory path for 14 different species of whale and dolphin: it's a kind of underwater highway where you can watch whales year-round. From June to August whales come close to the land to feed. Back on dry land there are seals and birds to ogle, and seafood to savour ('kai' is Maori for food, and 'koura' means crayfish). Fur seals, Kaikoura

4

Nelson

Anyone here into the arts, good coffee, seafood restaurants, Victorian architecture and careening around the Great Outdoors? The good people of Nelson (p212) deliver it all, partnered with equal measures of eco-awareness and urban bohemia. This funky town offers 'liveability' to its residents and plenty of enticements to keep the itinerant population (you and me) here for a day or three.

Victorian-era workers' cottages, Nelson

5

Picton

No doubt about it, Picton (p198) is underrated. Too many people just jump on/off the ferry here and continue on to wherever they're bound. But why not take a day to chill out? Picton is a photogenic wee town on one of the prettiest waterways you could imagine, with plenty of quality places to eat, sleep and drink.

Marlborough & Nelson's Best...

NZ Wildlife, Up Close

○ **Kaikoura** Famous boat and aerial whale-watching tours off the Kaikoura coast. (p207)

○ **Marlborough Sounds** Watch dolphins chase the North Island ferry or get closer on a guided tour. (p201)

○ **Abel Tasman National Park** A plethora of grunting seals. (p219)

○ **Albatross encounters** Check out the big birds on a tour from Kaikoura. (p209)

Scenic Highways & Byways

○ **Picton–Havelock** Wiggly tarmac along the Marlborough Sounds' southern reaches.

○ **Kaikoura–Blenheim** Route 1 passes surf beaches and lonesome coastlines.

○ **Rapaura Road** The Marlborough Wine Region's vine-lined 'Golden Mile'.

○ **Motueka–Takaka** Over the hills south of Abel Tasman National Park.

Places to Get Wet

○ **Abel Tasman National Park** Kayak around this spectacular coastline. (p219)

○ **Marahau** Clear, clean waters on the doorstep of Abel Tasman National Park. (p222)

○ **Tahunanui Beach** People-filled sandy stretch 5km south of Nelson. (p212)

○ **Queen Charlotte Track** Dunk a toe in the chilly, mirror-flat Marlborough Sounds. (p201)

Need to Know

Excuses for a Drink

- **Marlborough Wine Region** We all know why you're here...now get sipping! (p206)

- **Blenheim breweries** Sidestep the sav blanc with some microbrewed delights. (p202)

- **Nocturnal Nelson** When the sun goes down Nelson's beery bars light up. (p216)

- **Kaikoura Seafest** (www. seafest.co.nz) If you're here in October, don't miss this sensational seaside shindig.

ADVANCE PLANNING

- **One month before** Is it summertime? Book your kayak/hike in Abel Tasman National Park pronto, plus tickets on the *Coastal Pacific* train between Picton and Christchurch via Kaikoura.

- **Two weeks before** Book a ferry to/from Wellington on the North Island, and accommodation across the region.

- **One week before** Book a Marlborough Wine Region winery tour and a whale-watching expedition in Kaikoura.

RESOURCES

Swing into the local i-SITE visitor centres for bookings and information on regional accommodation, transport, wine, food and activities, plus Department of Conservation (DOC) info and contacts:

- **Blenheim i-SITE** (www. lovemarlborough.co.nz)

- **Kaikoura i-SITE** (www. kaikoura.co.nz)

- **Nelson i-SITE** (www. nelsonnz.com)

- **Picton i-SITE** (www. lovemarlborough.co.nz)

GETTING AROUND

- **Hike** Along the Queen Charlotte Track and Abel Tasman Coast Track.

- **Kayak** Along the craggy, sandy coastline in Abel Tasman National Park.

- **Minibus** Around the Marlborough Wine Region wineries.

- **Mountain bike** Along the Queen Charlotte Track.

- **Ferry** Between Picton (South Island) and Wellington (North Island).

- **Train** Between Picton and Christchurch (via Kaikoura) on the *Coastal Pacific*.

BE FOREWARNED

- **Abel Tasman Coast Track** It's one of NZ's Great Walks, and it is indeed great: book your accommodation en route many moons in advance to ensure you'll have somewhere to rest your weary bones at night.

- **Queen Charlotte Track** Unless you're camping, it pays to book your QCT accommodation *waaay* in advance, especially in summer.

eft: Whitebait fritters; **Above:** Golden Bay, Abel Tasman National Park (p219)

Marlborough & Nelson Itineraries

If the name 'Marlborough' conjures images of chilled white wine and autumnal vine rows, the region won't disappoint. But explore further for outstanding tramping, mountain biking, sea kayaking and other activities.

3 DAYS

MARLBOROUGH WINE REGION TO KAIKOURA
FOODIE MARLBOROUGH

With only three days to explore the top of the South Island, don't try to do too much. Change down a gear and focus on some of life's best things: food and wine done the Marlborough way. The first stop is the iconic ❶ **Marlborough Wine Region** (p206) where you can spend a day visiting cellar doors, sampling Gewürztraminer, pinot gris and, of course, the world-famous sauvignon blanc. If you're more of a beer boffin, there are some ace microbreweries, too.

Back in the calm, clean backwaters of the ❷ **Marlborough Sounds** (p201), greenshell mussels grow in preposterous numbers. You'll find them on most menus in ❸ **Picton** (p198)– a generous bowl steamed with fennel, shallots, white wine and butter will cure whatever ails you.

Head southeast around the coast to ❹ **Kaikoura** (p205) for a seafood frenzy. This is the town to try crayfish, paua (abalone), scallops and all manner of fresh ocean fish. Whip out one of those recently acquired bottles and crack into some crustaceans, then take a whale-watching tour out to see the sea.

Top Left: Marlborough vineyard; **Top Right:** Sea kayaking (p222), Abel Tasman National Park

5
DAYS

KAIKOURA TO ABEL TASMAN NATIONAL PARK

GET BUSY

Enough sitting around eating crayfish and swilling wine! Time to burn off some calories.

Around the ❶**Kaikoura** (p205) coast, sea kayaking is a great way to see dolphins and seals. To the northwest, the ❷**Marlborough Sounds** (p201) also offer sea kayaking and plenty of dolphins.

Rather stay dry? Saddle-up on a mountain bike and career along the superbly scenic ❸**Queen Charlotte Track** (p201). Traditionally a tramping route, water taxis now assist bikers to access remote sections of the track, and transport hikers' packs to the next campsite. Weightless walking!

The hills around ❹**Nelson** (p212) further west are also great for mountain biking, or you can defy gravity with a paragliding, kiteboarding or hang gliding lesson, or succumb to its pull with some skydiving. Ask at the i-SITE about local rock-climbing, horse riding and kayaking operators.

The main lure for trampers around here is the stellar Abel Tasman Coast Track in ❺**Abel Tasman National Park** (p219). Tailor your adventure to include sea kayaking along the spectacular coastline.

Discover Marlborough & Nelson

Boats moored at Picton
SIMON GREENWOOD/GETTY IMAGES ©

MARLBOROUGH REGION

Picton

Half asleep in winter, but hyperactive in summer (with up to eight fully laden ferry arrivals per day), boaty Picton clusters around a deep gulch at the head of Queen Charlotte Sound. It's the main traveller port for the South Island, and the best base for tackling the Marlborough Sounds and Queen Charlotte Track.

◎ Sights & Activities

Edwin Fox Maritime Museum   Museum
(www.edwinfoxsociety.co.nz; Dunbar Wharf; adult/child $10/4; ⊘9am-5pm) Purportedly the world's third-oldest wooden ship, the *Edwin Fox* was built in Calcutta and launched in 1853. During its chequered career it carried troops to the Crimean War, convicts to Australia and immigrants to NZ. This museum has maritime exhibits, including the venerable old dear herself.

Eco World Aquarium   Wildlife Centre
(www.ecoworldnz.co.nz; Dunbar Wharf; adult/child/family $22/10/55; ⊘10am-5.30pm Oct-Apr, to 4pm May-Sep) ✐
The primary purpose of this centre is animal rehabilitation: all sorts of critters come here for fix-ups and rest-ups, and the odd bit of hanky panky! Special specimens include NZ's 'living dinosaur' – the tuatara – as well as blue penguins, geckos and giant weta. Fish-feeding time (11am and 2pm) is a splashy spectacle.

Sleeping

Buccaneer Lodge
Lodge $

(☎03-573 5002; www.buccaneerlodge.co.nz; 314 Waikawa Rd; s/d/tr $75/85/110; @🛜) Enthusiastic owners have spruced up this Waikawa Bay lodge to offer good en suite rooms, many with expansive views from the 1st-floor balcony. It also has courtesy town transfers, free bike hire and the pretty foreshore just five minutes' walk away.

Harbour View Motel
Motel $$

(☎03-573 6259, 0800 101 133; www.harbourviewpicton.co.nz; 30 Waikawa Rd; d $125-200; 🛜) The elevated position of this motel commands good views of Picton's mast-filled harbour from its tastefully decorated, self-contained studios with timber decks.

Gables B&B
B&B $$

(☎03-573 6772; www.thegables.co.nz; 20 Waikawa Rd; s $100, d $140-170, units $155-200, all incl breakfast; @🛜) This historic B&B (once home to Picton's mayor) has three individually styled en suite rooms in the main house and two homely self-contained units out the back. Prices drop if you organise your own breakfast. Lovely hosts show good humour (ask about the Muffin Club).

Whatamonga Homestay
Homestay $$

(☎03-573 7192; www.whsl.co.nz; 425 Port Underwood Rd; d incl breakfast $175; @🛜) Follow Waikawa Rd, which becomes Port Underwood Rd, for 8km and you'll bump into this classy waterside option – two self-contained units with king-sized beds and balconies with magic views. Two other rooms under the main house (also with views) share a bathroom. Free kayaks, dinghies and fishing gear are available.

Eating

Picton Village Bakkerij
Bakery $

(cnr Auckland & Dublin Sts; bakery items $3-8; ⏰6am-4pm) Dutch owners bake trays of European goodies here, including interesting breads, filled rolls, cakes and custardy, tarty treats. An excellent stop before or after the ferry.

Gusto
Cafe $

(33 High St; meals $14-20; ⏰7.30am-2.30pm; 🍴) This friendly and hardworking joint does beaut breakfasts including first-class salmon-scrambled eggs and a 'Morning Glory' fry-up worth the calories. Lunch options may include local mussels or a steak sandwich.

Le Café
Cafe $$

(www.lecafepicton.co.nz; London Quay; lunch $12-24, dinner $20-34; ⏰7.30am-10.30pm; 🍴) A perennially popular spot both for its quayside location, dependable food and Havana coffee. The likes of salami sandwiches and sweets are in the cabinet, while a good antipasto platter, generous pasta, local mussels, lamb and fish dishes feature à la carte. Laid-back atmosphere, craft beer and occasional live gigs make this a good evening hang-out.

ℹ️ Information

Picton i-SITE (☎03-520 3113; www.lovemarlborough.co.nz; Foreshore; ⏰9am-5pm Mon-Fri, to 4pm Sat & Sun) All vital tourist info including maps, Queen Charlotte Track information, lockers and transport bookings. Dedicated Department of Conservation (DOC) counter.

ℹ️ Getting There & Away

Make bookings for nationwide transport at Picton i-SITE.

Air

Soundsair (☎03-520 3080, 0800 505 005; www.soundsair.co.nz) flies daily between Picton and Wellington (adult/child from $95/85); a shuttle bus to/from the airstrip at Koromiko, 8km south, costs $7.

Boat

There are two operators crossing Cook Strait between Picton and Wellington, and, although all ferries leave from more or less the same place, each has its own terminal. The main transport hub (with car-rental depots) is at the Interislander Terminal, which also has public showers, a cafe and internet facilities.

Picton

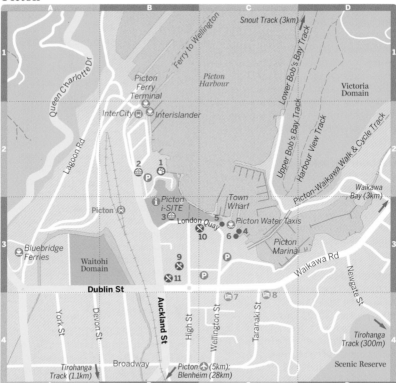

Picton

⊙ Sights
1 Eco World Aquarium B2
2 Edwin Fox Maritime Museum B2
3 Picton Museum B3

⊕ Activities, Courses & Tours
4 Cougar Line C3
5 Dolphin Watch Nature Tours C3
6 Marlborough Sounds
   Adventure Company C3

⊖ Sleeping
7 Gables B&B C4
8 Harbour View Motel C4

⊗ Eating
9 Gusto B3
10 Le Café C3
11 Picton Village Bakkerij B3

Bluebridge Ferries (📞0800 844 844, in
Wellington 04-471 6188; www.bluebridge.
co.nz; adult/child from $51/26; 🛜) Crossings

take 3½ hours, and the company runs up
to four sailings in each direction daily. Cars
and campervans from $118, motorbikes $51,
bicycles $10. The sleeper service arrives in
Picton at 6am.

Interislander (📞0800 802 802; www.
interislander.co.nz; adult/child $55/28)
Crossings take three hours 10 minutes; up to
five sailings in each direction daily. Cars are
priced from $118, campervans (up to 5.5m)
from $133, motorbikes $56, bicycles $15.

Bus

Buses serving Picton depart from the
Interislander terminal or nearby i-SITE.

InterCity (📞03-365 1113; www.intercity.
co.nz) runs south to Christchurch (5½ hours) via
Blenheim (30 minutes), Kaikoura (2½ hours),
with connections to Dunedin, Queenstown and
Invercargill. Services also run to/from Nelson
(2¼ hours), with connections to Motueka and the

Exploring the Marlborough Sounds

The Marlborough Sounds are a maze of peaks, bays, beaches and watery reaches, formed when the sea flooded deep river valleys after the last ice age. Roads are predominantly narrow and occasionally unsealed, so allow plenty of driving time and keep your wits about you.

Sounds travel is invariably quicker by boat (for example, Punga Cove from Picton by car takes two to three hours, but just 45 minutes by boat). Fortunately, an armada of vessels offer scheduled and on-demand boat services, with the bulk operating out of Picton for the Queen Charlotte Sound, and some from Havelock for Kenepuru and Pelorus Sounds.

TOURS & TRANSPORT

Cougar Line (03-573 7925, 0800 504 090; www.cougarlinecruises.co.nz; Town Wharf; track round trip $105, full-day tour from $80) Queen Charlotte Track transport, plus various half- and full-day cruise/walk trips, including the rather special (and flexible) ecocruise to Motuara Island and a Ship Cove picnic.

Marlborough Sounds Adventure Company (03-573 6078, 0800 283 283; www.marlboroughsounds.co.nz; Town Wharf; half- to 3-day packages $85-545) Bike-walk-kayak trips, with options to suit every inclination and duration. A top day option is the kayak & hike ($175).

Dolphin Watch Nature Tours (03-573 8040, 0800 945 354; www.naturetours.co.nz; Town Wharf; dolphin swimming/viewing $165/99, other tours from $75) Half-day 'swim with dolphins' and wildlife tours including trips to Motuara Island.

Myths & Legends Eco-Tours (03-573 6901; www.eco-tours.co.nz; half-/full-day cruises $200/250) A chance to get out on the water with a local Maori family – longtime locals, storytellers and environmentalists.

Picton Water Taxis (027 227 0284, 03-573 7853; www.pictonwatertaxis.co.nz) Water taxi and sightseeing trips around Queen Charlotte, on demand.

West Coast. At least one bus daily on each of these routes connects with a Wellington ferry service.

Smaller shuttle buses running from Picton to Christchurch include Atomic Shuttles (03-349 0697, 0508 108 359; www.atomictravel.co.nz), which can also be booked via Naked Bus (www.nakedbus.com).

Train

KiwiRail Scenic (04-495 0775, 0800 872 467; www.kiwirailscenic.co.nz) runs the *Coastal Pacific* service daily (October to May) each way between Picton and Christchurch via Blenheim and Kaikoura (and 22 tunnels and 175 bridges!), departing Christchurch at 7am and Picton at 1pm. Adult one-way Picton–Christchurch fares range from $79 to $159. The service connects with the Interislander ferry.

Queen Charlotte Track

The hugely popular, meandering, 70km **Queen Charlotte Track** (www.qctrack.co.nz; ⊙ some parts closed in summer) offers gorgeous coastal scenery on its way from historic Ship Cove to Anakiwa, passing through a mixture of privately owned land and DOC reserves.

Queen Charlotte is a well-defined track, suitable for people of average fitness. Numerous boat and tour operators service the track, allowing you to walk the whole three- to five-day journey, or start and finish where you like, on foot or by kayak or bike.

Detour:
Kenepuru & Pelorus Sounds

Kenepuru and Pelorus Sounds, to the west of Queen Charlotte Sound, are less populous and therefore offer fewer traveller services, including transport. There's some cracking scenery, however, and those with time to spare will be well rewarded by their explorations.

Havelock is the hub of this area, the western bookend of the 35km Queen Charlotte Drive (Picton being the eastern) and the self-proclaimed Greenshell Mussel Capital of the World. While hardly the most rock and roll of NZ towns, Havelock offers most necessities, including accommodation, fuel and food.

For finer detail, including a complete list of visitor services, visit www. pelorusnz.co.nz, which covers Havelock, Kenepuru and Pelorus Sounds, and the extremities of French Pass and D'Urville Island.

Sleeping & Eating

The beauty of the Queen Charlotte Track is that there are plenty of great day-trip options, allowing you to base yourself in Picton. However, there is also plenty of accommodation, nicely spaced along the way, and boat operators will transport your luggage along the track for you. Unless you're camping, it pays to book your accommodation *waaay* in advance, especially in summer.

Numerous cafes are also dotted along the track, the majority of which will only be in full swing during high summer. A complete list of sleeping and eating options can be found in the official Queen Charlotte Track Directory (www.qctrack.co.nz).

Information

The best place to get track information and advice is Picton i-SITE (p199), which also handles bookings for transport and accommodation. See also the online Queen Charlotte Track Directory (www.qctrack.co.nz).

Blenheim

Blenheim is an agricultural town 29km south of Picton on the Wairau Plain between the Wither Hills and the Richmond Ranges. The town demonstrates little power as a visitor magnet; it is the attractions beyond the back fence that pull in the punters.

Sights & Activities

Omaka Aviation Heritage Centre
Museum

(www.omaka.org.nz; 79 Aerodrome Rd; adult/child/family $25/10/62; ⊙10am-5pm) This captivating museum houses a splendid collection of original and replica Great War aircraft brought to life in a series of dioramas that depict dramatic wartime scenes, such as the death of the Red Baron. Memorabilia and photographic displays deepen the experience. The guided tour is an extra $5 extremely well spent. A cafe and shop are on-site, and next door is **Omaka Classic Cars** (www.omakaclassiccars.co.nz; adult/child $10/free; ⊙10am-4pm), which houses more than 100 vehicles from the '50s to the '80s.

High Country Horse Treks
Horse Riding

(☑03-577 9424; www.high-horse.co.nz; 961 Taylor Pass Rd; 1-3hr treks $50-120) These animal-mad folks run horse treks for all abilities from their base 11km southwest of town (call for directions).

Sleeping

BLENHEIM TOWN

171 on High Motel $$
(☑03-579 5098, 0800 587 856; www.171onhighmotel.co.nz; 171 High St; d $145-185; @ 🛜) A

welcoming option close to town, these tasteful, splash-o-colour studios and apartments are bright and breezy in the daytime, warm and shimmery in the evening. Expect a wide complement of facilities and 'extra mile' service.

WINE REGION ACCOMMODATION

Watson's Way Lodge
Lodge $

(☎03-572 8228; www.watsonswaylodge. com; 56 High St, Renwick; dm $30, d $70-90; ⊗closed Aug-Sep; @ 🛜) This traveller-focused, purpose-built hostel has spick-and-span rooms, mainly twins and doubles, some with en suite. There are spacious leafy gardens dotted with fruit trees and hammocks, an outdoor claw-foot bath, bikes for hire (guest/ public rate $18/28 per day) and local information aplenty.

Olde Mill House
B&B $$

(☎03-572 8458; www.oldemillhouse.co.nz; 9 Wilson St, Renwick; d $150; @ 🛜) On an elevated section in otherwise flat Renwick, this charming old house is a treat. Dyed-in-the-wool local hosts run a welcoming B&B, with stately decor, and home-grown fruit and homemade goodies for breakfast. Free bikes, outdoor spa and gardens make this a tip-top choice in the heart of the wine country.

St Leonards
Cottages $$

(☎03-577 8328; www.stleonards.co.nz; 18 St Leonards Rd; d $120-350, extra adult $35; 🛜⊠) Tucked into the grounds of an 1886 homestead, these four rustic cottages offer privacy and a reason to stay put. Each is unique in its layout and perspective on the gardens and vines. Our pick is the Stables, with its lemon-grove view. Anyone for tennis?

Vintners Hotel
Hotel $$$

(☎03-572 5094, 0800 684 190; www.mvh. co.nz; 190 Rapaura Rd; d $260-295; 🛜) Sixteen architecturally designed suites make the most of valley views and boast wet-room bathrooms and abstract art. The

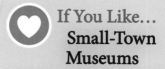

If You Like...
Small-Town Museums

If you like the rather amazing Omaka Aviation Heritage Centre in Blenheim, here are a few other small-town museums chock-full of local lore.

1 **MARLBOROUGH MUSEUM**
(www.marlboroughmuseum.org.nz; 26 Arthur Baker Pl, off New Renwick Rd, Blenheim; adult/child $10/5; ⊗10am-4pm) Besides a replica township, vintage mechanicals, and well-presented historical displays, there's the Wine Exhibition, for those looking to cap off their vineyard experiences.

2 **KAIKOURA MUSEUM**
(www.kaikoura.govt.nz; West End; adult/child $5/1; ⊗10am-4.30pm Mon-Fri, 2-4pm Sat & Sun) Housed in the new council building along with the library, this provincial museum displays historical photographs, Maori and colonial artefacts, a huge sperm-whale jaw and the fossilised remains of a plesiosaur.

3 **PICTON MUSEUM**
(London Quay; adult/child $5/1; ⊗10am-4pm) If you dig local history – whaling, sailing and the 1964 Roller Skating Champs – this will float your boat. The photo displays are well worth a look, especially for five bucks.

stylish reception building has a bar and restaurant opening out on to a cherry orchard and organic vegie garden.

Stonehaven
B&B $$$

(☎03-572 9730; www.stonehavenhomestay. co.nz; 414 Rapaura Rd; d incl breakfast $275-295; @ 🛜⊠) A stellar stone-and-timber B&B nestled among the picturesque vines, with two en suite guest rooms. Beds are piled high with pillows, breakfast is served in the summer house, and dinner is available by prior arrangement with rare wines from the cellar.

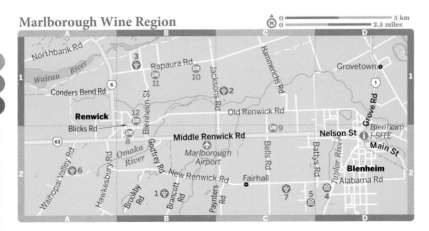

Marlborough Wine Region

Marlborough Wine Region

◎ Sights

✕ Eating & Drinking

Ritual Cafe   Cafe $

(10 Maxwell Rd; meals $7-18; ⊙7am-4pm Mon-Wed, to 10pm Thu-Sat) This hip joint, with its B-movie decor, booths and up-cycled furniture, is where Blenheim's cool cats come to purr over great coffee, all-day eggy brekkies and a counter-full of pastries and salads. Find excellent smoothie hangover cures here, too.

BV Gourmet   Deli, Cafe $

(www.bvgourmet.co.nz; 2a Park Tce; snacks $4-8; ⊙8am-5pm Mon-Fri, 9am-3pm Sat & Sun) Micro-sized cafe serving a compact range of pastries, salads, sweets and notable coffee. Picnickers will delight at the gluttonous selection of cheeses, meats and treats from NZ artisan producers and overseas.

Dodson Street   Craft Beer

(www.dodsonstreet.co.nz; 1 Dodson St) Pub and garden with a beer hall ambience and suitably Teutonic menu (mains $17 to $27) featuring pork knuckle, wurst and schnitzel. Stars of the show are the 24 taps pouring quality craft beer including next-door neighbour Renaissance, the 2013 Brewer's Guild champion.

ℹ Information

Blenheim i-SITE (☏03-577 8080, 0800 777 181; www.lovemarlborough.com; Railway Station; ⊙8.30am-5.30pm Mon-Fri, 9am-5pm Sat, 9am-4pm Sun) Information on Marlborough and beyond. Wine-trail maps and bookings for everything under the sun.

ℹ Getting There & Around

Air

Marlborough Airport (www.marlboroughairport. co.nz) is 6km west of town on Middle Renwick Rd.
Air New Zealand (☏0800 747 000; www. airnewzealand.co.nz) Has direct flights to/from Wellington, Auckland and Christchurch with onward connections.

Soundsair (☏0800 505 005, 03-520 3080; www.soundsair.com) Connects Blenheim with Wellington and Paraparaumu.

Bus

InterCity (☏03-365 1113; www.intercity.co.nz) Buses run daily from the Blenheim i-SITE to Picton (30 minutes) and Nelson (1¾ hours). Buses also head down south to Christchurch (two daily) via Kaikoura.

Naked Bus (www.nakedbus.com) Tickets bargain seats on some of the same services as InterCity, and on its own buses on major routes.

Blenheim Shuttles (☏03-577 5277, 0800 577 527; www.blenheimshuttles.co.nz) Offers shuttles (and tours) around Blenheim and the wider Marlborough region.

Train

KiwiRail Scenic (☏04-495 0775, 0800 872 467; www.kiwirailscenic.co.nz) runs the daily *Coastal Pacific* service, stopping at Blenheim en route to Picton (from $29; runs October to May) heading north, and Christchurch (from $79) via Kaikoura (from $49) heading south.

Kaikoura

Take SH1 132km southeast from Blenheim (or 183km north from Christchurch) and you'll encounter Kaikoura, a pretty peninsula town backed by the snow-capped Seaward Kaikoura Range. Few places in the world are home to such a variety of easily spottable wildlife: whales, dolphins, NZ fur seals, penguins, shearwaters, petrels and wandering albatross all live in the area or pass by.

◎ Sights

Point Kean
Seal Colony   Wildlife Reserve
At the end of the peninsula seals laze around in the grass and on the rocks, lapping up all the attention. Give them a wide berth (10m), and never get between them and the sea – they will attack if they feel cornered and can move surprisingly fast.

Fyffe House   Historic Building
(www.fyffehouse.co.nz; 62 Avoca St; adult/child $10/free; ◷10am-5.30pm daily Nov-Apr, to 4pm Thu-Mon May-Oct) Kaikoura's oldest

Taylor River, Blenheim (p202)

PHILIP NORTON/GETTY IMAGES ©

Don't Miss
Marlborough Wine Region

Marlborough is NZ's vinous colossus, producing around three quarters of the country's wine. Sunny days and cool nights create the perfect conditions for cool-climate grapes: world-famous sauvignon blanc, top-notch pinot noir, and notable chardonnay, riesling, Gewürztraminer, pinot gris and bubbly.

A TASTE OF THE TASTINGS

Pick up a copy of *The Marlborough Wine Trail* map from the Blenheim i-SITE (p204) or download a copy online at www.wine-marlborough.co.nz.

Brancott Estate (www.brancottestate.com; 180 Brancott Rd) Ubermodern cellar door and restaurant complex overlooking one of the original sauvignon blanc vineyards.

Cloudy Bay (www.cloudybay.co.nz; Jacksons Rd) 🍃 Globally coveted sauvignon blanc, bubbly and pinot noir, and Jack's Raw Bar Summer Sundays for shucked oysters and clams.

Spy Valley Wines (www.spyvalleywine.co.nz; 37 Lake Timara Rd, Waihopai Valley) 🍃 Stylish, edgy architecture at this espionage-themed winery, with great wines across the board.

Wither Hills (www.witherhills.co.nz; 211 New Renwick Rd) 🍃 One of the region's flagship wineries. Premium wines and enthralling winemaker-for-a-day tours ($45).

WINE TOURS

Wine tours are generally conducted in a minibus, last between four and seven hours, take in four to seven wineries and range in price from $65 to $95 (with a few grand tours up to around $200 for the day, including a winery lunch). **Highlight Wine Tours** (☎03-577-9046, 0800 494 638; www.highlightwinetours.co.nz) and **Bubbly Grape** (☎0800 228 2253, 027 672 2195; www.bubblygrape.co.nz) are the *grand crus*.

surviving building, Fyffe House's whalebone foundations were laid in 1844. Proudly positioned and fronted with a colourful garden, the little two-storey cottage offers a fascinating insight into the lives of colonial settlers. Interpretive displays are complemented by historic objects, while peeling wallpaper and the odd cobweb lend authenticity.

 Activities

There's a safe swimming **beach** in front of the Esplanade, alongside which is a **pool** (adult/child $3/2; 10am-5pm Nov-Mar) if you have a salt aversion.

Decent **surfing** can be found in the area, too, particularly at **Mangamaunu Beach** (15km north of town), where there's a 500m point break, which is fun in good conditions. Get the low-down, organise transport, learn to surf or hire gear from **Board Silly Surf Adventures** (☏ 027 418 8900, 0800 787 352; 134 Southbay Pde; 3hr lesson $75, board & wetsuit from $45) based at South Bay. Gear hire and advice is also available from **R&R Sport** (www.rrsport.co.nz; 14 West End) and **Surf Kaikoura** (www.surfkaikoura.co.nz; 4 Beach Rd).

Kaikoura Peninsula Walkway
Walking

A foray along this walkway is a must-do. Starting from the town, the three- to four-hour loop heads out to Point Kean, along the cliffs to South Bay, then back to town over the isthmus (or in reverse, of course). En route you'll see fur seals and red-billed seagull and shearwater colonies. Lookouts and interesting interpretive panels abound. Collect a map at the i-SITE or follow your nose.

Kaikoura Coast Track
Walking

(☏ 03-319 2715; www.kaikouratrack.co.nz; $230) This easy three-day, 37km, self-guided walk across private farmland combines coastal and alpine views. The price includes three nights' farm-cottage accommodation and pack transport; BYO sleeping bag and food. Starts 45km south of Kaikoura.

Tours

WHALE-WATCHING

Whale Watch Kaikoura
Ecotour

(☏ 03-319 6767, 0800 655 121; www.whalewatch. co.nz; Railway Station; 3hr tour adult/child $145/60) ✎ With knowledgeable guides and fascinating 'world of whales' onboard animation, Kaikoura's biggest operator heads out on boat trips to introduce you to some of the big fellas. It'll refund 80% of your fare if no whales are sighted (success rate: 98%). If this trip is a must for you, allow a few days flexibility in case the weather turns to custard.

Kaikoura Helicopters
Scenic Flights

(☏ 03-319 6609; www.worldofwhales.co.nz; Railway Station; 15-60min flight from $100-490) Reliable whale-spotting flights (standard 30-minute tour $220 each for three or more people), plus jaunts around the peninsula, Mt Fyffe and peaks beyond.

Wings over Whales
Ecotour

(☏ 0800 226 629, 03-319 6580; www.whales. co.nz; 30min flight adult/child $180/75) Light-plane flights departing from Kaikoura Airport, 7km south of town. Spotting success rate: 95%.

DOLPHIN- & SEAL-SPOTTING

Seal Swim Kaikoura
Ecotour

(☏ 03-319 6182, 0800 732 579; www.sealswim-kaikoura.co.nz; 58 West End; tours $70-110, viewing adult/child $55/35; ☺ Oct-May) Take a (warmly wetsuited) swim with Kaikoura's healthy population of playful seals – including very cute pups – on two-hour guided snorkelling tours run by the Chambers family. Shore or boat options available.

Dolphin Encounter
Ecotour

(☏ 0800 733 365, 03-319 6777; www.encounterkaikoura.co.nz; 96 Esplanade; swim adult/child $175/155, observation $90/45; ☺ tours 8.30am & 12.30pm year-round, plus 5.30am Nov-Apr) Here's your chance to rub shoulders with pods of dusky dolphins on three-hour tours. Limited numbers, so book in advance.

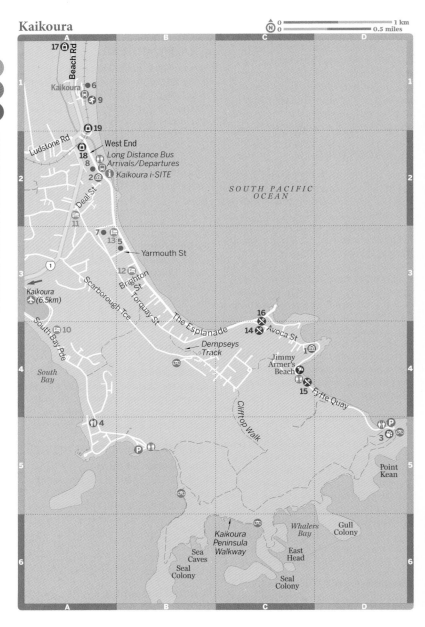

Kaikoura Kayaks
Kayaking

(03-319 7118, 0800 452 456; www.kaikour-akayaks.co.nz; 19 Killarney St; 3hr tours adult/child $95/70; tours 8.30am, 12.30pm & 4.30pm Nov-Apr, 9am & 1pm May-Oct) Excellent guided sea-kayak tours to view fur seals and explore the peninsula's coastline. Family-friendly, kayak fishing and other on-demand trips available, plus freedom kayak and paddle board hire.

Kaikoura

BIRDWATCHING

Albatross Encounter — Birdwatching

(☎03-319 6777, 0800 733 365; www.encounterkaikoura.co.nz; 96 Esplanade; adult/child $115/55; ⏱tours 9am & 1pm year-round, plus 6am Nov-Apr) Kaikoura is heaven for bird-nerds, who fly at the opportunity for a close encounter with pelagic species such as shearwaters, shags, mollymawks, petrels and the inimitable albatross.

FISHING

Fishing is a common obsession in Kaikoura, with local boaties angling for any excuse to go out for a little look-sea. It's a good opportunity to *kai koura* (eat crayfish). Trips start from around $60; the **i-SITE** (☎03-319 5641; www.kaikoura.co.nz; West End; ⏱9am-5pm Mon-Fri, to 4pm Sat & Sun, extended hours Dec-Mar) has a full list of operators.

Fishing at Kaikoura — Fishing

(☎03-319 3003; gerard.diedrichs@xtra.co.nz) Fishing, crayfishing, scenic tours and water-skiing, on the 6m *Sophie-Rose*.

Kaikoura Fishing Tours — Fishing

(☎0800 246 6597; www.kaikoura-fishing-tours.co.nz) Serious about scenery and seafood. Your catch is filleted ready for dinner.

WALKING & CYCLING

For town riding, hire bicycles from R&R Sport (p207) and Surf Kaikoura (p207).

Walks Kaikoura — Walking

(☎027 473 2659, 027 437 2426; www.walkskaikoura.com; half-/full day from $75/145) Experienced local guides offer tailored walks around the area, from mountains to coast with heli options, plus cycle tours on quiet sealed roads and the newly developed riverside trail.

OTHER TOURS

Maori Tours Kaikoura — Cultural Tour

(☎03-319 5567, 0800 866 267; www.maoritours.co.nz; 3½hr tour adult/child $134/74; ⏱tours 9am & 1.30pm) Fascinating half-day, small-group tours laced with Maori hospitality and local lore. Visit historic sites, hear legends and learn indigenous use of trees and plants. Advance bookings required.

🛏 Sleeping

Dylan's Country Cottages — Cottages $$

(☎03-319 5473; www.lavenderfarm.co.nz; 268 Postmans Rd; d $195; ⏱closed May-Aug; 🛜) On the grounds of the delightful Kaikoura Lavender Farm, northwest of town, these two self-contained cottages make for an aromatic escape from the seaside fray. One has a private outdoor bath and a shower emerging from a tree; the other an indoor spa and handkerchief lawn. Homemade scones, preserves and free-range eggs for breakfast. Sweet, stylish and romantic.

Kaikoura
Cottage Motels
Motel $$

(☎ 03-319 5599, 0800 526 882; www.kaikoura-cottagemotels.co.nz; cnr Old Beach & Mill Rds; d $140-160; ☎) This enclave of eight modern tourist flats looks mighty fine, surrounded by attractive native plantings. Oriented for mountain views, the self-contained units sleep four between an open plan studio-style living room and one private bedroom. Soothing sand-and-sky colour scheme and quality furnishings.

Bay Cottages
Motel $$

(☎ 03-319 5506; www.baycottages.co.nz; 29 South Bay Pde; cottage $100, motel $130; ☎) Here's a great-value option on South Bay, a few kilometres south of town: five tourist cottages with kitchenette and bathroom that sleep up to four, and two slick motel rooms with stainless-steel benches, a warm feel and clean lines. The cheery owner may even take you crayfishing in good weather.

Sails Motel
Motel $$

(☎ 03-319 6145; www.sailsmotel.co.nz; 134 Esplanade; d $120-140, q $170; ☎) There are no sea views (nor sails) at this motel, so the cherubic owners have to impress with quality. Their four secluded, tastefully appointed self-contained units are down a driveway in a garden setting (private outdoor areas abound).

Nikau Lodge
B&B $$$

(☎ 03-319 6973; www.nikaulodge.com; 53 Deal St; d $190-260; @ ☎) A waggly-tailed welcome awaits at this beautiful B&B high on the hill with grand-scale vistas. Five en suite rooms are plush and comfy, with additional satisfaction arriving in the form of cafe-quality breakfasts accompanied by fresh local coffee. Good humour, home baking, free wi-fi, complimentary drinks, a hot tub and blooming gardens: you may want to move in.

Waves on the
Esplanade
Apartments $$$

(☎ 03-319 5890, 0800 319 589; www.kaikouraapartments.co.nz; 78 Esplanade; apt $240-350; ☎) Can't do without the comforts of home? Here you go: spacious, luxury two-bedroom apartments with Sky TV, DVD player, two bathrooms, laundry facilities and full kitchen. Oh, and superb ocean views from the balcony. Rates are for up to four people.

Crayfish and green-lipped mussels in Kaikoura

✖ Eating & Drinking

Reserve Hutt
Cafe $

(72 West End; meals $10-20; ◷9am-3pm) The best coffee in the town centre, roasted on-site and espressed by dedicated baristas in Kaikoura's grooviest cafe. Puttin' out that rootsy retro-Kiwiana vibe we love so much, this is a neat place to linger over a couple of flatties and down a muffin, delicious ham croissant or the full eggy brunch.

Cafe Encounter
Cafe $

(96 Esplanade; meals $8-23; ◷7am-5pm; 📶✎) This cafe in the Encounter Kaikoura complex is more than just somewhere to wait for your trip. The cabinet houses respectable sandwiches, pastries and cakes, plus there's a tasteful range of daily specials such as pork schnitzel and fennel slaw. A sunny patio provides sea views.

Pier Hotel
Pub $$

(✎03-319 5037; www.thepierhotel.co.nz; 1 Avoca St; lunch $15-23, dinner $27-38; ◷11am-late) Situated in the town's primo seaside spot, with panoramic views, the historic Pier Hotel is a friendly and inviting place for a drink or a meal, whether outside or inside the character-filled public bar or dining rooms. Upstairs lodgings are worn and creaky, but good value (double room, including breakfast, from $90).

Green Dolphin
Modern NZ $$$

(✎03-319 6666; www.greendolphinkaikoura. com; 12 Avoca St; mains $25-39; ◷5-11pm) Kaikoura's consistent top-ender continues to dish up high-quality produce including seafood, beef, lamb and venison, as well as seasonal flavours such as fresh tomato soup. There are lovely home-made pasta dishes, too. The hefty drinks list demands attention, featuring exciting aperitifs, craft beer, interesting wines and more. Booking ahead is advisable, especially if you want to secure a table by the window and watch the daylight fade.

♥ If You Like...
Kaikoura Seafood

If you like the seafood offerings at Green Dolphin in Kaikoura, here are a few less-formal ways to get some *koura* (crayfish) on your plate. Unfortunately (some say unnecessarily), it's pricey – at a restaurant, you'll (pardon the pun) shell out around $55 for half a cray or over $100 for the whole beast. But the following options will save you a few dollars.

1 **KAIKOURA SEAFOOD BBQ**
(Fyffe Quay; items from $5; ◷10.30am-7pm) Conveniently located on the way to the Point Kean Seal Colony, this longstanding roadside barbecue is a great spot to sample local seafood, including crayfish and scallops, at an affordable price.

2 **NINS BIN**
(SH1; ◷8am-6pm) You can buy fresh, cooked or uncooked crays from the iconic Nins Bin, a surf-side caravan 23km north of town. Upwards of $50 should get you a decent specimen.

3 **CODS & CRAYFISH**
(81 Beach Rd; ◷8am-6pm) Fresh, cooked or uncooked crays.

---

❶ Information

Kaikoura i-SITE (✎03-319 5641; www.kaikoura. co.nz; West End; ◷9am-5pm Mon-Fri, to 4pm Sat & Sun, extended hours Dec-Mar) Helpful staff make tour, accommodation and transport bookings, and help with DOC-related matters.

❶ Getting There & Away

Bus

InterCity (✎03-365 1113; www.intercity.co.nz) Buses run between Kaikoura and Nelson (3½ hours), Picton (2¼ hours) and Christchurch (2¾ hours).

Atomic Shuttles (✎0508 108 359, 03-349 0697; www.atomictravel.co.nz) Services Kaikoura on its Christchurch to Picton run, which links with destinations as far afield as Nelson, Queenstown and Invercargill.

Naked Bus (📞0900 625 33; www.nakedbus.com) Tickets bargain seats on its own buses on major routes, and on other services dependent on capacity.

Train

KiwiRail Scenic (📞0800 872 467; www.kiwirailscenic.co.nz) runs the daily *Coastal Pacific* service, stopping at Kaikoura en route to Picton (from $59, 2¼ hours; runs October to May), and Christchurch (from $49, three hours). The northbound train departs Kaikoura at 9.54am; the southbound at 3.28pm.

NELSON REGION

Nelson

Dishing up a winning combination of great weather and beautiful surroundings, Nelson is hailed as one of New Zealand's most 'liveable' cities. In summer it fills up with local and international visitors, who lap up its diverse offerings.

🎯 Sights

Christ Church Cathedral   Church
(www.nelsoncathedral.org; Trafalgar Sq; ⏱8am-7pm Nov-Mar, to 5pm Apr-Oct) FREE The enduring symbol of Nelson, the art deco Christ Church Cathedral lords it over the city from the top of Trafalgar St. The best time to visit is during the 10am and 6pm Sunday services when you can hear the organist and choir on song.

Nelson Provincial Museum   Museum
(www.nelsonmuseum.co.nz; cnr Hardy & Trafalgar Sts; adult/child $7/5; ⏱10am-5pm Mon-Fri, to 4.30pm Sat & Sun) This modern museum space is filled with cultural heritage and natural history exhibits which have a regional bias, as well as regular touring exhibitions (for which admission fees vary). It also features a great rooftop garden.

Suter Art Gallery   Gallery
(www.thesuter.org.nz; 208 Bridge St; adult/child $3/50¢, free Sat; ⏱10.30am-4.30pm) Adjacent to Queen's Gardens, Nelson's public art gallery presents changing exhibitions, floor talks, musical and theatrical performances, and films. The Suter undergoes a major renovation from August 2014, so check the website for the re-opening date and details of relocated exhibits.

Tahuna Beach   Beach
Nelson's primo playground takes the form of an epic sandy beach (with lifeguards in summer), backed by a large grassy parkland with a playground, espresso cart, swimming pool, various other recreational facilities and an adjacent restaurant strip. Weekends can get verrrrry busy around here!

Trafalgar Street, Nelson
DAVID WALL PHOTO/GETTY IMAGES ©

Nelson

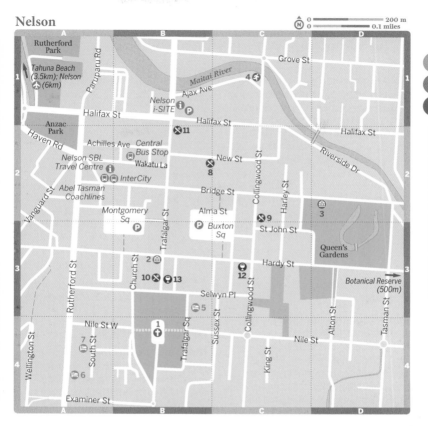

🏃 Activities

WALKING & CYCLING

The classic walk from town is to the **Centre of NZ** atop the **Botanical Reserve** (Milton St), and if you enjoy that then ask about the **Grampians**. The **Dun Mountain Trail** network ranging over the hills to the south of the city centre has lots of interesting options for fit, keen mountain bikers, as does **Codgers MTB Park**. The new **Great Taste Trail** offers flat riding through the craft-beer- and wine-soaked countryside.

UBike   Cycling

(☏0800 282 453; www.ubike.co.nz; Collingwood St Bridge; half-/full day $40/60) A short walk from the i-SITE, UBike hires city and mountain bikes from its riverside caravan.

Nelson

The Wondrous World of WearableArt

Nelson exudes creativity, so it's hardly surprising that NZ's most inspiring fashion show was born here. It began humbly in 1987 when creator Suzie Moncrieff held a local off-beat fashion show. The concept was to create a piece of art that could be worn and modelled. The idea caught on, and the World of WearableArt Awards Show became an annual event.

The awards show has been transplanted to Wellington, but you can ogle entries at Nelson's **World of WearableArt & Classic Cars Museum** (WOW; www. wowcars.co.nz; 1 Cadillac Way; adult/child $22/8; ☉10am-5pm). High-tech galleries include a carousel mimicking a catwalk, and a glow-in-the-dark room.

More car than bra? Under the same roof are around 50 mint-condition classic cars and motorbikes. Exhibits change, but may include a 1959 pink Cadillac, a yellow 1950 Bullet Nose Studebaker convertible and a BMW bubble car. You can view another 70 vehicles in *The Classic Collection* next door ($8 extra).

Has trail maps and tips, plus espresso to get you going.

Gentle Cycling Company   Cycling
(☏03-929 5652, 0800 932 453; www.gentlecy-cling.co.nz; 5-/8hr tours $75/80) Self-guided cycle tours along the Great Taste Trail, with drop-ins (and tastings) at wineries, breweries, cafes and occasional galleries. Freedom bike hire (per day $45) and shuttles also available.

Biking Nelson   Mountain Biking
(☏021 861 725, 0800 224 532; www.bikingnel-son.co.nz; 3hr guided ride $115, bike hire half-/full day $45/65) Hit Nelson's mountain-bike trails with Dave and crew, who run entry-level to hard-core guided rides (all gear provided) and offer freedom rental and advice.

PARAGLIDING, KITESURFING & PADDLE BOARDING

Nelson is a great place to get high or undry, with plenty of action in summer, particularly around the rather divine Tahuna Beach (p212). Tandem paragliding costs around $180, introductory kitesurf-ing starts at $150, and paddle-board hire is around $25 per hour. Operators include **Nelson Paragliding** (☏03-544 1182; www. nelsonparagliding.co.nz), **Kitescool** (☏021 354 837; www.kitescool.co.nz), **Kite Surf Nelson**

(☏0800 548 363; www.kitesurfnelson.co.nz) and **Supstar** (☏021 0268 5552; www.supstar-boards.co.nz).

OTHER ACTIVITIES

Nelson Bonecarving   Carving
(☏03-546 4275; www.carvingbone.co.nz; 87 Green St, Tahunanui; full-day course $79) Admir-ers of Maori design will love Stephan's acclaimed bonecarving course. He'll supply all materials, tools, instruction, encouragement and cups of tea (plus free pick-up/drop-off in town if needed); you supply inspiration and talent, and you'll emerge with your very own bone carving.

Tours

Bay Tours   Guided Tour
(☏03-548 6486, 0800 229 868; www. baytoursnelson.co.nz; half-/full-day tours from $75/144) Nelson city, region, wine, beer, food and art tours. The full-day scenic tour includes a visit to Kaiteriteri and a cruise in Abel Tasman National Park.

Nelson Tours & Travel   Guided Tour
(☏027 237 5007, 0800 222 373; www.nel-sontoursandtravel.co.nz) CJ and crew run various small-group, flexible tours honing in on Nelson's edible, drinkable elements. The five-hour 'Best of Both Worlds' visits wineries and breweries ($95), or venture

over to the Marlborough wineries on a day-long tour ($160).

Sleeping

Accents on the Park   Hostel $
(📞03-548 4335, 0800 888 335; www.accentsonthepark.com; 335 Trafalgar Sq; sites from $15, dm $20-28, d with/without bathroom from $92/60; @ 📶) This perfectly positioned hostel has a hotel feel with its professional staff, balconies, movie nights with free popcorn, free daily bread, wi-fi, soundproofed rooms, quality linen, fresh bathrooms and bikes for hire. On-site, there's also **East St**, a groovy vegetarian cafe and bar.

Te Maunga House   B&B $$
(📞03-548 8605; www.nelsoncityaccommodation.co.nz; 15 Dorothy Annie Way; s $90, d $125-140; 📶) Aptly named ('the mountain'), this grand old family home has exceptional views. Two doubles and a single, with their own bathrooms, are filled with characterful furniture and made up with good linens. Your hearty breakfast can be walked off up and down *that* hill. It's only a 10-minute climb (15 minutes in all, from town), but only the leggy ones will revel in it. Closed from May to September.

Palazzo Motor Lodge   Motel $$
(📞0800 472 5293, 03-545 8171; www.palazzomotorlodge.co.nz; 159 Rutherford St; studio $130-225, apt $230-390; @ 📶) Hosts with the most offer a cheerful welcome at this popular, modern, Italian-tinged motor lodge. The stylish studios and one- and two-room apartments feature enviable kitchens with decent cooking equipment, classy glassware and a dishwasher. The odd bit of dubious art is easily forgiven, particularly as Doris' sausage is available for breakfast.

South Street Cottages   Rental House $$$
(📞03-540 2769; www.cottageaccommodation.co.nz; South St; d from $230; 📶) Stay on NZ's oldest preserved street in one of three elegant, two-bedroom self-contained cottages built in the 1860s. Each has all the comforts of home, including kitchen, laundry and courtyard garden; breakfast provisions supplied. There is a two-night minimum stay.

Lake Rotoroa, Nelson Lakes National Park (p219)

DAVID WALL PHOTO/GETTY IMAGES ©

 Eating

Stefano's
Pizzeria $

(91 Trafalgar St; pizzas $6-29; ◷10am-late; ◿) Located upstairs in the State Cinema complex, this Italian-run joint turns out some of NZ's best pizza. Thin, crispy and delicious, with some variations an absolute bargain. Wash it down with a beer and chase it with a creamy dessert.

DeVille
Cafe $$

(22 New St; meals $11-20; ◷9am-4pm Mon-Sat; ◿) Most of DeVille's tables lie in its sweet walled courtyard, a hidden boho oasis in the inner city and the perfect place for a meal or morning tea. The food's good – from fresh baked goods to a chorizo-burrito brunch, caesar salad and sticky pork sandwich. Open late for live music Friday and Saturday in summer.

Hopgood's
Modern NZ $$$

(◿03-545 7191; www.hopgoods.co.nz; 284 Trafalgar St; mains $34-38; ◷5.30pm-late Mon-Sat, 11.30am-2pm Fri) Tongue-and-groove-lined Hopgood's is perfect for a romantic dinner or holiday treat. The food is decadent and skillfully prepared but unfussy, allowing quality local ingredients to shine. Try Asian crispy duck, or aged beef fillet with wild mushroom gratin. Desirable, predominantly Kiwi wine list. Bookings advisable.

Drinking & Nightlife

Free House
Craft Beer

(www.freehouse.co.nz; 95 Collingwood St) Come rejoice at this church of ales. Tastefully converted from its original, more reverent purpose, it's now home to an excellent, oft-changing selection of NZ craft beers. You can imbibe inside, out, or even in a yurt, where there's regular live music. Hallelujah!

Sprig & Fern
Craft Beer

(www.sprigandfern.co.nz; 280 Hardy St) This outpost of Richmond's Sprig & Fern brewery offers 18 brews on tap, from lager through to doppelbock and berry cider. No pokies, no TV, just decent beer, occasional live music and a pleasant outdoor

area. Pizzas can be ordered in. Look for a second Sprig at 143 Milton St, handy to Founders Park.

Vic
Pub

(www.vicbrewbar.co.nz; 281 Trafalgar St; ◷noon-late) A commendable example of a Mac's Brewbar, with trademark, quirky Kiwiana fit-out, including a knitted stag's head. Quaff a handle of ale, dine on honest pub grub (mains $12 to $33) and tap a toe to regular live music, including open-mic Mondays. Good afternoon sun and people-watching from streetside seating.

ℹ Information

Nelson i-SITE (◿03-548 2304; www.nelsonnz.com; cnr Trafalgar & Halifax Sts; ◷8.30am-5pm Mon-Fri, 9am-4pm Sat & Sun) A slick centre complete with DOC information desk for the low-down on national parks and walks (including Abel Tasman and Heaphy tracks). Pick up a copy of the Nelson Tasman Visitor Guide.

ℹ Getting There & Away

Air

Air New Zealand (◿0800 737 000; www.airnewzealand.co.nz) Has direct flights to/from Wellington, Auckland, Christchurch and Palmerston North.

Soundsair (◿03-520 3080, 0800 505 005; www.soundsair.co.nz) Flies daily between Nelson and Wellington.

Bus

Book Abel Tasman Coachlines, InterCity, KiwiRail Scenic and Interisland ferries at the Nelson SBL Travel Centre (◿03-548 1539; www.nelsoncoachlines.co.nz; 27 Bridge St) or the i-SITE.

Abel Tasman Coachlines (◿03-548 0285; www.abeltasmantravel.co.nz) Operates bus services to Motueka (one hour), Takaka (two hours), Kaiteriteri and Marahau (both two hours).

Atomic Shuttles (◿03-349 0697; www.atomictravel.co.nz) Runs from Nelson to Motueka (one hour), Picton (2¼ hours), Christchurch (7¾ hours) with a Greymouth connection, plus other southern destinations as far as Queenstown, Dunedin and Invercargill.

In Pursuit of Hoppiness

The Nelson region lays claim to the title of craft-brewing capital of New Zealand. World-class hops have been grown here since the 1840s, and a dozen breweries are spread between Nelson and Golden Bay. One is **McCashin's** (www.mccashins.co.nz; 660 Main Rd, Stoke), a ground-breaker in the new era of craft brewing in NZ. Visit them in their historic cider factory for a tasting or tour.

Pick up a copy of the **Nelson Craft Beer Trail** map (available from the i-SITE and other outlets, and online at www.craftbrewingcapital.co.nz) and wind your way between brewers and pubs. Top picks for a tipple include the Free House, McCashin's, the **Moutere Inn** (www.moutereinn.co.nz; 1406 Moutere Hwy; meals $12-30), **Golden Bear** (www.goldenbearbrewing.com; Mapua Wharf; meals $10-20) and the **Mussel Inn** (www.mussellinn.co.nz; 1259 SH60, Onekaka; all-day menu $5-18, dinner $23-30; ⊘11am-late, closed Jul-Aug).

InterCity (☎03-548 1538; www.intercity.co.nz; Bridge St, departs SBL Travel Centre) Runs from Nelson to most key South Island destinations including Picton (two hours), Kaikoura (3½ hours), Christchurch (seven hours) and Greymouth (six hours).

Motueka

Motueka (pronounced Mott-oo-ecka, meaning 'Island of Weka') is a bustling agricultural hub, and a great base from which to explore the region. Stock up here if you're en route to Golden Bay or the Abel Tasman and Kahurangi National Parks.

◎ Sights & Activities

Motueka District Museum
Museum

(140 High St; admission by donation; ⊘10am-4pm Mon-Fri Dec-Mar, 10am-3pm Tue-Fri Apr-Nov) An interesting collection of regional artefacts, housed in a dear old school building.

Hop Federation
Brewery

(☎03-528 0486; www.hopfederation.co.nz; 483 Main Rd, Riwaka) Pop in for tastings and takeaways (fill a flagon), or phone ahead to arrange a tour, at this teeny-weeny but terrific craft brewery 5km from Motueka.

Skydive Abel Tasman
Skydiving

(☎03-528 4091, 0800 422 899; www.skydive. co.nz; Motueka Aerodrome, College St; jumps 13,000ft/16,500ft $299/399) Move over Taupo: we've jumped both and think Mot takes the cake (presumably so do the many sports jumpers who favour this drop zone, some of whom you may see rocketing in).

Tasman Sky Adventures
Scenic Flights

(☎027 229 9693, 0800 114 386; www.skyad-ventures.co.nz; Motueka Aerodrome, 60 College St; 30min flight $205) A rare opportunity to fly in a microlight. Keep your eyes open and blow your mind on a scenic flight above Abel Tasman National Park. Wow. And there's tandem hang gliding for the brave (15/30 minutes, 2500ft/5280ft $195/275).

Sleeping

Equestrian Lodge Motel
Motel **$$**

(☎03-528 9369, 0800 668 782; www.equestri-anlodge.co.nz; Avalon Ct; d $120-156, q $165-220; @⊛⊠) No horses, no lodge, but no matter. This motel complex is close to town (off Tudor St), with expansive lawns, rose gardens, and a heated pool and spa. Rooms are plainly dressed but immaculate, and many have ovens.

Cheerful owners will hook you up with local activities.

Resurgence
Lodge, Chalets $$$

(☎03-528 4664; www.resurgence.co.nz; Riwaka Valley Rd; d lodge from $625, chalets from $525; @🛜🏊) 🍴 Choose a luxurious en suite lodge room or self-contained chalet at this magical green retreat 15 minutes' drive south of Abel Tasman National Park, and 30 minutes' walk from the picturesque source of the Riwaka River. Lodge rates include aperitifs and a four-course dinner, as well as breakfast; chalet rates are for B&B, with dinner an extra $100.

Eating & Drinking

Up the Garden Path
Cafe $$

(www.upthegardenpath.co.nz; 473 High St; meals $15-24; ⏰9am-4pm; 🖊) Perfect for lunch or a coffee break, this licensed cafe-gallery kicks back in an 1890s house amid idyllic gardens. Unleash the kids in the playroom and linger over your blueberry pancakes, chicken burger, lamb souvlaki, pasta or lemon tart. Vegetarian, gluten- and dairy-free options available.

Motueka Sunday Market
Market

(Wallace St; ⏰8am-1pm) On Sunday the car park behind the i-SITE fills up with trestle tables for the Motueka Sunday Market: produce, jewellery, buskers, arts, crafts and Doris' divine bratwurst.

Sprig & Fern
Craft Beer

(www.sprigandfern.co.nz; Wallace St; meals $14-19; ⏰2pm-late) A member of the Sprig & Fern family of taverns, this back-street tavern ups the ante among Motueka's drinking holes. Small but pleasant, with two courtyards, it offers 20 hand-pulled brews, simple food (burgers, pizza, platters) and occasional live music.

ℹ️ Information

Motueka i-SITE (☎03-528 6543; www.motuekaisite.co.nz; 20 Wallace St; ⏰8.30am-5pm Mon-Fri, 9am-4pm Sat & Sun) An excellent centre with helpful staff who handle bookings from Kaitaia to Bluff and provide local national-park expertise and necessaries.

ℹ️ Getting There & Away

Abel Tasman Coachlines (☎03-528 8850; www.abeltasmantravel.co.nz) Runs daily from Motueka to Nelson (one hour), Kaiteriteri (25 minutes) and Marahau (30 minutes).

Atomic Shuttles (☎03-349 0697, 0508 108 359; www.atomictravel.co.nz) Runs from Motueka to Nelson, connecting with further services via Christchurch over to Greymouth and down to Queenstown and Dunedin.

Abel Tasman Coast Track
DAVID WALL PHOTO/GETTY IMAGES ©

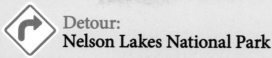

Detour:
Nelson Lakes National Park

Nelson Lakes National Park surrounds two lakes – Rotoiti and Rotoroa – fringed by sweet-smelling beech forest with a backdrop of greywacke mountains. Located at the northern end of the Southern Alps, and with a dramatic glacier-carved landscape, it's an awe-inspiring place to get up high. The park is flush with bird life, and is famous for brown-trout fishing.

Many spectacular walks allow you to appreciate this rugged landscape, but before you tackle them, stop by the **DOC Visitor Centre** (Department of Conservation; ☎ 03-521 1806; www.doc.govt.nz; View Rd; ☺ 8am-4.30pm, to 5pm in summer) for maps, track/weather updates and to pay your hut or camping fees.

The five-hour **Mt Robert Circuit Track** starts south of St Arnaud and circumnavigates the mountain. The optional side trip along Robert Ridge offers staggering views into the heart of the national park. Alternatively, the **St Arnaud Range Track** (five hours return), on the eastern side of the lake, climbs steadily to the ridgeline adjacent to Parachute Rocks.

There are also plenty of shorter (and flatter) walks from Lake Rotoiti's Kerr Bay and the road end at Lake Rotoroa. These and the longer day tramps are described in DOC's *Walks in Nelson Lakes National Park* pamphlet ($2).

The DOC Visitor Centre happily proffers park information (weather, activities), hut passes, plus displays on park ecology and history.

Abel Tasman National Park

Coastal Abel Tasman National Park blankets the northern end of a range of marble and limestone hills that extend from Kahurangi National Park. Various tracks in the park include an inland route, although the coast track is what everyone is here for – it's NZ's most popular Great Walk.

ABEL TASMAN COAST TRACK

This is arguably NZ's most beautiful Great Walk – 51km of sparkling seas, golden sand, quintessential coastal forest, and hidden surprises such as Cleopatra's Pool. A major attraction is the terrain: well cut, well graded and well marked. It's almost impossible to get lost and can be tramped in sneakers.

The entire tramp takes only three to five days, although with water taxi transport you can convert it into an almost endless array of options, particularly if you combine it with a kayak leg. If you can only spare a couple of days, a rewarding option is to loop around the northern end of the park, hiking the Coast Track from Totaranui, passing Anapai and Mutton Cove, overnighting at Whariwharangi Hut, then returning to Totaranui via the **Gibbs Hill Track**.

BOOKINGS & TRANSPORT

Along the Coast Track are four **Great Walk huts** ($32) with bunks, heating and flush toilets but no cooking facilities or lighting. There are also 19 designated **Great Walk campsites** ($14). As the Abel Tasman Track is a Great Walk, all huts and campsites must be booked in advance year-round, either online through **Great Walks Bookings** (☎ 0800 694 732; www.greatwalks.co.nz) or at DOC visitor centres, nationwide.

Moored permanently in Anchorage Bay, **Aquapackers** (☎ 0800 430 744; www.aquapackers.co.nz; Anchorage; dm/d incl

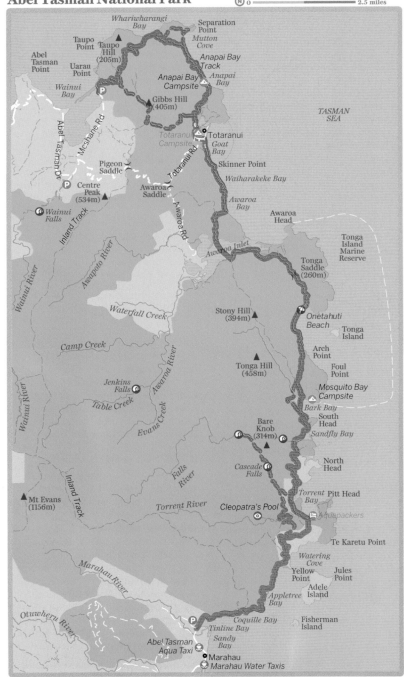

breakfast $75/195) is a converted 13m catamaran providing unusual but buoyant backpacker accommodation. **Totaranui Campsite** (☏03-528 8083; www.doc.govt. nz; summer/winter $15/10) is an extremely popular facility with a whopping capacity (850 campers) and a splendid setting next to the beach backed by some of the best bush in the park.

The closest big town to Abel Tasman is Motueka, with nearby Marahau as the southern gateway. All gateways are serviced between **Abel Tasman Coachlines** (☏03-548 0285; www. abeltasmantravel.co.nz) and **Golden Bay Coachlines** (☏03-525 8352; www. gbcoachlines.co.nz).

Once you hit the park, it is easy to get to/from any point on the track by water taxi, either from Kaiteriteri or Marahau. The following are key operators:

Abel Tasman Sea Shuttle Boat
(☏03-527 8688, 0800 732 748; www. abeltasmanseashuttles. co.nz; Kaiteriteri) Scheduled services with cruise/walk options.

Abel Tasman Aqua Taxi Boat
(☏03-527 8083, 0800 278 282; www. aquataxi.co.nz; Marahau-Sandy Bay Rd, Marahau) Scheduled and on-demand services as well as boat/walk options.

Wilsons Abel Tasman Boat
(☏03-528 2027, 0800 223 582; www. abeltasman.co.nz; 265 High St, Motueka; pass adult/child $150/75) Offers an explorer pass for unlimited taxi travel on three days over a five-day period, plus backpacker specials and an array of tours.

Marahau Water Taxis Boat
(☏03-527 8176, 0800 808 018; Abel Tasman Centre, Franklin St, Marahau) Scheduled services plus boat/walk options.

Local Knowledge

Abel Tasman National Park

RECOMMENDATIONS FROM STU HOUSTON, DEPARTMENT OF CONSERVATION (DOC)

1 SEA KAYAKING
The best way to see the park is by water, kayaking up the coastline – you see the beaches, the forests, mountains and rocks. Most people do kayaking as a day trip, but a three-day trip will give you a real feel for the area. You can do a quarter-day or half-day, but it's hard to get a full sense of the landscape on such a short trip. Ask the local kayak operators about options: walk a few kilometres, paddle a few...

2 TRAMP THE COAST TRACK
The Abel Tasman is one of those parks where the further into it you go, the better it gets. There are four huts on the Abel Tasman Coast Track and 19 campsites – the camp spots are primo, with some on the beach, right beside the sea. Most people start at Marahau and head north, tramp for three days and then get a water taxi out at the end.

3 WILDLIFE
There's a huge seal population here and many little blue penguins within the park – if you don't see them, you'll hear them: they make a lot of noise at night! We get quite a lot of dolphins travelling through and we see orcas two or three times a year. There are wood pigeons, tuis and bellbirds, too. A lot of the streams have native freshwater fish – kokopu, inanga – which trout and salmon have forced out in other areas.

4 TAKE A DIP
Swimming here is awesome! There's no glacial run-off and it's one of the few places in the country without any surf. In Marahau, where I live, the water temperature is around 21°C in summer (even down in Dunedin, which is not much further south, it's around 16°C).

JOHN WARBURTON-LEE/GETTY IMAGES ©

Don't Miss
Paddling the Abel Tasman

The Abel Tasman Coast Track has long been trampers' territory, but its coastal beauty makes it an equally seductive spot for sea kayaking, which can easily be combined with walking and camping. You can kayak from half a day to three days, camping, or staying in Department of Conservation (DOC) huts, bachs, even a floating backpackers, either fully catered for or self-catering. You can kayak one day, camp overnight then walk back, or walk further into the park and catch a water taxi back.

Most operators offer similar trips at similar prices. Marahau is the main base, but trips also depart from Kaiteriteri. A popular choice if time is tight is to spend a few hours kayaking in the Tonga Island Marine Reserve, followed by a walk from Tonga Quarry to Medlands Beach. This will cost around $195 including water taxis. Three-day trips usually drop you at the northern end of the park, then you paddle back (or vice versa) and cost from around $620 including food. One-day guided trips are around $200. Freedom rentals (double-kayak and equipment hire) are around $70/110 per person for one/two days.

November to Easter is the busiest time, with December to February the absolute peak. You can, however, paddle year-round.

Following are the main players in this competitive market (shop around):

Abel Tasman Kayaks (☏03-527 8022, 0800 732 529; www.abeltasmankayaks.co.nz; Main Rd, Marahau)

Kahu Kayaks (☏03-527 8300, 0800 300 101; www.kahukayaks.co.nz; cnr Marahau Valley Rd)

Kaiteriteri Kayaks (☏03-527 8383, 0800 252 925; www.seakayak.co.nz; Kaiteriteri Beach)

Marahau Sea Kayaks (☏03-527 8176, 0800 529 257; www.msk.co.nz; Abel Tasman Centre, Franklin St, Marahau)

Detour:
Farewell Spit

Bleak, exposed and positively sci-fi, Farewell Spit is a wetland of international importance and a renowned bird sanctuary – the summer home of thousands of migratory waders, notably the godwit (which flies all the way from the Arctic tundra), Caspian terns and Australasian gannets. The 35km beach features colossal, crescent-shaped dunes, from where panoramic views extend across Golden Bay and a vast low-tide salt marsh. Walkers can explore the first 4km of the spit via a network of tracks (see DOC's *Farewell Spit* brochure), but beyond that point access is via tours, scheduled according to tide.

Farewell Spit Eco Tours (☏ 03-524 8257, 0800 808 257; www.farewellspit.com; Tasman St, Collingwood; tours $120-155) Operating for nearly 70 years, Paddy and his expert guides run tours ranging from two to 6½ hours, departing from Collingwood, taking in the spit, lighthouse, and up to 20 species of bird which may include gannets and godwits. Expect ripping yarns aplenty.

Farewell Spit Nature Experience (☏ 03-524 8992, 0800 250 500; www.farewellspittours.com; Pakawau; tours $120-145) This air-conditioned operator runs a four-hour tour departing from Farewell Spit Visitor Centre, and a six-hour option leaving from the Old School Cafe, Pakawau.

Tours

Abel Tasman
Sailing Adventures
Sailing

(☏ 03-527 8375, 0800 467 245; www.sailingadventures.co.nz; Kaiteriteri; day trip $179) Scheduled and on-demand catamaran trips, with sail/walk/kayak combos available. The popular day trip includes lunch on Anchorage Beach.

Abel Tasman Tours
& Guided Walks
Guided Hike

(☏ 03-528 9602; www.abeltasmantours.co.nz; tours from $220) Small-group, day-long

walking tours (minimum two people) that include packed lunch and water taxis.

Wilsons Abel
Tasman
Walking, Kayaking

(☏ 03-528 2027, 0800 223 582; www.abeltasman.co.nz; 265 High St, Motueka; half-day cruise $78, cruise & walk $60-78, kayak & walk $80-195) Impressive array of cruises, walking, kayaking and combo tours, including a $35 backpacker day-walk and a barbecue cruise (great winter option). Luxurious beachfront lodges at Awaroa and Torrent Bay for guided-tour guests.

Christchurch & Central South

Nowhere in New Zealand is changing and developing as fast as post-earthquake Christchurch, and visiting the country's second-largest city as it's being rebuilt and reborn is both interesting and inspiring.

A short drive from Christchurch's dynamic re-emergence, Banks Peninsula conceals hidden bays and beaches – a backdrop for kayaking and wildlife cruises with a sunset return to the attractions of Akaroa. Throughout the seasons, Aoraki/Mt Cook, the country's tallest peak, stands sentinel over this diverse region.

Over the craggy Southern Alps, hemmed in by the wild Tasman Sea, the West Coast (aka Westland) is like nowhere else in NZ. During summer a phalanx of campervans and tourist buses tick off the must-see Pancake Rocks and Franz Josef and Fox Glaciers. Deviate from the trail even a short way, however, and you'll be awed by the spectacular sights that await you.

Akaroa Harbour, Banks Peninsula (p245)
DENNIS FLAHERTY/GETTY IMAGES ©

Wildflowers in Arthur's Pass National Park
BOB STEFKO/GETTY IMAGES ©

Christchurch & Central South

TASMAN SEA

0 — 50 km
0 — 25 miles

Lake Rotoroa

St Arnaud

Mt Travers (2338m)

Mt Uriah (1525m)

Punakaiki
Pancake Rocks

Paparoa National Park

Mt Ryall (1220m)

Nelson Lakes National Park

Mt Una (2301m)

Victoria Forest Park

Faerie Queen (2237m)

Hanmer Springs National Park

Greymouth

Grey River

Mt Haast (1587m)

Lewis Pass

St James Walkway

Kumara Junction

Lake Brunner (Moana Kotuku)

Mt Ajax (1832m)

Lake Sumner Forest Park

Hanmer Springs

Hokitika

Lake Mahinapua

Arthur's Pass National Park

Lake Sumner

Mt Longfellow (1898m)

Hokitika Gorge

Mt Rolleston (2272m)

Arthur's Pass (924m)

Arthur's Pass

Ross

Lake Kaniere

Pukekura

Mt Murchison (2400m)

Lake Pearson

Waipara

Lake Ianthe

Mt Bryce (2188m)

Woodend

Lake Wahapo

Westland Tai Poutini National Park

Mt Whitcombe (2638m)

Lake Coleridge

Porters Pass (945m)

Pegasus Bay

Franz Josef

Lake Mapourika

Mt Arrowsmith (2795m)

Mt Hutt Ski Area

Christchurch

Lyttelton

Aoraki/Mt Cook National Park

Lake Heron

Mt Hutt

Banks Peninsula

Aoraki/Mt Cook (3754m)

Methven

Lake Ellesmere

Akaroa

Rakaia

Rakaia River

Rangitata River

Lake Tekapo

Tekapo

Burkes Pass (701m)

Fairlie

Geraldine

Lake Pukaki

Timaru

Twizel

Lake Benmore

Canterbury Bight

Lake Aviemore

Waitaki River

Oamaru

1 Akaroa & Banks Peninsula
2 Aoraki/Mt Cook
3 Franz Josef & Fox Glaciers
4 TranzAlpine
5 Christchurch

Christchurch & Central South Highlights

Akaroa & Banks Peninsula

A haven for artists, gardeners and holidaymakers, Akaroa on the Banks Peninsula (p245) offers an engaging mix of volcanic landscapes, a gorgeous harbour and French colonial heritage. And with its own microclimate (locals grow grapes, olives and citrus), Akaroa is always a few degrees warmer than nearby Christchurch. Make a long day trip of it, or stay overnight to have a good look around. Akaroa Harbour

1

ROBIN SMITH/GETTY IMAGES ©

2 Aoraki/Mt Cook

Standing proud at 3754m, Aoraki/Mt Cook (p254) is something to behold. It's quite often cloud-covered, but on a clear day, the jagged, heaven-high peak is inspiring and humbling. But even when it is cloudy, this mountain's magnitude is undeniable: walking around the lake-strewn foothills in the crisp alpine air as avalanches rumble on distant slopes, you'll be forgiven for feeling a tad insignificant!

JOHN W BANAGAN/GETTY IMAGES ©

Franz Josef & Fox Glaciers

Quick, scoot over to the West Coast
and see Franz Josef (p260) and
Fox Glaciers (p264) before global
warming melts them! You probably
don't have to be there in the next
10 minutes – there's a heckuva lot
of ice here. Take a hike around the
jagged glacial faces (but not too
close – these things are moving!) or
a scenic flight above or onto these
massive rivers of ice. Helihikers on Franz
Josef Glacier

TranzAlpine

Are you a closet trainspotter? Can't
abstain from trains? Not a holiday without
a railway? The *TranzAlpine* (p260) is for
you! This improbably scenic rail journey
winds over the Southern Alps between
Christchurch on the South Island's east
coast and Greymouth in the west. It's not
an epic trip in terms of time – it takes
just five hours – but the landscapes and
outlooks en route are utterly photogenic.

Post-Quake Christchurch

On 22 February 2011 Christchurch (p234)
was wracked by a huge earthquake, killing
185 people and leaving hundreds of buildings requiring demolition. Reconstruction
is a long-term prospect, but around town
things are changing daily. There's a real
vigour and creative energy in the way locals
are redesigning their city and their lives. As
the saying goes, you can't keep a good man
(or city) down. Re:START Mall (p242)

Christchurch & Central South's Best...

Natural Wonders

o **Franz Josef & Fox Glaciers** There's only one word that fits – awesome! (p260)

o **Aoraki/Mt Cook** Nobody bagged this lofty peak until 1894 – it's *really* big. (p254)

o **Banks Peninsula** Spaghetti-like volcanic coastlines. (p245)

o **Pancake Rocks** Stacks of giant dolomite pancakes... Pass the maple syrup. (p259)

Walks

o **Mt John** A fab three-hour return hike to the summit above Lake Tekapo. (p253)

o **Banks Peninsula Track** Two- or four-day hop across farmland by the coast. (p246)

o **Hooker Valley Track** Glacial streams, swing bridges and Aoraki panoramas (hope for a sunny day). (p255)

o **Christchurch Botanic Gardens** Work the plane-seat kinks out of your legs in these beautiful gardens. (p234)

Places to Unwind

o **Banks of the Avon** While away a few hours by the riverside in central Christchurch. (p234)

o **Hanmer Springs** Slip into a hot spa, get your back massaged, or revel in après-ski good times. (p248)

o **Akaroa waterfront** Sip a strong coffee, munch a French pastry and assess the passers-by. (p245)

o **Monteith's Brewing Co** Big, beery and beautiful on the West Coast. (p258)

Places to Get Giddy

○ **Aoraki/Mt Cook from above** As high as Kiwis get without wings (take a scenic flight unless you're a hardcore mountaineer). (p255)

○ **Methven Hot-Air Balloons** Everybody sing: 'Up, up and away, my beautiful, my beautiful balloon...' (p251)

○ **TranzAlpine** Climb high over the Southern Alps on this epic train ride. (p260)

○ **Franz Josef & Fox Glaciers scenic flights** See them from above via wings, rotor blades or a parachute. (p260)

ADVANCE PLANNING

○ **One month before** Book a seat on the *TranzAlpine* train, and accommodation between Akaroa and Fox Glacier.

○ **Two weeks before** Organise a scenic flight above Aoraki/Mt Cook or the West Coast glaciers, or a balloon trip in Methven.

○ **One week before** Book a table at a top Christchurch restaurant (try Saggio di Vino) and a tour at Monteith's Brewing Co in Greymouth.

RESOURCES

○ **Christchurch & Canterbury** (www. christchurchnz.com) The low-down around town.

○ **Christchurch City Council** (www. christchurch.org.nz) City-centric info and post-quake updates.

○ **Neat Places** (www. neatplaces.co.nz) Christchurch eating and drinking blog.

○ **Akaroa Information Centre** (www.akaroa. com) Banks Peninsula and Akaroa info.

○ **Aoraki/Mt Cook National Park DOC Visitor Centre** (www.mtcooknz.com) Advises on weather conditions, guided tours and tramping.

○ **Westland Tai Poutini National Park Visitor Centre & i-SITE** (www. doc.govt.nz, www. glaciercountry.co.nz) At Franz Josef; also the regional DOC office.

GETTING AROUND

○ **Bus** From town to town across Canterbury.

○ **Car** To explore beyond the Christchurch city limits.

○ **Campervan** Up and down the wild, driftwood-strewn shores of the West Coast.

○ **Train** Across the snowy crags of the Southern Alps on the *TranzAlpine*.

○ **Punt** Along the lazy, languid Avon River (bring cucumber sandwiches and champagne).

BE FOREWARNED

○ **Mt Cook Village accommodation** Weary travellers without a reservation might find themselves without a bed at Mt Cook Village. Accommodation here is scant (especially midrange) and pricey: book well in advance.

Left: Hot-air ballooning over the Canterbury Plains; **Above:** Pancake Rocks (p259)
(LEFT) DAVID WALL/GETTY IMAGES ©; (ABOVE) MARCO SIMONI/ GETTY IMAGES ©

Christchurch & Central South Itineraries

Christchurch is the real deal: culture, class and southern spirit. Across Canterbury are incredible summits, peninsulas and lakes, while over the mountains are the West Coast's glaciers, rock formations and wilderness.

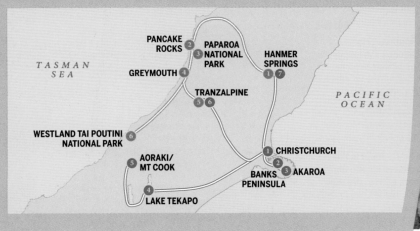

CHRISTCHURCH TO HANMER SPRINGS

3 DAYS

CHRISTCHURCH & CANTERBURY

There's too much to see and too much to do in Canterbury: don't waste time! Hit **1 Christchurch** (p234) running, with a kick-arse cafe coffee, a visit to the Canterbury Museum and a float through the Botanic Gardens on an Avon River punt. The city is rebuilding and reinventing itself: connect with the locals over a meal or a drink and discover a city getting back on its feet.

The next day cruise out to the formerly volcanic folds of **2 Banks Peninsula** (p245): explore the very Frenchy **3 Akaroa** (p245), with its wildlife-rich harbour, and the peninsula's photogenic outer bays. You

can also swim with dolphins here, and kayak around the coast.

Day three already! Give your Canterbury compass a twirl: you could wander west to **4 Lake Tekapo** (p253) and the snowy heights of **5 Aoraki/Mt Cook** (p254), where you can tramp, ski or take a scenic flight; or head over to the West Coast and back in a day on the **6 TranzAlpine** (p260) train. But our vote is to point the needle north to **7 Hanmer Springs** (p248), a chilled-out hot-springs resort town from which you can launch a wintertime skiing sortie or spa yourself silly.

 5 *DAYS*

HANMER SPRINGS TO WESTLAND TAI POUTINI NATIONAL PARK
HEADING FOR THE COAST

Shake yourself from your relaxed stupor in ❶ **Hanmer Springs** (p248) and take a day to cross the Alps to Westport and the ❷ **Pancake Rocks** (p259) south of town. You can also tramp near here in ❸ **Paparoa National Park** (p259).

Next day, head south to ❹ **Greymouth** (p258). The real highlight here is Monteith's Brewing Co, a West Coast brewery that started small but now has taps and barrels in pubs and bars across NZ. Then, if you're still not wild about the West Coast, the ❺ **TranzAlpine** (p260) train trundles back over the mountains from here to Christchurch.

The Big Daddies of West Coast tourism are another day further south: the momentous Franz Josef and Fox Glaciers in ❻ **Westland Tai Poutini National Park** (p260). Spend a day or two exploring the park, with a hike around (or actually on) one of the glaciers. A scenic flight is a terrific way to really grasp the enormity and power of these incredible ice rivers.

From the West Coast, you can save time with a short flight back to Christchurch from Hokitika.

Fox Glacier (p264)
OLIVER STREWE/GETTY IMAGES ©

Discover Christchurch & the Central South

CHRISTCHURCH

Welcome to a vibrant city in transition, coping creatively with the aftermath of New Zealand's second-worst natural disaster. Traditionally the most English of NZ cities, Christchurch's heritage heart was all but hollowed out following the 2010 and 2011 earthquakes that left 185 people dead.

Locals are genuinely keen to welcome sensitive visitors back to their city – and despite the heartache, they're the first to acknowledge how fascinating it all is.

◎ Sights

CITY CENTRE

Botanic Gardens   Gardens
(Map p240; www.ccc.govt.nz; Rolleston Ave; ⏲7am-8.30pm Oct-Mar, to 6.30pm Apr-Sep) **FREE** Strolling through these blissful 30 riverside hectares of arboreal and floral splendour is a consummate Christchurch experience. Gorgeous at any time of the year, it's particularly impressive in spring when the rhododendrons, azaleas and daffodil woodland are in riotous bloom. There are thematic gardens to explore, lawns to sprawl on, and a playground adjacent to the **Botanic Gardens Information Centre** (Map p240; ⏲9am-4pm Mon-Fri, 10.15am-4pm Sat & Sun).

Guided walks ($10) depart at 1.30pm (mid-September to April) from the Canterbury Museum, or you can tour around the gardens in the **Caterpillar train** (✆0800 882 223; www.gardentours.co.nz; adult/child $18/9; ⏲11am-3pm).

Canterbury Museum   Museum
(Map p240; ✆03-366 5000; www.canterbury-museum.com; Rolleston Ave; ⏲9am-5pm) **FREE** Yes, there's a mummy and dinosaur bones,

Botanic Gardens, Christchurch
LAURIE NOBLE/GETTY IMAGES ©

but the highlights of this museum are more local and more recent. The Maori galleries contain some beautiful *pounamu* (greenstone) pieces, while Christchurch Street is an atmospheric walk through the colonial past. The reproduction of Fred & Myrtle's gloriously kitsch Paua Shell House embraces Kiwiana at its best, and kids will enjoy the interactive displays in the Discovery Centre (admission $2). Hour-long guided tours commence at 3.30pm on Tuesday and Thursday.

Quake City — Museum

(Map p240; www.quakecity.co.nz; 99 Cashel St; adult/child $10/free; ☺10am-6pm) One of the new must-sees of Christchurch, this little museum tells the story of the earthquakes through photography, video footage and various artefacts, including bits fallen off the Cathedral and the statue of the 'founder of Canterbury' John Robert Godley that toppled from its perch in the square. Most affecting of all is the film featuring locals telling their own stories from that fateful day.

Cathedral Square — Square

(Map p240) Christchurch's historic hub sits at the heart of the grid of streets that delineate the devastated city centre. At its centre (at the time of writing, at least) is what remains of ChristChurch Cathedral.

The February 2011 earthquake brought down the Gothic church's 63m-high spire, leaving only the bottom half of the tower remaining. Despite the nave remaining largely intact, the deconstruction and demolition of the cathedral was announced in March 2012 by the Anglican Diocese.

Gap Filler — Outdoors

(www.gapfiller.org.nz) With so much empty space around the city, this organisation is doing its best to fill it with interesting things. Installations range from whimsical bits of art, to moving memorials to earthquake victims, to a minigolf course scattered around different abandoned lots. There are pianos to play, books to read and giant chess pieces to manoeuvre. One of the larger projects is the **Pallet Pavilion** (Map p240; www.palletpavilion.com;

cnr Kimore & Durham Sts; 🛜), a large cafe-bar–performance space demarcated by blue-painted storage pallets.

SUBURBS

International Antarctic Centre — Education Centre

(📞0508 736 4846; www.iceberg.co.nz; 38 Orchard Rd, Christchurch Airport; adult/child $39/19; ☺9am-5.30pm) Part of a huge complex built for the administration of the NZ, US and Italian Antarctic programs, this centre gives visitors the opportunity to see penguins and learn about the icy continent. Attractions include the Antarctic Storm chamber, where you can get a taste of -18°C wind chill.

The Xtreme Pass (adult/child $59/29) includes the '4D theatre' (a 3D film with moving seats and a water spray) and rides on a Hagglund all-terrain amphibious Antarctic vehicle.

Activities

Antigua Boat Sheds — Boating, Kayaking

(Map p240; 📞03-366 6768; www.boatsheds. co.nz; 2 Cambridge Tce; ☺7am-5pm) Dating from 1882, the photogenic green-and-white Antigua Boat Sheds hires out row boats ($35), kayaks ($12), Canadian canoes ($35) and bikes (adult/child $10/5); all prices are per hour. There's also an excellent cafe.

Punting on the Avon — Boating

(Map p240; www.punting.co.nz; 2 Cambridge Tce; adult/child $25/12; ☺9am-6pm Oct-Mar, 10am-4pm Apr-Sep) 🍃 The Antigua Boat Sheds are the starting point for half-hour punting trips through the botanical gardens. Relax in a flat-bottomed boat while a strapping lad in Edwardian clobber and a long pole does all the work. Other boats depart from the **Worcester St bridge** (Map p240) and punt through the ruined city centre.

City Cycle Hire — Bicycle Rental

(📞03-377 5952; www.cyclehire-tours.co.nz; bike half-/full day $25/35, mountain bike half-/full day $30/45) Offers door-to-door delivery

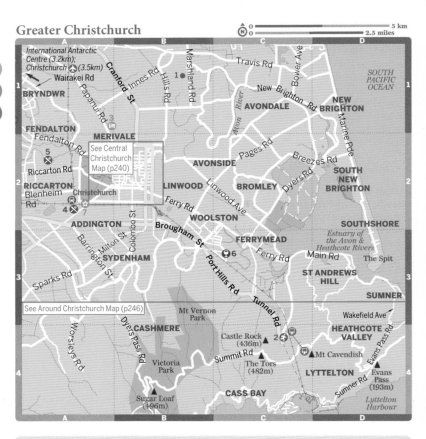

Greater Christchurch

of on- and off-road city bikes and touring bikes. They'll also meet you with a bike at the top of the gondola on Mt Cavendish if you fancy a 16km descent ($70 including gondola ride; 1½ hours).

Gondola
Cable Car

(Map p236; www.gondola.co.nz; 10 Bridle Path Rd; return adult/child $25/12; ⊙10am-5pm) Take a ride to the top of Mt Cavend-ish (500m) on this 945m cable car for wonderful views over the city, Lyttelton, Banks Peninsula and the Canterbury Plains. At the top there's a cafe and the child-focused *Time Tunnel* ride through historical scenes. You can also walk to Cavendish Bluff Lookout (30 minutes return) or the Pioneer Women's Memorial (one hour return).

Tram
Tram

(🕿03-377 4790; www.tram.co.nz; adult/child $10/free) Prior to the earthquakes, historic trams operated on a 2.5km inner-city loop. Limited services resumed in late 2013, heading between New Regent St and Canterbury Museum (35 minutes), but the route will expand as the rebuild continues.

Bone Dude
Carving Course

(Map p236; 🕿03-385 4509; www.thebonedude. co.nz; 153 Marshland Rd, Shirley; from $60; 🕘1-4pm Mon-Fri, 10am-1pm Sat) Creative types should consider booking a session with the Bone Dude, who'll show you how to carve your own bone pendant (allow three hours). Sessions are limited to eight participants, so book ahead.

Tours

Discovery Tours
Bus Tour

(🕿0800 372 879; www.discoverytravel.co.nz; tours from $130) Excursions to Akaroa, Aoraki/Mt Cook, Hanmer Springs, Kaikoura and the Waipara Valley wine region. The Arthur's Pass tour (adult/ child $355/178) packs the *TranzAlpine* train, jetboating and a farm tour into one action-packed day.

Hassle Free Tours
Bus Tour

(🕿03-385 5775; www.hasslefree.co.nz) Explore Christchurch on an open-top double-decker bus (adult/child $29/15).

Red Bus Rebuild Tour
Bus Tour

(🕿0800 500 929; www.redbus.co.nz; adult/ child $29/15) Commentaries focus on the past, present and future of earthquake-damaged sites in the city centre.

Christchurch Bike Tours
Cycling

(🕿0800 733 257; www.chchbiketours.co.nz; 2/4hr $50/160) Informative, two-hour tours loop around the city daily, heading to the Christchurch Farmers' Market on Saturday mornings. Also available is a four-hour gourmet food tour ending with a three-course lunch. Tours leave from the Antigua Boat Sheds.

Post-Quake Christchurch

RECOMMENDATIONS FROM JEFF PETERS, OWNER/MANAGER OF CENTREPOINT ON COLOMBO (P238)

1 THE SIGHTS
Christchurch is still the South Island's main gateway and hub: most tourist things are up and running, including the International Antarctic Centre, Canterbury Museum (which escaped with very little damage), and the Botanic Gardens. Sadly, we've lost the cathedral and the Arts Centre won't open for many years... But the city is still a great place to visit!

2 CREATIVE REBUILDING
Rebuilding will be a long process – 10, 15, 20 years. So people are finding creative opportunities to get on with things. The shipping-container mall Re:START (p242) really symbolises this kind of spirit.

3 EATING & DRINKING
We lost around half the pubs and restaurants around town, so the ones that are still operating are really busy! The service and food are usually pretty great. Christchurch has stood up and said, 'No earthquake's gonna beat us!'

4 EMERGING AREAS
Addington is emerging as an events area – Dux Live (p242), a music venue, and the Court Theatre (p242) are there now, plus some great cafes. The city centre will come back, but satellite areas around Christchurch are really going to thrive in the meantime.

5 QUAKE TOURISM
Take some time to understand what's happened here; walk around the city centre, chat with the locals and listen to their stories. 'Disaster tourism' is no problem, but it's probably best to stay away from residential areas.

The Canterbury Earthquakes

Christchurch's seismic nightmare began at 4.35am on 4 September 2010. Centred 40km west of the city, a 40-second, 7.1-magnitude earthquake jolted Cantabrians from their sleep, and caused widespread damage to older buildings in the central city.

Fast forward to 12.51pm on 22 February 2011, when central Christchurch was busy with shoppers and workers enjoying their lunch break. This time the 6.3-magnitude quake was much closer, centred just 10km southeast of the city and only 5km deep.

When the dust settled after 24 traumatic seconds, NZ's second-largest city had changed forever. The towering spire of the iconic ChristChurch Cathedral lay in ruins; walls and verandas had cascaded down on shopping strips; and two multistorey buildings had pancaked. Of the 185 deaths (across 20 nationalities), 115 occurred in the six-storey Canterbury TV building, where many international students at a language school were killed.

The impact of the events of a warm summer's day in early 2011 will take longer than a generation to resolve. Around 80% of the buildings within the city centre's famed four avenues have been or are due to be demolished, and at the time of writing, the empty blocks are an eerie sight, leaving much of the city centre looking like a giant car park.

Plans for the next 20 years of the city's rebuild include a compact, low-rise city centre, large green spaces, and parks and cycleways along the Avon River.

Christchurch Personal Guiding Service
Walking Tour

(Map p240; ☏03-383 2495; Rolleston Ave; tours $15; ☉1pm daily) Nonprofit organisation offering informative two-hour city walks. Buy tickets and join tours at the i-SITE or at the red-and-black kiosk nearby.

 Sleeping

Pomeroy's on Kilmore
B&B $$

(Map p240; ☏03-374 3532; www.pomeroysonk-ilmore.co.nz; 282 Kilmore St; r $145-195; P ☞) Even if this cute wooden cottage wasn't the sister and neighbour of Christchurch's best craft beer pub, it would still be one of our favourites. Three of the five elegantly furnished rooms open on to a sunny garden and rates include a self-serve continental breakfast.

Focus Motel
Motel $$

(Map p240; ☏03-943 0800; www.focusmotel.com; 344 Durham St N; r $150-200; P ☞)

Sleek and centrally located, this friendly motel offers studio and one-bedroom units with big-screen TVs, iPod docks, kitchenettes and super-modern decor. There's a guest barbecue and laundry, and pillowtop chocolates sweeten the deal.

CentrePoint on Colombo
Motel $$

(Map p240; ☏03-377 0859; www.centrepoin-toncolombo.co.nz; 859 Colombo St; r/apt from $165/190; P ☞) The friendly Kiwi-Japanese management have imbued this centrally located motel with style and comfort. Little extras like stereos, black-out curtains and spa baths (in the deluxe rooms) take it to the next level.

Merivale Manor
Motel $$

(Map p236; ☏03-355 7731; www.merivalemanor.co.nz; 122 Papanui Rd; d $145-180; P ☞) A gracious 19th-century Victorian mansion is the hub of this elegant motel, with units both in the main house and in the more typically motel-style blocks lining the drive. Accommodation ranges from studios to two-bedroom apartments.

Heritage Christchurch
Hotel $$$

(Map p240; ☎03-983 4800; www.heritageho-tels.co.nz; 28-30 Cathedral Sq; ste $235-440; ☎) ✦ Standing grandly on Cathedral Sq while all around is in ruins, the 1909 Old Government Building owes its survival to a thorough strengthening when it was converted to a hotel in the 1990s. After a three-year post-earthquake restoration, its spacious suites are more elegant than ever. All have full kitchens.

Orari B&B
B&B $$$

(Map p240; ☎03-365 6569; www.orari.co.nz; 42 Gloucester St; s $175-235, d $195-255; P ☎) Orari is an 1893 home that has been simply updated with light-filled, pastel-toned rooms and inviting guest areas, as well as a lovely front garden. A neighbouring block, constructed in a sympathetic style, contains five three-bedroom apartments.

 Eating

C1 Espresso
Cafe $

(Map p240; www.c1espresso.co.nz; 185 High St; mains $10-19; ⊙7am-10pm; ☎) ✦ Resurrected from the rubble, C1 has reopened better than ever in a grand former post office that somehow escaped the cataclysm. Recycled materials fill the interior (Victorian oak pannelling, bulbous 1970s light fixtures) and tables spill onto a little square. The food, coffee and service are excellent, too.

Beat Street
Cafe $

(Map p240; 324 Barbadoes St; mains $10-19; ⊙7am-5pm Sun-Tue, to 10pm Wed-Sat; ☝) Welcome to the grungy hub of Christchurch cafe-cool. Free range this and organic that combine with terrific eggy breakfasts, gourmet pies and robust coffee. Look out for open mic music and poetry nights.

Addington Coffee Co-op
Cafe $

(Map p236; www.addingtoncoffee.org.nz; 297 Lincoln Rd; mains $6-19; ⊙7.30am-4pm Mon-Fri, 9am-4pm Sat & Sun; ☎☝) One of Christ-urch's biggest and most bustling cafes is also one of its best. A compact stall selling organic cotton T-shirts jostles for attention with delicious cakes, gourmet pies and the legendary house breakfasts. An on-site laundry completes the deal for busy travellers.

Christchurch Farmers' Market
Market $

(Map p236; www.christchurchfarmersmarket. co.nz; 16 Kahu Rd, Riccarton; ⊙9am-noon Sat) Held in the pretty grounds of Riccarton House, this excellent farmers market offers a tasty array of organic fruit and vegies, South Island cheeses and salmon, local craft beer and ethnic treats.

King of Snake
Asian $$

(Map p240; ☎03-365 7363; www.kingofsnake. co.nz; 145 Victoria St; mains $24-37; ⊙11am-3.30pm Mon-Fri, 5.30-10pm daily) Dark wood, gold tiles and purple skull-patterned wallpaper fill this so-hip-right-now restaurant and cocktail bar with just the right amount of sinister opulence. The adventurous menu gainfully plunders the cuisines of Asia – from India to Korea – to delicious, if pricey, effect.

Saggio di Vino
European $$$

(Map p240; ☎03-379 4006; www.saggiodivino. co.nz; 179 Victoria St; mains $35-42; ⊙5-10pm) Despite the Italian name, the menu has a heavy French accent at this elegant restaurant, which is quite possibly Christ-urch's best. Expect delicious takes on terrine, duck *confit* and *Café de Paris* steak, and a well-laden cheese trolley to finish you off.

🍷 Drinking & Nightlife

Pomeroy's Old Brewery Inn
Pub

(Map p240; www.pomspub.co.nz; 292 Kilmore St; ⊙3-11pm Tue-Thu, noon-11pm Fri-Sun) Welcoming Pomeroy's is the city's hoppy hub for fans of NZ's rapidly expanding craft-beer scene. A wide range of guest taps showcase brews from around the country. There's regular live music, and the attached **Victoria's Kitchen** does great pub food (mains $22 to $26).

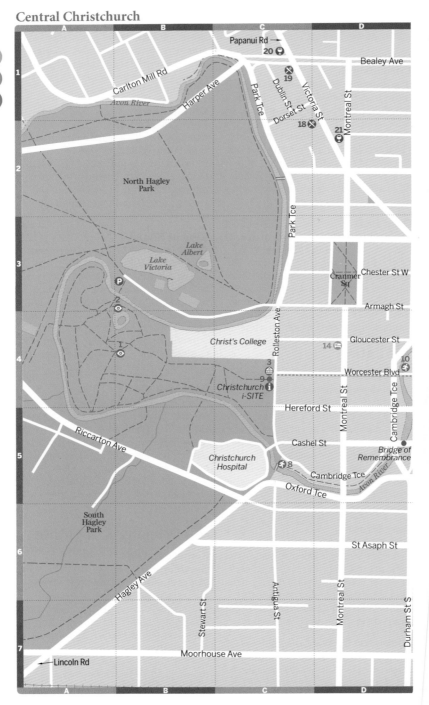

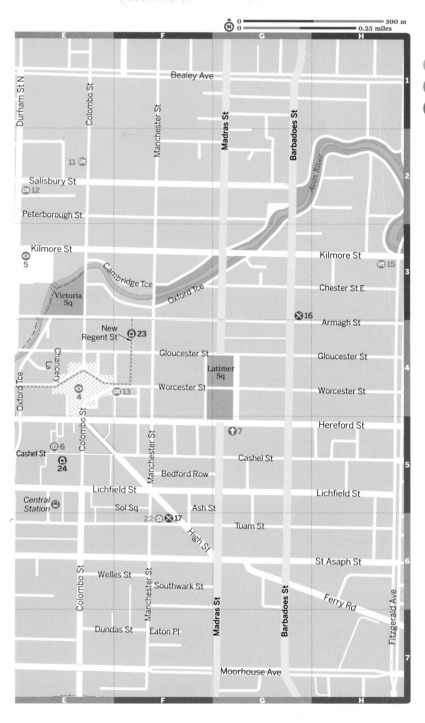

Central Christchurch

Carlton — Bar
(Map p240; www.carltonbar.co.nz; 1 Papanui Rd, Merivale; ⏰11am-midnight Sun-Wed, to 2am Thu-Sat) The rebuilt Carlton's ultramodern look includes old planning maps plastered to the walls and visual references to the shipping containers out of which it operated when the historic Carlton pub collapsed. The upstairs deck is a prime spot on a sunny afternoon.

Revival — Bar
(Map p240; www.revivalbar.co.nz; 94 Victoria St; ⏰4-9pm Mon & Tue, to midnight Wed, to 3am Thu-Sun) ✏ Revival is the hippest of Christchurch's container bars, with regular DJs and a funky lounge area dotted with a quirky collection of automotive rear ends and vintage steamer trunks.

The Brewery — Brewery
(Map p236; www.casselsbrewery.co.nz; 3 Garlands Rd, Woolston; ⏰7am-late) An essential destination for beer-loving travellers, the Cassels & Sons brewery crafts its beer using a wood-fired brew kettle, resulting in big, bold beers. Tasting trays are available for the curious and the indecisive, live bands perform most nights, and the food – including wood-fired pizzas – is top-notch, too.

Entertainment

Court Theatre — Theatre
(Map p236; ☎03-963 0870; www.courttheatre.org.nz; Bernard St, Addington) Christchurch's original Court Theatre was an integral part of the city's Arts Centre but was forced to relocate to this warehouse after the earthquakes. The new premises are much more spacious; it's a great venue to see popular international plays and works by NZ playwrights.

Dux Live — Live Music
(Map p236; www.duxlive.co.nz; 363 Lincoln Rd, Addington) One of the kingpins of the live-music scene, this intimate 250-capacity space has gigs most nights.

Alice Cinematheque — Cinema
(Map p240; ☎03-365 0615; www.aliceinvideoland.co.nz; 209 Tuam St; adult/child $16/12) There are only 38 seats at this Egyptian-themed art-house cinema, attached to the excellent Alice In Videoland specialty video and DVD store.

Shopping

Re:START Mall — Mall
(Map p240; www.restart.org.nz; Cashel Mall; ⏰10am-5pm; 🛜) This colourful labyrinth of shops based in shipping containers was

the first retail activity in the Christchurch CBD after the earthquakes. With a couple of decent cafes and a good selection of stores, it's a pleasant place to stroll. Note that Re:START is only intended to be temporary, so it may disappear at any time.

New Regent St
Mall

(Map p240; www.newregentstreet.co.nz) A forerunner to the modern mall, this pretty little stretch of pastel Spanish Mission–style shops was described as NZ's most beautiful street when it was completed in 1932. Fully restored post-earthquake, it's once again a pleasant place to stroll and peruse the tiny galleries, gift shops and cafes.

The Tannery
Shopping Centre

(Map p236; www.thetannery.co.nz; 3 Garlands Rd, Woolston; ⊗10am-5.30pm Mon-Sat, to 4pm Sun) In a city mourning the loss of its heritage, this post-earthquake conversion of a Victorian tannery couldn't be more welcome. The 19th-century industrial buildings have been zooshed up with period-style tiles, wrought iron and stained glass, and filled with boutique stores selling everything from books to fashion to surfboards.

ℹ Information

24 Hour Surgery (☎03-365 7777; www.24hoursurgery.co.nz; cnr Bealey Ave & Colombo St) No appointment necessary.

Airport i-SITE (☎03-353 7774; www.christchurchnz.com; ⊗7.30am-7pm)

Christchurch Hospital (☎03-364 0640, emergency dept 03-364 0270; www.cdhb.govt.nz; 2 Riccarton Ave) Has a 24-hour emergency department.

Christchurch i-SITE (Map p240; ☎03-379 9629; www.christchurchnz.com; Botanic Gardens, Rolleston Ave; ⊗8.30am-5pm, extended hours in summer)

ℹ Getting There & Away

Air

Christchurch Airport (CHC; ☎03-358 5029; www.christchurchairport.co.nz; Durey Rd) is the South Island's main international gateway.

Air New Zealand (☎0800 737 000; www.airnewzealand.co.nz) Air New Zealand–operated flights head to/from Auckland, Wellington, Dunedin and Queenstown. Code-share flights with smaller regional airlines head to/from Blenheim, Hamilton, Hokitika, Invercargill, Napier, Nelson, New Plymouth, Palmerston North, Paraparaumu, Rotorua and Tauranga.

Jetstar (☎0800 800 995; www.jetstar.com) Flies to/from Auckland, Wellington and Queenstown.

Bus

Atomic Shuttles (☎03-349 0697; www.atomictravel.co.nz) Destinations include Picton ($35, 5¼ hours), Greymouth ($45, 3¾ hours), Timaru ($25, 2½ hours), Dunedin ($30 to $35, 5¾ hours) and Queenstown ($50, seven hours).

InterCity (☎03-365 1113; www.intercity.co.nz) Coaches head to Picton (from $26, 5¼ hours), Timaru (from $28, 2½ hours), Dunedin (from

Re:START Mall
DAVID WALL PHOTO/GETTY IMAGES ©

Detour:
Lyttelton

Southeast of Christchurch are the prominent Port Hills, which slope down to the city's port on Lyttelton Harbour.

Lyttelton was badly damaged during the 2010 and 2011 earthquakes, and many of the town's heritage buildings along London St were subsequently demolished. However, Lyttelton has re-emerged as one of Christchurch's most interesting communities. The town's artsy, independent and bohemian vibe is stronger than ever, and it's once again a hub for good bars, cafes and restaurants. It's well worth catching the bus from Christchurch and getting immersed in the local scene, especially on a Saturday morning when the market's buzzing.

Buses 28 and 535 run from Christchurch to Lyttelton (adult/child $3.50/1.80, 25 minutes). At the time of writing, the Summit Rd to Christchurch and the road to Sumner were closed.

Lyttelton has a **visitor information centre** (☑03-328 9093; www.lytteltonharbour. info; 20 Oxford St; ◷10am-4pm).

$40, six hours) and Queenstown (from $55, eight to 11 hours) twice daily; and to Te Anau (from $61, 10¾ hours) daily.

Naked Bus (www.nakedbus.com; prices vary; 🛜) Destinations include Picton (4½ to 5¾ hours), Kaikoura (1½ hours), Dunedin (six hours), Wanaka (7½ hours) and Queenstown (eight hours).

Train

Christchurch railway station (☑03-341 2588; www.kiwirailscenic.co.nz; Troup Dr, Addington; ◷ticket office 6.30am-3pm) is the terminus for two highly scenic train journeys.

The *Coastal Pacific* runs daily from October to April departing from Christchurch at 7am and arriving at Picton at 12.13pm ($79 to $159). It then departs Picton at 1pm, returning to Christchurch at 6.21pm.

The *TranzAlpine* is widely considered one of the best train journeys in the world. It operates year-round with a daily train between Christchurch and Greymouth ($99 to $198, 4½ hours) via Springfield ($89, one hour), Arthur's Pass ($89, 2½ hours) and Lake Brunner ($99 to $198, 3½ hours).

ℹ Getting Around

To/From the Airport

Christchurch Airport is only 10km from the city centre but a taxi between the two can cost a hefty

$45 to $65. Alternatively, the airport is well served by **public buses** (www.metroinfo.co.nz).

Shuttle services include the following:
Steve's Shuttle (☑0800 101 021; www. steveshuttle.co.nz; city centre fare $18, plus $5 per additional passenger; ◷3am-6pm)

Super Shuttle (☑0800 748 885; www. supershuttle.co.nz; city centre fare $19, plus $5 for additional passengers; ◷24hr)

Public Transport

Christchurch's **Metro** (☑03-366 8855; www. metroinfo.co.nz) bus network is inexpensive and efficient. Most buses run from **Central Station** (Map p240; 46-50 Lichfield St). Get timetables from the i-SITE or the station's information kiosk. Tickets (adult/child $3.50/1.80) can be purchased on board and include one free transfer within two hours. Metrocards allow unlimited two-hour/full-day travel for $2.50/5, but the cards cost $10 and must be loaded up with a minimum of $10 additional credit.

Taxi

Blue Star (☑03-379 9799; www.bluestartaxis. org.nz)

First Direct (☑0800 505 555; www.firstdirect. net.nz)

AROUND CHRISTCHURCH

Banks Peninsula

Gorgeous Banks Peninsula (Horomaka) was formed by two giant volcanic eruptions about eight million years ago. Harbours and bays radiate out from the peninsula's centre, giving it an unusual cogwheel shape. The historic town of Akaroa (population 570), 80km from Christchurch, is a highlight, as is the absurdly beautiful drive along Summit Rd around the edge of one of the original craters.

Sights

AKAROA

Giant's House   Gardens
(Map p246; www.thegiantshouse.co.nz; 68 Rue Balguerie; adult/child $20/10; ⊙noon-5pm Jan-Apr, 2-4pm May-Dec) An ongoing labour of love from local artist Josie Martin, this playful and whimsical combination of sculpture and mosaics cascades down a hillside garden above Akaroa. Echoes of Gaudí and Miró can be found in the intricate collages of mirrors, tiles and broken china, and there are many surprising nooks and crannies to discover.

Akaroa Museum   Museum
(Map p248; www.akaroamuseum.org.nz; cnr Rues Lavaud & Balguerie; adult/child $4/1; ⊙10.30am-4.30pm) This interesting museum is spread over several historic buildings, including the old courthouse; the tiny 1858 Custom House by Daly's Wharf; and one of NZ's oldest houses, Langlois-Eteveneaux. It has interesting displays on the peninsula's once-significant Maori population, a courtroom diorama and a 20-minute audiovisual display on peninsular history.

 Activities

The visitor information centre can provide information and booklets on walks around the peninsula, including the three-hour

Akaroa Historic Area Walk, taking in the old wooden buildings and churches that give Akaroa its character.

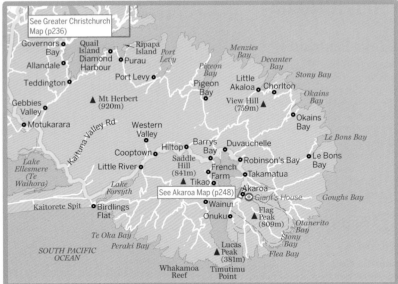

Banks Peninsula Track
Walking

(☎06-304 7612; www.bankstrack.co.nz; 2-/4-day from $150/230; ☺Oct-Apr) This privately owned and maintained 35km four-day walk traverses farmland and forest along the dramatic coast east of Akaroa. Fees include transport from Akaroa and hut accommodation. The two-day option covers the same ground at twice the pace.

Fox II Sailing
Sailing

(Map p248; ☎0800 369 7245; www.akaroafoxsail.co.nz; Daly's Wharf; adult/child $75/30; ☺departs 10.30am & 1.30pm Jan-May) Enjoy the scenery, observe the marine wildlife, learn about the history and try your hand at sailing on NZ's oldest gaff-rigged ketch.

Akaroa Guided Sea Kayaking Safari
Kayaking

(☎021 156 4591; www.akaroakayaks.com; 3hr/half-day $125/159) Paddle out at 7.30am on a three-hour guided Sunrise Nature Safari, or if early starts aren't your thing, try the 11.30am Bays & Nature Paddle. The half-day Try Sea Kayaking Experience is a more challenging option.

Akaroa Adventure Centre
Kayaking, Cycling

(Map p248; ☎03-304 8709; 74a Rue Lavaud; ☺9am-6pm) Rents out sea kayaks (per hour/day $20/60), bikes (per hour $15), fishing rods (per day $10) and surfboards (per day $28).

 ## Tours

Pohatu Plunge
Wildlife Tour

(☎03-304 8552; www.pohatu.co.nz) Runs evening tours to a white-flippered penguin colony (adult/child $70/55); they're best during the August to January breeding season, but possible throughout the year.

Black Cat Cruises
Boat Tour

(Map p248; ☎03-304 7641; www.blackcat.co.nz; Main Wharf; nature cruise $72/30, dolphin swim $145/120) As well as a two-hour nature cruise, Black Cat offers a three-hour 'swimming with dolphins' experience. Cruises have a 98% success rate in seeing dolphins, and an 81% success rate in actually swimming with them (there's a $50 refund if there's no swim).

🛏 Sleeping

AKAROA

La Rochelle
Motel $$

(Map p248; www.larochellemotel.co.nz; 1 Rue Grehan; d $140; 🛜) Tidy, central and reasonably priced, La Rochelle has a range of compact motel units, each of which opens onto a little semi-private terrace or balcony. Opt for a bigger bedroom and smaller bathroom or vice versa.

Tresori Motor Lodge
Motel $$

(Map p248; 📞03-304 7500; www.tresori.co.nz; cnr Rue Jolie & Church St; d $155-205; @🛜) Units are clean and smart at this modern 12-unit motel. They all have kitchenettes, but given that they're so close to Akaroa's waterfront cafe and restaurant strip, you needn't worry about using them.

Maison de la Mer
B&B $$$

(Map p248; 📞03-304 8907; www.maisondelamer.co.nz; 1 Rue Benoit; r $475-550; 🛜) If it were in France we'd call this lovely wooden house *Belle Époque,* but given it's in Akaroa let's stick with Edwardian. Either way, this luxury B&B is *magnifique.* The two rooms in the main house have a discreetly French feel, while the spacious boathouse is nautically themed. All have sublime views.

🍴 Eating & Drinking

Akaroa

Fish & Chips
Fish & Chips $

(Map p248; 59 Beach Rd; mains $6-19; ⏰11am-8pm) Order takeaways and sit by the ocean, or grab a table and tuck into blue cod, scallops, oysters and other assorted deep-fried goodness. Either way, keep a close eye on the local posse of eager cats and seagulls.

Little Bistro
French $$$

(Map p248; 📞03-304 7314; www.thelittlebistro.co.nz; 33 Rue Lavaud; mains $28-40; ⏰5pm-late Tue-Sat) *Très petite, très chic* and very tasty. Look forward to classic bistro style given a proud Kiwi spin with local seafood, South Island wines and Canterbury craft beers. The menu changes seasonally, but usually includes favourites such as crusted lamb or Akaroa salmon terrine.

Harbar
Bar, Cafe

(Map p248; www.harbar.co.nz; 83 Rue Jolie; ⏰10am-9.30pm) A perfect waterfront

Akaroa Harbour

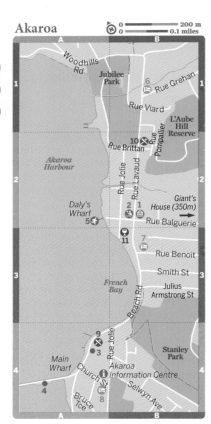

Akaroa

0 — 200 m
0 — 0.1 miles

Woodhills Rd
Jubilee Park
Rue Grehan
Rue Viard
L'Aube Hill Reserve
Rue Brittan
Rue Pompallier
Akaroa Harbour
Rue Jolie
Rue Lavaud
Daly's Wharf
Giant's House (350m)
Rue Balguerie
Rue Benoit
Smith St
French Bay
Julius Armstrong St
Beach Rd
Main Wharf
Church St
Akaroa Information Centre
Rue Jolie
Stanley Park
Selwyn Ave
Bruce Tce

Akaroa

location combines with rustic outdoor seating to produce Akaroa's best place for a sundowner drink. If you're peckish, tuck into pizza or fish and chips.

ⓘ Information

Akaroa Information Centre (Map p248; ☎03-304 8600; www.akaroa.com; 120 Rue Jolie; ⊙9am-5pm) Tours, activities, accommodation and postal services.

ⓘ Getting There & Away

Akaroa French Connection (☎0800 800 575; www.akaroabus.co.nz; one way/return $25/45) Daily shuttle service to/from Christchurch.

Akaroa Shuttle (☎0800 500 929; www.akaroashuttle.co.nz; one way/return $35/50) Heads to/from Christchurch daily, increasing to twice daily from November to April.

NORTH CANTERBURY

Hanmer Springs

Ringed by sculpted mountains, Hanmer Springs is the main thermal resort on the South Island. It's a pleasantly low-key spot to indulge yourself, whether soaking in hot pools, dining out or being pampered in the spa complex.

⊙ Sights & Activities

Wai Ariki Farm Park   Farm, Zoo
(☎03-315 7772; www.waiariki-farmpark.co.nz; 108 Rippingale Rd; adult/child $12/6; ⊙10am-4pm Tue-Sun, daily during school holidays) With more animals than Dr Dolittle's Facebook page, Wai Ariki is a great spot for kids. Llamas, Tibetan yaks, deer, rabbits, guinea pigs and goats all feature, and many of the critters can be hand-fed; horse treks for the young ones are also available (from $50).

Hanmer Springs Thermal Pools   Spa
(☎03-315 0000; www.hanmersprings.co.nz; 42 Amuri Ave; adult/child $20/10, locker $2; ⊙10am-9pm) 🏊 Maori legend has it that these springs formed as a result of embers from Mt Ngauruhoe in the North Island falling from the sky. The main pool

complex consists of a series of large pools of various temperatures, along with smaller landscaped rock pools, a freshwater 25m lap pool with a whirlpool attached, private thermal pools ($30 per 30 minutes) and a cafe. Kids of all ages will love the waterslides and speedy superbowl ride ($10).

The adjacent **Spa** (📞0800 873 529, 03-315 0029; www.hanmerspa.co.nz; ⏰10am-7pm) has massage and beauty treatments from $75. Entry to the pools is discounted to $12 if you partake of the spa's facilities.

Thrillseekers Adventures
Adventure Sports

(📞03-315 7046; www.thrillseekers.co.nz; Hanmer Springs Rd) Bungy off a 35m-high bridge ($169), jetboat the Waiau Gorge (adult/child $115/60), white-water raft (Grade II to III) down the Waiau River (adult/child $149/79) or get dirty on a quad-bike (adult/child $149/99).

Hanmer Springs Adventure Centre
Adventure Sports

(📞03-315 7233; www.hanmeradventure.co.nz; 20 Conical Hill Rd; ⏰8.30am-5pm) Offers quad-biking (from $129), mountainbike shuttles to the top of Jack's Pass ($115), clay-shooting ($35) and archery ($35). It also books local tours and rents mountain bikes (per hour/day from $19/45), fishing rods (per day $29) and ski/snowboard gear.

Hanmer Springs Ski Area
Skiing

(📞027 434 1806; www. skihanmer.co.nz; day pass adult/child $60/30) Only 17km from town via an unsealed road, this small complex has runs to suit all levels of ability.

Mt Lyford Alpine Resort
Skiing

(📞03-315 6178, snow-phone 03-366 1220; www. mtlyford.co.nz; day pass $70/35) This ski field is 60km from Hanmer, off the Inland Rd to Kaikoura.

Sleeping

Woodbank Park Cottages
Cottages $$

(📞03-315 5075; www.woodbankcottages.co.nz; 381 Woodbank Rd; d $200) These two matching cottages in a woodland setting are around 10 minutes' drive from Hanmer, but feel a million miles away. Decor is crisp and modern, bathrooms and kitchens are well appointed and wooden decks come equipped with gas barbecues and rural views.

Chalets Motel
Motel $$

(📞03-315 7097; www.chaletsmotel.co.nz; 56 Jacks Pass Rd; d $135-180; 📶) Soak up the mountain views from these tidy, reasonably priced, free-standing wooden chalets, set on the slopes behind the town

Hanmer Springs Thermal Pools
MATTHEW MICAH WRIGHT/GETTY IMAGES ©

If You Like...
Southern Wildlife

If you like dolphin swimming with Black Cat Cruises (p246), here are a few other ways to encounter some South Island wildlife in this neck of the woods.

1 ORANA WILDLIFE PARK
(www.oranawildlifepark.co.nz; McLeans Island Rd, McLeans Island; adult/child $28/9; ⏰10am-5pm) There's an excellent, walk-through native-bird aviary here, a nocturnal kiwi house, and a reptile exhibit featuring tuatara. Most of the 80-hectare grounds are devoted to Africana, including rhinos, giraffes, zebras, lemurs and cheetahs.

2 WILLOWBANK WILDLIFE RESERVE
(www.willowbank.co.nz; 60 Hussey Rd, Northwood; adult/child $28/11; ⏰9.30am-7pm Oct-Apr, to 5pm May-Sep) About 10km north of central Christchurch, Willowbank focuses on native NZ critters (including kiwis), heritage farmyard animals and hands-on enclosures with wallabies, deer and lemurs. There's also a re-created Maori village. In the evening this is the setting for the **Ko Tane** (www.kotane.co.nz; adult/child $135/68; ⏰5.30pm) cultural experience, which includes a traditional Maori welcome, cultural performance and *hangi* (earth oven) meal.

3 AKAROA DOLPHINS
(Map p248; ☎03-304 7866; www.akaroadolphins.co.nz; 65 Beach Rd, Akaroa; adult/child $74/35; ⏰12.45pm year-round, plus 10.15am & 3.15pm Oct-Apr) Two-hour wildlife cruises with a complimentary drink and home baking. Say hi to Murphy – wildlife-spotting dog extraordinaire – for us.

centre. All have full kitchens and the more expensive units have spa baths.

St James   Apartments $$$
(☎03-315 5225; www.thestjames.co.nz; 20 Chisholm Cres; apt $190-365; 📶) Luxuriate in a schmick modern apartment with all the mod cons, including an iPod dock and a kitchen with the latest Fisher & Paykel appliances. Sizes range from studios to two-bedroom apartments.

🍴 Eating & Drinking

Chantellini's   French $$$
(☎03-315 7667; www.chantellinis.com; 11 Jollies Pass Rd; mains $36-39; ⏰6-10pm Mon-Sat) Tucked away behind the main street, this quiet oasis offers a winning combination of classic French cooking, generous portions and charming service. Chandeliers and black drapes create an elegant ambience.

Monteith's Brewery Bar   Pub
(www.mbbh.co.nz; 47 Amuri Ave; ⏰9am-11pm) The best pub in town features lots of different Monteith's beers and tasty tucker from cooked breakfasts ($12 to $17), to bar snacks ($10 to $17) to full meals ($23 to $35). Live musicians kick off from 4pm Sundays.

ℹ Information

Hurunui i-SITE (☎03-315 0000; www.visithanmersprings.co.nz; 42 Amuri Ave; ⏰10am-5pm) Books transport, accommodation and activities.

ℹ Getting There & Away

Hanmer Connection (☎0800 242 663; www.hanmerconnection.co.nz; one way/return $30/50) Daily bus to/from Christchurch via Waipara and Amberley.

CENTRAL CANTERBURY

Methven

Methven is busiest in winter, when it fills up with snow bunnies heading to nearby Mt Hutt. Over summer it's a low-key and affordable base for hikers, bikers and fisher-folk.

Activities

Methven Heliski
Skiing

(☏03-302 8108; www.methvenheli.co.nz; Main St; 5-run day trips $975; ☺Jul-Sep) Trips include guide service, safety equipment and lunch.

Aoraki Balloon Safaris
Ballooning

(☏03-302 8172; www.nzballooning.com; flights $385) Early morning combos of snowcapped peaks and a breakfast with bubbly.

Skydiving NZ
Skydiving

(☏03-302 9143; www.skydivingnz.com; Pudding Hill Airfield) Offers tandem jumps from 12,000ft ($335) and 15,000ft ($440).

Sleeping

Redwood Lodge
Hostel $

(☏03-302 8964; www.redwoodlodge.co.nz; 3 Wayne Pl; s $50-60, d $90; @🛜) Despite being a BBH member there are no dorms at this charming family-friendly hostel. En suite doubles have their own TVs, and there's a large shared lounge and kitchen.

Bigger rooms can be reconfigured to accommodate families.

Whitestone Cottages
Rental Houses $$$

(☏021 179 0257; www.whitestonecottages.co.nz; 3016 Methven Hwy; house $210-350) For those mid-holiday moments when you just want to spread out, cook a meal, do your laundry and have your own space, these four large free-standing houses on the edge of town are just the ticket. Each sleeps six in two en suite bedrooms.

Eating & Drinking

Aqua
Japanese $

(112 Main St; mains $11-17; ☺5-9pm Jan-Oct) Dive into this tiny relaxed restaurant where kimono-clad servers deliver *yakisoba* (fried noodles), *ramen* (noodle soup) and *izakaya*-style dishes (small plates to share over drinks) to grateful guests. Top it off with sesame or green tea ice cream.

Blue Pub
Pub

(www.thebluepub.co.nz; Barkers Rd; mains $20-35; 🛜) Drink at the bar crafted from

The Southern Alps, near Methven

PETER UNGER/GETTY IMAGES ©

Don't Miss
Mt Hutt Ski Area

Canterbury's premier ski field, **Mt Hutt** has the largest skiable area of any of NZ's commercial fields (365 hectares), with its longest run stretching for 2km. Half of the terrain is suitable for intermediate skiers, with a quarter each for beginners and advanced. The season usually runs from mid-June to mid-October.

The ski field is only 26km from Methven, but in wintry conditions, the drive takes about 40 minutes; allow two hours from Christchurch. **Methven Travel** (☎03-302 8106, 0800 684 888; www.methventravel.co.nz) runs mountain buses in season ($20).

NEED TO KNOW
☎03-302 8811; www.nzski.com; day lift pass adult/child $95/53; ⏰9am-4pm

a huge slab of native timber, or tuck into robust meals in the quieter cafe. Afterwards, challenge the locals to a game of pool or watch the rugby on the big screen.

ℹ Information

Methven i-SITE (☎03-302 8955; www. amazingspace.co.nz; 160 Main St; ⏰7.30am-6pm Jul-Sep, 9am-5pm Mon-Fri, 10am-3pm Sat & Sun Oct-Jun; 🛜) The visitor information centre is housed in the Heritage Centre, which also includes a cafe, art gallery (free) and the hands-on *NZ Alpine & Agriculture Encounter* (adult/child $18/10).

ℹ Getting There & Around

Methven Travel (☎03-302 8106; www. methventravel.co.nz) Runs shuttles between Methven and Christchurch Airport ($42) three to four times a week, increasing to three times daily in the ski season.

SOUTH CANTERBURY

Lake Tekapo

At the southern end of its namesake lake, this little town has unobstructed views across turquoise water to a backdrop of rolling hills and snowcapped mountains. Rather than rushing on, it's worth staying to experience the region's glorious night sky from atop nearby Mt John.

 Sights & Activities

When the Mackenzie Basin was scoured out by glaciers, **Mt John** (1029m) remained as an island of tough bedrock in the centre of a vast river of ice. A road leads to the summit, or you can walk via a circuit track (2½ hours return).

Mountain bikes (per hour/half-day $10/25) and kayaks (per hour $25) can be hired from the Lake Tekapo YHA.

In winter Lake Tekapo is a base for downhill skiing at **Mt Dobson** or **Round Hill**, and cross-country skiing on the Two Thumb Range.

Church of the Good Shepherd
Church

(☉9am-5pm) The prime disgorging point for tour buses, this interdenominational lakeside church was built of stone and oak in 1935. Come early in the morning or late afternoon to avoid the peace-shattering hordes.

Tours

Earth & Sky
Tour

(☎03-680 6960; www.earthandsky.co.nz; SH8) 🍃 Nightly stargazing tours head up to the University of Canterbury's observatory on Mt John (adult/child $135/80).

Air Safaris
Scenic Flights

(☎03-680 6880; www.airsafaris.co.nz; SH8) 🍃 Unless you're a serious mountaineer with time to kill, you won't get better views of Aoraki/Mt Cook and its glaciers than those offered on the 'Grand Traverse' flights (adult/child $340/220).

Cruise Tekapo
Boat Tour

(☎027 479 7675; www.cruisetekapo.co.nz) 🍃 Lake cruises (from 25 minutes to two hours long) and fishing expeditions.

Sleeping

Chalet Boutique Motel
Apartments $$

(☎03-680 6774; www.thechalet.co.nz; 14 Pioneer Dr; units $185-295; 🛜) The 'boutique motel' tag doesn't do this superb lakeside complex justice. It might just about cover the four comfortable units in the main house, but doesn't come close to describing the modern two-bedroom house (with attached studio apartment) next door, or the wonderfully private 'Henkel hut' next to that.

Peppers Bluewater Resort
Resort $$

(☎03-360 1063; www.peppers.co.nz; SH8; d $111-226, apt $256-466; 🛜) Sprawling around rocky ponds and tussocky gardens, this huge resort offers a large variety of smart, contemporary accommodation, ranging from poky hotel rooms to spacious three-bedroom apartments and everything in between.

Eating

Astro Café
Cafe $

(Mt John Observatory, Godley Peaks Rd; mains $6-11; ☉10am-5pm) This glass-walled pavilion atop Mt John has spectacular 360-degree views across the entire Mackenzie Basin – quite possibly one of the planet's best locations for a cafe. Tuck into bagels with local Aoraki salmon, or fresh ham-off-the-bone sandwiches; the coffee and cake are good, too.

ℹ Information

Tekapo Springs Sales & Information Centre
(☎03-680 6579; SH8; ☉10am-6pm) Since the i-SITE closed, the folks from Tekapo Springs have filled the gap, dispensing brochures and advice. The only bookings they take are for its own complex though.

ⓘ Getting There & Away

Atomic Shuttles (☏03-349 0697; www.
atomictravel.co.nz) Daily buses to/from
Christchurch ($30, 3¼ hours), Geraldine ($20,
1¼ hours), Twizel ($20, 40 minutes), Cromwell
($30, three hours) and Queenstown ($30, 3¾
hours).

InterCity (☏03-365 1113; www.intercity.co.nz)
Daily coaches head to/from Christchurch (from
$36, 3¾ hours), Geraldine (from $21, 1¼ hours),
Mt Cook (from $30, 1½ hours), Cromwell (from
$36, 2¾ hours) and Queenstown (from $36, 4¾
hours).

Aoraki/Mt Cook National Park

The spectacular 700-sq-km Aoraki/Mt
Cook National Park, along with Fiordland,
and Mt Aspiring and Westland National
Parks, is part of the Southwest New Zealand (Te Wahipounamu) World Heritage Area, which extends from Westland's
Cook River down to Fiordland.

Of the 23 NZ mountains over 3000m,
19 are in this park. The highest is mighty
Aoraki/Mt Cook – at 3754m it's the tallest
peak in Australasia.

Aoraki/Mt Cook is a wonderful sight,
assuming there's no cloud in the way.
Most visitors arrive on tour buses, stop
at the Hermitage hotel for photos, and
then zoom off back down State Highway
80 (SH80). Hang around to soak up this
awesome peak and the surrounding
landscape, and to try the excellent short
walks.

◎ Sights

DOC Aoraki/ Mt Cook Visitor Centre
Interpretation Centre

(Department of Conservation; ☏03-435 1186;
www.doc.govt.nz; 1 Larch Grove; ☻8.30am-
4.30pm) **FREE** As well as being the font of
all knowledge about tramping routes and
weather conditions, DOC's visitor centre
has excellent displays on local flora,
fauna and history, as well as videos and
a sunken garden showcasing a historic
mountain hut. Most activities can be
booked here.

Sir Edmund Hillary Alpine Centre
Museum

(www.hermitage.co.nz; The Hermitage;
adult/child $20/10; ☻7am-8.30pm
Oct-Mar, 8am-7pm Apr-Sep) This
multimedia museum opened
just three weeks before the
January 2008 death of the
man widely regarded as
the greatest New Zea-
lander of all time. As well
as memorabilia and dis-
plays about mountain-
eering, there's a domed
digital planetarium
(showing four different
digital presentations)
and a cinema (screen-
ing four documentaries,
including the *Mt Cook
Magic* 3D movie and a

Aoraki/Mt Cook National Park

fascinating 75-minute film about Sir Ed's conquest of Mt Everest).

Tasman Glacier — Glacier

At 27km long and up to 3km wide, the Tasman is the largest of NZ's glaciers, but it's melting fast, losing hundreds of metres from its length each year. **Tasman Lake**, at the foot of the glacier, only started to form in the early 1970s and now stretches to 7km. The lake is covered by a maze of huge icebergs which are continuously being sheared off the glacier's terminal face.

In the glacier's last major advance (17,000 years ago), the glacier crept south far enough to carve out Lake Pukaki. A later advance did not reach out to the valley sides, so there's a gap between the outer valley walls and the lateral moraines of this later advance. The unsealed Tasman Valley Rd, which branches off Mt Cook Rd 800m south of the village, travels through this gap. From the Blue Lakes shelter, 8km along the road, the **Tasman Glacier View Track** (40 minutes return) leads to a viewpoint on the moraine wall, passing the Blue Lakes on the way.

🏃 Activities

Various easy walks from the Hermitage area are outlined in brochures available from DOC.

Hooker Valley Track — Hiking

Perhaps the best of the day walks, this track (three hours return from the Mt Cook Village) heads up the Hooker Valley and crosses three swing bridges to the Stocking Stream and the terminus of the Hooker Glacier. After the second swing bridge, Aoraki/Mt Cook totally dominates the valley, and you'll often see icebergs floating in Hooker Lake.

Kea Point Track — Hiking

The trail to Kea Point (two hours return from Mt Cook Village) is lined with native plants and ends at a platform with excellent views of Aoraki/Mt Cook, the Hooker Valley and the ice faces of Mt Sefton and the Footstool.

Glacier Sea-Kayaking — Kayaking

(☎03-435 1890; www.mtcook.com; per person $145; ⏰Oct–Apr) Guided trips head out on the terminal lake of the Tasman or the Mueller Glacier. There are usually icebergs to negotiate, but if this is your prime reason for taking the trip, it pays to check in advance whether there actually are any.

Southern Alps Guiding — Snow Sports

(☎03-435 1890; www.mtcook.com; Old Mountaineers, 3 Larch Grove Rd) From June to October heliskiers can head up Tasman Glacier for a 10km to 12km downhill run ($830 to $870). Private guiding is also available, as well as three- to four-hour helihiking trips on Tasman Glacier year-round ($450).

Glentanner Horse Trekking — Horse Riding

(☎03-435 1855; www.glentanner.co.nz; 1/2/3hr ride $70/90/150; ⏰Nov-Apr) Leads guided treks on a high-country sheep station with options suited to all levels of experience.

🎫 Tours

Tasman Valley 4WD & Argo Tours — Tour

(☎0800 686 800; www.mountcooktours.co.nz; adult/child $75/38) Offers a 90-minute Argo (8WD all-terrain vehicle) tour checking out the Tasman Glacier and its terminal lake. Expect plenty of alpine flora and an interesting commentary along the way.

Glacier Explorers — Boat Tour

(☎03-435 1641; www.glacierexplorers.com; adult/child $145/70) Head out on the terminal lake of the Tasman Glacier onboard a custom-built MAC boat and get up close and personal with 300-year-old icebergs. Book at the activities desk at the Hermitage.

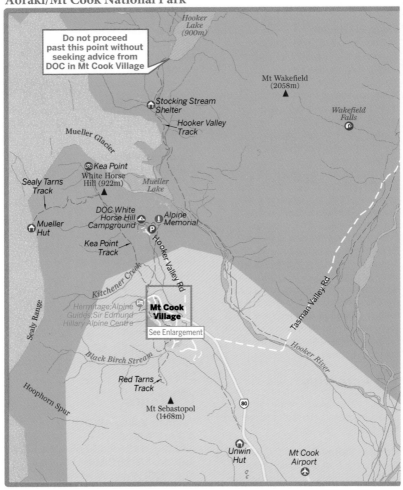

Do not proceed past this point without seeking advice from DOC in Mt Cook Village

Helicopter Line   Scenic Flights

(📞03-435 1801; www.helicopter.co.nz) From Glentanner Park, the Helicopter Line offers 20-minute Alpine Vista flights ($230), an exhilarating 35-minute flight over the Ben Ohau Range ($345) and a 40-minute Mountains High flight over the Tasman Glacier and alongside Aoraki/Mt Cook ($425). All feature snow landings.

Mount Cook Ski Planes   Scenic Flights

(📞03-430 8034; www.mtcookskiplanes. com) Based at Mt Cook Airport, offering 40-minute (adult/child $405/295) and 55-minute (adult/child $530/405) flights, both with snow landings. Flightseeing without a landing is a cheaper option; try the 25-minute Mini Tasman trip (adult/child $275/255) or 45-minute Alpine Wonderland (adult/child $370/275).

Hermitage
Hotel $$$

(📞03-435 1809; www.hermitage.co.nz; Terrace Rd; r $239-599; @ 🛜) Completely dominating Mt Cook Village, this famous hotel offers fantastic mountain views. While the corridors in some of the older wings can seem a little hospital-like, all of the rooms have been renovated to a high standard. As well as the hotel, the Hermitage offers motel rooms and well-equipped A-frame chalets.

Eating & Drinking

Old Mountaineers
Cafe, Bar $$

(www.mtcook.com; Bowen Dr; breakfast $10-15, lunch $15-26, dinner $18-35; ⏱10am-9pm daily Nov-Apr, Tue-Sun May & Jul-Oct; 🛜) 🍴 A good-value alternative to the eateries at the Hermitage, this large cafe-bar provides mountain views through picture windows or from outside tables in summer. As well as cooked breakfasts, it delivers top-notch burgers, pizza, pasta and salad. Linger to study the old black-and-white pics and mountaineering memorabilia.

Chamois Bar & Grill
Pub

(www.mountcookbackpackers.co.nz; Bowen Dr; ⏱4pm-late) Upstairs in Mt Cook Backpacker Lodge, in the heart of the village, this large bar offers pub grub, a pool table, a big-screen TV and the occasional live gig.

Information

The DOC Visitor Centre (p254) is the best source of local information. The nearest ATM and supermarket are in Twizel.

Getting There & Away

Cook Connection (📞0800 266 526; www.cookconnect.co.nz) Shuttle services to Lake Tekapo ($35, 1½ hours) and Twizel ($25, one hour).

InterCity (📞03-365 1113; www.intercity.co.nz) Daily coaches head to/from Christchurch (from $67, 5¼ hours), Geraldine (from $38, three hours), Lake Tekapo, (from $30, 1½ hours), Cromwell (from $59, 2¾ hours) and Queenstown (from $64, four hours).

Sleeping

Aoraki/Mt Cook Alpine Lodge
Lodge $$

(📞03-435 1860; www.aorakialpinelodge.co.nz; Bowen Dr; d $164-189; @) This modern lodge has comfortable en suite rooms and a huge lounge and kitchen area. The superb mountain views from the barbecue area will have you arguing for the privilege of grilling the sausages for dinner.

THE WEST COAST

Greymouth

The West Coast's largest town has gold in its veins, and today its fortunes still ebb and flow with the tide of mining, although dairy farming and tourism top up the coffers.

Sights & Activities

Shantytown Museum

(www.shantytown.co.nz; Rutherglen Rd, Paroa; adult/child/family $31.50/15.50/74; ⏱8.30am-5pm) Eight kilometres south of Greymouth and 2km inland from SH6, Shantytown re-creates a 1860s gold-mining town, complete with steam-train rides, post-office, pub and Rosie's House of Ill Repute. There's also gold panning, a flying fox, sawmill, a gory hospital and 10-minute holographic movies in the Princess Theatre.

Left Bank Art Gallery Gallery

(www.leftbankarts.org.nz; 1 Tainui St; admission by donation; ⏱10am-4pm daily) This 90-year old former bank houses contemporary NZ jade carvings, prints, paintings, photographs and ceramics. The gallery also fosters and supports a wide society of West Coast artists.

Monteith's Brewing Co Brewery

(☎03-768 4149; www.monteiths.co.nz; cnr Turumaha & Herbert Sts; ⏱10.30am-7.30pm) The original Monteith's brewhouse may simply be brand HQ for mainstream product largely brewed elsewhere, but it still delivers heritage in spades through its excellent-value tour (one hour, $20, includes generous samples; three to five tours per day). The flash tasting room-cum-bar is now Greymouth's most exciting watering hole (tasty snacks $7 to $18) – shame it shuts up shop so early.

Sleeping

Ardwyn House B&B $

(☎03-768 6107; ardwynhouse@hotmail.com; 48 Chapel St; s/d incl breakfast from $60/90;

📶) This old-fashioned B&B nestles amid steep gardens on a quiet dead-end street. Mary, the well-travelled host, cooks a splendid breakfast.

Paroa Hotel Hotel $$

(☎03-762 6860, 0800 762 6860; www.paroa.co.nz; 508 Main South Rd, Paroa; d $128-140; 📶) Opposite the Shantytown turn-off, this family-owned hotel (60 years and counting) has spacious units sharing a large lawned garden next to the beach. The notable bar and restaurant dishes up warm hospitality in the form of roast, pavlova (mains $18 to $32), and beer, amid local clientele.

Eating & Drinking

DP:One Cafe Cafe $

(104 Mawhera Quay; meals $7-23; ⏱8am-8pm Mon-Fri, 9am-5pm Sat & Sun; 📶) A stalwart of the Greymouth cafe scene, this hip joint serves great espresso, along with good-value grub. Groovy tunes, wi-fi, a relaxed vibe and quayside tables make this a welcoming spot to linger.

Freddy's Cafe Cafe $

(115 Mackay St; snacks $4-7, meals $8-18; ⏱8am-5pm) Don't miss the doorway because upstairs the restrained-retro Freddy's beckons with good espresso, all-day hot meals (pancakes, seafood chowder, pasta) alongside an appealing selection of cabinet food.

Information

Greymouth i-SITE (☎03-768 5101, 0800 473 966; www.greydistrict.co.nz; Railway Station, 164 Mackay St; ⏱9am-5pm Mon-Fri, 9.30am-4pm Sat & Sun; 📶) The helpful crew at the railway station can assist with all manner of advice and bookings, including those for DOC huts and walks. See also www.westcoastnz.com.

Getting There & Around

Combined with the i-SITE in the railway station, the **West Coast Travel Centre** (☎03-768 7080; www.westcoasttravel.co.nz; Railway Station, 164 Mackay St; ⏱9am-5pm Mon-Fri, 10am-4pm Sat & Sun; 📶) books local and national transport and offers luggage storage.

PAUL KENNEDY/GETTY IMAGES ©

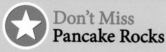

Don't Miss
Pancake Rocks

Located midway between Westport and Greymouth is Punakaiki, a small settlement beside the rugged 38,000-hectare Paparoa National Park.

Punakaiki is famous for its fantastic Pancake Rocks and blowholes. Through a layering-weathering process called stylobedding, the Dolomite Point limestone has formed into what looks like piles of thick pancakes. Aim for high tide (tide times are posted at the visitor centre) when the sea surges into caverns and booms menacingly through blowholes. See it on a wild day and be reminded that Mother Nature really is the boss. An easy 15-minute walk loops from the highway out to the rocks and blowholes.

Tramps around Punakaiki include the **Truman Track** (30 minutes return) and the **Punakaiki–Pororari Loop** (3½ hours), which goes up the spectacular limestone Pororari River Gorge before popping over a hill and coming down the bouldery Punakaiki River to rejoin the highway.

The **Paparoa National Park Visitor Centre and i-SITE** (☎03-731 1895; www.doc. govt.nz; SH6; ⊙9am-5pm Oct-Nov, to 6pm Dec-Mar, to 4.30pm Apr-Sep) has information on the park and track conditions, and handles bookings for local attractions and accommodation including hut tickets.

Bus

InterCity (☎03-365 1113; www.intercity.co.nz) has daily buses north to Westport (two hours) and Nelson (six hours), and south to Franz Josef Glacier (3½ hours). **Naked Bus** (www.nakedbus. com) runs the same route three days a week.

Both companies offer connections to destinations further afield.

Atomic Travel (☎03-349 0697, 0508 108 359; www.atomictravel.co.nz) passes Greymouth on its daily Nelson to Franz Josef Glacier service (and onward to Queenstown), as well as running across Arthur's Pass to Christchurch. **West Coast**

MERTEN SNIJDERS/GETTY IMAGES ©

Don't Miss
TranzAlpine

The *TranzAlpine* is one of the world's great train journeys, traversing the Southern Alps between Christchurch and Greymouth, from the Pacific Ocean to the Tasman Sea, passing through Arthur's Pass National Park. En route is a sequence of dramatic landscapes, from the flat, alluvial Canterbury Plains, through narrow alpine gorges, an 8.5km tunnel, beech-forested river valleys, and alongside a lake fringed with cabbage trees. The 4½-hour journey is unforgettable, even in bad weather (if it's raining on one coast, it's probably fine on the other).

NEED TO KNOW
☑ 03-341 2588, 0800 872 467; www.kiwirailscenic.co.nz; adult/child one way from $99/69; ⏲ departs Christchurch 8.15am, Greymouth 1.45pm

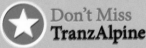 Shuttle (☑ 03-768 0028, 0274 927 000; www.westcoastshuttle.co.nz) also runs a daily service between Greymouth and Christchurch.

Westland Tai Poutini National Park

The biggest highlights of the Westland Tai Poutini National Park are the Franz Josef and Fox glaciers. Nowhere else at this latitude do glaciers come so close to the ocean.

Some say Franz Josef is the superior ice experience, and, while it's visually more impressive, the walk to Fox is shorter, more interesting and often gets you closer to the ice.

FRANZ JOSEF GLACIER

The early Maori knew Franz Josef as Ka Roimata o Hine Hukatere (Tears of the Avalanche Girl). Legend tells of a girl losing her lover who fell from the local peaks, and her flood of tears freezing into the glacier. The glacier was first explored by Europeans in 1865, with Austrian Julius Haast naming it after the Austrian emperor. The glacier car park is 5km from Franz Josef village; the primary viewpoint is a 40-minute walk from there.

⊙ Sights & Activities

West Coast Wildlife Centre
Wildlife

(www.wildkiwi.co.nz; cnr Cron & Cowan Sts; day pass adult/child/family $30/18/80, with backstage pass $50/30/125; ☎) 🖉 This feel-good attraction ticks all the right boxes (exhibition, cafe, retail, wi-fi), then goes a whole lot further by actually breeding the rowi – the rarest kiwi in the world. The day pass is well worthwhile by the time you've viewed the conservation, glacier and heritage displays, and hung out with real, live kiwi in their ferny enclosure.

INDEPENDENT WALKS

A rewarding alternative to driving to the glacier car park is the richly rainforested **Te Ara a Waiau Walkway/Cycleway**, starting from near the fire station at the southern end of town. It's a one-hour walk (each way) or half that by bicycle; bicycles are available for hire from **Across Country Quad Bikes** (☎ 03-752 0123, 0800 234 288; www.acrosscountryquad-bikes.co.nz; Air Safaris Bldg, SH6) or the **YHA** (☎ 03-752 0754; www.yha.co.nz; 2-4 Cron St; dm $23-30, s $57, d $85-110; @☎).

Several glacier viewpoints are accessed from the car park, including **Sentinel Rock** (20 minutes return) and the **Ka Roimata o Hine Hukatere Walk** (1½ hours return), leading you to the terminal face (read the signs; respect the barriers).

Other longer walks include the **Douglas Walk** (one hour return), off the Glacier Access Rd, which passes moraine from the 1750 advance, and **Peter's Pool**, a small kettle lake. The **Terrace Track** (30 minutes return) is an easy amble over bushy terraces behind the village, with Waiho River views. Two good rainforest walks, **Tatare Tunnels** and **Callery Gorge Walk** (both around 1½ hours return), start from Cowan St.

GUIDED WALKS & HELIHIKES

Small group walks with experienced guides (boots, jackets and equipment supplied) are offered by **Franz Josef Glacier Guides** (☎ 03-752 0763, 0800 484 337; www.franzjosefglacier.com; 6 Main Rd). Both standard tours require helicopter transfers to and from the ice; the 'Ice Explorer' ($325) is bookended by a four-minute flight, with around three hours on the ice; the easier 'Heli Hike' ($429) explores higher reaches of the glacier, requiring a 10-minute flight with around two hours on the ice. Taking

Mountaineer on Franz Josef Glacier
BO TORNVIG/GETTY IMAGES ©

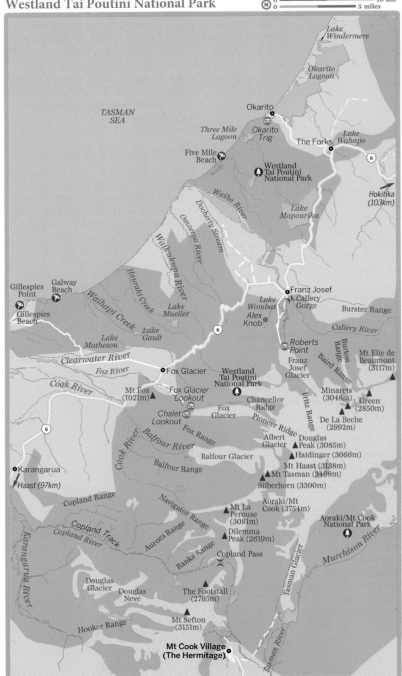

N 0 — 10 km
0 — 5 miles

Lake Windermere

Okarito Lagoon

TASMAN SEA

Three Mile Lagoon

Okarito

Okarito Trig

The Forks

Lake Wahapo

6

Five Mile Beach

Westland Tai Poutini National Park

Hokitika (103km)

Waiho River

Docherty Stream

Omoeroa River

Lake Mapourika

Waikukupa River

Hauraki Creek

Lake Mueller

6

Franz Josef

Callery Gorge

Burster Range

Lake Wombat

Alex Knob

Callery River

Gillespies Point

Galway Beach

Gillespies Beach

Waihapi Creek

Lake Matheson

Lake Gault

Roberts Point

Baird Range

Burton Range

Mt Elie de Beaumont (3117m)

Clearwater River

Fox River

Fox Glacier

Franz Josef Glacier

Cook River

Mt Fox (1021m)

Fox Glacier Lookout

Westland Tai Poutini National Park

Chancellor Ridge

Pioneer Ridge

Fritz Range

Minarets (3048m)

Green (2850m)

De La Beche (2992m)

Chalet Lookout

Fox Glacier

Fox Range

Albert Glacier

Douglas Peak (3085m)

6

Balfour River

Balfour Glacier

Haidinger (3066m)

Mt Haast (3138m)

Karangarua

Haast (97km)

Cook River

Balfour Range

Copland Range

Navigator Range

Aurora Range

Mt Tasman (3498m)

Silberhorn (3300m)

Aoraki/Mt Cook (3754m)

Aoraki/Mt Cook National Park

Copland Track

Copland River

Mt La Perouse (3081m)

Dilemma Peak (2619m)

Murchison River

Karangarua River

Banks Range

Copland Pass

Tasman Glacier

Douglas Glacier

Douglas Neve

The Footstall (2765m)

Hooker Range

Mt Sefton (3151m)

Tasman River

Mt Cook Village (The Hermitage)

around three hours, the 'Glacier Valley Walk' ($75) follows the Waiho River up to the moraine, offering a chance to get beyond the public barriers for close-up views of the ice. All trips are $10 to $30 cheaper for children.

OTHER ACTIVITIES

Glacier Hot Pools Hot Pools
(www.glacierhotpools.co.nz; 63 Cron St; adult/child $25/18; ☺1-9pm) Skillfully embedded into pretty rainforest greenery on the edge of town, this stylish outdoor hot-pool complex is perfect après hike or on a rainy day.

Skydive Franz Skydiving
(☎03-752 0714, 0800 458 677; www.skydive-franz.co.nz; Main Rd) Claiming NZ's highest jump (18,000ft, 80 seconds freefall, $559), this company also offers 15,000ft for $419, and 12,000ft for $319.

Tours

SKYDIVING & AERIAL SIGHTSEEING

A short, scenic helicopter or fixed-wing flight above the glaciers is a terrific way to grasp the impressive size of them. Booking offices line the main street.

Air Safaris Scenic Flights
(☎03-752 0716, 0800 723 274; www.airsafaris.co.nz) Franz' only fixed-wing flyer offers a 30-minute 'twin glacier' ($250) and a 50-minute 'grand traverse' ($340) flight.

Fox & Franz Josef Heliservices Scenic Flights
(☎03-752 0793, 0800 800 793; www.scenic-flights.co.nz)

Glacier Helicopters Scenic Flights
(☎03-752 0755, 0800 800 732; www.glacierheli-copters.co.nz)

Helicopter Line Scenic Flights
(☎03-752 0767, 0800 807 767; www.helicopter.co.nz)

Mountain Helicopters Scenic Flights
(☎03-752 0046, 0800 369 432; www.mountain-helicopters.co.nz)

OTHER TOURS

Glacier Valley Eco Tours Guided Tour
(☎03-752 0699, 0800 999 739; www.gla-ciervalley.co.nz) Offers leisurely three- to eight-hour walking tours around local sights ($70 to $160), packed with local knowledge. Glacier shuttle service ($12.50 return).

Sleeping

58 on Cron Motel $$
(☎03-752 0627, 0800 662 766; www.58oncron.co.nz; 58 Cron St; d $175-245; ☎) Lacking imagination in both name and decor, these motel units nevertheless impress with their comfort, cleanliness, mod cons and considerate attitude to guests.

Glenfern Villas Apartment $$$
(☎03-752 005, 0800 453 6334; www.glenfern.co.nz; SH6; d $230-289; ☎) A handy 3km out of the tourist hubbub, these delightful one- and two-bedroom villas sit amid groomed grounds with private decks surveying mountain scenery. Top-notch beds, full kitchens, bike hire and family-friendly facilities strongly suggest 'holiday', not 'stop-off'.

Holly Homestead B&B $$$
(☎03-752 0299; www.hollyhomestead.co.nz; SH6; d $265-430; @☎) Guests are welcomed with fresh home baking at this wisteria-draped 1926 B&B. Choose from three characterful en suite rooms or a suite, all of which share a deck perfect for that sundowner. Children over 12 welcome.

Eating

Landing Bar & Restaurant Pub $$
(www.thelandingbar.co.nz; SH6; mains $20-40; ☺7.30am-late; ☎) This busy but well-run pub offers an inordinately huge menu of crowd-pleasing food such as burgers, steaks and pizza. The patio – complete

Detour:
Okarito

Fifteen kilometres south of Whataroa is the turn-off to the Forks, branching west for 13km to the magical seaside hamlet of Okarito (population 30ish). It sits alongside **Okarito Lagoon**, the largest unmodified wetland in NZ and a superb place for spotting birds including rare kiwi and the majestic kotuku.

From a car park on the Strand you can begin the easy **Wetland Walk** (20 minutes), a longer walk to **Three Mile Lagoon** (2¾ hours return), and a jolly good puff up to **Okarito Trig** (1½ hours return), which rewards the effort with spectacular Southern Alps and Okarito Lagoon views (weather contingent).

Okarito Nature Tours (☏ 050 865 2748, 03-753 4014; www.okarito.co.nz; kayak half-/full day $60/70; 🕿) hires out kayaks for paddles into the lagoon and up into the luxuriant rainforest channels where all sorts of birds hang out. Guided tours are available (from $85), while overnight rentals ($80) allow experienced paddlers to explore further afield.

Okarito Boat Tours (☏ 03-753 4223; www.okaritoboattours.co.nz) runs bird-spotting lagoon tours, the most fruitful of which is the Early Bird (7.30am, 1½ hrs, $70). Other worthy options include the one-hour sightseeing tour (2.30pm, $45), and the two-hour nature tours (9am and 11.30am, $85).

---

with sunshine and gas heaters – is a good place to warm up after a day on the ice.

Information

Westland Tai Poutini National Park Visitor Centre & i-SITE (☏ 03-752 0796; www.doc.govt.nz; Cron St; ◷ 8.30am-6pm summer, to 5pm winter) Regional DOC office with good exhibits, weather information and track updates; the i-SITE desk books major nationwide transport except the Interislander ferry. See also www.glaciercountry.co.nz.

Getting There & Around

InterCity (☏ 03-365 1113; www.intercity.co.nz) has daily buses south to Fox Glacier (35 minutes) and Queenstown (eight hours); and north to Nelson (10 hours). **Naked Bus** (www.nakedbus.com) services the same routes three times a week. Both provide connections to destinations further afield.

Glacier Valley Shuttle (☏ 03-752 0699, 0800 999 739; www.glaciervalley.co.nz) runs scheduled shuttle services to the glacier car park (return trip $12.50).

FOX GLACIER

Fox is smaller and quieter than Franz Josef, with a farmy feel and more open aspect. Beautiful Lake Matheson is a highlight, as are the historic sites and the beach itself down at Gillespies Beach.

◉ Sights & Activities

GLACIER VALLEY WALKS

It's 1.5km from Fox Village to the glacier turn-off, and a further 2km to the car park, which you can reach under your own steam via **Te Weheka Walkway/Cycleway**, a pleasant rainforest trail starting just south of the Bella Vista motel.

From the car park the terminal face is 30 to 40 minutes' walk. How close you can get to it depends on conditions. Obey all signs: this place is dangerously dynamic.

Short walks near the glacier include the **Moraine Walk** (over a major 18th-century advance) and **Minnehaha Walk**. The **River Walk** extends to the **Chalet Lookout Track** (1½ hours return) leading to a glacier lookout. The fully accessible

River Walk Lookout Track (20 minutes return) starts from the Glacier View Road car park and allows people of all abilities the chance to view the glacier.

Fox Glacier Guiding   Guided Walk
(📞03-751 0825, 0800 111 600; www.foxguides.co.nz; 44 Main Rd) Guided walks (equipment provided) are organised by Fox Glacier Guiding. Half-day walks cost $132/105 per adult/child; full-day walks are $185. There are also easygoing two-hour interpretive walks to the glacier (adult/child $49/35). Longer guided helihike adventures are also available.

OTHER WALKS

Lake Matheson   Lake
The famous 'mirror lake' can be found about 6km down Cook Flat Rd. Wandering slowly (as you should), it will take 1½ hours to complete the circuit. The best time to visit is early morning, or when the sun is low in the late afternoon, although the presence of the Matheson Cafe means that any time is a good time.

 Tours

Skydive Fox Glacier   Skydiving
(📞03-751 0080, 0800 751 0080; www.skydivefox.co.nz; Fox Glacier Airfield, SH6) Eye-popping scenery abounds on leaps from 16,000ft ($399) or 12,000ft ($299). The airfield is conveniently located three minutes' walk from the centre of town.

Fox & Franz Josef Heliservices   Scenic Flights
(📞03-751 0866, 0800 800 793; www.scenic-flights.co.nz)

 Sleeping

Fox Glacier Top 10 Holiday Park   Holiday Park $
(📞03-751 0821, 0800 154 366; www.fghp.co.nz; Kerrs Rd; sites from $20 per person, s/d $70, cabins & units $70-215; @ 🛜) Options to suit all budgets, from well-draining tent sites and gravel campervan sites, to lodge rooms and upscale motel units. Shipshape amenities include a splendid communal kitchen/dining room, and a playground for the kids.

Rainforest Motel   Motel $$
(📞03-751 0140, 0800 724 636; www.rainforest-motel.co.nz; 15 Cook flat Rd; d $115-145; 🛜) Rustic log cabins on the outside with neutral decor on the inside. Epic lawns for running around on or simply enjoying the mountain views. A tidy, good-value option.

Westhaven   Motel $$
(📞03-751 0084, 0800 369 452; www.thewesthaven.co.nz; SH6; d $145-185; @ 🛜) These architecturally precise suites are a classy combo of corrugated steel and local stone amid burnt-red and ivory walls. The deluxe king rooms have spa baths, and there are bikes to hire (half-/full day $20/40).

 Eating

Matheson Cafe   Modern NZ $$
(📞03-751 0878; www.lakematheson.com; Lake Matheson Rd; breakfast & lunch $9-20, dinner $17-33; ⏰8am-late Nov-Mar, to 4pm Apr-Oct) This cafe does everything right: sharp architecture that maximises inspiring mountain views, strong coffee, craft beers and upmarket fare from a smoked salmon breakfast bagel, to slow-cooked lamb followed by berry crumble.

 Information

DOC South Westland Weheka Area Office
(📞03-751 0807; SH6; ⏰10am-2pm Mon-Fri) This is no longer a general visitor information centre, but has the usual DOC information, Backcountry Hut Passes and weather/track updates.

 Getting There & Around

InterCity (📞03-365 1113; www.intercity.co.nz) Runs two buses a day north to Franz Josef (40 minutes), the morning bus continuing to Nelson (11 hours). Daily southbound services run to Queenstown (7½ hours).

Naked Bus (www.nakedbus.com) Runs three times a week north along the coast all the way through to Nelson, and south to Queenstown.

Fox Glacier Shuttles (📞0800 369 287) Staffed by the inimitable Murray, who will drive you around the area from Franz Josef to the Copland Valley, and including Lake Matheson, Gillespies Beach and the glaciers. Look for him parked opposite Fox Glacier Motors.

Queenstown & the South

With a cinematic background of mountains and lakes you actually might have seen in the movies, and a 'what can we think of next' array of adventure activities, it's little wonder Queenstown tops many travellers' Kiwi itineraries. You can slow down (slightly) in Wanaka, Queenstown's junior cousin, which also has good bars and outdoor adventures on tap.

To the east, Otago is overflowing with picturesque scenery. The region's historic heart is Dunedin, with excellent restaurants and cafes, and a vibrant student-based culture. If you're seeking wildlife, head to the Otago Peninsula, where penguins, albatross, sea lions and seals are easily sighted.

The bottom end of the South Island offers some of the country's most spectacular landscapes: Fiordland National Park, with jagged peaks, glistening lakes and Milford and Doubtful Sounds; and the peaceful Catlins, with bird-rich native forests and a rugged, coastline.

Seaplane on Lake Te Anau (p308)
JOHN ELK/GETTY IMAGES ©

Queenstown & the South

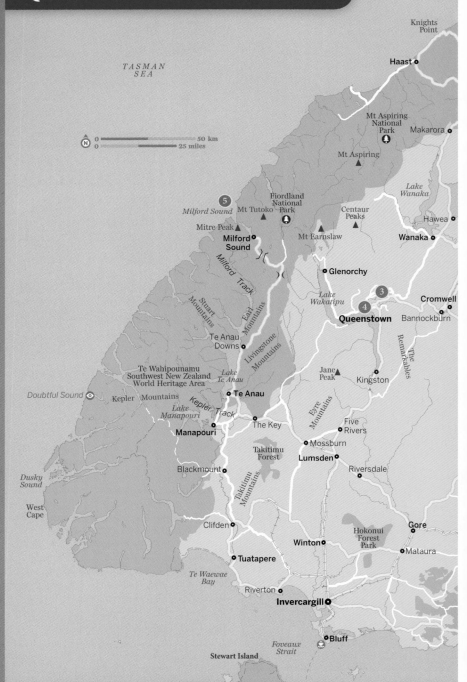

TASMAN
SEA

Knights
Point

Haast

Mt Aspiring
National
Park

Makarora

Mt Aspiring

0   50 km
0   25 miles

Lake
Wanaka

5

Milford Sound

Mt Tutoko

Fiordland
National
Park

Centaur
Peaks

Hawea

Mitre Peak

Milford
Sound

Mt Earnslaw

Wanaka

Glenorchy

Lake
Wakatipu

3

Cromwell

Stuart
Mountains

Earl
Mountains

4

Queenstown

Bannockburn

Te Anau
Downs

Livingstone
Mountains

Te Wahipounamu
Southwest New Zealand
World Heritage Area

Lake
Te Anau

Jane
Peak

Kingston

Doubtful Sound

Kepler   Mountains

Kepler Track

Te Anau

Eyre
Mountains

Lake
Manapouri

The Key

Manapouri

Five
Rivers

Takitimu
Forest

Mossburn

Lumsden

Riversdale

Dusky
Sound

Takitimu
Mountains

Blackmount

West
Cape

Hokonui
Forest
Park

Gore

Clifden

Winton

Mataura

Tuatapere

Te Waewae
Bay

Riverton

Invercargill

Stewart Island

Foveaux
Strait

Bluff

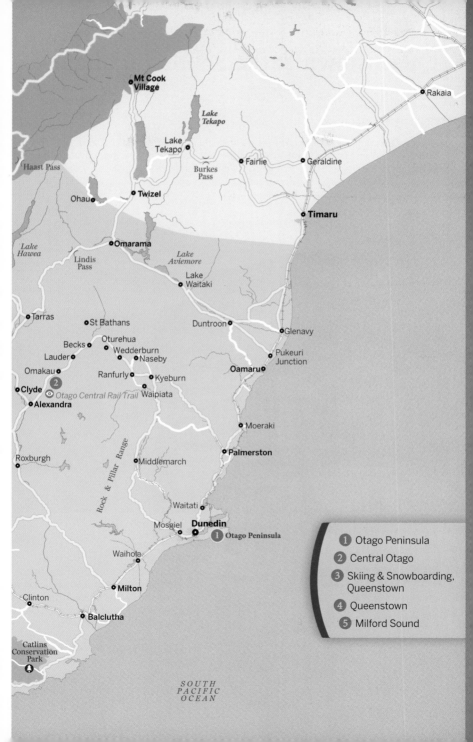

Mt Cook Village

Rakaia

Lake Tekapo

Lake Tekapo

Haast Pass

Burkes Pass

Fairlie

Geraldine

Ohau

Twizel

Timaru

Lake Hawea

Omarama

Lake Aviemore

Lindis Pass

Lake Waitaki

Tarras

St Bathans

Duntroon

Glenavy

Becks

Oturehua

Wedderburn

Pukeuri Junction

Lauder

Naseby

Omakau

Ranfurly

Kyeburn

Oamaru

Clyde

Otago Central Rail Trail

Waipiata

Alexandra

Moeraki

Roxburgh

Rock & Pillar Range

Middlemarch

Palmerston

Waitati

Mosgiel

Dunedin

Otago Peninsula

Waihola

Clinton

Milton

Balclutha

Catlins Conservation Park

SOUTH PACIFIC OCEAN

1 Otago Peninsula
2 Central Otago
3 Skiing & Snowboarding, Queenstown
4 Queenstown
5 Milford Sound

Queenstown & the South Highlights

Otago Peninsula

Like a Jackson Pollock paint spillage on the map, the Otago Peninsula (p302) makes a brilliant day trip from Dunedin. Jump in a rental car and meander around the convoluted bays, headlands and inlets. En route you can check out some southern wildlife – royal albatrosses, sea lions and yellow-eyed penguins are all here, happily soaring, grunting and waddling. Taiaroa Head (p303)

GRANT DIXON/GETTY IMAGES ©

Central Otago

In Central Otago (p305) rolling hills turn from green to gold, providing the backdrop to a succession of tiny, charming gold-rush towns, where rugged 'Southern Man' types prop up the bars in lost-in-time pubs. This is one of the country's top wine regions, producing world-class pinot noir. There are also fantastic opportunities for mountain bikers here, including the fab Otago Central Rail Trail. Cyclist, Otago Central Rail Trail (p306)

ANDREW BAIN/GETTY IMAGES ©

Skiing & Snowboarding

The Southern Alps jag up high and mighty down here, and with rain-weighty clouds streaming in from the Tasman Sea, expect plenty of winter snow. Queenstown (p276) has, of course, long been a hot spot for powder-hounds. Coronet Peak and the Remarkables are the main ski spots near here, but there's also Treble Cone and Cardrona, and great cross-country (Nordic) skiing and snowboarding near Wanaka (p289). Skiing, Coronet Peak (p281)

Queenstown

Queenstown (p276) gets plenty of publicity for its ski fields, jetboating, bungy jumps, après-ski nightlife and ritzy restaurants. And deservedly so! But there's other interesting stuff to do around here, too. Glenorchy, about 46km to the northwest on Lake Wakatipu, is blessed with good weather and has magical, end-of-the-world appeal; while Wanaka, about 120km north-west, offers a dose Queenstown hip without the hype. Gondala Resturant, Skyline Gondola (p276)

Milford Sound

Exploring this far corner of New Zealand's rain-hazed wilderness mightn't be on your hit-list if you're only here for a few weeks... But trust us, Milford Sound (p312) in photogenic Fiordland National Park will linger in your memories for years. Not convinced? The drive from Te Anau to Milford illustrates what we're talking about: mountains, forests, mirror-perfect waterways... It's even beautiful in the rain!

Queenstown & the South's Best...

Wild Rides

○ **Queenstown bungy jumping** The original is still the best. (p277)

○ **Wanaka paragliding** Float down off the top of Treble Cone under a paraglide plume. (p291)

○ **Otago Central Rail Trail** Mountain bike 150km through the Otago countryside, with plenty of interesting detours, pubs and B&B pit stops. (p306)

○ **Helicopter sightseeing** Sound-out Milford Sound from above. (p309)

Snow Zones

○ **Coronet Peak** Queenstown region's oldest ski field also has night skiing! (p281)

○ **The Remarkables** Downhill for all comers; tackle the remarkable, sweeping 'Homeward Bound' run. (p281)

○ **Cardrona** Close to Wanaka, and featuring the 'Heavy Metal' snowboard park. (p295)

○ **Snow Farm New Zealand** Spectacular cross-country (Nordic) skiing high above Lake Wanaka. (p295)

Urban Moments

○ **Eating out in Queenstown** From fine dining to perfect pizza, Queenstown serves it up. (p283)

○ **Sammy's** The live-music scene in Dunedin is pumping. (p301)

○ **Cinema Paradiso** Fab flicks at one of Wanaka's art-house cinemas. (p293)

○ **Caffeine fix** Dunedin's cool cafes keep the southern chills at bay. (p302)

Need to Know

Natural Splendours

○ **Milford Sound** Tranquil, reflective, serene... We hope your cruise boat is quiet! (p312)

○ **Doubtful Sound** Like Milford, but much bigger and with less tourists. (p311)

○ **Otago Peninsula** Wildlife havens and harbour inlets near Dunedin. (p302)

○ **The Catlins** Compact wilderness with waterfalls, forests and wild coast. (p313)

ADVANCE PLANNING

○ **One month before** Book internal flights, car hire and accommodation (especially in summer around Milford Sound, and in Queenstown and Wanaka, during ski season).

○ **Two weeks before** Book a cruise or a kayak on Milford Sound or Doubtful Sound, or a tour through the underrated Catlins.

○ **One week before** Book a bungy jump in Queenstown, check www. dunedinmusic.co.nz to see who's rocking Dunedin, and reserve a table for a top-shelf dinner in Queenstown.

RESOURCES

○ **Queenstown i-SITE** (www.queenstownnz. co.nz) The official local visitor info centre.

○ **Lake Wanaka i-SITE** (www.lakewanaka.co.nz) For Wanaka-centric advice and info.

○ **Dunedin i-SITE** (www. dunedinnz.com) The best spot for information on Dunedin and the Otago Peninsula.

○ **Otago Daily Times** (www.odt.co.nz) The best news and current-affairs source down south.

○ **Ski & Snowboard New Zealand** (www. brownbearski.co.nz) Online info for all the southern ski resorts.

GETTING AROUND

○ **Boat** Cruise across the mirror-flat waters of Milford Sound.

○ **Car** Drive along the superscenic Te Anau– Milford Hwy (keep at least one hand on the wheel as you snap photos).

○ **Sea kayak** Paddle around the shores of Doubtful Sound.

○ **Minibus** Head through the Catlins on a guided tour.

○ **Hike** Tramp along the 53.5km Milford Track.

BE FOREWARNED

○ **Queenstown in summer** Queenstown is a happening ski town, but don't arrive in summer expecting solitude! Mountain bikers and hikers are here in their hundreds. Accommodation books out and prices rocket; book well in advance.

○ **Royal Albatross Centre, Otago Peninsula** No viewing mid-September to late November; limited sightings late November to December.

Left: The Remarkables (p281);
Above: Coronet Peak ski area (p281)

Queenstown & the South Itineraries

Everyone in Queenstown is from somewhere else. They're here to bungy jump, jetboat, ski and party. Beyond 'QT' is the sublime wilderness of Fiordland and the Catlins, with student-cool Dunedin further east.

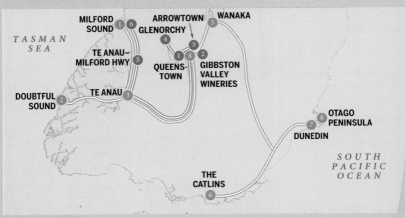

QUEENSTOWN TO MILFORD SOUND

QUEENSTOWN & AROUND

3 DAYS

Kick-start your ❶**Queenstown** (p276) experience with a hefty breakfast, then devote the day to bungy jumping, hang gliding, downhill skiing, paragliding, skydiving, mountain biking or white-water rafting – whichever white-knuckle ride suits your mood (or season). In the evening, chow down at a sassy restaurant then hit the bars for some mellow tunes and a nocturnal tipple.

On day two, take things a bit more slowly with a leisurely hot-air balloon flight, an indulgent cellar-door tour of the nearby

❷**Gibbston Valley wineries** (p284), or a visit to the local shops and Chinese settlement in ❸**Arrowtown** (p286). Alternatively, drive the 46km around Lake Wakatipu to tiny ❹**Glenorchy** (p286) for lunch at the Glenorchy Cafe and a short walk in the area.

Get up early on day three and fill your camera's memory card along the gorgeous ❺**Te Anau–Milford Hwy** (p312). Next up is a truly magical experience: a boat cruise across the hushed, mesmerising waters of ❻**Milford Sound** (p312).

MILFORD SOUND TO OTAGO PENINSULA

5 DAYS

THE SOUNDS OF SILENCE

Fiordland National Park is just so darn *pure*... Do places like this really still exist?

South of ❶ **Milford Sound** (p312) the coastline fractures: ❷ **Doubtful Sound** (p311) is one of Fiordland's biggest and most spectacular sounds, with waterfalls, thick forest and glass-flat waters. Book a cruise, overnight adventure or kayaking trip.

Backtrack for an evening in laid-back ❸ **Te Anau** (p308), or drive further for a night's drinking and carousing in ❹ **Queenstown** (p276) or an art-house movie in ❺ **Wanaka** (p289).

Veering back southeast into Southland for a day or two, explore the beautiful,

lonesome ❻ **Catlins** (p313) region, either on a tour or under your own steam.

Trundle north to ❼ **Dunedin** (p294) for some reggae, rock and coffee (the three pillars of modern civilisation). If the sun is shining, go surfing at the local St Clair or St Kilda beach. Warm up afterwards at a Dunedin cafe, then lurch into the night for some bar-hopping and live tunes.

On day five, day trip to ❽ **Otago Peninsula** (p302), exploring little beaches and fishing towns and ogling fur seals, penguins and seabirds up close.

Fiordland National Park (p308)
JOHN BORTHWICK/GETTY IMAGES ©

Discover Queenstown & the South

At a Glance

○ **Queenstown & Wanaka** (p276 & p289) Savvy ski towns.

○ **Dunedin** (p294) Students, cafes, coffee and bars.

○ **Otago Peninsula** (p302) Wildlife and scenery on Dunedin's doorstep.

○ **Central Otago** (p305) Gold-mining towns, mountain-bike trails and wineries.

○ **Fiordland & Southland** (p308) Epic wilderness areas...a bit like a virginal Norway crossed with a lost Scotland.

QUEENSTOWN

No one's ever visited Queenstown and said, 'I'm bored.' Looking like a small town, but displaying the energy of a small city, Queenstown wears its 'Global Adventure Capital' badge proudly, and most visitors take the time to do crazy things they've never done before. The town's restaurants and bars are regularly packed with a mainly young crowd that really knows how to holiday.

◎ Sights

Queenstown Gardens
Park

(Map p278; Park St) Set on its own little tongue of land framing Queenstown Bay, this pretty park was laid out by those garden-loving Victorians as a place to promenade. The clothes may have changed (they've certainly shrunk), but people still flock to this leafy peninsula to stroll, picnic and laze about.

Kiwi Birdlife Park
Bird Sanctuary

(Map p282; www.kiwibird.co.nz; Brecon St; adult/child $42/21; ⊙9am-5pm, shows 11am & 3pm) These five acres are home to 10,000 native plants, tuatara and scores of birds, including kiwi, kea, moreporks, parakeets and extremely rare black stilts. Stroll around the aviaries, watch the conservation show, and tiptoe quietly into the darkened kiwi houses.

Skyline Gondola
Cable Car

(Map p278; www.skyline.co.nz; Brecon St; adult/child return $27/16) Hop aboard for fantastic views. At the top there's the inevitable cafe, restaurant, souvenir shop and observation deck, as well as the Queenstown Bike Park (p279) and Skyline Luge (p280). At night there are Maori culture shows from Kiwi

Skyline Gondola, Queenstown
GERARD WALKER/GETTY IMAGES ©

Haka (p285) and stargazing tours (including gondola adult/child $79/39).

 Activities

TRAMPING

Queenstown Hill Walkway Tramping
(Map p278) The strenuous tramp up 900m Queenstown Hill takes two to three hours return. Access is from Belfast Tce.

Guided Nature Walks Walking
(☏ 03-442 7126; www.nzwalks.com; adult/child from $105/65) Excellent walks in the Queenstown area, including a *Walk & Wine* option and snow-shoeing in winter.

Ultimate Hikes Tramping
(Map p282; ☏ 03-450 1940; www.ultimatehikes. co.nz; 9 Duke St; ⏱8am-6pm Nov-Apr) Offers day tramps on the Routeburn Track (adult/child $169/85) and the Milford Track (adult/child $295/95) from Queenstown.

BUNGY & SWINGS

AJ Hackett Bungy Bungy
(Map p282; ☏ 03-450 1300; www.bungy.co.nz; The Station, cnr Camp & Shotover Sts) The bungy originators now operate bungy from three sites in the Queenstown area, with giant swings available at two of them. It all started at the historic 1880 **Kawarau Bridge** (Map p287; adult/child $180/130), 23km from Queenstown (transport included). The closest to Queenstown are the **Ledge Bungy** (Map p278; adult/child $180/130) and **Ledge Swing** (Map p278; adult/child $150/100) at the top of the Skyline Gondola; the leap is only 47m, but it's 400m above town.

Last but most pant-wetting is the **Nevis Bungy** (per person $260) – the highest bungy in Australasia. The **Nevis Swing** (solo/tandem $320/180) starts 160m above the river and cuts a 300-degree arc across the canyon on a rope longer than a rugby field – yes, it's the world's biggest swing.

WHITE-WATER RAFTING & SLEDGING

Queenstown Rafting Rafting
(Map p282; ☏ 03-442 9792; www.rafting.co.nz; 35 Shotover St; rafting/heli-rafting $199/285)

Rafts year-round on the choppy Shotover River (Grade III to V) and calmer Kawarau River (Grade II to III). Trips take four to five hours with two to three hours on the water. Heli-rafting trips are an exciting alternative.

Family Adventures Rafting
(☏ 03-442 8836; www.familyadventures.co.nz; adult/child $179/120) Gentle (Grade I to II) trips on the Shotover suitable for children three years and older. Operates in summer only.

Serious Fun Extreme Sports
(☏ 03-442 5262; www.riversurfing.co.nz; per person $195) The only company to surf the infamous Chinese Dogleg section of the Kawarau River, on what's basically a glorified boogie board.

JETBOATING

Skippers Canyon Jet Jetboating
(☏ 03-442 9434; www.skipperscanyonjet.co.nz; Skippers Rd; adult/child $129/79) Incorporates a 30-minute blast through the narrow gorges of the remote **Skippers Canyon** (Map p287), on the upper reaches of the Shotover River.

Shotover Jet Jetboating
(☏ 03-442 8570; www.shotoverjet.com; Gorge Rd, Arthurs Point; adult/child $129/69) Half-hour trips through the rocky Shotover Canyons, with lots of thrilling 360-degree spins.

K Jet Jetboating
(Map p282; ☏ 03-409 0000; www.kjet.co.nz; adult/child $119/69) One-hour trips on the Kawarau and Lower Shotover Rivers, leaving from the main jetty.

SKYDIVING & PARAGLIDING

NZone Skydiving
(Map p282; ☏ 03-442 5867; www.nzone.biz; 35 Shotover St; 9000-15,000ft jumps $269-439) Jump out of a perfectly good aeroplane – with a tandem skydiving expert.

G Force Paragliding Paragliding
(Map p278; ☏ 03-441 8581; www.nzgforce.com; per person $199) Tandem paragliding from the top of the gondola or from Coronet Peak (9am departures are $20 cheaper).

Queenstown

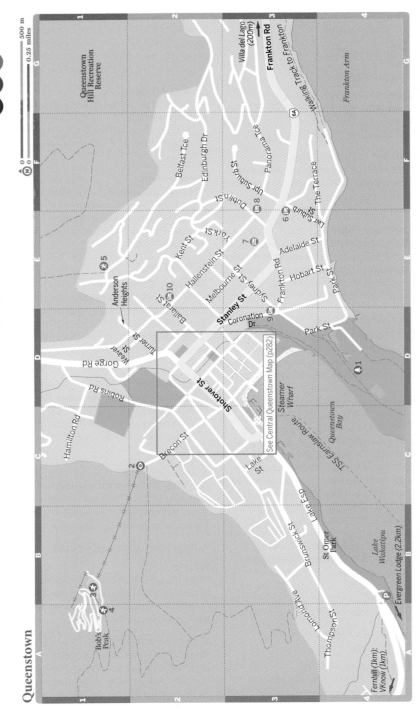

Queenstown

MOUNTAIN BIKING

The **Queenstown Trail** – more than 100km in total – links five scenic smaller trails showcasing Queenstown, Arrowtown, Gibbston, Lake Wakatipu and Lake Hayes. The trail is suitable for cyclists of all levels.

Queenstown Bike Park
Mountain Biking

(Map p278; ☏03-441 0101; www.queenstownbikepark.co.nz; Skyline; half-/full day $60/85; ⊙10am-6pm Sep-Nov, Mar & Apr, to 8pm Dec-Feb) Thirteen different trails – from easy (green) to extreme (double black) – traverse Bob's Peak high above the lake. Once you've descended on two wheels, simply jump on the gondola and do it all over again.

Vertigo Bikes
Mountain Biking

(Map p282; ☏03-442 8378; www.vertigobikes.co.nz; 4 Brecon St; rental half-/full day from $39/59) If you're serious about getting into mountain biking QT-style, Vertigo is an essential first stop. Options include skills training clinics (from $149), guided sessions in the Queenstown Bike Park ($159), downhill rides into Skippers Canyon (two runs $159) and Remarkables helibiking ($399).

Outside Sports
Bicycle Rental

(Map p282; ☏03-441 0074; www.outsidesports.co.nz; 36-38 Shotover St) One-stop shop for bike rentals and trail information.

Tours

TSS Earnslaw
Boat Tour

(Map p282; ☏0800 656 501; www.realjourneys.co.nz; Steamer Wharf, Beach St; tours from $55) Climb aboard for the standard 1½-hour Lake Wakatipu tour (adult/child $55/22) or take a 3½-hour excursion to the high-country **Walter Peak Farm** (Map p287) for sheep-shearing demonstrations and sheep-dog performances (adult/child $75/22).

Air Milford
Scenic Flights

(☏03-442 2351; www.airmilford.co.nz) Options include a Milford Sound flyover (adult/child $420/255), a fly-cruise-fly combo ($499/300), and longer flights to Doubtful Sound and Aoraki/Mt Cook.

Over the Top Helicopters
Helicopter

(☏03-442 2233; www.flynz.co.nz; from $265) Around Queenstown and beyond.

Sunrise Balloons
Ballooning

(☏03-442 0781; www.ballooningnz.com; adult/child $445/295) One-hour sunrise rides including a champagne breakfast.

Queenstown Wine Trail
Wine Tasting

(☏03-441 3990; www.queenstownwinetrail.co.nz) Choose from a five-hour tour with tastings at four wineries ($139) or a shorter *Summer Sampler* tour with lunch included ($160).

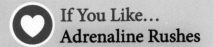

If You Like…
Adrenaline Rushes

If you like the rush of the AJ Hackett Bungy (p277), here are a few other Queenstown heart-starters for you to try.

1 SHOTOVER CANYON SWING
(Map p282; ☑03-442 6990; www.canyonswing. co.nz; booking office 35 Shotover St; per person $215, additional swings $35) Be released loads of different ways – backwards, in a chair, upside down. From there it's a 60m free fall and a wild swing across the canyon at 150km/h.

2 FROGZ
(☑03-441 2318; www.frogz.co.nz; per person $195) Steer buoyant sleds on the rapids and whirlpools of the Kawarau River.

3 ZIPTREK ECOTOURS
(Map p278; ☑03-441 2102; www.ziptrek.com; Skyline) Incorporating a series of ziplines (flying foxes), this harness-clad thrill-ride takes you from treetop to treetop high above Queenstown.

4 SKYLINE LUGE
(Map p278; ☑03-441 0101; www.skyline.co.nz; Skyline; 1/2/3/5 rides incl gondola $36/39/45/50; ⏱10am-dusk) Ride the gondola to the top, then hop on a three-wheeled cart to ride the 800m track.

5 QUEENSTOWN PARAFLIGHTS
(Map p282; ☑0800 225 520; www.paraflights. co.nz; solo/tandem per person $159/129) Float 200m above the lake as you're pulled behind a boat. Departs from the main pier.

🛏 Sleeping

Adventure Queenstown   Hostel $
(Map p282; ☑03-409 0862; www.aqhostel. co.nz; 36 Camp St; dm $29-35, d/tr $120/135; @🛜) Run by experienced travellers (as evidenced by the photos displayed throughout), this central hostel has spotless dorms, a modern kitchen and envy-inducing balconies. Free stuff includes

unlimited internet, international calling to 30 countries, bicycles and frisbees. Private rooms have en suites bathrooms (as do some of the dorms), iPod docks and Blueray players.

Amity Lodge   Motel $$
(Map p278; ☑03-442 7288; www.amitylodge. co.nz; 7 Melbourne St; unit from $170; P🛜) In a quiet street around a five-minute walk up from the town centre, this angular white block has renovated one- and two-bedroom units and friendly owners. The triple-glazing is more about keeping out the cold than noise.

Coronation Lodge   Lodge $$
(Map p278; ☑03-442 0860; www.coronationlodge.co.nz; 10 Coronation Dr; d $165-185; P🛜) Right beside Queenstown Gardens, this tidy block has basement parking, plush bed linen, wooden floors and Turkish rugs. Larger rooms have kitchenettes.

Alexis Queenstown   Motel $$
(Map p278; ☑03-409 0052; www.alexisqueenstown.co.nz; 69 Frankton Rd; unit from $155; P🛜) This modern hillside motel is an easy 10-minute walk from town along the lakefront. The pleasant self-contained units have thoughtful extras such as stereos and robes, along with beaut lake views.

Lomond Lodge   Lodge $$
(Map p282; ☑03-442 8235; www.lomondlodge.com; 33 Man St; d $145-169; P@🛜) A makeover has modernised Lomond Lodge's cosy decor. Share your on-the-road stories with fellow travellers around the garden barbecue. Larger family apartments ($299 for up to four people) are also available.

Little Paradise Lodge   Lodge $$
(Map p287; ☑03-442 6196; www.littleparadise. co.nz; Glenorchy-Queenstown Rd, Mt Creighton; dm $45, r with/without bathroom $140/120) Wonderfully eclectic, this slice of arty paradise is the singular vision of the Swiss/Filipina owners. Each rustic room features wooden floors, quirky artwork and handmade furniture. Outside the fun

WILL SALTER/GETTY IMAGES ©

Don't Miss
Skiing & Snowboarding

Queenstowners have two excellent ski fields to chose between in the **Remarkables** (Map p287; ☎03-442 4615, snow-phone 03-442 4615; www.nzski.com; daily lift pass adult/child $87/48) and **Coronet Peak** (Map p287; ☎03-450 1970, snow-phone 03-442 4620; www.nzski.com; daily lift pass adult/child $97/54), and when they fancy a change of scenery, there's always Cardrona and Treble Cone near Wanaka. Coronet Peak is the only field to offer night skiing, which on a star-filled night is an experience not to be missed.

The ski season generally lasts from around June to September. Tune into 99.2FM from 6.45am to 9am to hear snow reports. In winter, the shops are full of ski gear for purchase and hire; Outside Sports (p279) is a reliable option.

Even outside of the main season, heliskiing is an option for cashed-up serious skiiers; try Over the Top Helicopters (p279), **Harris Mountains Heli-Ski** (☎03-442 6722; www.heliski.co.nz; from $825) or **Southern Lakes Heliski** (☎03-442 6222; www.heliskinz.com; from $820).

continues with a back-to-nature swimming hole and well-crafted walkways through beautiful gardens.

The Dairy   Boutique Hotel $$$
(Map p282; ☎03-442 5164; www.thedairy.co.nz; 10 Isle St; s $435-465, d $465-495; P@🛜)
🍴 Once a corner store, the Dairy is now a luxury B&B with 13 rooms packed with classy touches like designer bed linen, silk cushions and luxurious mohair rugs.

Rates include cooked breakfasts and freshly baked afternoon teas.

Historic Stone
House   Apartments $$$
(Map p278; ☎03-442 9812; www.historicstone-house.co.nz; 47 Hallenstein St; apt from $225; P🛜) Formerly the mayor's digs, this lovely stone building (1874) has been converted into a three-bedroom apartment, with an additional one-bedroom unit in an exten-

Central Queenstown

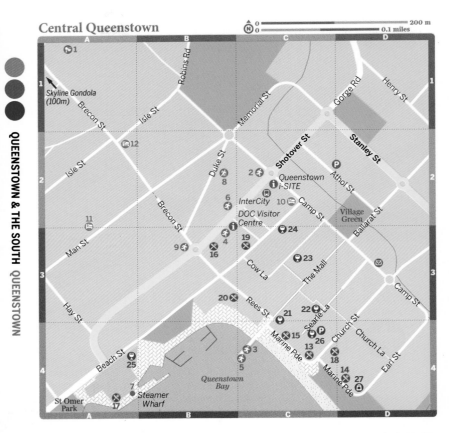

Central Queenstown

◎ Sights

1 Kiwi Birdlife Park A1

❸ Activities, Courses & Tours

2 AJ Hackett Bungy C2
3 K Jet C4
  NZone ....(see 6)
4 Outside Sports B3
5 Queenstown Paraflights C4
6 Queenstown Rafting B2
  Shotover Canyon Swing ....(see 6)
7 TSS Earnslaw A4
8 Ultimate Hikes B2
9 Vertigo Bikes B3

◎ Sleeping

10 Adventure Queenstown C2
11 Lomond Lodge A2
12 The Dairy A2

❸ Eating

13 Aggy's Shack C4
14 Botswana Butchery D4
15 Eichardt's Bar C4
16 Fergburger B3
17 Public Kitchen & Bar A4
18 Sasso C4
19 Vudu Cafe C3
20 Vudu Cafe & Larder B3

❻ Drinking & Nightlife

21 Ballarat Trading Company C3
22 Bardeaux C3
23 Debajo C3
24 New Zealand Wine Experience C3
25 Pub on Wharf A4
26 Zephyr C4

❻ Shopping

27 Vesta D4

sion and another in an elevated building behind it. Modern kitchens and bathrooms meld with antique furniture, and there are established gardens and a spa pool.

Chalet Queenstown B&B
B&B $$$

(Map p278; ☏ 03-442 7117; www.chaletqueenstown.co.nz; 1 Dublin St; s/d $195/245; P 🛜) The seven perfectly appointed rooms at this stylish B&B are decked out with interesting artworks and quality bed linen. All have balconies with views; get in early and request one looking over the lake.

Eating

Fergburger
Burgers $

(Map p282; www.fergburger.com; 42 Shotover St; burgers $10-19; ⏱8.30am-5am) Queenstown's famous Fergburger has now become a tourist attraction in itself, forcing many locals to look elsewhere for their big-as-your-head gourmet burger fix. We think the original is still worth the wait.

Aggy's Shack
Fish & Chips $

(Map p282; cnr Marine Pde & Church St; $9-20; ⏱11am-10pm) Head to this simple lakeside gazebo for fish and chips, including juicy blue cod, and the opportunity to try a few Maori flavours like smoked eel, kina (sea urchin) and titi (muttonbird).

Public Kitchen & Bar
Modern NZ $$

(Map p282; ☏ 03-442 5969; www.publickitchen.co.nz; Steamer Wharf, Beach St; dishes $15-45; ⏱noon-11pm) The trend towards informal, shared dining has come to Queenstown in the form of this excellent waterfront eatery. Grab a posse and order a selection of plates of varying sizes from the menu; the meaty dishes are particularly excellent.

Vudu Cafe & Larder
Cafe $$

(Map p282; www.vudu.co.nz; 16 Rees St; mains $13-19; ⏱7.30am-6pm) Excellent home-style baking combines with great coffee and tasty cooked breakfasts at this cosmopolitan cafe. Admire the huge photo of a much less-populated Queenstown from an inside table, or head through to the rear garden for lake and mountain views. There's another **branch** (Map p282; 23 Beach St) around the corner.

Eichardt's Bar
Tapas $$

(Map p282; www.eichardtshotel.co.nz; 1-3 Marine Pde; breakfast $16-18, lunch $24-26, tapas $7-10; ⏱7.30am-10pm) Elegant without being stuffy, this small bar attached to Eichardt's Private Hotel is a wonderful refuge from the buzz of the streets. Foodwise, tapas is the main focus – and although the selection isn't particularly Spanish, it is particularly delicious.

Sasso
Italian $$

(Map p282; ☏ 03-409 0994; www.sasso.co.nz; 14-16 Church St; mains $25-36; ⏱4-10pm) Whether you're snuggled by one of

Amisfield winery (p284)
GERARD WALKER/GETTY IMAGES ©

Detour:
Gibbston Valley Wineries

Gung-ho visitors to Queenstown might be happiest dangling off a giant rubber band, but as they're plunging towards the Kawarau River, they might not realise they're in the heart of Gibbston, one of Central Otago's main wine subregions, accounting for around 20% of plantings.

Almost opposite the Kawarau Bridge, a precipitous 2km gravel road leads to **Chard Farm** (Map p287; ☏03-442 6110; www.chardfarm.co.nz; Chard Rd; ⏰11am-5pm), the most picturesque of the Gibbston wineries. A further 800m along the Gibbston Hwy (SH6) is **Gibbston Valley Wines** (Map p287; www.gibbstonvalleynz.com; tastings $5-12; ⏰10am-5pm), a large complex with a 'cheesery' and a restaurant.

A further 3km along SH6, **Peregrine** (Map p287; ☏03-442 4000; www.peregrinewines.co.nz; ⏰10am-5pm) is one of Gibbston's top wineries, producing excellent sauvignon blanc, pinot gris, riesling and, of course, pinot noir.

Although it's just outside Gibbston (and most of its grapes are grown near Cromwell), the best of all the wineries in the Queenstown region is **Amisfield** (Map p287; ☏03-442 0556; www.amisfield.co.nz; 10 Lake Hayes Rd; dishes $18-34; ⏰tasting 10am-6pm, restaurant 11am-3pm & 5.30-8pm), by the shores of Lake Hayes.

Ask at the Queenstown i-SITE or Department of Conservation (DOC) centre for maps and information about touring the area.

---

the fireplaces inside the stone cottage (1882) or you've landed a table under the summer stars on the front terrace, this upmarket Italian eatery isn't short on atmosphere. Thankfully the food's excellent, too.

Botswana Butchery
Modern NZ $$$

(Map p282; ☏03-442 6994; www.botswanabutchery.co.nz; 17 Marine Pde; mains $34-45; ⏰noon-11pm) Lake views and schmick interiors set the scene for a scintillating menu that's predominantly but not exclusively meaty, and a wine list of telephone directory dimensions. The $15 Express Lunch is a great deal.

🍷 Drinking & Nightlife

Ballarat Trading Company
Pub

(Map p282; www.ballarat.co.nz; 7-9 The Mall; ⏰11am-late) Stuffed bears, rampant wall-mounted ducks and a re-created colonial general store – there's really no competition for the title of Queenstown's most eclectic decor. Beyond the grab-bag of influences, Ballarat is quite a traditional

spot, with gleaming beer taps, sports on TV, occasional lapses into 1980s music and robust meals.

Zephyr
Bar

(Map p282; 1 Searle Lane; ⏰8pm-4am) Queenstown's coolest indie-rock bar is located – as all such places should be – in a grungy basement off a back lane.

Pub on Wharf
Pub

(Map p282; www.pubonwharf.co.nz; 88 Beach St; ⏰10am-late; 📶) Ubercool interior design combines with handsome woodwork and lighting fit for a hipster hideaway. Fake sheep heads reinforce that you're still in New Zealand, and Mac's beers on tap, scrummy nibbles and a decent wine list make this a great place to settle in for the evening. There's live music nightly.

New Zealand Wine Experience
Wine Bar

(Map p282; ☏03-409 2226; www.winetastes.com; 14 Beach St; ⏰10.30am-10pm) Here's something different: load up cash on a smart card and then help yourself to tasting pours or glasses of more than 90 NZ wines dispensed through an automated gas-closure system. There's also a whisky corner, and cheese platters are available.

Bardeaux
Wine Bar

(Map p282; Eureka Arcade, Searle Lane; ☺4pm-4am) This small, low-key, cavelike wine bar is all class. Under a low ceiling are plush leather armchairs and a fireplace made from Central Otago schist. The wine list is extraordinary, with the price of several bottles reaching four digits.

Debajo
Club

(Map p282; www.facebook.com/Debajoqueens-town; Cow Lane; ☺10pm-4am) The perennial end-of-night boogie spot – house and big-beat get the dance floor heaving till closing time.

Entertainment

Kiwi Haka
Traditional Dance

(Map p278; ☏03-441 0101; www.skyline.co.nz; Skyline; adult/child excl gondola $39/26) For a traditional Maori cultural experience, head to the top of the gondola. There are three 30-minute shows nightly; bookings are essential.

Shopping

Vesta
Arts & Crafts

(Map p282; www.vestadesign.co.nz; 19 Marine Pde; ☺10.30am-5.30pm) Showcasing really cool NZ-made art and craft, Vesta is full of interesting prints, paintings, glass art and gifts. It's housed in Williams Cottage (1864), Queenstown's oldest home. It's worth visiting just to check out the 1930s wallpaper and 1920s garden.

Information

DOC Visitor Centre
(Department of Conservation; Map p282; 03-442 7935; www.doc.govt.nz; 38 Shotover St; ☺8.30am-5pm)

Queenstown i-SITE (Map p282; ☏03-442 4100; www.queenstown-vacation.com; cnr Shotover & Camp Sts; ☺8.30am-7pm) Friendly and informative despite being perpetually frantic, the saintly staff can help with bookings and information on Queenstown, Gibbston, Arrowtown and Glenorchy.

ℹ Getting There & Away

Air

For information on international flights, see the transport chapter. Both Air New Zealand (☏0800 737 000; www.airnewzealand.co.nz) and Jetstar (☏0800 800 995; www.jetstar.com) fly to Queenstown from Auckland, Wellington and Christchurch.

Bus

Alpine Connexions (☏03-443 9120; www.alpinecoachlines.co.nz) Shuttles head to/from Cardrona ($35), Wanaka ($35), Cromwell ($25), Alexandra ($35) and Dunedin ($45), as well as key stops on the Otago Central Rail Trail.

Shops and restaurants in Queenstown

JOHN ELK/GETTY IMAGES ©

Atomic Shuttles (03-349 0697; www.atomictravel.co.nz) Daily bus to Cromwell ($15, 50 minutes), Omarama ($30, 2¼ hours), Twizel ($30, 3¼ hours), Lake Tekapo ($30, 3¾ hours) and Christchurch ($50, seven hours).

InterCity (Map p282; 03-442 4922; www.intercity.co.nz) Daily coaches to/from Wanaka (from $17, 1½ hours), Franz Josef (from $62, eight hours), Dunedin (from $22, 4¼ hours) and Invercargill ($48, three hours), and twice daily to Christchurch (from $55, eight to 11 hours).

Naked Bus (www.nakedbus.com) Two buses to Wanaka (1¼ hours) daily; one to Cromwell (one hour), Franz Josef (six hours) and Christchurch (nine hours); and less frequent services to Te Anau (2¾ hours). Prices vary.

ⓘ Getting Around

To/From the Airport

Queenstown Airport (ZQN; Map p287; 03-450 9031; www.queenstownairport.co.nz; Sir Henry Wrigley Dr, Frankton) is 7km east of the town centre. Queenstown Taxis (03-450 3000; www.queenstown.bluebubbletaxi.co.nz) and Green Cabs (0508 447 336; www.greencabs.co.nz) charge around $35.

Connnectabus (03-441 4471; www.connectabus.com) Route 11 runs to to the airport from Camp St every 15 minutes from 6.50am to 11pm (adult/child $8/5). There are also services to Arrowtown and Wanaka.

Super Shuttle (0800 748 885; www.supershuttle.co.nz; fare $16) Picks up and drops off in Queenstown.

AROUND QUEENSTOWN

Arrowtown

Beloved by day-trippers from Queenstown, exceedingly quaint Arrowtown sprang up in the 1860s following the discovery of gold in the Arrow River. Today pretty, tree-lined avenues retain more than 60 of their original gold-rush buildings, but the only gold flaunted these days are the credit cards being waved in the expanding array of fashionable shops.

Sights & Activities

Chinese Settlement   Historic Site
(Map p287; Buckingham St; ⏱24hr) **FREE**
Arrowtown has NZ's best example of a gold-era Chinese settlement. Interpretive signs explain the lives of Chinese diggers during and after the gold rush (the last resident died in 1932), while restored huts and shops make the story more tangible.

ⓕ Tours

Arrowtown Legends Tour   Bus Tour
(Map p287; 0800 405 066; www.connectabus.com; Ramshaw Lane; tour $20; ⏱10am, 11am, 1pm, 2pm, 3pm & 4pm) Arrowtown is tiny but this double-decker bus (an ex-London Routemaster) manages a 30-minute loop, complete with an interesting commentary.

ⓘ Information

Arrowtown Visitor Information Centre (Map p287; 03-442 1824; www.arrowtown.com; 49 Buckingham St; ⏱8.30am-5pm) Shares premises with the Lake District Museum & Gallery.

 Getting There & Away

Connectabus (Map p287; 03-441 4471; www.connectabus.com) runs regular services (7.45am to 11pm) on its No 10 route from Frankton to Arrowtown. From Queenstown, you'll need to catch a No 11 bus to the corner of Frankton and Kawarau Rds, and change there. The only direct service is the double-decker bus heading out on the first Arrowtown Legends Tour of the day, which departs Queenstown at 9.30am ($8).

Glenorchy & Around

Set in achingly beautiful surroundings, postage-stamp-sized Glenorchy is the perfect low-key antidote to Queenstown.

🏃 Activities

DOC's *Head of Lake Wakatipu* and *Wakatipu Walks* brochures (both $5) detail day walks taking in the Routeburn

Around Queenstown

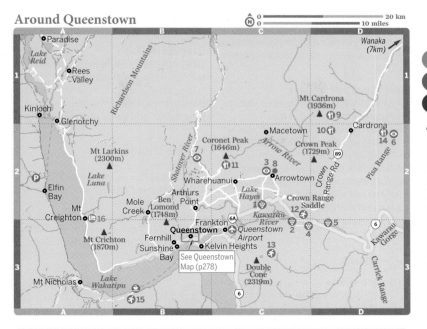

Around Queenstown

Valley, Lake Sylvan, Dart River and Lake Rere. Two of the best short tracks are the **Routeburn Nature Walk** (one hour), at the start of the Routeburn Track, and the **Lake Sylvan tramp** (one hour 40 minutes).

Routeburn Track   Tramping
(www.doc.govt.nz; hut/campsite Nov-Apr $54/18, May-Oct $15/5) Passing through a huge variety of landscapes with fantastic views, the 32km-long, two- to four-day Routeburn Track is one of the most popular rainforest/subalpine tracks in NZ. It's one of NZ's nine designated Great Walks, and many trampers rate it as the very best.

The track can be started from either end. En route, you'll take in breathtaking views from **Harris Saddle** and the top of nearby **Conical Hill**, from where you can see waves breaking at Martins Bay. From **Key Summit**, there are panoramic views of the Hollyford Valley and the Eglinton and Greenstone River Valleys.

Dart Stables   Horse Riding
(☏03-442 5688; www.dartstables.com; Coll St) Options include a two-hour 'River Wild'

ride ($135) and a 1½-hour 'Ride of the Rings' trip ($175) for Hobbity types. If you're really keen, consider the overnight two-day trek with a sleepover in Paradise ($705).

Dart River Jet Safaris Jetboating
(📞03-442 9992; www.dartriver.co.nz; adult/child $219/119; ⏱departs 9am & 1pm) Journeys into the heart of the spectacular Dart River wilderness, including a short walk through the beech forest and a 4WD trip. The return trip from Glenorchy takes three hours. You can also combine a jetboat ride with a river descent in an inflatable three-seater 'funyak' (adult/child $319/219). Prices include Queenstown pickups.

👉 Tours

Ultimate Hikes Walking Tour
(📞03-450 1940; www.ultimatehikes.co.nz; ⏱Nov–mid-Apr) If you fancy comfort while adventuring, Ultimate Hikes offers a three-day guided tramp on the Routeburn (from $1225). All trips include meals and accommodation in Ultimate's own comfortable huts. They also offer a one-day Routeburn Encounter ($169).

Glenorchy Base Walking Tour
(📞03-409 0960; www.glenorchybase.co.nz; half-/full day from $350/420) Specialises in guided walks around the Glenorchy area. Highlights include birdwatching around Lake Sylvan and a Routeburn Track day walk.

Private Discovery Tours  Driving Tour
(📞03-442 2299; www.rdtours.co.nz) Half-day 4WD tours head through a high-country sheep station in a remote valley between Mts Earnslaw and Alfred (adult/child $185/92). Full-day tours include *Lord of the Rings* sites around Paradise (adult/child $295/150). Prices include pick-up from Queenstown.

🛏 Sleeping & Eating

Kinloch Lodge Lodge, Cafe $
(📞03-442 4900; www.kinlochlodge.co.nz; Kinloch Rd; dm $35, d with/without bathroom from $140/85; @🔊) 🖋 Across Lake Wakatipu

Campervan, near Wanaka

JOHN HAY/GETTY IMAGES ©

from Glenorchy (26km by road; five minutes by boat), this wonderfully remote 1868 lodge rents mountain bikes, offers guided kayaking and provides transfers to tramping trailheads. The Heritage Rooms are small but stylish, with shared bathrooms. Rooms in the YHA-associated hostel are comfy and colourful, and there's a post-tramp hot tub. The excellent cafe-bar is open for lunch year-round and for à la carte dinners in summer and set dinners in winter.

Glenorchy Cafe Cafe $$
(Mull St, Glenorchy; mains $10-20, pizza $25; ⊙9am-5pm Sun-Wed, to 9pm Thu-Sat Jan-Apr, 10am-5pm Sun-Fri, to 9pm Sat May-Dec) Grab a sunny table out the back of this cute little cottage and tuck into cooked breakfasts, sandwiches and soup. Head inside at night to partake in pizza and beer underneath the oddball light fixtures.

❶ Information

Glenorchy Information Centre & Store
(☏03-409 2049; www.glenorchy-nz.co.nz; Mull St, Glenorchy; ⊙9am-6pm) Attached to the Glenorchy Hotel, this little shop is a good source of updated weather and track information.

❶ Getting There & Away

Glenorchy lies at the head of Lake Wakatipu, a scenic 40-minute (46km) drive northwest from Queenstown. With sweeping vistas and gem-coloured waters, the sealed road is wonderfully scenic but its constant hills are a killer for cyclists. There are no bus services.

WANAKA

Which is better, Queenstown or Wanaka? Unlike its amped-up sibling across the Crown Range, Wanaka retains a laid-back, small-town feel. It's definitely not a sleepy hamlet anymore though, and new restaurants and bars are adding a veneer of sophistication.

Local Knowledge

Glenorchy Area

RECOMMENDATIONS FROM JANE CAMPION, FILM DIRECTOR AND SCREENWRITER

1 **GLENORCHY**
Glenorchy offers jetboating on the Dart River, and coffee and home-baked bread at the Glenorchy Cafe, but the best thing to do is to take yourself on a bush walk. I recommend the two-hour loop to Lake Sylvan: it's a fairly short walk for this scale of landscape, but it immediately gives you a sense of the delight and intimacy of the bush. And the lake is phenomenal for swimming!

2 **LAKE RERE WALK**
My favourite day walk in the area is Lake Rere, a loop walk from Greenstone, about an hour from Glenorchy. The walk takes about five hours, but allow six or seven to picnic at the lake, a magical place where I am yet to see a sandfly (both the curse and protector of this area: reasonably rare in Glenorchy, they proliferate in the bush).

3 **ROUTEBURN TRACK**
The legendary, four-day Routeburn Track (p287) also starts near Glenorchy. The track here is very well maintained – a highway for walkers. For a day walk, go about 2½ hours into the flats and loll about amid the yellow tussocks.

4 **HORSE TREKKING**
Horse treks at Dart Stables (p287) are excellent – the horses are well cared for, and the landscape is magnificent. I had a horse as a kid, so organised treks are a little bit tame for me, but I have ridden the Dart River horses on some stunning rides along the riverbanks.

◉ Sights

Puzzling World Amusement Park
(www.puzzlingworld.com; 188 Wanaka Luggate Hwy/SH84; adult/child $18/12; ⊙8.30am-

5.30pm) A 3D Great Maze and lots of fascinating brain-bending visual illusions to keep people of all ages bemused, bothered and bewildered. It's en route to Cromwell, 2km from town.

National Transport & Toy Museum
Museum

(www.wanakatransportandtoymuseum.com; 851 Wanaka Luggate Hwy/SH6; adult/child $15/5; ⊙8.30am-5pm) Small armies of Smurfs, *Star Wars* figurines and Barbie dolls share billing with dozens of classic cars and a mysteriously acquired MiG jet fighter in this vast collection, which fills four giant hangers near the airport.

Activities

TRAMPING

For walks close to town, including various lakeside walks, pick up the DOC brochure *Wanaka Outdoor Pursuits* ($3.50). The short climb to the top of **Mt Iron** (527m, 1½ hours return) reveals panoramic views.

Alpinism & Ski Wanaka
Tramping, Skiing

(☑03-442 6593; www.alpinismski.co.nz; from $135) Guided day walks and overnight tramps, and more full-on mountain assaults, courses and ski touring.

MOUNTAIN BIKING

Pick up the DOC brochure *Wanaka Outdoor Pursuits* ($3.50), describing mountain-bike rides ranging from 2km to 24km, including the **Deans Bank Loop Track** (12km).

One particularly scenic new route is the **Newcastle Track** (12km), which follows the raging blue waters of the Clutha River from the Albert Town Bridge to Red Bridge.

Thunderbikes
Bicycle Rental

(☑03-443 2558; www.thunderbikes.co.nz; 16 Helwick St; ⊙9am-5pm) Hires bikes (half-/full day from $20/35) and carries out repairs.

OTHER ACTIVITIES

Deep Canyon
Canyoning

(☑03-443 7922; www.deepcanyon.co.nz; from $220; ⊙Oct-Apr) Loads of climbing, walking and waterfall-abseiling through confined, wild gorges.

Skydive Lake Wanaka
Skydiving

(☑03-443 7207; www.skydivewanaka.com; from $329) Jump from 12,000ft or go the whole hog with a 15,000ft leap and 60 seconds of freefall.

Wanaka Kayaks
Kayaking

(☑0800 926 925; www.wanakakayaks.co.nz; from per hour $12; ⊙9am-6pm Dec-Mar) Rents kayaks ($14 per hour), stand up paddle boards ($18 per hour), and catamarans ($60

Heliskiers, Mt Aspiring National Park
DAVID WALL/GETTY IMAGES ©

Wanaka

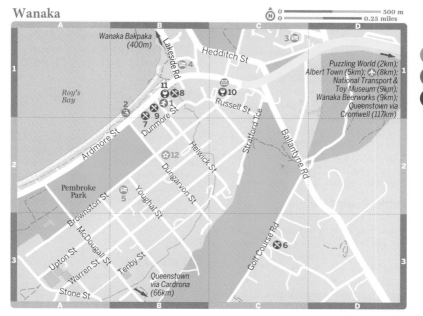

Wanaka

Activities, Courses & Tours
1 Thunderbikes B1
2 Wanaka Kayaks B1

Sleeping
3 Criffel Peak View C1
4 Lakeside B1
5 Wanaka View Motel B2

Eating
6 Bistro Gentil C3

7 Boaboa Food Company B1
8 Francesca's Italian Kitchen B1
9 Kai Whakapai B1

Drinking & Nightlife
10 Barluga & Woody's C1
11 Lalaland B1

Entertainment
12 Cinema Paradiso B2

per hour), and offers guided paddle-powered tours of the lake (half-/full day $75/149).

Wanaka Paragliding   Paragliding
(☏0800 359 754; www.wanakaparagliding.co.nz; tandem $199) Count on around 20 minutes soaring on the summer thermals around Treble Cone.

Tours

Wanaka Helicopters   Helicopter
(☏03-443 1085; www.wanakahelicopters.co.nz) Options range from 15-minute tasters ($95) to two-hour-plus trips to Milford Sound ($995).

Wanaka Flightseeing   Scenic Flights
(☏03-443 8787; www.flightseeing.co.nz) Spectacular flyovers of Mt Aspiring ($240), Aoraki/Mt Cook ($435) and Milford Sound ($490).

Adventure Wanaka   Cruise, Fishing
(☏03-443 6665; www.adventurewanaka.com) Offers lake cruises and fishing trips in an 8m launch.

Wanaka Bike Tours   Mountain Biking
(☏0800 862 453; www.wanakabiketours.co.nz; from $99) Guided trips including helibiking.

🛏 Sleeping

Wanaka Bakpaka — Hostel $

(📞03-443 7837; www.wanakabakpaka.co.nz; 117 Lakeside Rd; dm $28-29, d with/without bathroom $90/70; @🛜) An energetic husband-and-wife team run this friendly hostel above the lake with just about the best views in town. Amenities are top-shelf and the onto-it staff consistently offer a red-carpet welcome to weary travellers. It's worth considering paying a bit extra for the en suite double with the gorgeous views.

Criffel Peak View — B&B $$

(📞03-443 5511; www.criffelpeakview.co.nz; 98 Hedditch St; s $130, d $160-165, apt $270) Situated in a quiet cul-de-sac, this excellent B&B has three rooms sharing a large lounge with a log fire and a sunny wisteria-draped deck. The charming hostesses live in a separate house behind, which has a self-contained two-bedroom apartment attached.

Wanaka View Motel — Motel $$

(📞03-443 7480; www.wanakaviewmotel.co.nz; 122 Brownston St; unit $120-195; 🛜) The refurbished Wanaka View has five apartments with Sky TV, spa baths, full kitchens and lake views; the largest has three bedrooms. There's also a comfortable studio unit tucked around the back, which is cheaper but doesn't have a kitchen or view.

Riversong — B&B $$

(📞03-443 8567; www.riversongwanaka.co.nz; 5 Wicklow Tce; d $160-190; 🛜) Across from the Clutha River in nearby Albert Town, River-song has two guest bedrooms in a lovely weatherboard house. The well-travelled owner has a fabulous nonfiction library. If you can tear yourself away from the books, there's excellent trout fishing just metres away.

Lakeside — Apartments $$$

(📞03-443 0188; www.lakesidewanaka.co.nz; 7 Lakeside Rd; apt $295-795; 🛜🈴) 🥢 Luxuriate in a modern apartment in a prime position overlooking the lake, right by the town centre. All have three bedrooms but can be rented with only one or two bedrooms open. The swimming pool is a rarity in these parts and an appealing alternative to the frigid lake on a sweltering day.

Eating

Boaboa Food Company — Fast Food $

(www.facebook.com/boaboafc; 137 Ardmore St; mains $10-18; ☺10am-9pm) Fancy burgers (spiced pulled pork, high-country salmon, porterhouse steak) are the mainstay of this white-tiled takeway bar, but they also do fish and chips and fried chicken. There are only a handful of high tables, but the lakefront beckons.

Kai Whakapai — Cafe, Bar $

(cnr Helwick & Ardmore Sts; brunch $7-18, dinner $17-22; ☺7am-11pm) An absolute Wanaka institution, Kai (the Maori word for food) is the place to be for a liquid sundowner accompanied by a massive sandwich or pizza. Locally brewed Wanaka Beerworks beers are on tap and there are Central Otago wines as well.

Francesca's Italian Kitchen — Italian $$

(📞03-443 5599; www.fransitalian.co.nz; 93 Ardmore St; mains $20-25; ☺noon-3pm & 5.30pm-late) Ebullient expat Francesca has brought the big flavours and easy conviviality of an authentic Italian family trattoria to Wanaka in the form of this stylish and perennially busy eatery. Even simple things like pizza, pasta and polenta chips are exceptional. She also runs a pizza cart from the New World car park.

Bistro Gentil — French $$$

(📞03-443 2299; www.bistrogentil.co.nz; 76a Golf Course Rd; mains $30-42; ☺11.30am-2pm Sat & Sun, 5-9pm Wed-Sun, extended hours Dec-Feb) Lake views, fabulous NZ art, oodles of wines by the glass and delicious modern French cuisine – Gentil ticks plenty of boxes for a memorable night out. On a balmy night, request an outside table.

Drinking & Nightlife

Barluga & Woody's   Bar
(Post Office Lane, 33 Ardmore St; ⏰4pm-
2.30am) The tucked-away Post Office Lane
complex is Wanaka's coolest drinking
destination – despite the lack of lake
views. Sharing both a courtyard and
owners, these neighbouring bars operate
more-or-less in tandem, especially when
there's a DJ event on. Barluga's leather
armchairs and retro wallpaper bring to
mind a refined gentleman's club. Wicked
cocktails and killer back-to-back beats
soon smash that illusion. Woody's plays
the role of the younger brother, with pool
tables and indie sounds.

Lalaland   Cocktail Bar
(www.lalalandwanaka.co.nz; Level 1, 99 Ardmore
St; ⏰3pm-2am) Keep a watchful eye on the
lake or sink into a comfy chair at this little,
low-lit, completely over-the-top cocktail
palace/bordello. The young barmeister-
owner truly knows his stuff, concocting
elixers to suit every mood. Entry is via the
rear stairs.

Entertainment

Cinema Paradiso   Cinema
(📞03-443 1505; www.paradiso.net.nz; 72 Brownston St; adult/child $15/9) Stretch out on a
comfy couch or in an old Morris Minor
at this Wanaka institution, screening the
best of Hollywood and art-house flicks.
At intermission the smell of freshly baked
cookies wafts through the theatre, although the homemade ice cream is just
as alluring.

Information

Lake Wanaka i-SITE (📞03-443 1233; www.
lakewanaka.co.nz; 103 Ardmore St; ⏰8.30am-
5.30pm) Extremely helpful but always busy.

Getting There & Away

Alpine Connexions (📞03-443 9120; www.
alpinecoachlines.co.nz) Links Wanaka with
Queenstown, Cromwell, Alexandra, Dunedin and
the Rail Trail towns of Central Otago.

Atomic Shuttles (📞03-349 0697; www.
atomictravel.co.nz) Daily bus to/from Dunedin
($35, 4½ hours) via Cromwell ($15, 50 minutes),

Picnic with a view of Lake Wanaka

JOHN HAY/GETTY IMAGES ©

Alexandra ($20, 1¾ hours) and Roxburgh ($30, 2¼ hours).

Connectabus (📞0800 405 066; www.connectabus.com; 1-way/return $35/65) Handy twice-daily service linking Wanaka with Queenstown airport (1¼ hours) and Queenstown (1½ hours).

InterCity (📞03-442 4922; www.intercity.co.nz) Coaches depart from outside the Log Cabin on the lakefront, with daily services to Cromwell (from $10, 44 minutes), Queenstown (from $17, 1½ hours), Lake Hawea (from $10, 24 minutes), Makarora (from $12, 1¾ hours) and Franz Josef (from $43, 6½ hours).

Naked Bus (www.nakedbus.com) Services to Queenstown, Cromwell, Franz Josef, Lake Tekapo and Christchurch. Prices vary.

ℹ️ Getting Around

Adventure Rentals (📞03-443 6050; www.adventurerentals.co.nz; 20 Ardmore St) Hires cars and 4WDs.

Yello (📞03-443 5555; www.yello.co.nz) Taxis and shuttles.

DUNEDIN & OTAGO

Dunedin

Two words immediately spring to mind when Kiwis think of their seventh largest city: 'Scotland' and 'students'. The 'Edinburgh of the South' is immensely proud of its Scottish heritage, never missing an opportunity to break out the haggis and bagpipes on civic occasions.

◉ Sights

Toitu Otago Settlers Museum Museum
(Map p296; www.toituosm.com; 31 Queens Gardens; ⏰10am-4pm Fri-Wed, to 8pm Thu; 📶) **FREE** Storytelling is the focus of this excellent interactive museum. The engrossing Maori section is followed by a large gallery where floor-to-ceiling portraits of Victorian-era settlers stare out from behind their whiskers and lace; click on the terminal to learn more about the individuals that catch your eye.

Railway Station Historic Building
(Map p296; Anzac Ave) Featuring mosaic-tile floors and glorious stained-glass windows, Dunedin's striking bluestone railway station (built between 1903 and 1906) claims to be NZ's most-photographed building.

Dunedin Public Art Gallery Gallery
(Map p296; www.dunedin.art.museum; 30 The Octagon; ⏰10am-5pm; 📶) **FREE** Explore NZ's art scene at this expansive and airy gallery. Only a fraction of the collection is displayed at any given time, with most of the space given over to often-edgy temporary shows.

Baldwin Street, Dunedin
JOHN ELK/GETTY IMAGES ©

294

Detour:
Cardrona

The cute hamlet of Cardrona reached it's zenith in the 1870s at the height of the gold rush when its population numbered over a thousand. Now it's a sleepy little place which wakes up with a jolt for the ski season.

With views of foothills and countless snowy peaks, the **Crown Range Road** from Cardrona to Queenstown is one of the South Island's most scenic drives. At 1076m, it's the highest sealed road in NZ. It passes through tall, swaying tussock grass in the **Pisa Conservation Area** (Map p287), which has several short walking trails. There are some great places to stop and drink in the view, particularly at the Queenstown end of the road before you start the switchback down towards Arrowtown.

The **Cardrona Alpine Resort** (Map p287; ☎03-443 7341; www.cardrona.com; off Cardrona Valley Rd; day pass adult/child $99/51; � 9am-4pm Jul-Sep), a 345-hectare ski field which is well organised and professional, offers runs to suit all abilities (25% beginners, 50% intermediate, 25% advanced) at elevations ranging from 1670m to 1860m.

In winter **Snow Farm New Zealand** (Map p287; ☎03-443 7542; www.snowfarmnz.com; off Cardrona Valley Rd; day pass adult/child $40/20) is home to fantastic cross-country (Nordic) skiing, snow-shoeing, sledding and dog-sled tours, with over 40km of groomed trails.

The **Cardrona Hotel** (☎03-443 8153; www.cardronahotel.co.nz; Crown Range Rd; d $185; ☉ bar 10am-2am), a classic southern pub, first opened its doors in 1863, and today you'll find a good restaurant (mains $20 to $32) and a great garden bar. The lovingly restored rooms have snug, country-style furnishings and patios opening onto the garden (expect some noise on summer nights).

Otago Museum
Museum

(Map p296; www.otagomuseum.govt.nz; 419 Great King St; admission by donation; ☉10am-5pm) The centrepiece of this august institution is *Southern Land, Southern People,* showcasing Otago's cultural and physical past and present, from geology and dinosaurs to the modern day. The Tangata Whenua Maori gallery houses an impressive *waka taua* (war canoe), wonderfully worn old carvings, and some lovely *pounamu* (greenstone) weapons, tools and jewellery.

Check the timing of the daily guided tours ($12) and free gallery talks on the website.

Speight's Brewery
Brewery

(Map p296; ☎03-477 7697; www.speights.co.nz; 200 Rattray St; adult/child $25/10; ☉noon, 2pm, 4pm & 6pm Jun-Sep, plus 5pm & 7pm Oct-May) Speight's has been churning out beer on this site since the late 1800s. The 90-minute tour offers samples of six different brews, and there's an option to combine a tour with a meal at the neighbouring Ale House (lunch/dinner $55/61).

Baldwin St
Street

The world's steepest residential street (or so says the *Guinness Book of World Records*), Baldwin St has a gradient of 1 in 2.86 (19 degrees).

🏃 Activities

St Clair and St Kilda are both popular swimming beaches (though you need to watch for rips at St Clair). Both have consistently good left-hand breaks.

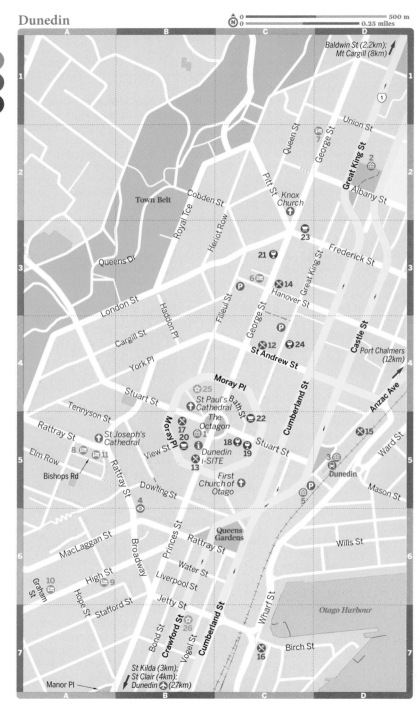

0 — 500 m
0 — 0.25 miles

Baldwin St (2.2km);
Mt Cargill (8km)

Union St

Queen St

George St

Great King St

Albany St

Town Belt

Cobden St

Royal Tce

Heriot Row

Pitt St

Knox Church

Queens Dr

23

Frederick St

21

London St

Haddon Pl

Filleul St

6

14

Hanover St

Great King St

Cargill St

George St

Castle St

Port Chalmers (12km)

York Pl

12

24

St Andrew St

Cumberland St

Anzac Ave

Stuart St

Moray Pl

25

Tennyson St

St Paul's Cathedral

Bath St

The Octagon

22

Rattray St

St Joseph's Cathedral

17

20

Moray Pl

Ward St

Elm Row

8

11

View St

18

19

Stuart St

15

Bishops Rd

13

Dunedin i-SITE

1

First Church of Otago

3

Dunedin

Mason St

Dowling St

4

MacLaggan St

Broadway

Princes St

Rattray St

Queens Gardens

5

Wills St

High St

9

Water St

Liverpool St

10

Graham St

Hope St

Stafford St

Jetty St

Crawford St

Cumberland St

Otago Harbour

Bond St

Vogel St

26

16

Birch St

Wharf St

St Kilda (3km);
St Clair (4km);
Dunedin (27km)

Manor Pl

296

St Clair Hot Salt Water Pool
Swimming

(Esplanade, St Clair; adult/child $5.70/2.60; ◷7am-7pm Oct-Mar) This heated, outdoor pool sits on the western headland of St Clair Beach.

Esplanade Surf School
Surfing

(☎0800 484 141; www.espsurfschool.co.nz; 1½hr group lessons $60, private instruction $120) Operating from a van parked at St Clair Beach in summer (call at other times), this experienced crew provides equipment and lessons.

Tunnel Beach Walkway
Walking

(Tunnel Beach Rd, Blackhead) This short but extremely steep track (15 minutes down, 30 back up) accesses a dramatic stretch of coast where the wild Pacific has carved sea stacks, arches and unusual formations out of the limestone. The track is 7km southwest of central Dunedin.

Tours

Back to Nature Tours
Bus Tour

(☎0800 286 000; www.backtonaturetours. co.nz) The full-day Royal Peninsula tour (adult/child $189/125) heads to points of interest around Dunedin before hitting the Otago Peninsula. Stops include Larnach Castle's gardens (castle entry is extra), a pub lunch, Penguin Place and the Royal Albatross Centre.

First City Tours
Bus Tour

(adult/child $25/15; ◷buses depart the i-SITE 9am, 10.30am, 1pm & 2.30pm) Double-decker bus tours loop around the city, stopping at the Otago Museum, Speight's, Botanic Gardens and Baldwin St.

Walk Dunedin
Walking Tour

(☎03-434 3300; www.toituosm.com; 2hr walk $30; ◷10am) History-themed strolls around the city organised by the Settlers Museum. They depart from the i-SITE.

Sleeping

Hogwartz
Hostel $

(Map p296; ☎03-474 1487; www.hogwartz.co.nz; 277 Rattray St; dm $29, s $60, d with/without bathroom from $80/64, apt $110-165; @ 🛜) The Catholic bishop's residence from 1872 to 1999, this beautiful building is now a fascinating warren of comfortable and sunny rooms, many with harbour views. The old coach house and stables have recently been converted into swankier en suite rooms and apartments.

315 Euro
Motel $$

(Map p296; ☎03-477 9929; www.eurodunedin. co.nz; 315 George St; d $160-200; P 🛜) This sleek complex is accessed by an unlikely-looking alley off Dunedin's main retail strip. Choose from modern studios or larger one-bedroom apartments with full kitchens. Double-glazing keeps George St's irresistible buzz at bay.

Below: Otago Farmers Market; **Right:** Tunnel Beach coastline (p297)

(BELOW) DAVID WALL/GETTY IMAGES ©; (RIGHT) JANETTE ASCHE/GETTY IMAGES ©

858 George St — Motel $$

(☏ 03-474 0903; www.858georgestreetmotel.
co.nz; 858 George St; units $135-280; P 🖥) ✒
Cleverly designed to blend harmoniously
with the neighbourhood's two-storey
Victorian houses, this top-quality motel
complex has units ranging in size from
studios to two bedrooms. Each has a terrace or small balcony.

Dunedin Palms Motel — Motel $$

(Map p296; ☏ 03-477 8293; www.dunedinpalms-
motel.co.nz; 185-195 High St; unit $155-250;
P 🖥) A mercifully short stroll up from the
city centre, the Palms has smartly renovated studio, one- and two-bedroom units
arrayed around a central car park.

Majestic Mansions — Apartments $$

(☏ 03-456 5000; www.st-clair.co.nz; 15 Bedford
St; apt $139-210; P 🖥) One street back
from St Clair beach, this venerable 1920s
apartment block has been thoroughly
renovated, keeping the
layout of the original little flats
but sprucing them up with feature
wallpaper and smart furnishings.

Fletcher Lodge — B&B $$$

(Map p296; ☏ 03-477 5552; www.fletcherlodge.
co.nz; 276 High St; s $295-500, d $335-595, apt
$650-775; P @ 🖥) ✒ Originally home
to one of NZ's wealthiest industrialists,
this gorgeous redbrick mansion is just
minutes from the city, but the secluded
gardens feel wonderfully remote. Rooms
are elegantly trimmed with antique furniture and ornate plaster ceilings.

Brothers Boutique Hotel — Hotel $$$

(Map p296; ☏ 03-477 0043; www.brothersho-
tel.co.nz; 295 Rattray St; d $170-395; P 🖥)
Rooms in this 1920s Christian Brothers
residence have been refurbished beyond
any monk's dreams. The chapel room
($320) includes the original arched
stained-glass windows. There are great
views from the rooftop units.

Bluestone on George
Apartments $$$

(Map p296; ☎03-477 9201; www.bluestonedunedin.co.nz; 571 George St; apt $190-235; P 🛜)
If you're expecting an imposing old bluestone building, think again: this four-storey block couldn't be more contemporary. The elegant studio units are decked out in muted tones, with kitchenettes, laundry facilities and tiny balconies.

Hotel St Clair
Hotel $$$

(☎03-456 0555; www.hotelstclair.com; 24 Esplanade; r $205-255, ste $370; P 🛜) Soak up St Clair's surfy vibe from the balcony of your chic room in this contemporary medium-rise hotel. All but the cheapest have ocean views, and the beach is only metres from the front door.

Eating

Otago Farmers Market
Market $

(Map p296; www.otagofarmersmarket.org.nz; Dunedin Railway Station; ◷8am-12.30pm Sat) This thriving market is all local, all edible (or drinkable) and mostly organic. Grab felafels or espresso to sustain you while you browse, and stock up on fresh meats, seafood, vegies and cheese for your journey. Also pick up some locally brewed Green Man organic beer. Sorted.

Good Oil
Cafe $

(Map p296; 314 George St; mains $9-17; ◷7.30am-4pm) This sleek little cafe is Dunedin's top spot for coffee and cake. If you're still waking up, kickstart the day with imaginative brunches such as kumara hash with hot smoked salmon.

Circadian Rhythm
Vegan, Vegetarian $

(Map p296; www.circadianrhythm.co.nz; 72 St Andrew St; mains $9-13; ◷11am-9pm Mon-Sat; 🍴) Specialising in organic curries, felafels and stir-fries, this meat-free cafe is also a music venue, with jazz on Friday nights from 5.30pm. Dunedin's Emerson's and Green Man beers are both available, so you don't have to be *too* healthy.

299

Detour:
Moeraki

The name Moeraki means 'sleepy sky', which should give you some clue as to the pace of life in this little fishing village. The main attraction is the collection of large spherical boulders scattered along a beautiful stretch of beach like a kid's giant discarded marbles. The famed **Moeraki Boulders** (Te Kaihinaki) lie just off SH1, a kilometre north of the Moeraki turn-off. Try to time your visit with low tide.

It's a pleasant 45-minute walk along the beach from the village to the boulders. Head in the other direction on the **Kaiks Wildlife Trail** and you'll reach a cute old wooden lighthouse. You might even spot yellow-eyed penguins and fur seals (be sure to keep your distance).

Fleur's Place (☑ 03-439 4480; www.fleursplace.com; Old Jetty, 169 Haven St; mains $32-42; ⊙9.30am-late Wed-Sun) has a rumble-tumble look about it, but this timber hut houses one of the South Island's best seafood restaurants. Head for the upstairs deck and tuck into fresh chowder, tender muttonbird and other ocean bounty. Bookings are strongly recommended.

Etrusco at the Savoy   Italian $$
(Map p296; ☑ 03-477 3737; www.etrusco.co.nz; 8a Moray Pl; mains $17-21; ⊙5.30pm-late) NZ has very few dining rooms to match the Edwardian elegance of the Savoy, with its moulded ceilings, stained glass crests, brass chandeliers, green Ionian columns and fabulously over-the-top lamps. Pizza and pasta might seem like an odd fit, but Etrusco's deliciously rustic dishes absolutely hold their own.

Scotia   Modern Scottish $$
(Map p296; ☑ 03-477 7704; www.scotiadunedin. co.nz; 199 Stuart St; mains $18-32; ⊙4pm-late Tue-Sun) Occupying a cosy heritage townhouse, Scotia toasts all things Scottish with a wall full of single malt whisky and hearty fare such as smoked salmon and Otago hare. The two Scottish Robbies – Burns and Coltrane – look down approvingly on a menu that also includes haggis and whisky-laced pâté.

Starfish   Cafe, Bar $$
(☑ 03-455 5940; www.starfishcafe.co.nz; 7/240 Forbury Rd, St Clair; brunch $14-20, dinner $20-30; ⊙7am-5pm Sun-Tue, to late Wed-Sat) Starfish is the coolest creature in the growing restaurant scene at St Clair Beach. Pop out on a weekday to score an outside table, and tuck into gourmet pizza and wine. Dinner is a more sophisticated beast.

Plato   Modern NZ $$$
(Map p296; ☑ 03-477 4235; www.platocafe. co.nz; 2 Birch St; brunch $16-22, dinner $32-33; ⊙11am-2pm Sun, 6pm-late daily) The kooky decor (including collections of toys and beer tankards) gives little indication of the seriously good food on offer at this relaxed eatery by the harbour. Seafood features prominently on a menu full of international flavours.

🍷 Drinking & Nightlife

Mou Very   Bar
(Map p296; www.facebook.com/MouVeryBar; 357 George St; ⊙7am-12.30am) Welcome to one of the world's smallest bars – it's only 1.8m wide, but is still big enough to host regular DJs, live bands and poetry readings. There are just six bar stools, so patrons spill out into an adjacent laneway.

Albar

Bar

(Map p296; 135 Stuart St; ⏱11am-late) This former butcher is now a bohemian little bar attracting maybe the widest age range in Dunedin. Most punters are drawn by the many single-malt whiskies, interesting tap beers and cheap-as-chips bar snacks ($6 to $9).

Di Lusso

Cocktail Bar

(Map p296; www.dilusso.co.nz; 117 Stuart St; ⏱4pm-3am Mon-Sat) Upmarket and designery with wood panelling, chandeliers and a backlit drinks display, Di Lusso serves seriously good cocktails. DJs play from Thursday to Saturday.

Carousel

Cocktail Bar

(Map p296; www.carouselbar.co.nz; upstairs 141 Stuart St; ⏱5pm-late Tue-Sat) Tartan wallpaper, a roof deck and great cocktails leave the dressed-up clientele looking pleased to be seen somewhere so deadly cool. DJs spin deep house until late on the weekends, and there's live jazz on Friday evenings.

Speight's Ale House

Pub

(Map p296; www.thealehouse.co.nz; 200 Rattray St; ⏱11.30am-late) Busy even in the non-university months, the Ale House is a favourite of strapping young lads in their cleanest dirty shirts. It's a good spot to watch the rugby on TV and to try the full range of Speight's beers.

Urban Factory

Club

(Map p296; www.urbanfactory.co.nz; 101 Great King St; ⏱10pm-3am) The hippest of NZ's touring bands, regular DJ sessions and carefully crafted cocktails.

✪ Entertainment

Metro Cinema

Cinema

(Map p296; ☎03-471 9635; www.metrocinema. co.nz; Moray Pl; adult/student $13/12) Within the town hall, Metro shows art-house and foreign flicks.

Sammy's

Live Music

(Map p296; 65 Crawford St) Dunedin's premier live-music venue draws an eclectic mix of genres from noisy-as-hell punk to chilled reggae and gritty dubstep. It's the venue of choice for visiting Kiwi bands and up-and-coming international acts.

ⓘ Information

Dunedin Hospital (☎03-474 0999, emergency department 0800 611 116; www.southerndhb. govt.nz; 201 Great King St)

Dunedin i-SITE (Map p296; ☎03-474 3300; www.isitedunedin.co.nz; 26 Princes St; ⏱8.30am-5pm)

Urgent Doctors & Accident Centre (☎03-479 2900; www.dunedinurgentdoctors.com; 95

Speight's Ale House
DAVID WALL PHOTO/GETTY IMAGES ©

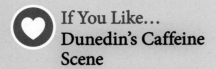

If You Like...
Dunedin's Caffeine Scene

If you like the coffee at the Good Oil (p302), here are a few other spots where you can nurture your bean addiction.

1 THE FIX
(Map p299; 15 Frederick St; ⏰Mon-Sat) Wage slaves queue at the pavement window every morning at this coffee bar, while students and others with time on their hands relax in the courtyard. Fix don't serve food, but you can bring along your own or takeaways.

2 MAZAGRAN ESPRESSO BAR
(Map p299; 36 Moray Pl; ⏰8am-6pm Mon-Fri, 10am-2pm Sat) The godfather of Dunedin's coffee scene, this compact coffee house is the source of the magic bean for many of the city's restaurants and cafes.

3 STRICTLY COFFEE COMPANY
(Map p299; www.strictlycoffee.co.nz; 23 Bath St; ⏰7.30am-4pm Mon-Fri) Stylish, retro option hidden down grungy Bath St. Different rooms provide varying views and artworks to enjoy while you sip and sup.

Hanover St; ⏰8am-11.30pm) There's also a late-night pharmacy next door.

Getting There & Away

Air

Air New Zealand (☎0800 737 000; www.airnewzealand.co.nz) Flies to/from Auckland, Wellington and Christchurch.

Jetstar (☎0800 800 995; www.jetstar.com) Flies to/from Auckland.

Bus

InterCity (☎03-471 7143; www.intercity.co.nz; 7 Halsey St) Coaches to/from Christchurch (from $40, six hours) and Oamaru (from $14, 40 minutes) twice daily; and Cromwell (from $20,

3¼ hours), Queenstown (from $22, 4¼ hours) and Te Anau (from $37, 4½ hours) daily.

Alpine Connexions (☎03-443 9120; www.alpineconnexions.co.nz) Shuttles head to/from Alexandra ($40), Clyde ($40), Cromwell ($45), Queenstown ($45) and Wanaka ($45), as well as key stops on the Otago Central Rail Trail.

Atomic Shuttles (☎03-349 0697; www.atomictravel.co.nz) To/from Christchurch (from $30, 5¾ hours), Oamaru ($20, 1¾ hours), Cromwell ($30, 3¾ hours), Wanaka ($35, 4½ hours) and Invercargill ($37, 3¼ hours).

Getting Around

To & From the Airport

Dunedin Airport (DUD; ☎03-486 2879; www.flydunedin.com; Airport Rd, Momona) is 27km southwest of the city. A standard taxi ride between the city and the airport costs $80 to $90. For door-to-door shuttles, try **Kiwi Shuttles** (☎03-487 9790; www.kiwishuttles.co.nz; per 1/2/3/4 passengers $20/36/48/60) or **Super Shuttle** (☎0800 748 885; www.supershuttle.co.nz; per 1/2/3/4 passengers $25/35/45/55).

Bus

Dunedin's **GoBus** (☎03-474 0287; www.orc.govt.nz; adult fare $2-6.70) network extends across the city.

Taxi

Dunedin Taxis (☎03-477 7777; www.dunedintaxis.co.nz)

Otago Taxis (☎03-477 3333)

Otago Peninsula

The Otago Peninsula has the South Island's most accessible diversity of wild-life. Albatross, penguins, fur seals and sea lions are some of the highlights, as well as rugged countryside, wild walks, beaches, and interesting historical sites. Call into the Dunedin i-SITE (p301) for brochures and maps, or visit www.otago-peninsula.co.nz.

DAVID WALL PHOTO/GETTY IMAGES ©

 Don't Miss
Royal Albatross Centre & Fort Taiaroa

Taiaroa Head, at the Otago Peninsula's northern tip, has the world's only mainland royal albatross colony, along with a late-19th-century military fort, built to defend NZ against a feared invasion by the Russians.

Albatross are present throughout the year, but the best time to see them is from December to February, when one parent is constantly guarding the young while the other delivers food throughout the day. Sightings are most common in the afternoon when the winds pick up; calm days don't see much bird action. The main glassed-in observation area is closed during the breeding season, from mid-September to late November. From late November to December the birds are nestbound so it's difficult to see their magnificent wingspan.

The only public access to the area is by guided tour. The hour-long Classic tour (adult/child $39/19) focusses on the albatross, or there's a 30-minute Fort tour (adult/child $19/9); the two can be combined on the Unique tour ($49/24).

Little penguins swim ashore at Pilots Beach (just below the car park) around dusk to head to their nests in the dunes. For their protection, the beach is closed to the public every evening, but viewing is possible from a specially constructed wooden platform (adult/child $20/10). Depending on the time of year, 50 to 500 penguins might waddle past.

NEED TO KNOW
🗹 03-478 0499; www.albatross.org.nz; Taiaroa Head; ⊙11.30am-dusk

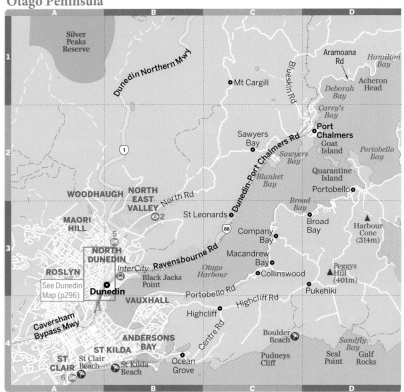

Sights

Nature's Wonders Naturally
Wildlife Reserve

(☎03-478 1150; www.natureswonders.co.nz; Taiaroa Head; adult/child $55/45; ⏱tours from 10.15am) What makes the improbably beautiful beaches of this coastal sheep farm different from other important wildlife habitats is that (apart from pest eradication and the like) they're left completely alone. No tagging or weighing is carried out, and many of the multiple private beaches haven't suffered a human footprint in years.

The result is that yellow-eyed penguins can often be spotted (through binoculars) at any time of the day, and NZ fur seals laze around rocky swimming holes, blissfully unphased by tour groups passing by. Depending on the time of year, you might also see whales and little penguin chicks.

Penguin Place
Bird Sanctuary

(☎03-478 0286; www.penguinplace.co.nz; 45 Pakihau Rd; adult/child $49/15) Situated on private farmland, this reserve protects nesting sites of the yellow-eyed penguin. Ninety-minute tours focus on penguin conservation and close-up viewing from a system of hides.

Activities

A popular walking destination is beautiful **Sandfly Bay**, reached from Seal Point Rd (moderate, one hour return). From the end of Sandymount Rd, you can fol-

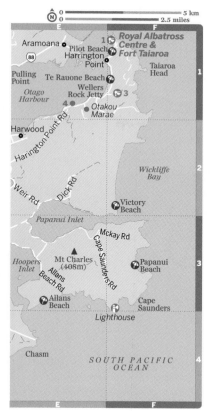

Monarch Cruise. Pick-up and drop-off from Dunedin is included.

Monarch Wildlife Cruises & Tours

Boat Tour

(☎03-477 4276; www.wildlife.co.nz) ✆ One-hour boat trips from Wellers Rock (adult/child $49/22), and half- ($89/32) and full-day ($235/118) tours from Dunedin. You may spot sea lions, penguins, albatross and seals.

❶ Getting There & Around

On weekdays, 13 buses travel between Dunedin's Cumberland St and Portobello (adult/child $5.80/3.40), the closest town to the albatross colony 10km away. On Saturdays this reduces to 10, and on Sundays to four. Once on the peninsula, it's tough to get around without your own transport. Most tours will pick you up from your Dunedin accommodation.

There's no petrol on the peninsula.

---

low a trail to the impressive **Chasm** (20 minutes).

Wild Earth Adventures

Kayaking

(☎03-489 1951; www.wildearth.co.nz; trips from $115) Offers trips in double sea kayaks, with wildlife often sighted en route. Trips take between three hours and a full day, with pick-ups from the Octagon in Dunedin.

Tours

Elm Wildlife Tours

Wildlife Tour

(☎03-454 4121; www.elmwildlifetours.co.nz; tours from $105) ✆ Well-regarded, small-group, wildlife-focused tours, with options to add the Royal Albatross Centre or a

Central Otago

ALEXANDRA

Unless you've come especially for the Easter Bunny Hunt or September's NZ Merino Shearing Championships, the main reason to visit unassuming Alexandra is mountain biking.

MATTHEW MICAH WRIGHT/GETTY IMAGES ©

 Don't Miss
Otago Central Rail Trail

Stretching from Dunedin to Clyde, the Central Otago rail branch linked small, inland goldfield towns with the big city from the early 20th century through to the 1990s. After the 150km stretch from Middlemarch to Clyde was permanently closed, the rails were ripped up and the trail resurfaced. The result is a year-round mainly gravel trail that takes bikers, walkers and horseback riders along a historic route containing old rail bridges, viaducts and tunnels.

With excellent trail-side facilities (toilets, shelters and information), few hills, gob-smacking scenery and profound remoteness, the trail attracts well over 25,000 visitors annually.

The trail can be followed in either direction. The entire trail takes approximately four to five days to complete by bike (or a week on foot), but you can obviously choose to do as short or long a stretch as suits your plans.

Mountain bikes can be rented in Dunedin, Middlemarch, Alexandra and Clyde. Any of the area's i-SITEs can provide detailed information. See www.otagocentralrailtrail.co.nz and www.otagorailtrail.co.nz for track information, recommended timings, accommodation options and tour companies.

 ## Sights & Activities

Walkers and mountain bikers will love the old gold trails weaving through the hills; collect maps from the i-SITE.

Central Stories   Museum
(www.centralstories.com; 21 Centennial Ave; admission by donation; ☺10am-4pm) Central Otago's history of gold mining, winemaking, orcharding and sheep farming is

covered in this excellent regional museum which shares a building with the i-SITE.

Altitude Bikes
Bicycle Rental

(☏03-448 8917; www.altitudeadventures.co.nz; 88 Centennial Ave; from $25 per day) Rents bikes and organises logistics for riders on the Otago Central Rail, Clutha Gold and Roxburgh Gorge trails.

Sleeping

Quail Rock
B&B $$

(☏03-448 7224; www.quailrock.co.nz; 5 Fairway Dr; s/d from $100/150) Perched high above town, this very comfortable B&B offers equal servings of privacy and mountain views. Homemade preserves give breakfast a unique touch, and dinners are also available.

Information

Alexandra i-SITE (☏03-448 9515; www.centralotagonz.com; 21 Centennial Ave; ⏱9am-5pm; 🛜) Pick up a free map of this very spread-out town.

Getting There & Away

InterCity (☏03-471 7143; www.intercity.co.nz) A daily coach heads to/from Dunedin (from $21, three hours), Roxburgh (from $14, 34 minutes), Clyde (from $15, nine minutes), Cromwell (from $18, 24 minutes) and Queenstown (from $22, 1½ hours).

Atomic Shuttles (☏03-349 0697; www.atomictravel.co.nz) A daily bus heads to/from Dunedin ($30, 2¼ hours), Roxburgh ($15, 30 minutes), Cromwell ($15, 50 minutes) and Wanaka ($20, 1¾ hours).

Alpine Connexions (☏03-443 9120; www.alpineconnexions.co.nz) Shuttles head to/from Dunedin ($40), Clyde ($15), Cromwell ($24), Queenstown ($35) and Wanaka ($35), as well as key stops on the Otago Central Rail Trail.

CLYDE

Much more charming than his buddy Alex, 8km down the road, Clyde looks more like a 19th-century gold-rush film set than a real town. It's also one end of the Otago Central Rail Trail.

Sights & Activities

Clyde Historical Museums
Museum

(5 Blyth St; admission by donation; ⏱2-4pm Tue-Sun Sep-Apr) The main building showcases Maori and Victorian exhibits and provides information about the Clyde Dam. Larger exhibits (machinery, horse-drawn carts etc) are housed in the Herb Factory complex at 12 Fraser St.

Trail Journeys
Bicycle Rental

(☏03-449 2150; www.trailjourneys.co.nz; 16 Springvale Rd; ⏱tours Sep-Apr) 🚲 Right by the Rail Trailhead, Trail Journeys rents bikes (from $40 per day) and arranges cycling tours, baggage transfers and shuttles. It also has a depot in Middlemarch.

Sleeping

Dunstan House
B&B $$

(☏03-449 2295; www.dunstanhouse.co.nz; 29 Sunderland St; s $95, d with/without bathroom from $160/120; ⏱Oct-Apr; 🛜) This restored late-Victorian balconied inn has lovely bar and lounge areas, and rooms decorated in period style. The less expensive rooms share bathrooms but are just as comfortable and atmospheric.

Getting There & Away

InterCity (☏03-471 7143; www.intercity.co.nz) A daily coach heads to/from Dunedin (from $19, 3¼ hours), Roxburgh (from $12, 44 minutes), Alexandra (from $15, nine minutes), Cromwell (from $10, 14 minutes) and Queenstown (from $13, 1½ hours).

Alpine Connexions (☏03-443 9120; www.alpineconnexions.co.nz) Shuttles head to/from Dunedin ($40), Alexandra ($15), Cromwell ($24), Queenstown ($35) and Wanaka ($35), as well as key stops on the Otago Central Rail Trail.

FIORDLAND & SOUTHLAND

Fiordland

Formidable Fiordland is NZ's largest and most impenetrable wilderness, a jagged, mountainous, densely forested landmass ribbed with deeply recessed sounds (which are technically fiords) reaching inland like crooked fingers from the Tasman Sea.

TE ANAU

Peaceful, lakeside Te Anau township is the main gateway to Fiordland National Park tramps and the ever-popular Milford Sound, as well as a pleasant place to while away a few days.

Sights & Activities

**Te Anau
Glowworm Caves**   Cave

Once present only in Maori legends, these impressive caves were rediscovered in 1948. Accessible only by boat, the 200m-long system of caves is a magical place with sculpted rocks, waterfalls small and large, whirlpools and a glittering glow-worm grotto in its inner reaches.

**DOC Te Anau
Wildlife Centre**   Wildlife Centre

(Te Anau-Manapouri Rd; admission by donation; ⏲dawn-dusk) Here's a chance to see native bird species difficult to spot in the wild, including the precious icon of Fiordland, the extremely rare takahe.

SHORT WALKS & BIKE RIDES

Te Anau's **Lakeside Track** makes for a delightful stroll in either direction – north to the marina and around to the Upukerora River (around an hour return), or south past the National Park Visitor Centre and on to the control gates and start of the Kepler Track (50 minutes). Hire bikes and obtain cycle track maps from **Outside Sports** (www.outsidesports.co.nz; 38 Town Centre; ⏲9am-5pm) or **Te Anau Bike Hire** (7 Mokonui St; mountain bikes per hour/day from $12/30; ⏲from 10am Sep-Apr).

During summer, **Trips & Tramps** (☎0800 305 807, 03-249 7081; www.tripsandtramps.com; ⏲Oct-Apr) offers small-group, guided hikes on the Kepler and

Mitre Peak, Milford Sound (p312)

Routeburn, among other tracks. Real Journeys runs guided day hikes (adult/child $195/127, November to mid-April) along an 11km stretch of the Milford Track. A number of day walks can also be completed by linking with regular bus services run by Tracknet.

For self-guided adventures, pick up DOC's *Fiordland National Park Day Walks* brochure ($2) from Te Anau i-SITE or Fiordland National Park Visitor Centre or download it at www.doc.govt.nz.

Tours

Real Journeys
Tour

(☎ 0800 656 501; www.realjourneys.co.nz) Real Journeys runs 2¼-hour guided tours ($75/22 per adult/child), reaching the heart of the Te Anau Glowworm Caves by a walkway and a short underground boat ride.

Southern Lakes Helicopters
Scenic Flights

(☎ 03-249 7167; www.southernlakeshelicopters.co.nz; Lakefront Dr) Flights over Te Anau for 25 minutes ($195); longer trips over Doubtful, Dusky and Milford Sounds (from $540); and a chopper/walk/boat option on the Kepler Track ($185).

Wings & Water Te Anau
Scenic Flights

(☎ 03-249 7405; www.wingsandwater.co.nz; Lakefront Dr) Ten-minute local flights (adult/child $95/55), and longer flights over the Kepler Track and Doubtful and Milford Sounds (from $225).

Sleeping

Te Anau Lakeview Holiday Park
Holiday Park $

(☎ 03-249 7457, 0800 483 262; www.teanauholidaypark.co.nz; 77 Manapouri-Te Anau Hwy; sites per person from $17, dm/s $28/36, units $70-260; @ 🛜) This 22-acre grassy lakeside holiday park has plenty of room to pitch your tent or park your van. It also has a wide range of accommodation from basic dorms and singles, through to tidy cabins and motels, and the rather swanky Mar-akura Apartments with enviable lake and

mountain views. Friendly staff will hook you up with local activities and transport.

Keiko's Cottages B&B
B&B $$

(☎ 03-249 9248; www.keikos.co.nz; 228 Milford Rd; d $165-195; 🕐 closed Jun-Aug; 🛜) The private, self-contained cottages here are lovely, and surrounded by Japanese-style gardens. A Japanese breakfast in the morning and a bamboo-bordered hot tub in the evening are worthy extras.

Te Anau Lodge B&B
B&B $$$

(☎03-249 7477; www.teanaulodge.com; 52 Howden St; d $240-350; @ ☎) The former 1930s-built Sisters of Mercy Convent, relocated to a grand location just north of town, is a heavenly accommodation option. Sip your complimentary wine in a chesterfield in front of the fire, retire to your spa before collapsing on a king-size bed, then awaken to a fresh, delicious breakfast in the old chapel.

Eating & Drinking

Miles Better Pies
Bakery $

(cnr Town Centre & Mokonui St; pies $5-7) The bumper selection includes venison, lamb and mint, and fruit pies. There are a few pavement tables, but sitting beside the lake is nicer.

Redcliff Cafe
Restaurant $$$

(www.theredcliff.co.nz; 12 Mokonui St; mains $31-39; ⊙4-10pm) Housed in a replica old settler's cottage, relaxed Redcliff offers generous fine-dining in a convivial atmosphere backed by sharp service. The predominantly locally sourced food is truly terrific: try the wild venison or hare. Kick off or wind it up with a drink in the rustic front bar, which often hosts live music.

Fat Duck
Bar, Restaurant

(124 Town Centre; ⊙8.30am-late; ☎) This corner bar with alfresco seating is a sound choice for supping a pint or two of Mac's. Marginally trendy gastropub style is reflected in fair modern fare (breakfast $13 to $20, dinner $22 to $39).

ⓘ Information

Fiordland i-SITE (☎03-249 8900; www.fiordland.org.nz; 85 Lakefront Dr; ⊙8.30am-5.30pm) Activities, accommodation and transport bookings.

Fiordland Medical Centre (☎03-249 7007; 25 Luxmore Dr; ⊙8am-5.30pm Mon-Fri, 8.30am-noon Sat)

Fiordland National Park Visitor Centre (DOC; ☎03-249 0200; www.doc.govt.nz; cnr Lakefront Dr & Te Anau-Manapouri Rd; ⊙8.30am-4.30pm) Can assist with Great Walks bookings, general hut tickets and information, with the bonus of a natural history display and a shop stocking essential topographical maps for backcountry trips.

ⓘ Getting There & Away

InterCity has daily bus services between Te Anau and Queenstown (2½ hours), Invercargill (2½ hours) and Dunedin (4¾ hours). Buses depart outside Kiwi Country on Miro St.

AROUND TE ANAU

Milford Track

The best-known track in NZ and routinely touted as 'the finest walk in the world', the Milford is an absolute stunner, complete with rainforest, deep glaciated valleys, a glorious alpine pass surrounded by towering peaks, and powerful waterfalls including the legendary Sutherland Falls, one of the loftiest in the world. All these account for its popularity: more than 14,000 trampers complete the 54km-long track each year.

During the Great Walks season, the track is also frequented by guided tramping parties, which stay at cosy, carpeted lodges with hot showers and proper food. If that sounds appealing, contact **Ultimate Hikes** (☎03-450 1940, 0800 659 255; www.ultimatehikes.co.nz; 5-day tramp $1930-2095), the only operator permitted to run guided tramps of the Milford.

Bookings

The Milford Track is one of NZ's Great Walks. Between late October and mid-April, you need a Great Walks pass ($162) to cover your three nights in the huts. Passes must be obtained in advance (book early to avoid disappointment), either online via DOC's Great Walks Bookings or in person at a DOC visitor centre.

★ Don't Miss
Doubtful Sound

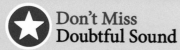

Magnificent Doubtful Sound is a wilderness area of fractured and gouged mountains, dense forest and thundering waterfalls. One of NZ's largest sounds – three times the length and 10 times the area of Milford – Doubtful is technically a fiord (being carved by glaciers, rather than rivers). It is also much, *much* less visited. If you have the time and the money, it's an essential experience.

Until relatively recently, only the most intrepid tramper or sailor ever explored Doubtful Sound. Even Captain Cook only observed it from off the coast in 1770, because he was 'doubtful' whether there would be enough puff in the winds within the sound to carry his ship back out to the coast.

Getting to Doubtful Sound involves boarding a boat at Pearl Harbour in Manapouri for a one-hour trip to West Arm power station, followed by a 22km (40-minute) drive over Wilmot Pass to Deep Cove (permanent population: two) where you hop aboard a boat for your cruise on the sound.

Fiordland Cruises (☏ 0800 368 283; www.fiordlandcruises.co.nz; s/d $600/1200) runs an overnight cruise on the *Southern Secret* (maximum 12 passengers); cabins are en suite doubles.

Deep Cove Charters (☏ 0800 249 682; www.deepcovecharters.co.nz; s bunk $500, tw/d cabin $1100/1200) runs overnight cruises on board the *Seafinn* (maximum 12 passengers).

Real Journeys (☏ 0800 656 501; www.realjourneys.co.nz) runs a day-long Wilderness Cruise (adult $245 to $265, child $65), which includes a three-hour journey aboard a modern catamaran with a specialist nature guide. Its overnight cruise, which runs from September to May, is aboard the *Fiordland Navigator* which sleeps 70 in en suite cabins: twin-share (adult $417 to $595, child $209 to $298), and quad-share (adult $263 to $375, child $132 to $188).

Te Anau–Milford Hwy

The 119km road from Te Anau to Milford (SH94) offers the most easily accessible experience of Fiordland. The trip takes two to 2½ hours if you drive straight through, but take time to stop and experience the majestic landscape. Pull off the road and explore the many viewpoints and nature walks en route. Pick up DOC's *Fiordland National Park Day Walks* brochure ($2) from Te Anau i-SITE or Fiordland National Park Visitor Centre or download it at www.doc.govt.nz.

MILFORD SOUND

The first sight of Milford Sound (Piopio-tahi in Maori) is stunning. Sheer rocky cliffs rise out of still, dark waters, and forests clinging to the slopes sometimes relinquish their hold, causing a 'tree avalanche' into the waters. The spectacular, photogenic 1692m-high Mitre Peak rises dead ahead.

Activities

Rosco's Milford Kayaks
Kayaking

(📞0800 476 726, 03-249 8500; www.roscos-milfordkayaks.com; 72 Town Centre, Te Anau; trips $99-255) Guided, tandem-kayak trips including the 'Morning Glory' ($189), a challenging paddle the full length of the fiord to Anita Bay, and the easier 'Stirling Sunriser' ($189), which ventures beneath the 151m-high Stirling Falls. Among many other options are trips 'your grandmother could do', and kayak-walk combos on the Milford Track.

Fiordland Wilderness Experiences
Kayaking

(📞03-249-7700, 0800 200 434; www.seakayakfiordland.co.nz; Sandy Brown Rd, Te Anau; per person $145; ⏱Sep-Apr) Offers guided six-hour trips on Milford Sound, with four to five hours on the water.

Tours

A cruise on Milford Sound is Fiordland's most accessible experience, as evident from the slew of cruise companies located in the flash **cruise terminal** (⏱8am-5.15pm Oct-Apr, 9am-4.15pm May-Sep), a 10-minute walk from the cafe and car park.

Real Journeys
Boat Tour

(📞0800 656 501, 03-249 7416; www.realjourneys.co.nz; adult/child from $70/22) Milford's biggest operator runs various trips including the popular 1¾-hour scenic cruise (adult $70 to $93, child $22). The nature cruise (adult $85 to $95, child $22, 2½ hours) hones in on wildlife with a specialist nature guide providing commentary. Overnight cruises are also available, on which you can kayak

Milford Sound
THIENTHONGTHAI WORACHAT/GETTY IMAGES ©

and take nature tours in tender crafts en route.

Go Orange — Boat Tour
(📞03-249 8585, 0800 246 672; www.goorange. co.nz; adult $49-70, child $15) Real Journeys' low-cost two-hour cruises (leaving 9am, 12.30pm and 3.30pm) along the full length of the sound with the bonus of a complimentary snack.

Jucy Cruize — Boat Tour
(📞0800 500 121; www.jucycruize.co.nz; adult/ child from $50/15) Offers 1½-hour trips on a 200-seater boat.

Mitre Peak Cruises — Boat Tour
(📞0800 744 633; www.mitrepeak.com; adult/ child from $70/17) Two-hour cruises in smallish boats (maximum capacity 75). The 4.30pm cruise is good because many larger boats are heading back at this time.

Southern Discoveries — Boat Tour
(📞0800 264 536; www.southerndiscoveries. co.nz; adult/child from $70/16) A range of trips exploring Milford Sound, all lasting around two hours. The 2¼-hour wildlife cruise operates on a smaller (75-person) boat.

Sleeping & Eating

Milford Sound Lodge — Lodge $
(📞03-249 8071; www.milfordlodge.com; SH94; campsites from $20, dm $33; @ 🛜) Along-side the Cleddau River, 1.5km from the Milford hub, this simple but comfortable lodge has a down-to-earth, active vibe. Travellers and trampers commune in the lounge or at on-site **Pio Pio Cafe** which provides meals ($7 to $22), wine and espresso. Very comfortable chalets ($195 to $295) enjoy an absolute river-side location. Booking ahead is strongly recommended.

Blue Duck Café & Bar — Cafe $$
(lunch $6-18, dinner $16-27; ⏰cafe 8.30am-4.30pm, bar 4pm-late) Catering to a captive audience, this unpredictable cafe serves pies, sandwiches and suchlike during the day, then turns the tables for evenings of pizza and beer in the bar. You'll find the Blue Duck on the edge of the main Milford car park; activity booking office on site.

 Getting There & Away

Bus
InterCity runs daily bus services to Milford Sound from Te Anau (three hours) and Queenstown (six hours) on to which you can add a cruise when you book. Naked Bus also runs from Te Anau to the sound.

Te Anau–based Tracknet provides regular Milford Sound services, with connections south from Invercargill, and north from Queenstown.

Car
Fill up with petrol in Te Anau before setting off. Chains must be carried on avalanche-risk days from May to November (there will be signs on the road), and can be hired from service stations in Te Anau.

Southland

SOUTHERN SCENIC ROUTE

The quiet Southern Scenic Route begins in Queenstown and heads south via Te Anau to Manapouri, Tuatapere, River-ton and Invercargill. From Invercargill it continues north through the Catlins to Dunedin. See www.southernscenicroute. co.nz or pick up the free *Southern Scenic Route* map to join all the dots.

THE CATLINS

The most direct route between Inver-cargill and Dunedin is via SH1. The pastoral scenery is pretty, but not as spectacular as the SH92 route via the Catlins coast. The Catlins is an enchant-ing region, combining lush farmland, native forests, usual coastal landmarks and empty beaches, bush walks and wildlife-spotting opportunities. On a clear summer's day it is a beauty to behold. In the face of an Antarctic southerly it's an entirely different kettle of fish. Good luck.

Pubilc transport is limited to the **Bottom Bus** (📞03-477 9083; www. bottombus.co.nz; from $175), which travels swiftly through from Dunedin three days a week. By far the best way to explore the area is with your own wheels. Allow a few

The Catlins

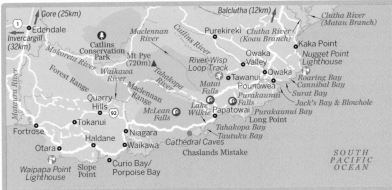

days if at all possible, and make sure you have on hand the *Southern Scenic Route* brochure and the purple *Catlins* brochure and map, which detail every dot.

Activities

Catlins Surf School — Surfing
(☏03-246 8552; www.catlins-surf.co.nz)
Located in Porpoise Bay, the Catlins Surf School runs 90-minute surfing lessons for $50. The occasional group of dolphin spectators is free of charge. If you're already confident on the waves, hire a board and wetsuit (very necessary) for three hours ($40). Owner Nick also offers tuition in stand up paddle boarding ($75, two hours).

Catlins Horse Riding — Horse Riding
(☏027 269 2904, 03-415 8368; www.catlinshorseriding.co.nz; 41 Newhaven Rd, Owaka; 1/2/3hr rides $60/100/150) Explore the idiosyncratic coastline and landscapes on four legs with Catlins Horse Riding. Learners treks and the full gallop available.

Tours

Catlins Wildlife Trackers — Wildlife Tours
(☏03-415 8613, 0800 228 5467; www.catlins-ecotours.co.nz) Based near Papatowai and running since 1990, Catlins Wildlife Trackers offer customised guided walks and tours with a focus on ecology. If you want to see the beloved mohua, penguins, sea lions or other wildlife, Mary and Fergus will track it down for you. Their fully guided three-night/two-day package costs $800, including all food, accommodation and transport.

Information

The i-SITEs in Invercargill and Balclutha have lots of Catlins information. On the road, you'll pass two information centres: the small Catlins Info Centre in Owaka or even smaller Waikawa Information Centre (☏03-246 8464; waikawamuseum@hyper.net.nz; Main Rd; ☉10am-5pm). Online, see www.catlins.org.nz and www.catlins-nz.com.

The Best of the Rest

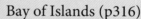

Bay of Islands (p316)

Much more than a gorgeous bay festooned with islands and dolphins, this part of Northland is where both Maori and Pakeha New Zealanders have their roots.

Taranaki (p321)

New Zealand's best-looking peak is well worth checking out. Down below on the coast is New Plymouth with its impressive museum, art gallery and caffeine scene.

Stewart Island (p325)

NZ's third-biggest island is oft overlooked. But if you're looking for quirky, far-flung wilderness and wildlife experiences, look no further.

Top: Rakiura National Park, Stewart Island;
Bottom: Mt Taranaki (p324)

Bay of Islands

HIGHLIGHTS

1 **Sailing & cruising** Count dolphins and gorgeous uninhabited islands.

2 **Russell** (p318) Hell-hole turned holiday haven.

3 **Waitangi Treaty Grounds** (p319) The birthplace of modern NZ.

Bottlenose dolphins, Bay of Islands
STEVE CLANCY PHOTOGRAPHY/GETTY IMAGES ©

The Bay of Islands ranks as one of NZ's top tourist drawcards, and the turquoise waters of the bay are punctuated by around 150 undeveloped islands. The Bay of Islands is also a place of enormous historical significance. Maori knew it as Pewhairangi and settled here early in their migrations. As the site of NZ's first permanent British settlement (at Russell), it is the birthplace of European colonisation in the country.

 Activities

The Bay of Islands offers some fine sub-tropical diving, made even better by the sinking of the 113m navy frigate HMNZS *Canterbury* in Deep Water Cove near Cape Brett.

There are plenty of opportunities for kayaking or sailing around the bay, either on a guided tour or by renting and going it alone. Cruises and dolphin swimming are also available.

Paihia Dive   Diving
(☎09-402 7551; www.divenz.com; Williams Rd, Paihia; reef & wreck $229) Combined reef and wreck trips to either the *Canterbury* or the *Rainbow Warrior*.

Coastal Kayakers   Kayaking
(☎0800 334 661; www.coastalkayakers.co.nz; Te Karuwha Pde, Paihia) Runs guided tours (half-/full day $85/115, minimum two people) and multiday adventures. Kayaks (per hour/half-/full day $15/40/50) can also be rented for independent exploration.

Flying Kiwi Parasail   Parasailing
(☎0800 359 691; www.parasail-nz.co.nz; solo $99, tandem per person $89, child $69) Departs from both Paihia and Russell wharves for NZ's highest parasail (1200ft).

**Tango Jet Ski &
Island Boat
Tours**   Jet Skiing
(☎0800 253 8752; www.tangojetskitours. co.nz; boat tours/jet ski hire from $65/100) Zip around the bay in a speedy inflatable boat or skipper your own jet ski. Jet skis can take two people.

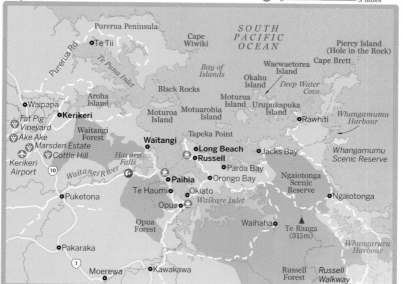

Tours

BOAT

One of the bay's most striking islands is **Piercy Island (Motukokako)** off Cape Brett, at the bay's eastern edge. This steep-walled rock fortress features a vast natural arch – the famous **Hole in the Rock**.

The best way to explore the bay is under sail. Either help crew the boat (no experience required), or just spend the afternoon island-hopping, sunbathing, swimming, snorkelling, kayaking and fishing.

Explore NZ   Cruise, Sailing

(☏09-402 8234; www.explorenz.co.nz; cnr Marsden & Williams Rds, Paihia) ✈ The four-hour Swim with the Dolphins Cruise (adult/child $89/45, additional $15 to swim) departs at 8am and 12.30pm. The four-hour Discover the Bay Cruise (adult/child $99/49) departs at 9am and 1.30pm, heading to the Hole in the Rock and stopping at Urupukapuka Island.

Fullers Great Sights   Cruise

(☏0800 653 339; www.dolphincruises.co.nz; Paihia Wharf) ✈ The four-hour Dolphin Cruise (adult/child $95/50) departs daily at 9am and 1.30pm, actively seeking out dolphins en route to the Hole in the Rock, and stopping at Urupukapuka Island on the way back. You won't visit the Hole in the Rock on the four-hour Dolphin Eco Experience (adult/child $109/55, departs 8am and 12.30pm); the focus is finding dolphins to swim with.

The full-day Cream Trip (adult/child $119/60) follows the mail route around the bay and includes dolphin swimming. A glamorous option for an overnight cruise from September to April is on the launch *Ipipiri*, with accommodation in en suite state rooms from $299 per person. Meals and kayaking, snorkelling and island walks are included.

R Tucker Thompson   Sailing

(☏09-402 8430; www.tucker.co.nz) ✈ Run by a charitable trust with an education focus, the *Tucker* is a majestic tall ship offering day sails (adult/child $145/73, including a barbecue lunch) and late-afternoon cruises (adult/child $59/30).

Carino
Sailing

(☎09-402 8040; www.sailingdolphins.co.nz; adult/child $114/69) This 50ft catamaran is the only yacht licensed for swimming with dolphins. A barbecue lunch is available for $6.

Ecocruz
Sailing

(☎0800 432 627; www.ecocruz.co.nz; dm/d $650/1500) Three-day/two-night sailing cruise aboard the 72ft ocean-going yacht *Manawanui*. Prices include accommodation, food, fishing, kayaking and snorkelling.

She's a Lady
Sailing

(☎0800 724 584; www.bay-of-islands.com; day sail $97) On day sails go snorkelling or paddle a see-through-bottomed kayak. Charter boats for longer trips and a sailing school.

Mack Attack
Jetboating

(☎0800 622 528; www.mackattack.co.nz; 9 Williams Rd, Paihia; adult/child $95/40) An exhilarating, high-speed 1½-hour jetboat trip to the Hole in the Rock.

CULTURAL TOURS

Native Nature Tours
Cultural, Tramping

(☎0800 668 873; www.nativenaturetours.co.nz; 581 Tipene Rd, Motatau; day tramps $145-235, overnight $375) A local Maori couple formally welcome you to their *marae* (meeting house) and lead tramps on their ancestral lands, including visits to sacred sites and an introduction to Maori food and medicine. Other options include tree planting, and overnight stays include a traditional *hangi* (earth-cooked meal) and glowworm spotting.

OTHER TOURS

Salt Air
Scenic Flights

(☎09-402 8338; www.saltair.co.nz; Marsden Rd, Paihia) Scenic flights include a five-hour light aircraft and 4WD tour to Cape Reinga and Ninety Mile Beach ($425), and helicopter flights out to the Hole in the Rock ($230). A new tour even lands on the famed island (from $379).

Russell

POP 720

Although it was once known as 'the hellhole of the Pacific', those coming to Russell for debauchery will be sadly disappointed: they've missed the orgies on the beach by 170 years. Instead they'll find a historic town with gift shops and B&Bs, and, in summer, you can rent kayaks and dinghies along the Strand.

◉ Sights

Pompallier Mission
Historic Building

(www.pompallier.co.nz; The Strand; tours adult/child $10/free; ☺10am-4pm) Built in 1842 to house the Catholic mission's printing press, this is the mission's last remaining building in the Western Pacific. A staggering 40,000 books were printed here in Maori. In the 1870s it was converted into a private home, but it is now restored to its original state, with tannery and printing workshop.

Christ Church
Church

(Church St) English naturalist Charles Darwin made a donation towards the cost of building the country's oldest church (1836). The graveyard's biggest memorial commemorates Tamati Waka Nene, a powerful Ngapuhi chief from the Hokianga who sided against Hone Heke in the Northland War. The church's exterior has musket and cannonball holes from the 1845 battle.

Russell Museum
Museum

(www.russellmuseum.org.nz; 2 York St; adult/child $7.50/2; ☺10am-4pm) This small museum has a well-presented Maori section, a large 1:5-scale model of Captain Cook's *Endeavour*, and a video on the town's history.

ⒻTours

Russell Mini Tours
Bus Tour

(☎0800 64 64 86; www.russellminitours.com; cnr The Strand & Cass St; adult/child $29/15; ☺tours 10am, 11am, 1pm, 2pm, 3pm & 4pm) Minibus tour around historic Russell. Tours departing Paihia (adult/child $40/20) visiting Kawakawa and the Kawiti Glowworm Caves are also available.

AMOS CHAPPLE/GETTY IMAGES ©

 Don't Miss
Waitangi Treaty Grounds

Occupying a headland draped in lawns and bush, this is NZ's most significant historic site. Here, on 6 February 1840, the first 43 Maori chiefs, after much discussion, signed the Treaty of Waitangi with the British Crown; eventually, over 500 chiefs would sign it.

The Treaty House was built in 1832 as the four-room home of British resident James Busby. It's now preserved as a memorial and museum containing displays, including a copy of the treaty. Just across the lawn, the magnificently detailed *whare runanga* (meeting house) was completed in 1940 to mark the centenary of the treaty.

International visitors will get more out of what is already quite a pricy admission fee if they pay extra for a guided tour ($10) or cultural performance ($15). The 30-minute performance (11am and 1pm) demonstrates traditional Maori song and dance, including the *haka* (war dance). The Ultimate Combo (adult/child $40/free) is a combined ticket including tour and performance. Other options include a Maori Cultural Workshop (adult/child $60/35), and a *hangi* and concert (adult/child $105/50, Wednesday and Saturday December to March) at the Treaty Ground's **Whare Waka** (Waitangi Treaty Grounds; mains $15-24; ⊙9am-5pm) cafe.

NEED TO KNOW

☑09-402 7437; www.waitangi.net.nz; 1 Tau Henare Dr; adult/child $25/free; ⊙9am-5pm Mar-Dec, to 7pm Jan-Feb

🛏️ Sleeping

Lesley's B&B Homestay   B&B $$

(📞09-403 7099; www.lesleys.co.nz; 1 Pomare Rd; s $110-150, d $140-180; 🛜) Rooms are bright and colourful at this welcoming B&B owned by a well-travelled local artist. Breakfasts are legendary – the owner Lesley is also a trained chef – and the guests can fire up the barbecue. Gardens and palms surround the property, and the attractions and cafes of Russell are a 10-minute walk away.

Russell Motel   Motel $$

(📞09-403 7854; www.motelrussell.co.nz; 16 Matauwhi Rd; units $130-165; 🛜🏊) Sitting amid well-tended gardens, this old-fashioned motel offers a good range of units and a pool that the kids will love. The studios are a little dark but you really can't quibble for this price in central Russell.

Duke of Marlborough   Historic Hotel $$

(📞09-403 7829; www.theduke.co.nz; 35 The Strand; r $165-360; 🛜) Holding NZ's oldest pub licence, the Duke boasts about 'serving rascals and reprobates since 1827', although the building has burnt down twice since then. The upstairs accommodation ranges from small, bright rooms in a 1930s extension, to snazzy, spacious doubles facing the water.

✕ Eating

Gables   Modern NZ $$

(📞09-403 7670; www.thegablesrestaurant. co.nz; 19 The Strand; lunch $19-25, dinner $25-32; 🕐noon-3pm Fri-Mon, from 6pm Thu-Mon) Serving an imaginative take on Kiwi classics (lamb, beef and lots of seafood), the Gables occupies an 1847 building on the waterfront, built using whale vertebrae for foundations. Ask for a table by the windows for watery views and look forward to local produce including oysters, cheese and Kerikeri citrus fruits.

Tuk Tuk   Thai $$

(www.tuktukrestaurant.co.nz; 19 York St; mains $18-24; 🕐10.30am-11pm; 🍴) Thai fabrics adorn the tables and Thai favourites fill

the menu. In clement weather grab a table out front and watch Russell's little world go by.

ℹ️ Information

Russell Booking & Information Centre (📞09-403 8020; www.russellinfo.co.nz; Russell Pier; 🕐8am-5pm, extended hours summer)

ℹ️ Getting There & Away

The quickest way to reach Russell by car is via the car ferry (car/motorcycle/passenger $11/5.50/1), which runs every 10 minutes from Opua (5km from Paihia) to Okiato (8km from Russell), between 6.40am and 10pm.

Paihia & Waitangi

POP 1800

The birthplace of NZ (as opposed to Aotearoa), Waitangi inhabits a special, somewhat complex place in the national psyche – aptly demonstrated by the mixture of celebration, commemoration, protest and apathy that accompanies the nation's birthday (Waitangi Day, 6 February).

It was here that the long-neglected and much-contested Treaty of Waitangi was first signed between Maori chiefs and the British Crown, establishing British sovereignty or something a bit like it, depending on whether you're reading the English or Maori version of the document.

Joined to Waitangi by a bridge, Paihia would be a fairly nondescript coastal town if it wasn't the main entry point to the Bay of Islands. If you're not on a tight budget, catch a ferry to Russell, which is far nicer.

ℹ️ Information

Bay of Islands i-SITE (📞09-402 7345; www. northlandnz.com; Marsden Rd; 🕐8am-5pm Mar–mid-Dec, 8am-7pm mid-Dec–Feb) Information and bookings.

ℹ️ Getting There & Around

All buses serving Paihia, such as InterCity and Naked Bus, stop at the Maritime Building by the wharf.

Ferries depart regularly for Russell.

Taranaki

HIGHLIGHTS

① **Mt Taranaki** (p324) So pretty it hurts.

② **Puke Ariki** (p321) Innovative, contemporary and socially astute museum.

③ **Govett-Brewster Art Gallery** (p321) One of the best regional art galleries in NZ.

Dawson Falls (p324), Mt Taranaki
JOCHEN SCHLENKER/GETTY IMAGES ©

New Plymouth

POP 53,400

Dominated (in the best possible way) by Mt Taranaki and surrounded by lush farmland, New Plymouth is this part of NZ's only international deep-water port. The city has a bubbling arts scene, some fab cafes and a rootsy, outdoorsy focus, with surf beaches and Egmont National Park a short hop away.

◉ Sights

Puke Ariki   Museum
(www.pukeariki.com; 1 Ariki St; ☉9am-6pm Mon, Tue, Thu & Fri, to 9pm Wed, to 5pm Sat & Sun) **FREE** Translating as 'Hill of Chiefs', Puke Ariki is home to the i-SITE (p322), a museum, library, a cafe and the fabulous Arborio (p322) restaurant. The excellent museum has an extensive collection of Maori artefacts, plus colonial, mountain geology and wildlife exhibits.

Pukekura Park   Gardens
(www.pukekura.org.nz; Liardet St; ☉7.30am-6pm, to 8pm Nov-Mar) Pukekura has 49 hectares of gardens, playgrounds, trails, streams, waterfalls, ponds and display houses. **Rowboats** (per half-hour $10; ☉Dec & Jan) meander across the main lake (full of arm-sized eels), next to which the **Tea House** (Liardet St; snacks $4-9, mains $10-12; ☉9am-4pm Mar-Nov, 9am-late Dec-Feb) serves light meals (and fudge!). The technicoloured **Festival of Lights** (www.festival-oflights.co.nz) here draws the summer crowds, as does the classically English **cricket oval**.

**Govett-Brewster
Art Gallery**   Gallery
(☏06-759 6060; www.govettbrewster.com; 42 Queen St; ☉10am-5pm) **FREE** Arguably the country's best regional art gallery. Presenting contemporary – often experimental – local and international shows, it's most famous for its connection with famous NZ sculptor, filmmaker and artist Len Lye (1901–80). There's a cool cafe here too. Closed temporarily for earthquake proofing when we visited: call or or check the website for updates.

Activities

SURFING

Taranaki's black, volcanic-sand beaches are terrific for surfing! Close to the eastern edge of town are **Fitzroy Beach** and **East End Beach** (allegedly the cleanest beach in Oceania).

Beach Street Surf Shop   Surfing
(☎06-758 0400; beachstreet@xtra.co.nz; 39 Beach St; 90min lesson $75; ⊙10am-5pm Mon-Thu, to 6pm Fri, to 3pm Sat & Sun) Close to Fitzroy Beach, this surf shop offers lessons, gear hire (surfboard/wetsuit per hour $10/5) and surf tours.

TRAMPING

The excellent **Coastal Walkway** (11km) from Bell Block to Port Taranaki, gives you a surf-side perspective on New Plymouth and crosses the sexily engineered **Te Rewa Rewa Bridge**.

Sleeping

Fitzroy Beach Motel   Motel $$
(☎06-757 2925; www.fitzroybeachmotel.co.nz; 25 Beach St; 1-/2-bedroom unit from $155/190; 🛜) This quiet, old-time motel (just 160m from Fitzroy Beach) has been thoroughly redeemed with a major overhaul and extension. Highlights include quality carpets, double glazing, lovely bathrooms, LCD TVs, and an absence of poky studio-style units (all one- or two-bedroom).

Dawson Motel   Motel $$
(☎06-758 1177; www.thedawsonmotel.co.nz; 16 Dawson St; d from $150, 1-/2-bedroom unit from $180/210; 🛜) Just a couple of years old, the corporate Dawson is a sharp-looking, two-storey number – all white, red and black inside – with sea and mountain views from the top-floor rooms. The location is primo: a five-minute walk into town and 50m to the Coastal Walkway.

King & Queen Hotel Suites   Boutique Hotel $$$
(☎06-757 2999; www.kingandqueen.co.nz; cnr King & Queen Sts; ste $200-400) The new kid on the New Plymouth accommodation block is this regal boutique hotel. Run by unerringly professional staff, it's an interesting 17-room affair over two levels. Each suite features antique Moroccan and Euro furnishings, plush carpets, lustrous black tiles, hip art, retro leather couches and *real* flowers. Cafe/bean roastery on-site.

Eating

Federal Store   Cafe $$
(440 Devon St E; mains $10-20; ⊙7am-5pm Mon-Fri, 9am-5pm Sat & Sun; 🖼) Super-popular and crammed with retro furniture, Federal conjures up a 1950s corner-store vibe. Switched-on staff in dinky head scarves take your coffee order as you queue to order at the counter, keeping you buoyant until your hot cakes, New Yorker sandwich or spicy beans arrive. Terrific cakes, tarts and premade counter food (love the veggie frittata), and very kid-friendly, too.

Arborio   Mediterranean $$
(☎06-759 1241; www.arborio.co.nz; Puke Ariki, 1 Ariki St; mains $13-34; ⊙9am-late) Despite looking like a cheese grater, Arborio, in the Puke Ariki building, is the star of New Plymouth's food show. It's airy, arty and modern, with sea views and faultless service. The Med-influenced menu ranges from an awesome tandoori chicken pizza to pastas, risottos and spicy calamari with garlic and coriander.

Frederic's   Tapas $$
(www.frederics.co.nz; 34 Egmont St; plates $12-19, mains $18-25; ⊙11am-late) Freddy's is a fab gastro-bar with quirky interior design (rusty medieval chandeliers, peacock-feather wallpaper, religious icon paintings), serving generous share plates. Order some lemon-crusted calamari, or some green-lipped mussels with coconut cream, chilli and coriander to go with your Monteith's pale ale.

Information

New Plymouth i-SITE (☎06-759 6060; www.taranaki.co.nz; Puke Ariki, 1 Ariki St; ⊙9am-6pm Mon-Tue & Thu-Fri, to 9pm Wed, to 5pm Sat & Sun) In the Puke Ariki building, with a fantastic interactive tourist-info database.

Taranaki

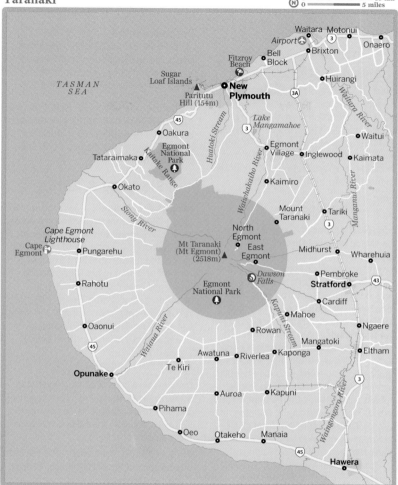

Getting There & Away

Air

New Plymouth Airport (www.newplymouthairport.com; Airport Dr) is 11km east of the centre off SH3. **Scott's Airport Shuttle** (☎0800 373 001, 06-769 5974; www.npairportshuttle.co.nz; adult from $25) operates a door-to-door shuttle.

Air New Zealand (☎06-757 3300; www.airnewzealand.co.nz; 12-14 Devon St E; ☺9am-5pm Mon-Fri) Daily direct flights to/from Auckland, Wellington and Christchurch, with onward connections.

Bus

Services run from the **bus centre (cnr Egmont & Ariki Sts).**

InterCity (www.intercity.co.nz) Services include: Auckland ($73, six hours, two daily), Hamilton ($49, four hours, two daily), Palmerston North ($35, four hours, one daily), Wellington ($45, seven hours, one daily) and Whanganui ($29, 2½ hours, one daily).

Naked Bus (www.nakedbus.com) Services include: Auckland ($30, six hours, one daily), Hamilton ($30, four hours, one daily), Palmerston North ($23, 3½ hours, one daily),

Wellington ($20, 6¼ hours, one daily) and Whanganui ($18, 2½ hours, one daily).

Mt Taranaki (Egmont National Park)

A classic 2518m volcanic cone dominating the landscape, Mt Taranaki is a magnet to all who catch his eye. With the last eruption over 350 years ago, experts say that the mountain is overdue for another go. But don't let that put you off – this mountain is an absolute beauty and the highlight of any visit to the region.

Activities

From **North Egmont**, the main walk is the scenic **Pouakai Circuit**, a two- to three-day, 25km loop through alpine, swamp and tussock areas with awesome mountain views. Short, easy walks from here include the **Ngatoro Loop Track** (one hour), **Veronica Loop** (two hours) and **Nature Walk** (15-minute loop). The **Summit Track** also starts from North Egmont. It's a 14km poled route taking eight to 10 hours return, and should not be attempted by inexperienced people, especially in icy conditions and snow.

East Egmont has the **Potaema Track** (wheelchair accessible; 30 minutes return), **East Egmont Lookout** (10 minutes return) and the steep **Enchanted Track** (two to three hours return).

At Dawson Falls you can do several short walks including **Wilkies Pools Loop** (1¼ hours return) or the excellent but challenging **Fanthams Peak Return** (five hours return), which is snowed-in during winter. The **Kapuni Loop Track** (one-hour loop) runs to the impressive 18m **Dawson Falls** themselves. You can also see the falls from the visitor centre via a 10-minute walk to a viewpoint.

Tours

Mt Taranaki Guided Tours   Tramping
(☏ 027 441 7042; www.mttaranakiguidedtours.co.nz) Guided hikes on the mountain from

one to three days, with the appropriately named Ian McAlpine. Price on application.

Taranaki Tours   Guided Tour
(☏ 0800 886 877, 06-757 9888; www.taranakitours.com; per person from $130) Runs an around-the-mountain day tour, strong on Maori culture and natural history.

Heliview   Scenic Flights
(☏ 0800 767 886, 06-753 0123; www.heliview.co.nz; flights from $149) A 25-minute 'Port to Peak' summit flight costs $249 per passenger.

Sleeping & Eating

Mountain House   Lodge $$
(☏ 06-765 6100; www.stratfordmountainhouse.co.nz; 998 Pembroke Rd; d $155, extra person $20) This upbeat lodge, on the Stratford side of the mountain (15km from the SH3 turn-off and 3km to the Manganui ski area), has recently renovated, motel-style rooms and a mod, European-style **restaurant-cafe** (mains brunch $13-38, dinner $34-42; ☉ 9am-late Wed-Sun). Dinner plus B&B packages available (from $295).

Information

Dawson Falls Visitor Centre (☏ 443 0248; www.doc.govt.nz; Manaia Rd; ☉ 9am-4pm Thu-Sun, daily school holidays) On the southeastern side of the mountain, fronted by an awesome totem pole.

North Egmont Visitor Centre (☏ 06-756 0990; www.doc.govt.nz; Egmont Rd; ☉ 8am-4.30pm) Current and comprehensive national park info.

Getting There & Away

There are no public buses to the national park but numerous shuttle-bus/tour operators will gladly take you there for around $40/55 one-way/return (usually cheaper for groups).

Cruise NZ Tours (☏ 0800 688 687) Mountain shuttle bus departing New Plymouth 7.30am for North Egmont; returns 4.30pm. Other pick-ups/drop-offs by arrangement. Tours also available.

Eastern Taranaki Experience (☏ 06-765 7482; www.eastern-taranaki.co.nz) Shuttle services as well as tours and accommodation in Stratford.

Stewart Island

HIGHLIGHTS

1 **Rakiura Track** (p326) One of NZ's greatest Great Walks.

2 **Spotting a kiwi** (p329) Wait! What's that? There, in the bushes...

3 **Meeting the locals** Bend an elbow at the bar with some islanders.

Ulva Island
MATTHEW MICAH WRIGHT/GETTY IMAGES ©

Travellers who undertake the short jaunt to Stewart Island/Rakiura will be rewarded with a warm welcome from both the local kiwi and the local Kiwis. NZ's 'third' island is a good place to spy the country's shy, feathered icon in the wild, and the close-knit community of Stewart Islanders (population 381) are relaxed hosts.

Sights

Ulva Island
Island

A tiny paradise covering only 250 hectares, Ulva Island/Te Wharawhara is a great place to see lots of birds. Established as a bird sanctuary in 1922, it remains one of Stewart Island/Rakiura's wildest corners – 'a rare taste of how NZ once was and perhaps could be again', according to DOC. Today the air is alive with birdsong, which can be appreciated on walking tracks in the island's northwest as detailed in *Ulva: Self-Guided Tour* ($2), available from the DOC visitor centre. Any water-taxi company will run you to the island from Golden Bay wharf, with scheduled services run by **Ulva Island Ferry** (☏03-219 1013; return adult/child $20/10; ⊙departs 9am, noon, 4pm; returns noon, 4pm, 6pm). To get the most out of Ulva Island, go on a tour with Ulva's Guided Walks (p327).

Rakiura Museum
Museum

(Ayr St, Oban; adult/child $2/50¢; ⊙10am-1.30pm Mon-Sat, noon-2pm Sun) Historic photographs are stars of this small museum focused on local natural and human history, and featuring Maori artifacts, whaling gear and household items.

Activities

Rakiura National Park protects 85% of the island, making it a mecca for trampers and birdwatchers.

Numerous operators offer guided tours: walking, driving, boating and by air, most focusing on wildlife with history slotted in. Independent walkers have plenty to choose from; visit Rakiura National Park Visitor Centre for details on local tramps, long and short, and huts along the way.

Stewart Island (North)

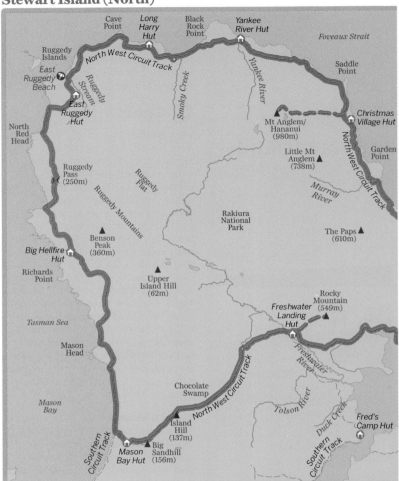

Cave Point
Long Harry Hut
Black Rock Point
Yankee River Hut
Foveaux Strait

Ruggedy Islands
North West Circuit Track
Saddle Point

East Ruggedy Beach
Ruggedy Stream
Christmas Village Hut

East Ruggedy Hut
Mt Anglem/ Hananui (980m)
Garden Point

North Red Head
Little Mt Anglem (738m)
North West Circuit Track

Ruggedy Pass (250m)
Ruggedy Flat
Murray River

Rakiura National Park

Ruggedy Mountains
The Paps (610m)

Benson Peak (360m)

Big Hellfire Hut
Richards Point
Upper Island Hill (62m)

Tasman Sea
Rocky Mountain (549m)
Freshwater Landing Hut

Mason Head
Freshwater River

Mason Bay
Chocolate Swamp
North West Circuit Track
Tolson River
Duck Creek
Fred's Camp Hut

Southern Circuit Track
Island Hill (137m)
Mason Bay Hut
Big Sandhill (156m)
Southern Circuit Track

DAY WALKS

Observation Rock
Walking

This short but quite sharp 15-minute climb reaches the Observation Rock lookout where there are panoramic views of Paterson Inlet, Mount Anglem and Mount Rakeahua. The trail is clearly marked from the end of Leonard Rd, off Ayr St, Oban.

Ackers Point
Walking

This three-hour return walk from Oban features an amble around the bay to a bushy track passing the historic Stone House (built 1835) at **Harrald Bay** before reaching **Ackers Point Lighthouse** where there are wide views of Foveaux Strait and the chance to see blue penguins and a colony of tïtï.

OVERNIGHT TRAMPS

Rakiura Track
Tramping

(www.doc.govt.nz) One of NZ's nine Great Walks, the 39km, three-day Rakiura Track is a peaceful and leisurely loop, which sidles around beautiful beaches before climbing over a 250m-high forested ridge

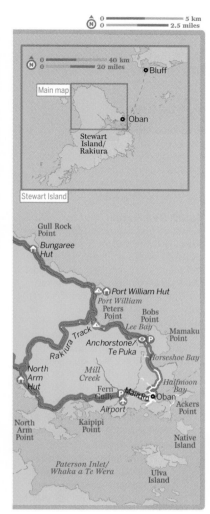

naturalists, these excellent half-day tours ($125; transport included) explore Ulva Island. Book at the Fernery.

Stewart Island Experience
Guided Tours

(☎03-219 0056, 0800 000 511; www.stewartis-landexperience.co.nz; ⏱12 Elgin Tce) Runs 2½-hour Paterson Inlet cruises (adult/child $90/22) via Ulva Island; 1½-hour minibus tours of Oban and the surrounding bays ($45/25); and 2½-hour marine-life nature cruises with semisubmersible viewing ($90/45).

Bravo Adventure Cruises
Birdwatching

(☎03-219 1144; www.kiwispotting.co.nz) Departing around sunset, Bravo runs small-group kiwi-spotting tours ($140) on a scenic reserve reached by a 30-minute boat trip and involving gentle walking through forest and on a beach.

Phil's Sea Kayak
Kayaking

(☎03-219 1444, 027 444 2323; trips from $79) Stewart Island/Rakiura's only kayaking guide, Phil runs trips on Paterson Inlet tailored for all abilities which include Ulva Island and sandy beaches, with sightings of wildlife along the way. Watch for good weather and give him a bell.

Ruggedy Range Wilderness Experience
Birdwatching

(☎0274 784 433, 03-219 1066; www.rug-gedyrange.com; Main Rd) Nature-guide Furhana runs small-group guided walks include half- and full-day trips to Ulva Island ($120/185); and overnight trips to see kiwi in the wild ($525).

Sleeping

Jo & Andy's B&B
B&B $

(☎03-219 1230; jariksem@clear.net.nz; cnr Morris St & Main Rd, Oban; s $60, d/tw $90; @🖥) A great option for budget travellers, this cosy blue home squeezes in twin, double and single rooms. A big breakfast of muesli, fruit and homemade bread prepares you for the most active of days. Jo and Andy are splendid company and

and traversing the sheltered shores of Paterson Inlet/Whaka a Te Wera. It passes sites of historical interest and introduces many of the common sea- and forest birds of the island. It's a well-defined circuit requiring a moderate level of fitness, suitable for tramping year-round.

Tours

Ulva's Guided Walks
Walking Tour

(☎03-219 1216; www.ulva.co.nz) Focused firmly on birding and guided by expert

there's hundreds of books if the weather packs up.

Stewart Island Lodge
Lodge $$

(☎03-219 0085; www.stewartislandlodge.co.nz; Nichol Rd; d incl breakfast $195; @🛜) On a hill overlooking the bay, five minutes' walk from Oban, this grand lodge has six comfortable en suite rooms. Shared facilities include a sunny balcony, lounge and dining patio for partaking of the continental breakfast or your own meals prepared in the guest kitchen. As it's owned by Stewart Island Experience; enquire about island tours and transport.

Latt 47
Rental House $$

(☎03-219 1330; john.barry@clear.net.nz; 12a Excelsior Rd, Oban; d $180) This modern, hillside house sleeps up to four. Debbie can also hook you up with other suitable Stewart Island/Rakiura accommodation.

Bay Motel
Motel $$

(☎03-219 1119; www.baymotel.co.nz; 9 Dundee St, Oban; d $175-200; 🛜) Modern, comfortable units with lots of light and views over the harbour. Some rooms have spa baths, all have kitchens and two are wheelchair-accessible. When you've exhausted the island's bustling after-dark scene, Sky TV's on hand for on-tap entertainment.

🍴 Eating

Bird on a Pear
Cafe $

(Oban; meals $10-18; ⏱7am-3.30pm) Upstairs on the wharf with Halfmoon Bay views, the Bird is a bright and breezy spot to enjoy a cooked breakfast, lunch or coffee and fresh home baking.

South Sea Hotel
Pub $$

(www.stewart-island.co.nz; 26 Elgin Tce, Oban; mains $16-30; ⏱7am-9pm; 🛜) Welcome to one of NZ's classic pubs, complete with stellar cod and chips, beer by the quart, civilised cafe ambience in the dining room, and plenty of friendly banter in the public bar. Great at any time of day (or night), try to wash up for the Sunday-night quiz – an unforgettable, fun slice of island life hosted by Quizmistress Vicki. Basic rooms available (double $90 to $115) and studio motels out back ($165).

ℹ️ Information

The best place for information on the mainland is Invercargill i-SITE. Online, see www.stewartisland.co.nz.

Rakiura National Park Visitor Centre (☎03-219 0008; www.doc.govt.nz; Main Rd, Oban; ⏱8am-5pm Jan-Mar, reduced hours Apr-Dec) Information displays introduce Stewart Island/Rakiura's flora and fauna, while a video library provides entertainment and education (a good rainy day Plan B).

Stewart Island Experience Red Shed (☎03-219 0056, 0800 000 511; www.stewartislandexperience.co.nz; 12 Elgin Tce, Oban;

Stewart Island brown kiwi
TERRY WHITTAKER / ALAMY ©

Spotting a Kiwi: A Brush with the Gods

Stewart Island/Rakiura is one of the few places on earth where you can spot a kiwi in the wild. Considered the king of the forest by Maori, the bird has been around for 70 million years and is related to the now extinct moa.

As big as a barnyard chicken and estimated to number around 20,000 birds, the Stewart Island/Rakiura brown kiwi (*Apteryx australis lawryi*, also known as the tokoeka) is larger in size, longer in the beak, and thicker in the legs than its northern cousins. They are also the only kiwi active during daylight hours, and birds may be seen around sunrise and sunset foraging for food in grassed areas and on beaches where they mine sandhoppers under washed-up kelp.

7.30am-6.30pm) Conveniently located next to the wharf, the helpful crew at the Red Shed can hook you up with nearly everything on and around the island including accommodation, guided tours, boat trips, bikes, scooters and rental cars.

ⓘ Getting There & Away

Air

Stewart Island Flights (☏03-218 9129; www.stewartislandflights.com; Elgin Tce, Oban; adult/child one-way $117.50/75, return $203/118) Flies between the island and Invercargill three times daily, with good standby and over-60s discounts.

Boat

Stewart Island Experience (☏0800 000 511, 03-212 7660; www.stewartislandexperience.co.nz; Main Wharf, Oban) The passenger-only ferry runs between Bluff and Oban (adult/child $75/38 one-way) up to four times daily (reduced in winter). Book a few days ahead in summer. The crossing takes one hour and can be a rough ride. Cars and campervans can be stored in a secure car park at Bluff for an additional cost.

ⓘ Getting Around

Water taxis offer pick-ups and drop-offs to remote parts of the island – a handy service for trampers. The taxis also service Ulva Island (return $25).
Aihe Eco Charters & Water Taxi (☏03-219 1066; www.aihe.co.nz)
Rakiura Water Taxi (☏027 354 9991, 0800 725 487; www.rakiurawatertaxi.co.nz)
Stewart Island Water Taxi & Eco Guiding (☏03-219 1394, 0800 469 283; www.stewartislandwatertaxi.co.nz)

Rent a scooter (per half-/full day from $60/70) or a car (per half-/full day from $65/95) from Stewart Island Experience.

New Zealand
In Focus

Maori dancers performing *kapa haka*
PAUL KENNEDY/GETTY IMAGES ©

New Zealand Today

Lord of the Rings film set

> ❝ *New Zealanders have little difficulty in finding something to feel proud about* ❞

where they live
(% of New Zealanders)

63	20	10	5	2
North Island	South Island	Australia	Rest of the World	Travelling

if New Zealand were 100 people

69 would be European
14 would be Maori
9 would be Asian
7 would be Pacific Islanders
1 would be other

population per sq km

≈ 3 people

NEW ZEALAND AUSTRALIA USA

New Zealand has had a bad run on the disaster front in recent years, between devastating earthquakes and a mining tragedy – not to mention the usual storms, droughts, drownings, sinkings and suchlike that make headline news. The global financial crisis hasn't helped either, with money troubles well and truly trickling down to ground level. Despite this, a typically plucky NZ public turns to the sporting arena – and increasingly the arts – to put a smile on its dial.

Shaky Isles

In September 2010, just as the country was edging out of its worst recession in 30 years, a magnitude 7.1 earthquake struck near Christchurch, the nation's second-largest city. The damage was extensive but miraculously no lives were lost, partly because the earthquake occurred in the early hours of the morning when people were in their beds.

Then, in the early afternoon of 22 February 2011, a magnitude 6.3 earthquake struck

MATT MUNRO/LONELY PLANET ©

about. While the All Blacks remain a foundation – not only for their sporting achievements but as figureheads for 'brand NZ' – the depth of Kiwi talent ranges far beyond the rugby pitch. Following the All Blacks' success at the 2011 Rugby World Cup, this feather-weight country punched well above its weight in the 2012 London Olympics. Claiming six gold medals, Team NZ gave traditional rival and sporting giant Australia a run for its money as it only managed to win one more. Other Kiwi sporting stars making their mark around the globe include young golfing sensation Lydia Ko, NBA rookie Steve Adams, IndyCar speedster Scott Dixon, and Valerie Adams: the greatest female shot-putter the world has ever seen.

While Sir Peter Jackson holds his position as a heavyweight in cinema with his blockbusting adaptations of *The Hobbit*, another major player has thrown his hat into the ring. Canadian director James Cameron has set up a rural home base near Wellington, and will create the *Avatar* sequels in the capital, bringing substantial investment and cementing NZ's reputation as a world-class filmmaking destination.

Pop pundits are also taking note of new Kiwi stars, with Grammy award-winning Lorde (of *Pure Heroine,* one of *Rolling Stone*'s albums of 2013) and Kimbra (of Goyte's 2012 smash-hit *Somebody That I Used to Know*) making huge impressions. Pages are also being turned on the international literary scene, as evidenced by Cantabrian Eleanor Catton. Her voluminous historical novel *The Luminaries* claimed one of the world's most coveted publishing accolades, the Man Booker Prize, in 2013, only the second New Zealander to do so.

Christchurch. This time, 185 people lost their lives. Numerous buildings, already weakened by the September 2010 quake and its aftershocks, were damaged beyond repair and had to be demolished completely.

The city's rebuild has been slow; the city centre didn't re-open fully until mid-2013. Cantabrians, however, have displayed admirable resilience and innovation, helping Christchurch to re-emerge as one of NZ's most exciting cities. Fringe suburbs have been reinvigorated, such as Woolston ('Coolston') and Addington, while a cardboard (yes cardboard!) cathedral has been brought into the fold. The city was named by Lonely Planet as one of the world's top 10 cities in *Best in Travel 2013*.

Reasons to be Cheerful

New Zealanders have little difficulty in finding something to feel proud

History

By Professor James Belich

Bridge over the Clutha River built in 1882, Alexandra (p305)

PETER WALTON/GETTY IMAGES ©

New Zealand's history isn't long but it is fast. In less than a thousand years these islands have produced two new peoples: the Polynesian Maori and European New Zealanders. The latter are often known by their Maori name 'Pakeha' (white person; though not all like the term). NZ shares some of its history with the rest of Polynesia, and with some other European settler societies, but also has its own unique features.

Making Maori

The first settlers of NZ were the Polynesian forebears of today's Maori. Beyond that, there are a lot of question marks. Exactly where in east Polynesia did they come from: the Cook Islands, Tahiti, the Marquesas? When did they arrive? Did the first settlers come in one group or several?

Prime sites for first settlement were warm coastal gardens for the food plants

AD 1000–1200

Archaeological evidence suggests Maori arrived in NZ around AD 1200, but earlier dates have also been suggested.

brought from Polynesia (kumara or sweet potato, gourd, yam and taro); sources of workable stone for knives and adzes; and areas with abundant big game. The first settlers spread far and fast, from the top of the North Island to the bottom of the South Island within the first 100 years. High-protein diets are likely to have boosted population growth.

By about 1400, however, with big-game supply of large, slow-moving moa (flightless birds) dwindling, Maori economics turned from big game to small game – forest birds and rats – and from hunting to gardening and fishing. A good living could still be made, but it required detailed local knowledge, steady effort and complex communal organisation, hence the rise of the Maori tribes. Competition for resources increased, as did conflict, and this led to the building of increasingly sophisticated fortifications, known as *pa*.

The Maori had no metals and no written language (and no alcoholic drinks or drugs). But their culture and spiritual life was rich and distinctive. Below Ranginui (sky father) and Papatuanuku (earth mother) were various gods of land, forest and sea, joined by deified ancestors over time. The mischievous demigod Maui was particularly important.

Maori traditional performance art, and the group singing and dancing known as *kapa haka,* has real power, even for modern audiences. Visual art, notably woodcarving, is something special – 'like nothing but itself' in the words of 18th-century explorer-scientist Joseph Banks.

Enter Europe

NZ became an official British colony in 1840, but the first authenticated contact between Maori and the outside world took place almost two centuries earlier in 1642, in Golden Bay at the top of the South Island. Two Dutch ships sailed from Indonesia to search for a southern land and anything valuable it might contain.

When Abel Tasman's ships anchored in the bay, local Maori came out in their canoes to make the traditional challenge: friends or foes? Misunderstanding this, the Dutch

1642
First European contact: Abel Tasman arrives, but leaves without landing after a skirmish with Maori.

1769
James Cook and Jean de Surville visit; despite some violence, both communicate with Maori.

1790s
Whaling ships and sealing gangs arrive. Europeans depend on Maori for food, water and protection.

challenged back, by blowing trumpets. When a boat was lowered to take a party between the two ships, it was attacked by Maori. Four crewmen were killed. Tasman sailed away and did not come back; nor did any other European for 127 years. But the Dutch did leave a name: 'Nieuw Zeeland' or 'New Sealand'.

Contact between Maori and Europeans was renewed in 1769, when English and French explorers arrived, under James Cook and Jean de Surville. Relations were more sympathetic, and exploration continued, motivated by science, profit and great power rivalry. Cook made two more visits between 1773 and 1777, and there were further French expeditions.

Unofficial visits, by whaling ships in the north and sealing gangs in the south, began in the 1790s. The first mission station was founded in 1814, in the Bay of Islands, and was followed by dozens of others: Anglican, Methodist and Catholic. Surprisingly, the most numerous category of visitor was probably American. New England whaling ships favoured the Bay of Islands for rest and recreation; 271 called there between 1833 and 1839 alone. To whalers, 'rest and recreation' meant sex and drink. Their favourite haunt, the little town of Kororareka (now Russell), was known to the missionaries as 'the hellhole of the Pacific'.

One or two dozen bloody clashes dot the history of Maori–European contact before 1840, but given the number of visits, interracial conflict was modest. Most warfare was between Maori and Maori: the terrible intertribal 'Musket Wars' of 1818–36 are evidence of this.

Europe brought such things as pigs (at last) and potatoes, which benefited Maori, while muskets and diseases had the opposite effect. The Musket Wars killed perhaps 20,000 people, and new diseases did considerable damage, too. By 1840 the Maori population had been reduced to about 70,000, a decline of at least 20%. Maori bent under the weight of European contact, but they certainly did not break.

Making Pakeha

By 1840 Maori tribes described local Europeans as 'their Pakeha', and valued the profit and prestige they brought. Maori wanted more of both, and concluded that accepting nominal British authority was the way to get them. In 1840 the two peoples struck a deal, symbolised by the treaty first signed at Waitangi on 6 February that year. The Treaty of Waitangi now has a standing not dissimilar to that of the Constitution in the US, but it is even more contested. The original problem was a discrepancy between British and Maori understandings of the treaty. The English version promised Maori full equality as British subjects in return for complete rights of government. The Maori version also promised that Maori would retain their chieftainship, which implied local rights of government.

1840
Treaty of Waitangi signed by 40 chiefs in a sovereignty settlement. NZ becomes a nominal British colony.

1853–56
Provincial and central elected governments are established, and the first elections held for the NZ parliament.

1860–61
Conflict with the government over Maori land at Waitara sparks the First Taranaki War; Waikato tribes get involved.

In 1840 there were only about 2000 Europeans in NZ, with the shanty town of Kororareka (now Russell) as the capital and biggest settlement. By 1850 six new settlements had been formed with 22,000 settlers between them. About half of these had arrived under the auspices of the New Zealand Company and its associates. The company was the brainchild of Edward Gibbon Wakefield, who also influenced the settlement of South Australia. From the 1850s, his settlers, who included a high proportion of upper-middle-class gentlefolk, were swamped by succeeding waves of immigrants that continued to wash in until the 1880s. These people were part of the great British and Irish diaspora that also populated Australia and much of North America. Small groups of Germans, Scandinavians and Chinese made their way in, though the last faced increasing racial prejudice from the 1880s, when the Pakeha population reached half a million.

Much of the mass immigration from the 1850s to the 1870s was assisted by the provincial and central governments, which also mounted large-scale public works schemes, especially in the 1870s under Julius Vogel. In 1876 Vogel abolished the provinces on the grounds that they were hampering his development efforts. The last imperial governor with substantial power was the talented but Machiavellian George Grey, who ended his second governorship in 1868. Thereafter, the governors (governors-general from 1917) were largely just nominal heads of state; the head of government (the premier or prime minister) had more power. The central government – originally weaker than the provincial governments, the imperial governor and the Maori tribes – eventually exceeded the power of all three.

The Maori tribes did not go down without a fight, however. The first clash took place in 1843 in the Wairau Valley, now a winegrowing district. In 1845 more serious fighting broke out in the Bay of Islands, when Maori chief Hone Heke sacked a British settlement. Pakeha were able to swamp the few Maori living in the South Island, but the fighting of the 1840s confirmed that the North Island at that time comprised a European fringe around an independent Maori heartland.

In the 1850s settler population and aspirations grew, and fighting broke out again in 1860. The wars burned on sporadically over much of the North Island

Talk the Talk

Linguistic similarities between Maori and Tahitian indicate neighbourly relations in the distant past as well as their shared origin. Maori is about as similar to Tahitian as Spanish is to French, despite the 4294km separating these island groups.

1861
Gold is discovered in Otago; the regional population climbs from 13,000 to over 30,000 in six months.

1865–69
Second Taranaki War: Maori resist First Taranaki War land confiscations and come close to victory.

1893
NZ becomes the first country in the world to grant the vote to women.

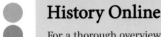

History Online

For a thorough overview of New Zealand history from Gondwanaland to today, visit www.history-nz.org. The Ministry for Culture & Heritage's history website (www.nzhistory.net.nz) is also an excellent source of info on NZ history, including the New Zealand Land Wars.

until 1872. In the early years, a Maori nationalist organisation, the King Movement, was the backbone of resistance. In later years, some remarkable prophet-generals, notably Titokowaru and Te Kooti, took over. Most wars were small-scale, but the Waikato War of 1863–64 was not, resulting in around 1700 casualties. This conflict, fought at the same time as the American Civil War, involved armoured steamships, ultramodern heavy artillery, telegraph and 10 proud British regular regiments. Maori political, though not cultural, independence ebbed away in the last decades of the 19th century. It finally expired when police invaded its last sanctuary, the Urewera Mountains, in 1916.

Welfare & Warfare

From the 1850s to the 1880s, despite conflict with Maori, the Pakeha economy boomed on the back of wool exports, gold rushes and massive overseas borrowing for development. The crash came in the 1880s, when NZ experienced its Long Depression. In 1890 the Liberals came to power, and stayed there until 1912, helped by a recovering economy. NZ became the first country in the world to give women the vote in 1893, and introduced old-age pensions in 1898. The Liberals also introduced a long-lasting system of industrial arbitration, but this was not enough to prevent bitter industrial unrest in 1912–13. This happened under the conservative 'Reform' government, which had replaced the Liberals in 1912. Reform remained in power until 1928, and later transformed itself into the National Party. Renewed depression struck in 1929, and the NZ experience of it was as grim as any.

In 1935 a second reforming government took office: the First Labour government, led by Michael Joseph Savage, easily NZ's favourite Australian. For a time, the Labour government was considered the most socialist government outside Soviet Russia. But, when the chips were down in Europe in 1939, Labour had little hesitation in backing Britain.

NZ had also backed Britain in the Boer War (1899–1902) and WWI (1914–18), with dramatic losses in WWI in particular. NZ, a peaceful-seeming country, has spent much of its history at war. In the 19th century it fought at home; in the 20th, overseas.

1914–18
WWI: 100,000 NZ troops suffer almost 60,000 casualties, mostly in France.

1939–45
WWII: 200,000 NZ troops participate; 100,000 Americans arrive to defend NZ from the Japanese.

1975
Waitangi Tribunal is set up to investigate grievances of Maori people in relation to the Treaty of Waitangi.

Better Britons?

British visitors have long found NZ hauntingly familiar. This is not simply a matter of the British and Irish origin of most Pakeha. It also stems from the tightening of NZ links with Britain from 1882, when refrigerated cargoes of food were first shipped to London. By the 1930s giant ships carried frozen meat, cheese and butter, as well as wool, on regular voyages taking about five weeks one way. The NZ economy adapted to the feeding of London, and cultural links were also enhanced. This tight relationship has been described as 'recolonial', but it is a mistake to see NZ as an exploited colony. Average living standards in NZ were normally better than in Britain, as were the welfare and lower-level education systems. New Zealanders had access to British markets and culture, and they contributed their share to the latter as equals. Indeed, New Zealanders, especially in war and sport, sometimes saw themselves as a superior version of the British – the Better Britons of the south.

'Recolonial' NZ prided itself, with some justice, on its affluence, equality and social harmony. But it was also conformist, even puritanical. Until the 1950s it was

Maori *hongi* greeting (p349)
MIKE POWELL/GETTY IMAGES ©

1981
Rugby tour by South African Springboks divides NZ; many Kiwis take a strong anti-apartheid stance.

1985
Greenpeace antinuclear protest ship *Rainbow Warrior* is sunk in Auckland Harbour by French spies.

1992
The government begins reparations for land confiscated in the Land Wars and confirms Maori fishing rights.

The Best...
Historic
Buildings

1 Auckland Art Gallery
(p65)

2 Dunedin Railway
Station (p294)

3 National Tobacco
Company Building
(p181), Napier

4 Civic Theatre (p60),
Auckland

5 Embassy Theatre
(p170), Wellington

6 Antigua Boat Sheds
(p235), Christchurch

technically illegal for farmers to allow their cattle to mate in fields fronting public roads, for moral reasons. The 1953 American movie, *The Wild One,* was banned until 1977. Sunday newspapers were illegal until 1969, and full Sunday trading was not allowed until 1989. Licensed restaurants hardly existed in 1960, nor did supermarkets or TV. Notoriously, from 1917 to 1967, pubs were obliged to shut at 6pm.

Coming In, Coming Out

The 'recolonial' system was shaken several times after 1935, but managed to survive until 1973, when Mother England ran off and joined the Franco-German commune now known as the EU. NZ was beginning to develop alternative markets to Britain, and alternative exports to wool, meat and dairy products. Wide-bodied jet aircraft were allowing the world and NZ to visit each other on an increasing scale. NZ had only 36,000 tourists in 1960, compared with more than two million a year now. Women were beginning to penetrate first the upper reaches of the workforce and then the political sphere. Gay people came out of the closet, despite vigorous efforts by moral conservatives to push them back in. University-educated youths were becoming more numerous and more assertive.

From 1945 Maori experienced both a population explosion and massive urbanisation. In 1936, Maori were 17% urban and 83% rural. Fifty years later, these proportions had reversed. The immigration gates – which until 1960 were pretty much labelled 'whites only' – widened, first to allow in Pacific Islanders for their labour, and then to allow in (East) Asians for their money.

In 1984 NZ's third great reforming government was elected – the Fourth Labour government, led nominally by David Lange and in fact by Roger Douglas, the Minister of Finance. This government adopted an antinuclear foreign policy, delighting the Left, and a more market-driven economic policy, delighting the Right. NZ's numerous economic controls were dismantled with breakneck speed. Middle NZ was uneasy about the antinuclear policy, which threatened NZ's ANZUS alliance with Australia and the US. But in 1985 French spies sank the antinuclear protest ship *Rainbow Warrior* in Auckland Harbour, killing one crewman. The

2004
Maori TV begins broadcasting, committed to NZ content and Maori language and culture.

2005
Helen Clark is returned in NZ's third successive Labour government. The Maori Party takes four seats.

2008
John Key's National Party ousts Clark's Labour after nine years in government.

lukewarm US condemnation of the French act brought middle NZ in behind the antinuclear policy, which became associated with national independence. Revelling in their new freedom, NZ investors engaged in a frenzy of speculation, and suffered even more than the rest of the world from the economic crash of 1987.

The early 21st century is an interesting time for NZ. Like NZ food and wine, its film and literature are flowering as never before, and the new ethnic mix is creating something very special in popular music. There are continuities, however – the pub, the sportsground, the quarter-acre section, the bush, the beach and the bach (holiday home) – and they are part of the reason people like to come here.

Meanwhile, Christchurch continues to rebuild after the 2011 earthquakes, and the national rugby team, the All Blacks, are gearing up for their World Cup title defence in England in 2015.

IN FOCUS HISTORY

The Six O'Clock Swill

From 1917 to 1967, NZ liquor laws dictated that pubs shut their doors at 6pm – a puritanical concession aimed at preserving morality in Kiwi society. In the cities, after-work hordes would storm the pubs at 5.05pm, chugging down as many beers as possible before 6pm – the 'Six O'Clock Swill'. In the country, however, the dictum was often ignored, especially on the South Island's marvellously idiosyncratic West Coast.

The art-deco Embassy Theatre (p170), Wellington
OLIVER STREWE/GETTY IMAGES ©

2011
185 people die in a 6.3-magnitude earthquake in Christchurch.

2011
New Zealand hosts the Rugby World Cup: the All Blacks (only just!) win the final.

2013
New Zealand becomes one of just 15 countries in the world to legally recognise same-sex marriage.

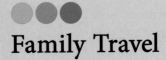

Family Travel

Mahia Peninsula, Hawke's Bay (p179)

DOUGLAS PEARSON/GETTY IMAGES ©

New Zealand is super-easy to tackle with the kids in tow. Accommodation is usually kid-friendly, the public health care system is world class, and Kiwi food doesn't usually have chilli in it! Baby formula and disposable nappies (diapers) are widely available in cities and towns, most of which have public rooms where parents can go to nurse a baby or change a nappy.

Sights & Activities

Fabulous kids' playgrounds (with slides, swings, see-saws etc) proliferate across NZ; local visitor information centres can point you in the right direction.

Some regions produce free information booklets geared towards kids' sights and activities; one example is **Kidz Go!** (www.kidzgo.co.nz), which details child-friendly activities and restaurants in the larger urban centres. Other handy websites for families include www.kidspot.co.nz and www.kidsnewzealand.com.

Practicalities

With family-friendly accommodation, accessible babysitting resources, straightforward car-hire/car-seat arrangements and myriad children's discounts and kid-centric eating options, NZ is a wonderfully practical place for getting around with the kids.

Accommodation

Many motels and holiday parks have playgrounds, games and DVDs, and occasionally fenced swimming pools and trampolines. Cots and highchairs aren't always available at budget and midrange accommodation, but top-end hotels supply them and often provide child-minding services. B&Bs aren't usually amenable to families – many promote themselves as kid-free. Most hostels focusing on the backpacker party demographic don't welcome kids either, but some of the bigger operators do (including YHA hostels).

Car Hire

Procuring a kiddie car-seat for your rental car is no problem with the larger companies (Avis, Budget, Europcar etc), but some smaller car-hire companies struggle with the concept. Double-check that the company you choose can supply and fit the correctly sized seat for your child. Some companies may legally require you to fit the seat yourself. Note that kids under six months old may require a baby 'capsule' instead. Have this conversation with your car-hire company well in advance.

Discounts

Child concessions are often available for accommodation, tours and attraction entry fees, along with air, bus and train transport, with discounts of as much as 50% off the adult rate. Note that the definition of 'child' can vary from under 12 to under 18 years; toddlers (under four years) usually get free admission and transport.

Eating Out

There are plenty of family-friendly restaurants in NZ with highchairs and kids' menus. Pubs often serve kids' meals and most cafes and restaurants (with the exception of upmarket eateries) can handle the idea of child-sized portions.

The Best...
Children's Highlights

1 Geysers and mud bubbles, Rotorua

2 Auckland Zoo (p65)

3 Cable Car (p159), Wellington

4 Shotover Jet (p277), Queenstown

5 Punting on the Avon (p235), Christchurch

Need To Know

- **Babysitting** Try www.rockmybaby.co.nz or www.babysitters4u.co.nz.
- **Changing facilities** In most towns and shopping malls.
- **Cots** Usually available in midrange and top-end accommodation.
- **Health** High first-world standards.
- **Highchairs** Widely available in restaurants and cafes.
- **Kids' menus** Often available in pubs and less-formal restaurants and cafes.
- **Nappies (diapers)** Widely available.
- **Strollers** Even on public transport you'll get a helping hand.
- **Transport** Most public transport caters for young passengers.

Environment
By Vaughan Yarwood

Great spotted kiwis

ROBIN BUSH/GETTY IMAGES ©

One of the main reasons travellers come to New Zealand is to experience the country's superb landscapes. From snowy summits and volcanoes to glaciers, beaches and ancient forests, NZ has a wealth of natural assets. But this is also a fragile environment, and the pressures of agriculture, forestry and population growth have all taken a toll.

The Land

NZ is geologically young – less than 10,000 years old. Straddling two vast tectonic plates, nature's strongest forces are at work here: volcanoes, geothermal geysers, hot springs and mud pools abound...not to mention earthquakes.

The South Island has the higher mountains: the 650km-long, 3754m-high Southern Alps. Moisture-laden westerly winds dump an incredible 15m of rain annually on the Alps' western slopes. The North Island has a more even rainfall, snares most of the country's volcanic activity (especially around Rotorua and Taupo) and is spared the temperature extremes of the South – which can plunge when a wind blows in from Antarctica.

But on either island, the important thing to remember, especially if you are tramping at high altitude, is that NZ has a maritime climate. This means weather can change with lightning speed, catching out the unprepared.

A third of NZ – more than 50,000 sq km – is protected in national parks and reserves, administered by the **DOC** (Department of Conservation; www.doc.govt.nz).

Environmental Issues

The NZ Forest Accord protects native forests, and NZ is also famous for its strong antinuclear stance, but to describe NZ as entirely 'clean and green' would be inaccurate.

European grazing systems have left many hillsides barren and eroded, and despite increasing demand for organic food, most NZ farming still relies on chemical fertilisers, pesticides and herbicides.

NZ's energy consumption has grown phenomenally over the last 20 years – NZ is one of the most inefficient energy users in the developed world. Public transport is often inadequate and ecological values still play little part in urban planning.

Other hot issues include *Didymosphenia geminata* (aka Didymo or 'rock snot') algae in waterways, fixed-net fishing endangering dolphins, and the curse of introduced possums, rats and stoats.

The Best...
Places to See a Kiwi

1 Auckland Zoo (p65)

2 Rainbow Springs (p113), Rotorua

3 Willowbank Wildlife Reserve (p250), Christchurch

4 Zealandia (p159), Wellington

5 Kiwi Birdlife Park (p276), Queenstown

Flora & Fauna

NZ may be relatively young, geologically speaking, but its plants and animals go back a long way. The tuatara, for instance, an ancient reptile unique to these islands, is a Gondwanaland survivor closely related to the dinosaurs, while many of the distinctive flightless birds (ratites) have distant African and South American cousins.

Birds

The now-extinct, flightless moa was 3.5m tall and weighed more than 200kg; you can see skeletons at Auckland Museum. Rumours of late survivals of this giant bird abound, but none have been authenticated. So if you see a chunky ostrichlike bird in your travels, photograph it – you may have just made the greatest zoological discovery of the last 100 years!

Kiwis are threatened and nocturnal, so it's rare to spot one in the wild. Other bird-nerd favourites include royal albatrosses, white herons, Fiordland crested and yellow-eyed penguins, Australasian gannets and dotterels. More common are tuis, bellbirds, fantails, pukeko, morepork owls and weka.

If you spend any time in the South Island high country, you are likely to come up against the fearless and inquisitive kea – an uncharacteristically drab green parrot with bright red underwings. Kea are common in the car parks of the Fox and Franz Josef Glaciers, where they hang out for food scraps or tear rubber from car windscreens.

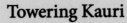

Towering Kauri

'When Chaucer was born this was a sturdy young tree. When Shakespeare was born it was 300 years old. It predates most of the great cathedrals of Europe. Its trunk is sky-rocket straight and sky-rocket bulky, limbless for half its height. Ferns sprout from its crevices. Its crown is an asymmetric mess, like an inverted root system. I lean against it, give it a slap. It's like slapping a building. This is a tree out of Tolkien. It's a kauri.'

Joe Bennett, A Land of Two Halves, *referring to the McKinney kauri in Northland.*

Marine Mammals

Cruising the waters off NZ are whales, orcas, seals and dolphins. Kaikoura, on the east coast of the South Island, is the place to see them – sperm whales, fur seals and dusky dolphins are here year-round, and you'll also see migrating humpback, pilot, blue and southern right whales. You can swim with dolphins and seals here, too, and also at Akaroa and Tauranga.

Trees

Keep an eye out for yellow-flowering kowhai in spring, and red pohutukawa and rata in summer. Mature, centuries-old kauri are stately emblems of former days: see them at Northland's Waipoua Kauri Forest. Also look for rimu (red pines), totara (favoured for Maori war canoes), mamuka (black tree ferns) and ponga (silver tree ferns).

You won't get far into the bush without coming across one of its most prominent features: tree ferns. NZ is a land of ferns (more than 80 species) and most easily recognised are the mamaku (black tree fern) – which grows to 20m and can be seen in damp gullies throughout the country – and the 10m-high ponga (silver tree fern) with its distinctive white underside.

Maori Culture
By John Huria

Maori wood carving

WILFRIED KRECICHWOST/GETTY IMAGES ©

If you're looking for a Maori experience in New Zealand you'll find it – a performance, a conversation, an art gallery, a tour. Maori are a diverse people: some are engaged with traditional cultural networks and pursuits; others are occupied with adapting tradition and placing it into a dialogue with our rapidly globalising culture.

Maori Then

Three millennia ago people began moving eastwards into the Pacific, sailing against the prevailing winds and currents (hard to go out, easier to return safely) in large, double-hulled ocean-going craft. Some stopped at Tonga and Samoa; others settled the central East Polynesian tropical islands.

The first arrival in Aotearoa (NZ's Maori name) was the great navigator Kupe, whose wife Kuramarotini gave Aotearoa its name: *'He ao, he ao tea, he ao tea roa!'* (A cloud, a white cloud, a long white cloud!)

The early settlers moved around a lot, but when they settled, Maori established *mana whenua* (regional authority), whether by military campaigns or by peaceful intermarriage and diplomacy.

Maori lived in *kainga* (small villages) with associated gardens. From time to time people would leave their home base and go to harvest seasonal foods. When peaceful life was interrupted by conflict, Maori would withdraw to a *pa* (fortified village).

Then Europeans arrived.

Maori Today

Today's Maori culture is marked by new developments in arts, business, sport and politics. Many historical grievances still stand (see the History chapter, p334), but some *iwi* (tribes; Ngai Tahu and Tainui, for example) have settled historical issues and are major forces in the NZ economy. Maori have also addressed the decline in Maori language use by establishing *kohanga reo, kura kaupapa Maori* and *wananga* (Maori-medium schools). Maori radio stations abound; **Maori Television** (www.maoritelevision.com) and the Maori-language station **Te Reo** (www.maoritelevision.com/tv/te-reo-channel) occupy TV screens. In late May or early June, *Matariki* (Maori New Year) is a time for learning, planning and preparing as well as singing, dancing and celebrating.

Religion

Christian churches and denominations are important in the Maori world: there are televangelists, mainstream churches for regular and occasional worship, and two major Maori churches (Ringatu and Ratana).

But in the (non-Judeo Christian) beginning there were the *atua Maori,* the Maori gods, and for many Maori the gods remain a vital and relevant force. They are spoken of on the *marae* (meeting place) and in wider Maori contexts. The traditional Maori creation story is well known and widely celebrated.

Visiting Marae

As you travel around NZ, you will see many *marae* complexes, which should only be visited by arrangement with the owners. *Marae* complexes include a *wharenui* (meeting house), which often embodies an ancestor. Its ridge is the backbone, the rafters are ribs, and it shelters the descendants.

Hui (gatherings) are held at *marae.* Issues are discussed, classes conducted, milestones celebrated and the dead farewelled. *Te reo Maori* (the Maori language) is prominent, sometimes exclusively so.

If you visit a *marae* as part of an organised group, you'll be welcomed in a *powhiri* – a process involving a ceremonial *wero* (challenge), a *karanga* (ceremonial call) between women, *whaikorero* (speech making) and a *waiata* (song). The visitors' speaker then places *koha* (a gift, usually an envelope of cash) on the *marae.* The hosts then invite the visitors to *hariru* (shake hands) and *hongi (greet).* Visitors and hosts are now united and share food and drink.

Traditional Maori Arts

Some of the largest collections of Maori arts (or *taonga,* meaning 'treasures') are at Wellington's Te Papa museum, Auckland Museum and Canterbury Museum in Christchurch.

Carving

Traditional Maori carving, with its intricate detailing and curved lines, can transport the viewer. It's quite amazing to consider that it was traditionally done with painstakingly made stone tools, until the advent of iron (when nails suddenly became very popular). The apex of carving today is the *whare whakairo* (carved meeting house), with traditional motifs used to interpret stories and embody ancestors.

The Hongi

The Maori *hongi* greeting involves pressing the forehead and nose together firmly, shaking hands and perhaps offering a greeting such as *'Kia ora'* or *'Tena koe'*. Some prefer one press (for two or three seconds, or longer); others prefer two shorter ones (press, release, press).

Weaving

Weaving was an essential art that provided clothing, nets and cordage, footwear, mats and *kete* (bags). Flax was (and still is) the preferred medium for weaving, but contemporary weavers use everything in their work: raffia, copper wire, rubber – even polar fleece and garden hoses!

Haka

As any All Blacks rugby fan will tell you, experiencing the awe-inspiring, uplifting *haka* – chanted words, vigorous body movements and *pukana* (when performers distort their faces, eyes bulging with the whites showing, perhaps with tongue extended) – can get the adrenaline flowing. The *haka* isn't just a war dance; it's also used to welcome visitors, honour achievement, express identity or to present strong opinions.

Ta Moko

Ta moko is the Maori art of tattoo, traditionally worn by men on their faces, thighs and buttocks, and by women on their chins and lips. Historically, *moko* were tapped into the skin using pigment and a bone chisel, but the modern tattooist's gun is now more common. Many Maori wear *moko* with quiet pride and humility.

Contemporary Maori Arts

A distinctive theme in much contemporary Maori art is the tension between traditional Maori ideas and modern artistic mediums and trends. For general information on Maori arts today, see www.maoriart.org.nz.

Writing

Key Maori authors to scan the shelves for include Patricia Grace (*Potiki; Cousins; Dogside Story; Tu*), Witi Ihimaera (*Pounamu, Pounamu; The Matriarch; Bulibasha; The Whale Rider*), Keri Hulme (*The Bone People*, winner of the 1985 Booker Prize), Alan Duff (*Once Were Warriors*), James George (*Hummingbird; Ocean Roads*) and Eleanor Catton (*The Luminaries*, winner of the 2013 Man Booker Prize). Poetry buffs should seek out anything by the late, lamented Hone Tuwhare (*Deep River Talk: Collected Poems*).

Theatre

Theatre is a strong area of the Maori arts today. Instead of dimming the lights and immediately beginning the performance, many Maori theatre groups begin with a stylised *powhiri*, with space for audience members to respond to the play, and end with a *karakia* (blessing or prayer) or farewell.

The Best...
Places to Experience Haka

1 Whakarewarewa Thermal Village (p105)

2 Waitangi Treaty Grounds (p319)

3 Tamaki Maori Village (p112)

4 Te Papa (p162)

5 Auckland Museum (p66)

It's worth looking out for **Taki Rua** (www.takirua. co.nz), a prominent theatre group and veteran independent producer of Maori work.

Film

Barry Barclay's *Ngati* (1987) was NZ's first nondocumentary, feature-length movie by a Maori director. Merata Mita was the first Maori woman to direct a fiction feature: *Mauri* (1988). Other films with significant Maori input include the harrowing *Once Were Warriors* and the uplifting *Whale Rider*. Oscar-shortlisted Taika Waititi wrote and directed *Eagle vs Shark* and *Boy*.

The **New Zealand Film Archive** (www.filmarchive. org.nz) in Auckland and Wellington is a great place to experience Maori film, with most showings either free or inexpensive.

Dance

Contemporary Maori dance often takes its inspiration from *kapa haka* (group cultural dance) and traditional Maori imagery. The exploration of pre-European life also provides inspiration.

NZ's leading Maori dance company is the **Atamira Dance Company** (www.atamiradance.co.nz), which produces critically acclaimed, beautiful and challenging work.

Active New Zealand

Bungy jumping from Kawarau Bridge (p277), Queenstown

New Zealand's astounding natural assets encourage even the laziest lounge lizards to drag themselves outside. Outdoor activities across the nation are accessible and supremely well organised. Commercial operators can hook you up with whatever kind of experience floats your boat – from bungy jumping off a canyon to sea kayaking around a national park.

Hiking

Hiking (aka bush walking, trekking or tramping, as Kiwis call it) is the perfect vehicle for a close encounter with NZ's natural beauty. There are thousands of kilometres of tracks here, plus an excellent network of huts and camping grounds.

Before plodding off into the forest, get up-to-date track and weather info and maps from the appropriate authority – usually the **Department of Conservation** (DOC; www.doc.govt.nz) or regional i-SITE visitor information centres. If you have your heart set on a summer walk along one of the Great Walks, check out the booking requirements and get in as many months in advance as you can. DOC staff can also help plan tramps on lesser-known tracks.

Online, www.tramper.co.nz is a fantastic website with track descriptions and ratings.

The Best...
Non-Great Walks Tracks

1 Tongariro Alpine Crossing (p134)

2 Queen Charlotte Track (p201)

3 Kaikoura Coast Track (p207)

4 Banks Peninsula Track (p246)

5 Mauao Base Track (p119), Mt Maunganui

For safety tips, see www.mountainsafety.org.nz. Log your walk intentions online at www.adventuresmart.org.nz.

The Great Walks

NZ's nine official 'Great Walks' (one of which is actually a canoeing trip; see www.greatwalks.co.nz) are the country's most popular tracks. Natural beauty abounds, but prepare yourself for crowds, especially over summer.

On the North Island, the 46km, three- to four-day **Lake Waikaremoana Track** in Te Urewera National Park is easy to medium in difficulty and offers lake views, bush-clad slopes and swimming. Through the volcanic landscape of Tongariro National Park, the **Tongariro Northern Circuit** is a medium-to-hard, three- to four-day tramp over 43km. The easy **Whanganui Journey** is a 145km, five-day canoe or kayak trip down the Whanganui River in Whanganui National Park.

Down south, the hugely popular, two- to five-day **Abel Tasman Coast Track** is rated easy and takes in 54km of beaches and bays of Abel Tasman National Park. The 78km **Heaphy Track** in Kahurangi National Park is a medium-hard-rated walk over four to six days. The easy-to-medium 60km **Kepler Track** in Fiordland National Park passes lakes, rivers, gorges, glacial valleys and beech forest over three or four days. Also in Fiordland are the easy, four-day **Milford Track** over 53.5km, and the medium-difficulty **Routeburn Track** over two to four days and 32km. On remote Stewart Island, the **Rakiura Track** (39km over three days) is a medium-difficulty track with bird life (kiwi!), beaches and lush bush.

Passes & Bookings

To tramp these tracks you'll need to buy Great Walk Tickets (p219). These track-specific tickets cover you for hut accommodation (from $22 to $54 per adult per night) and/or camping ($6 to $18 per adult per night). You can camp only at designated camping grounds; note there's no camping on the Milford Track.

In the off-peak season (May to September), you can use **Backcountry Hut Passes** ($92 per adult, valid for six months) or pay-as-you-go **Hut Tickets** ($5) instead of Great Walk Tickets on all Great Walks except for the Lake Waikaremoana Track, Heaphy Track, Abel Tasman Coast Track and Rakiura Track (for which Great Walk Tickets are required year-round). Kids under 17 stay in huts and camp for free on all Great Walks.

Bookings can be made online or via phone or email. Alternatively, visit DOC visitor centres close to the tracks. Trampers must book and pay for accommodation in advance and specify dates.

Guided Walks

If you're new to tramping or just want a more comfortable experience than the DIY alternative, several companies can escort you through the wilds, usually staying in comfortable huts (showers!), with meals cooked and equipment carried for you.

On the North Island, sign up for a guided walk at Mt Taranaki, Lake Waikaremoana or Tongariro National Park. On the South Island try Kaikoura, the Banks Peninsula, Milford Track, Queen Charlotte Track, Heaphy Track or Hollyford Track. Prices for a five-day/four-night guided walk start at around $1800, rising towards $2200 for deluxe experiences.

Skiing & Snowboarding

New Zealand is an essential southern-hemisphere destination for snow bunnies, with downhill skiing, cross-country (Nordic) skiing and snowboarding all passionately pursued. The NZ ski season is generally June to October, though it can run as late as November.

NZ's commercial ski areas aren't generally set up as 'resorts' with chalets, lodges or hotels. Rather, accommodation and après-ski carousing are often in surrounding towns, connected with the slopes via daily shuttles.

Club areas are publicly accessible and usually less crowded and cheaper than commercial fields, even though non-members pay a higher fee. Many club areas have lodges you can stay at (subject to availability).

Visitor information centres in NZ and **Tourism New Zealand** (www.newzealand. com) have info on the various ski areas and can make bookings and organise packages. Lift passes cost anywhere from $50 to $100 per adult per day (half price for kids). Ski and snowboard equipment rental starts at around $50 per day.

Online, see www.brownbearski.co.nz, www.snow.co.nz and www.nzsnowboard.com.

North Island

The key North Island ski spots are Whakapapa and Turoa on **Mt Ruapehu** (www. mtruapehu.com) in Tongariro National Park, and **Tukino** (www.tukino.co.nz) on the eastern side of Mt Ruapehu. **Manganui** (www.skitaranaki.co.nz) on Mt Taranaki offers volcano-slope, club-run skiing.

South Island

Most of the South Island action revolves around the resort towns of Queenstown and Wanaka. Iconic ski fields near here include **Coronet Peak** (www.nzski.com), the **Remarkables** (www.nzski.com), **Treble Cone** (www.treblecone.com) and **Cardrona** (www.cardrona.com). NZ's only commercial Nordic (cross-country) ski area is **Snow Farm New Zealand** (www.snowfarmnz.com) near Wanaka.

In South Canterbury there's **Ohau** (www.ohau.co.nz) on Mt Sutton, **Mt Dobson** (www.dobson.co.nz), **Fox Peak** (www.foxpeak.co.nz) and **Roundhill** (www.roundhill.co.nz), which is perfect for beginners and intermediates.

In Central Canterbury try **Mt Hutt** (www.nzski.com), **Porters** (www.skiporters.co.nz), **Temple Basin** (www.templebasin.co.nz), **Craigieburn Valley** (www.craigieburn.co.nz), **Broken River** (www.brokenriver.co.nz), **Mt Olympus** (www.mtolympus.co.nz) or the family-friendly **Mt Cheeseman** (www.mtcheeseman.co.nz) near Christchurch.

Northern Canterbury opportunities include **Hanmer Springs** (www.skihanmer.co.nz) and **Mt Lyford** (www.mtlyford.co.nz). In the Nelson region is the low-key **Rainbow** (www.skirainbow.

Heliskiing

NZ's remote heights are tailor-made for heliskiing, with operators covering a wide off-piste area along the Southern Alps. Costs range from around $825 to $1450 for three to eight runs. **HeliPark New Zealand** (www.helipark.co.nz) at Mt Potts is a dedicated heliski park. Heliskiing is also available at Coronet Peak, Treble Cone, Cardrona, Mt Hutt, Mt Lyford, Ohau and Hanmer Springs.

co.nz), with minimal crowds and good cross-country skiing. **Awakino** (www.skiawakino.com) in North Otago is a small player, but good for intermediate skiers.

Extreme Stuff

The fact that a pant-wetting, illogical activity such as bungy jumping is now an every-day pursuit in NZ says much about how 'extreme sports' have evolved here. Bungy, skydiving, jetboating and white-water rafting are all well established, and all great fun!

Bungy Jumping

Bungy jumping (hurtling earthwards from bridges with nothing between you and eternity but a gigantic rubber band strapped to your ankles) has plenty of daredevil panache.

Queenstown is a spider-web of bungy cords, including a 43m jump off the Kawarau Bridge, a 47m leap from the top of a gondola, and the big daddy, the 134m Nevis Bungy. Other South Island bungy jumps include above the Waiau River near Hanmer Springs, and Mt Hutt ski field.

On the North Island head to Taihape, Rotorua, Auckland and Taupo. Varying the theme, try the 109m-high Shotover Canyon Swing or Nevis Swing in Queenstown, both seriously high rope swings: *swoosh...*

Skydiving

Ejecting yourself from a plane at high altitude is big business in NZ. For most first-time skydivers, a tandem skydive will help you make the leap. The thrill is worth every dollar – around $250/300/350 for a 8000/10,000/12,000ft jump. The **New Zealand Parachute Federation** (www.nzpf.org) is the governing body. Ask your operator if they have Civil Aviation Authority (CAA) acDavid Wall Photo/getty images ©
ation before you take the plunge.

Jetboating

Hold onto your breakfast – it's passenger-drenching 360-degree spins ahoy! On the South Island, the Shotover and Kawarau Rivers (Queenstown) and the Buller River (Westport) have fab jetboating. On the North Island the Whanganui, Motu, Rangitaiki and Waikato Rivers offer excellent jetboating, and there are sprint jets at the Agrodome in Rotorua. Jetboating around the Bay of Islands in Northland is also de rigueur.

White-Water Rafting

There are almost as many white-water rafting possibilities as there are rivers in the country, and there's no shortage of companies to get you into the rapids. **Whitewater NZ** (www.rivers.org.nz) covers all things white-water. The **New Zealand Rafting Association** (NZRA; www.nz-rafting.co.nz) has an online river guide, and lists registered operators.

Mountain Biking

NZ is laced with quality mountain-biking opportunities, including the 22 'Great Rides' comprising the **Nga Haerenga, New Zealand Cycle Trail** (www.nzcycletrail.com). Mountain bikes can be hired in towns such as Queenstown, Wanaka, Nelson, Picton, Taupo and Rotorua.

Various companies will take you up to the tops of mountains and volcanoes (such as Mt Ruapehu, Christchurch's Port Hills, Cardrona and the Remarkables) so you can hurtle back down. Rotorua's Redwoods Whakarewarewa Forest offers famously good mountain biking, as do the 42 Traverse (close to Tongariro National Park), the Alexandra goldfield trails in Central Otago, the Queenstown Bike Park, and Twizel near Mt Cook. Also try Waitati Valley and Hayward Point near Dunedin, Canaan Downs near Abel Tasman National Park, Mt Hutt, Methven and the Banks Peninsula.

Sea Kayaking

Sea kayaking is a fantastic way to see the coast, and get close to wildlife you'd otherwise never see.

Highly rated sea-kayaking areas around NZ include the Hauraki Gulf, the Bay of Islands, Coromandel Peninsula, Marlborough Sounds, Abel Tasman National Park and Fiordland. The **Kiwi Association of Sea Kayakers** (KASK; www.kask.org.nz) is the main NZ organisation. The **Sea Kayak Operators Association of New Zealand** (www.skoanz.org.nz) website has a map of paddling destinations with links to operators.

Surfing

NZ has a sensational mix of quality waves perfect for both beginners and experienced surfers. Point breaks, reefs, rocky shelves and hollow, sandy beach breaks can all be found.

NZ water temperatures and climate vary greatly from north to south. For comfort while surfing, wear a wetsuit. In summer on the North Island, you can get away with wearing a spring suit and boardies; on the South Island, a 2mm to 3mm steamer

Jetboating on the Shotover River (p277), Queenstown
TIM GERARD BARKER/GETTY IMAGES ©

Cycle Touring

With good roads and even better scenery, cycle touring is a magical way to see NZ. Most towns offer touring-bike hire at either backpacker hostels or specialist bike shops, and there are repair shops in the bigger towns. Anyone planning a cycling tour (particularly of the South Island) should check out the guided and self-guided tour options at www.cyclehire.co.nz, as well as Lonely Planet's *Cycling New Zealand*.

can do the job. Steamers are essential in winter.

Top North Island surf spots include Raglan, Mt Maunganui, Taranaki's Surf Highway 45 and the East Coast around Mahia Peninsula. Down south try the Kaikoura Peninsula, Dunedin and the Punakaiki on the West Coast.

Online, www.surfingnz.co.nz lists surf schools, while www.surf.co.nz provides information on the top spots.

Horse Trekking

Unlike some other parts of the world where beginners get led by the nose around a paddock, here you can really get out into the countryside on a farm, forest or beach. Rides range from one-hour jaunts (from around $60) to week-long, fully catered treks.

For equine info online, including trek-operator listings, see www.truenz.co.nz/horsetrekking and www.newzealand.com.

Mountain biking with a view of Lake Wakatipu, near Queenstown

Survival
Guide

Sea kayaking at Cathedral Cove (p93), Coromandel Peninsula
DAVID WALL PHOTO/GETTY IMAGES ©

Directory

Accommodation

Across New Zealand, you can bed down in historic guesthouses, facility-laden hotels, uniform motel units, beautifully situated campsites, and hostels that range in character from clean-living to tirelessly party-prone.

If you're travelling during peak tourist seasons, book your bed well in advance. Accommodation is most in demand (and at its priciest) during the summer holidays from Christmas to late January, at Easter, and during winter in snowy resort towns like Queenstown.

Visitor information centres provide reams of local accommodation information, often in the form of folders detailing facilities and up-to-date prices; many can also make bookings on your behalf.

For online listings, check out: **Automobile Association** (AA; ☎0800 500 444; www.aa.co.nz) and **Jasons** (www.jasons.com).

Farmstays

Farmstays open the door to the agricultural side of NZ life, with visitors encouraged to get some dirt beneath their fingernails at orchards and dairy, sheep and cattle farms. Costs can vary widely, with B&Bs generally ranging from $80 to $120. Some farms have separate cottages where you can fix your own food, while others offer low-cost, shared, backpacker-style accommodation.

Pubs, Hotels & Motels

The least expensive form of NZ hotel accommodation is the humble pub. NZ's old pubs are often full of character (and characters), while others are

grotty, ramshackle places that are best avoided, especially by women travelling solo. Also check whether there's a band playing the night you're staying – you could be in for a sleepless night. In the cheapest pubs, singles/doubles might cost as little as $30/60 (with a shared bathroom down the hall), though $50/80 is more common.

At the top end of the hotel scale are five-star international chains, resort complexes and architecturally splendorous boutique hotels, all of which charge a hefty premium for their mod cons, snappy service and/or historic opulence. We quote 'rack rates' (official advertised rates) for such places, but discounts and special deals often apply.

NZ's towns have a glut of nondescript, low-rise motels and 'motor lodges', charging between $80 and $180 for double rooms. Most are modernish (though decor is often mired in the early 2000s) and have similar facilities, namely tea- and coffee-making equipment, fridge, and TV. Prices vary with standard.

Sleeping Price Ranges

The following price indicators used throughout this book refer to a double room with bathroom during high season:

- **$** less than $100
- **$$** $100–200
- **$$$** more than $200

Price ranges generally increase by 20% to 25% in Auckland, Wellington and Christchurch. Here you can still find budget accommodation at up to $100 per double, but midrange stretches from $100 to $240, with top-end rooms more than $240.

Customs Regulations

For the low-down on what you can and can't bring into NZ, see the **New Zealand Customs Service** (www.customs. govt.nz) website. Per-person duty-free allowances:

- 1125mL of spirits or liqueur
- 4.5L of wine or beer

Book Your Stay Online

For more accommodation reviews by Lonely Planet authors, check out http://hotels.lonelyplanet.com. You'll find independent reviews, as well as recommendations on the best places to stay. Best of all, you can book online.

- 200 cigarettes (or 50 cigars or 250g of tobacco)
- dutiable goods up to the value of $700

It's a good idea to declare any unusual medicines. You must declare any plant or animal products (including anything made of wood), and food of any kind. Weapons and firearms are either prohibited or require a permit and safety testing.

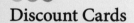

Discount Cards

The internationally recognised **International Student Identity Card** is produced by the **International Student Travel Confederation** (ISTC; www.istc.org), and issued to full-time students aged 12 and over. It provides discounts on accommodation, transport and admission to attractions.

The **New Zealand Card** (www.newzealandcard.com) is a $35 discount pass that will score you between 5% and 50% off a range of accommodation, tours, sights and activities.

Travellers over 60 with some form of identification (eg an official seniors card from your home country) are often eligible for concession prices.

Electricity

230V/50Hz

Food & Drink

New Zealand's restaurants and cafes are adept at throwing together traditional staples (lamb, beef, venison, green-lipped mussels) with Asian, European and pan-Pacific flair. Tipping is not mandatory, but feel free if you've had a happy culinary experience (about 10% of the bill). For online listings see:

- www.dineout.co.nz
- www.menus.co.nz

On the liquid front, NZ wine is world class (especially sauvignon blanc and pinot noir), and you'll be hard-pressed to find a NZ town of any size without decent espresso. NZ microbrewed beers have also become mainstream.

Vegetarians & Vegans

Most large urban centres have at least one dedicated vegetarian cafe or restaurant: see the **Vegetarians New Zealand** (www.vegetarians.co.nz) website for listings. Beyond this, almost all restaurants and cafes offer some vegetarian menu choices (although sometimes only one or two). Many eateries also provide gluten-free and vegan options. Always check that stocks and sauces are vegetarian, too.

In this book, the vegetarian icon () in Eating listings indicates a good vegetarian selection.

Price Ranges

The following price indicators refer to the average price of a main course:

- $ less than $15
- $$ $15–32
- $$$ more than $32

Gay & Lesbian Travellers

The gay and lesbian tourism industry in NZ isn't as high-profile as it is in neighbouring Australia, but homosexual communities are prominent in Auckland and Wellington, with myriad support organisations across both islands. NZ has progressive laws protecting the rights of gays and lesbians: same-sex marriage was legalised here in 2013, while the legal minimum age for sex between consenting persons is 16. Generally speaking, Kiwis are fairly relaxed and accepting about homosexuality, but that's not to say that homophobia doesn't exist.

Resources

There are loads of websites dedicated to gay and lesbian travel in NZ. **Gay Tourism New Zealand** (www.gaytourismnewzealand.com) is a good starting point, with links to various sites. Other worthwhile queer websites:

- www.gaynz.com
- www.gaynz.net.nz
- www.lesbian.net.nz
- www.gaystay.co.nz

Check out the nationwide magazine *express* (www.gayexpress.co.nz) every second Wednesday for the latest happenings, reviews and listings on the NZ gay scene.

Health

New Zealand is one of the healthiest countries in the world in which to travel.

Diseases such as malaria and typhoid are unheard of, and the absence of poisonous snakes or other dangerous animals makes outdoor adventures here less risky than in neighbouring Australia.

Before You Go

Vaccinations

NZ has no vaccination requirements for any traveller, but the World Health Organization recommends that all travellers should be covered for diphtheria, tetanus, measles, mumps, rubella, chickenpox and polio, as well as hepatitis B, regardless of their destination. Ask your doctor for an *International Certificate of Vaccination* (or 'the yellow booklet'), which will list all the vaccinations you've received.

Health Insurance

Health insurance is essential for all travellers. If your current health insurance doesn't cover you for medical expenses incurred overseas, consider extra insurance – see www.lonelyplanet.com/travel-insurance for more information. Find out in advance if your insurance plan will make payments directly to providers or reimburse you later for overseas health expenditures.

In New Zealand

Availability & Cost of Health Care

NZ's public hospitals offer a high standard of care (free for residents). All travellers are covered for medical care resulting from accidents that occur while in NZ (eg motor-

Climate

Auckland
°C/°F Temp — Rainfall inches/mm

Christchurch
°C/°F Temp — Rainfall inches/mm

Queenstown
°C/°F Temp — Rainfall inches/mm

vehicle accidents, adventure-activity accidents) by the Accident Compensation Corporation. Costs incurred due to treatment of a medical illness that occurs while in NZ will only be covered by travel insurance. For more details, see www.moh.govt.nz and www.acc.co.nz.

The 24-hour, free-call **Healthline** (📞 0800 611 116; **www.health.govt.nz**) offers health advice throughout NZ.

Pharmaceuticals

Over-the-counter medications are widely available in NZ through private chemists. These include painkillers, antihistamines and skin-care products. Some medications, such as antibiotics and the contraceptive pill, are only available via a prescription obtained from a general practitioner.

Insurance

○ A watertight travel insurance policy covering theft, loss and medical problems is essential. Some policies specifically exclude designated 'dangerous activities' such as scuba diving, bungy jumping, white-water rafting, skiing and even tramping. If you plan on doing any of these things (a distinct possibility in NZ!), make sure your policy covers you fully.

○ It's worth mentioning that under NZ law, you cannot sue for personal injury (other than exemplary damages). Instead, the country's **Accident Compensation Corporation** (ACC; www.acc. co.nz) administers an accident compensation scheme that provides accident insurance for NZ residents and visitors to the country, regardless of fault. This scheme, however, does not negate the necessity for your own comprehensive travel-insurance policy, as it doesn't cover you for such things as income loss, treatment at home or ongoing illness.

○ Consider a policy that pays doctors or hospitals directly, rather than you paying on the spot and claiming later. If you have to claim later, keep all documentation. Check that the policy covers ambulances and emergency medical evacuations by air.

○ Worldwide travel insurance is available at www.lonelyplanet.com/travel-insurance. You can buy, extend and claim online anytime – even if you're already on the road.

Practicalities

○ **News** Leaf through Auckland's *New Zealand Herald,* Wellington's *Dominion Post* or Christchurch's *The Press* newspapers. Online, see www.nzherald.co.nz or www.stuff.co.nz.

○ **TV** Watch one of the national government-owned TV stations (TV One, TV2, TVNZ 6, Maori TV and the 100% Maori language Te Reo) or the subscriber-only Sky TV (www.skytv.co.nz).

○ **Radio** Tune in to Radio National for current affairs and Concert FM for classical and jazz (see www.radionz.co.nz for frequencies). Kiwi FM (www.kiwifm.co.nz) showcases NZ music; Radio Hauraki (www.hauraki.co.nz) cranks out the rock.

○ **DVDs** Kiwi DVDs are encoded for Region 4, which includes Mexico, South America, Central America, Australia, the Pacific and the Caribbean.

○ **Weights & measures** NZ uses the metric system.

Internet Access

Wi-fi & Internet Service Providers

○ You'll be able to find wi-fi access around the country, from hotel rooms to pub beer gardens to hostel dorms. Usually you have to be a guest or customer to log-on; you'll be issued with an access code. Sometimes it's free, sometimes there's a charge.

○ The country's main telecommunications company is Telecom New Zealand (www.telecom.co.nz), which has wireless hotspots around the country where you can purchase prepaid access cards. Alternatively, purchase a prepaid number from the login page at any wireless hotspot using your credit card. See Telecom's website for hotspot listings.

- If you've brought your palmtop or laptop, consider buying a prepay USB modem (aka a 'dongle') with a local SIM card: both Telecom and Vodafone sell these from around $100. If you want to get connected via a local internet service provider (ISP), options include the following:

Clearnet (☏ 0508 888 800; www.clearnet.co.nz)

Earthlight (☏ 03-479 0303; www.earthlight.co.nz)

Slingshot (☏ 0800 892 000; www.slingshot.co.nz)

Internet Cafes

There are fewer internet cafes around these days than there were five years ago (thanks to the advent of iPhones/iPads and wi-fi) but you'll still find them in most sizeable towns. Access at cafes ranges anywhere from $4 to $6 per hour.

Many public libraries have internet access, including wi-fi, but generally it's provided for research, not for travellers to check Facebook.

●●●
Legal Matters

Marijuana is widely indulged in but illegal: anyone caught carrying this or other illicit drugs will have the book thrown at them.

Drink-driving is a serious offence and remains a significant problem in NZ. The legal blood alcohol limit is 0.08% for drivers over 20, and zero for those under 20.

If you are arrested, it's your right to consult a lawyer before any formal questioning begins.

●●●
Money

ATMs & Eftpos

Branches of the country's major banks across both islands have ATMs, but you won't find them everywhere (eg not in small towns).

Many NZ businesses use electronic funds transfer at point of sale (Eftpos), allowing you to use your bank card (credit or debit) to make direct purchases and often withdraw cash as well. Eftpos is available practically everywhere: just like an ATM, you'll need a personal identification number (PIN).

Credit & Debit Cards

Credit Cards

Credit cards such as Visa and MasterCard are widely accepted for everything from a hostel bed to a bungy jump, and are pretty much essential for car hire. They can also be used for over-the-counter cash advances at banks and from ATMs, but be aware that such transactions incur charges. Diners Club and American Express cards are not as widely accepted.

Debit Cards

Debit cards enable you to withdraw money directly from your home bank account using ATMs, banks or Eftpos facilities. Any card connected to the international banking network (Cirrus, Maestro, Visa Plus and Eurocard) should work with your PIN. Fees will vary depending on your home bank; ask before you leave. Alternatively, companies such as Travelex offer debit cards with set withdrawal fees and a balance you can top-up from your personal bank account while on the road.

Currency

NZ's currency is the NZ dollar, comprising 100 cents. There are 10c, 20c, 50c, $1 and $2 coins, and $5, $10, $20, $50 and $100 notes. Prices are often still marked in single cents and then rounded to the nearest 10c when you hand over your money.

Moneychangers

Changing foreign currency or travellers cheques is usually no problem at NZ banks or at licensed moneychangers (eg Travelex) in the major cities. Moneychangers can be found in all major tourist areas, cities and airports.

Taxes & Refunds

The Goods and Services Tax (GST) is a flat 15% tax on all domestic goods and services. Prices in this book include GST. There's no GST refund available when you leave NZ.

Travellers Cheques

Amex, Travelex and other international brands of travellers cheques are a bit old-fashioned these days, but they're easily exchanged at banks and moneychangers.

Opening Hours

Note that most attractions close on Christmas Day and Good Friday.

Shops & businesses 9am to 5.30pm Monday to Friday, and 9am to 12.30pm or 5pm Saturday. Late-night shopping (until 9pm) in larger cities on Thursday and/or Friday nights. Sunday trading in most big towns and cities.

Supermarkets 8am to 7pm, often 9pm or later in cities.

Banks 9.30am to 4.30pm Monday to Friday; some city branches also open Saturday mornings.

Post offices 8.30am to 5pm Monday to Friday; larger branches also 9.30am to 1pm Saturday. Postal desks in newsagents open later.

Restaurants Noon to 2.30pm and 6.30 to 9pm, often until 11pm Fridays and Saturdays.

Cafes 7am to 4pm or 5pm.

Pubs Noon until late; food from noon to 2pm and from 6pm to 8pm.

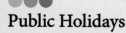

Public Holidays

NZ's main public holidays:

New Year 1 and 2 January

Waitangi Day 6 February

Easter Good Friday and Easter Monday; March/April

Anzac Day 25 April

Queen's Birthday First Monday in June

Labour Day Fourth Monday in October

Christmas Day 25 December

Boxing Day 26 December

In addition, each NZ province has its own anniversary-day holiday. The dates of these provincial holidays vary. When they fall on Friday to Sunday, they're usually observed the following Monday; if they fall on Tuesday to Thursday, they're held on the preceding Monday.

Provincial anniversary holidays:

Southland 17 January

Wellington 22 January

Auckland 29 January

Northland 29 January

Nelson 1 February

Otago 23 March

Taranaki 31 March

South Canterbury 25 September

Hawke's Bay 1 November

Marlborough 1 November

Chatham Islands 30 November

Westland 1 December

Canterbury 16 December

School Holidays

The Christmas holiday season, from mid-December to late January, is part of the summer school vacation: expect transport and accommodation to book out in advance, and queues at tourist attractions. There are three shorter school-holiday periods during the year: from mid- to late April, early to mid-July, and mid-September to early October. For exact dates see the **Ministry of Education** (www.minedu.govt.nz) website.

Safe Travel

Although it's no more dangerous than other developed countries, violent crime does happen in NZ, so it's worth taking sensible precautions on the streets at night or if staying in remote areas. Gang culture permeates some parts of the country; give any black-jacketed, insignia-wearing groups a wide berth.

Theft from cars is a problem around NZ and travellers are viewed as easy marks. Avoid leaving valuables in vehicles, no matter where they're parked; you're tempting fate at tourist parking areas and trailhead car parks.

Don't underestimate the dangers posed by NZ's unpredictable, ever-changing climate, especially in high-altitude areas. Hypothermia is a real risk.

NZ has been spared the proliferation of venomous creatures found in neighbouring Australia (spiders, snakes, jellyfish etc). Sharks patrol NZ waters, but rarely nibble on humans. Much greater ocean hazards are rips and undertows, which can quickly drag swimmers out to sea: heed local warnings.

Kiwi roads are often made hazardous by speeding locals, wide-cornering campervans and traffic-ignorant sheep. Set yourself a reasonable itinerary and keep your eyes on the road. Cyclists take care: motorists can't always overtake easily on skinny roads.

In the annoyances category, NZ's sandflies are a royal pain (the intense itching can last for months). Lather yourself with insect repellent in coastal areas, even if you're only sitting on the edge of a beach for a minute or two.

●●●
Telephone

Telecom New Zealand (www.telecom.co.nz) The country's key domestic player, with a stake in the local mobile (cell) market.

Vodafone (www.vodafone.co.nz) Mobile-network option.

2 Degrees (www.2degreesmobile.co.nz) Mobile-network option.

Emergencies

The number for emergency services (ambulance, fire, police) is ☎111.

Mobile Phones

Local mobile phone numbers are preceded by the prefix ☎021, ☎022, ☎025 or ☎027. Mobile phone coverage is good in cities and towns and most parts of the North Island, but can be patchy away from urban centres on the South Island.

If you want to bring your own phone and use a prepaid service with a local SIM card, Vodafone is a practical option. Any Vodafone shop (found in most major towns) will set you up with a SIM card and phone number (about $40); top-ups can be purchased at newsagents, post offices and petrol stations practically anywhere.

Alternatively, if you don't bring your own phone from home, you can rent one from **Vodafone Rental** (www.vodarent.co.nz) priced from

$5 per day (for which you'll also need a local SIM card), with pick-up and drop-off outlets at NZ's major airports. We've also had some positive feedback on **Phone Hire New Zealand** (www.phonehirenz.com), which hires out mobile phones, SIM cards, modems and GPS systems.

Local Calls

Local calls from private phones are free! Local calls from payphones cost $1 for the first 15 minutes, and $0.20 per minute thereafter, though coin-operated payphones are scarce (and if you do find one, chances are the coin slot will be gummed up); you'll generally need a phonecard. Calls to mobile phones attract higher rates.

International Calls

Payphones allow international calls, but the cost and international dialling code for calls will vary depending on which provider you're using.

To make international calls from NZ, you need to dial the international access code ☎00, then the country code and the area code (without the initial zero). So for a London number, you'd dial ☎00-44-20, then the number. If dialling NZ from overseas, the country code is ☎64, followed by the appropriate area code minus the initial zero.

Long Distance Calls & Area Codes

NZ uses regional two-digit area codes for long-distance calls, which can be made from any payphone. If you're making a local call (ie to someone else in the same town), you don't need to dial the area code. But if you're dialling within a region (even if it's to a nearby town with the same area code), you do have to dial the area code.

Information & Toll-Free Calls

Numbers starting with 0900 are usually recorded information services, charging upwards of $1 per minute (more from mobiles); these numbers cannot be dialled from payphones.

Toll-free numbers in NZ have the prefix 0800 or 0508 and can be called free of charge from anywhere in the country, though they may not be accessible from certain areas or from mobile phones. Telephone numbers beginning with 0508, 0800 or 0900 cannot be dialled from outside NZ.

Phonecards

NZ has a wide range of phonecards available, which can be bought at hostels, newsagents and post offices for a fixed-dollar value (usually $5, $10, $20 and $50). These can be used with any public or private phone by dialling a toll-free access number and then the PIN number on the card. Shop around – rates vary from company to company.

●●●
Time

NZ is 12 hours ahead of GMT/UTC and two hours ahead of Australian Eastern Standard Time. The Chathams are 45 minutes ahead of NZ's main islands.

In summer, NZ observes daylight-saving time, where clocks are wound forward by one hour on the last Sunday in September; clocks are wound back on the first Sunday of the following April.

●●●
Tourist Information

Tourism New Zealand

The website for the official national tourism body, **Tourism New Zealand** (www. newzealand.com), is the best place for pretrip research. Emblazoned with the hugely successful 100% Pure New Zealand branding, the site has information in several languages, including German and Japanese, and also list Tourism New Zealand contact offices overseas (Australia, UK, USA etc).

Local Tourist Offices

Almost every Kiwi city or town seems to have a visitor information centre. The bigger centres stand united within the outstanding **i-SITE** (www. newzealand.com/travel/i-sites) network – around 80 info centres affiliated with Tourism New Zealand. i-SITEs have trained staff, information on local activities and attractions, and free brochures and maps. Staff can also book activities, transport and accommodation.

There's also a network of **Department of Conservation** (DOC; www. doc.govt.nz) visitor centres to help you plan activities and make bookings. DOC visitor centres – in national parks, regional centres and major cities – usually also have displays on local lore, flora, fauna and biodiversity.

●●●
Travellers with Disabilities

Kiwi accommodation generally caters fairly well for travellers with disabilities, with a significant number of hostels, hotels, motels and B&Bs equipped with wheelchair-accessible rooms. Many tourist attractions similarly provide wheelchair access, with wheelchairs often available.

Tour operators with accessible vehicles operate from most major centres. Key cities are also serviced by 'kneeling' buses (buses that hydraulically stoop down to kerb level to allow easy access), and taxi companies offer wheelchair-accessible vans. Large car-hire firms (Avis, Hertz etc) provide cars with hand controls at no extra charge (advance notice required).

Resources

Weka (www.weka.net.nz) Good general information, with categories including Transport and Travel.

Royal New Zealand Foundation of the Blind (www.rnzfb.org.nz)

National Foundation for the Deaf (www.nfd.org.nz)

Mobility Parking (www. mobilityparking.org.nz) Info on mobility parking permits and online applications.

Climate Change & Travel

Every form of transport that relies on carbon-based fuel generates CO_2, the main cause of human-induced climate change. Modern travel is dependent on aeroplanes, which might use less fuel per kilometre per person than most cars but travel much greater distances. The altitude at which aircraft emit gases (including CO_2) and particles also contributes to their climate change impact. Many websites offer 'carbon calculators' that allow people to estimate the carbon emissions generated by their journey and, for those who wish to do so, to offset the impact of the greenhouse gases emitted with contributions to portfolios of climate-friendly initiatives throughout the world. Lonely Planet offsets the carbon footprint of all staff and author travel.

Visas

Visa application forms are available from NZ diplomatic missions overseas, travel agents and **Immigration New Zealand** (☎09-914 4100, 0508 558 855; www.immigration.govt.nz). Immigration New Zealand has over a dozen offices overseas; consult the website.

Visitor Visa

Citizens of Australia don't need a visa to visit NZ and can stay indefinitely (provided they have no criminal convictions). UK citizens don't need a visa either and can stay in the country for up to six months.

Citizens of another 56 countries that have visa-waiver agreements with NZ don't need a visa for stays of up to three months, provided they have an onward ticket and sufficient funds to support their stay: see the website for details. Nations in this group include Canada, France, Germany, Ireland, Japan, the Netherlands, South Africa and the USA.

Citizens of other countries must obtain a visa before entering NZ. Visas come with three months' standard validity and cost NZ$130 if processed in Australia or certain South Pacific countries (eg Samoa, Fiji), or around NZ$165 if processed elsewhere in the world.

Women Travellers

NZ is generally a very safe place for women travellers, although the usual sensible precautions apply: avoid walking alone late at night and never hitchhike alone. If you're out on the town, always keep enough money aside for a taxi back to your accommodation. Lone women should also be wary of staying in basic pub accommodation unless it looks safe and well managed. Sexual harassment is not a widely reported problem in NZ, but of course it does happen.

For more information, see www.womentravel.co.nz.

Transport

Getting There & Away

New Zealand is a long way from almost everywhere – most travellers jet in from afar. Flights, tours and rail tickets can be booked online at lonelyplanet.com/bookings.

Entering the Country

Disembarkation in New Zealand is generally a straightforward affair, with only the usual customs declarations and the luggage carousel scramble to endure. Under the Orwellian title of 'Advance Passenger Screening', documents that used to be checked after you touched down in NZ (passport, visa etc) are now checked before you board your flight – make sure all your documentation is in order so that your check-in is stress-free.

Passport

There are no restrictions when it comes to foreign citizens entering NZ. If you have a current passport and visa (or don't require one), you should be fine.

✈ Air

The high season for flights into NZ is during summer (December to February), with slightly less of a premium on fares over the shoulder months (October/November and March/April). The low season generally tallies with the winter months (June to August), though this is still a busy time for airlines ferrying ski bunnies and powder hounds.

International Airports

A number of NZ airports handle international flights, with Auckland receiving most traffic:

Auckland International Airport (AKL; ☎ 09-275 0789; www.aucklandairport.co.nz; Ray Emery Dr, Mangere)

Christchurch International Airport (CHC; ☎ 03-358 5029; www.christchurchairport.co.nz; 30 Durey Rd)

Dunedin International Airport (DUD; ☎ 03-486 2879; www.dnairport.co.nz; 25 Miller Rd, Momona)

Hamilton International Airport (HIA; ☎ 07-848 9027; www.hamiltonairport.co.nz; Airport Rd)

Queenstown Airport (ZQN; ☎ 03-450 9031; www.queenstownairport.co.nz; Sir Henry Wrigley Dr)

Rotorua International Airport (ROT; ☎ 07-345 8800; www.rotorua-airport.co.nz; SH30)

Wellington Airport (WLG; ☎ 04-385 5100; www.wellingtonairport.co.nz; Stewart Duff Dr, Rongotai)

Departure Tax

An international departure tax of NZ$25 applies when leaving three of NZ's smaller international airports: Hamilton, Rotorua and the sporadically international Palmerston North. At all other airports the tax has been replaced with a NZ$12.50 Passenger Service Charge (PSC), which is included in your ticket price. At Hamilton, Rotorua and Palmerston North, departure tax must be paid separately at the airport before you board your flight (via credit card or cash). For kids under 12 it's NZ$10, and free for kids under two.

Getting Around

✈ Air

Those who have limited time to get between NZ's attractions can make the most of a widespread (and very reliable and safe) network of intra- and inter-island flights.

Airlines in New Zealand

The country's major domestic carrier, Air New Zealand, has an aerial network covering most of the country, often operating under the Air New Zealand Link moniker on less popular routes. Australia-based Jetstar also flies between main urban areas. Beyond this, several small-scale regional operators provide essential transport services to outlying islands such as Great Barrier Island in the Hauraki Gulf, to Stewart Island and the Chathams. Operators include the following:

Air Chathams (www.airchathams.co.nz) Services to the remote Chatham Islands from Wellington, Christchurch and Auckland.

Air Fiordland (www.airfiordland.com) Services around Milford Sound, Te Anau and Queenstown.

Air New Zealand (www.airnewzealand.co.nz) Offers flights between 30-plus domestic destinations, plus myriad overseas destinations.

Air West Coast (www.airwestcoast.co.nz) Operates charter/scenic flights ex-Greymouth, winging over the West Coast glaciers and Aoraki/Mt Cook, and stopping in Milford Sound, Queenstown and Christchurch.

Air2there.com (www.air2there.com) Connects destinations across Cook Strait, including Paraparaumu, Wellington, Nelson and Blenheim.

FlyMySky (www.flymysky.co.nz) At least three flights daily from Auckland to Great Barrier Island.

Golden Bay Air (www.goldenbayair.co.nz) Flies regularly between Wellington, Nelson and Takaka in Golden Bay. Also connects to Karamea for Heaphy Track trampers.

Great Barrier Airlines
(www.greatbarrierairlines.co.nz)
Plies the skies over Great
Barrier Island, Auckland,
Tauranga and Whangarei.

Jetstar (www.jetstar.com)
Joins the dots between key
tourism centres: Auckland,
Wellington, Christchurch,
Dunedin and Queenstown (and
flies Queenstown to Melbourne
and Sydney; Christchurch to
Melbourne, Sydney and the
Gold Coast; and Auckland to
Melbourne, Adelaide, the Gold
Coast and Cairns).

Salt Air (www.saltair.co.nz)
Charter flights from Auckland
to the Bay of Islands.

Soundsair (www.soundsair.
co.nz) Numerous flights
each day between Picton
and Wellington, plus flights
from Wellington to Blenheim,
Nelson and Whanganui.

Stewart Island Flights
(www.stewartislandflights.com)
Flies between Invercargill and
Stewart Island.

Sunair (www.sunair.co.nz)
Flies to Whitianga from
Auckland, Great Barrier
Island and Tauranga, plus
numerous other North
Island connections between
Hamilton, Napier, Rotorua and
Gisborne and New Plymouth.

Air Passes
Available exclusively to travel-
lers from the USA or Canada
who have bought an Air New
Zealand fare to NZ from the
USA or Canada, Australia or
the Pacific Islands, Air New
Zealand offers the good-value
New Zealand Explorer Pass.
The pass lets you fly between
up to 27 destinations in New

Zealand, Australia and the
South Pacific islands (including Norfolk Island, Tonga, Van-
uatu, Tahiti, Fiji, Niue and the
Cook Islands). Fares are broken down into four discounted,
distance-based zones: zone
one flights start at US$79 (eg
Auckland to Christchurch);
zone two from US$109 (eg
Auckland to Queenstown);
zone three from US$214 (eg
Wellington to Sydney); and
zone four from US$295 (eg
Tahiti to Auckland). You can
buy the pass before you travel,
or after you arrive in NZ.

    Star Alliance (www.
staralliance.com) offers the
sector-based **South Pacific
Airpass**, valid for selected
journeys within NZ, and
between NZ, Australia and
several Pacific islands,
including Fiji, New Caledonia,
Tonga, the Cook Islands and
Samoa. Passes are available
to nonresidents of these
countries, must be issued
outside NZ in conjunction with
Star Alliance international
tickets, and are valid for three
months. A typical Sydney–
Christchurch–Wellington–
Auckland–Nadi pass cost
NZ$1050 at the time of
research.

Bicycle
Touring cyclists proliferate in
NZ, particularly over summer.
The roads are generally in good
nick, and the climate is generally not too hot or cold. Road
traffic is the biggest danger:
trucks overtaking too close
to cyclists are a particular
threat. Bikes and cycling gear
are readily available to rent or
buy in the main centres, as are
bicycle repair shops.

    By law all cyclists must wear
an approved safety helmet

(or risk a fine); it's also vital
to have good reflective safety
clothing. For more bike safety
and legal tips, see www.nzta.
govt.nz/traffic/ways/bike.

Hire
Rates offered by most outfits
for renting road or mountain
bikes range from $10 to $20
per hour and $30 to $50 per
day. Longer-term rentals may
be available by negotiation.
You can often hire bikes
from your accommodation
(hostels, camping grounds,
etc), or rent more reputable
machines from bike shops in
the larger towns.

Boat
NZ may be an island nation
but there's virtually no long-
distance water transport
around the country. Obvious
exceptions include the boat
services between Auckland
and various islands in the
Hauraki Gulf, the inter-island
ferries that chug across Cook
Strait between Wellington and
Picton, and the passenger
ferry that negotiates Foveaux
Strait between Bluff and the
town of Oban on Stewart
Island.

Bus
Bus travel in NZ is relatively
easy and well organised, with
services transporting you to
the far reaches of both islands
(including the start/end of
various walking tracks), but it
can be expensive, tedious and
time-consuming.

    NZ's dominant bus
company is **InterCity**
(www.intercity.co.nz), which
can drive you to just about
anywhere on the North and
South Islands. **Naked Bus**
(www.nakedbus.com) has

similar routes and remains the main competition.

Seat Classes & Smoking

There are no allocated economy or luxury classes on NZ buses (very democratic), and smoking on the bus is a definite no-no.

Reservations

Over summer, school holidays and public holidays, book well in advance on popular routes (a week or two if possible). At other times a day or two ahead is usually fine. The best prices are generally available online, booked a few weeks in advance.

Bus Passes

If you're covering a lot of ground, both InterCity and Naked Bus offer bus passes that can be cheaper than paying as you go, but they do of course lock you into using their respective networks. Passes are generally valid for 12 months.

NATIONWIDE PASSES

Flexipass A hop-on/hop-off InterCity pass, allowing travel to pretty much anywhere in NZ, in any direction, including the Interislander ferry across Cook Strait. The pass is purchased in blocks of travel time: minimum 15 hours ($119), maximum 60 hours ($449). The average cost of each block becomes cheaper the more hours you buy. You can top up the pass if you need more time.

Flexitrips An InterCity bus-pass system whereby you purchase a specific number of bus trips (eg Auckland to Tauranga would count as one trip) in blocks of five, with or without the Cook Strait ferry

trip included. Five/15/30 trips including the ferry cost $210/383/550 (subtract $54 if you don't need the ferry).

Aotearoa Adventurer, **Kiwi Explorer**, **Kia Ora New Zealand** and **Tiki Tour New Zealand** Hop-on/hop-off, fixed-itinerary nationwide passes offered by InterCity. These passes link up tourist hot spots and range in price from $645 to $1219. See www.travelpass.co.nz for details.

Naked Passport (www.nakedpassport.com) A Naked Bus pass that allows you to buy trips in blocks of five, which you can add to any time, and book each trip as needed. Five/15/30 trips cost $151/318/491. An unlimited pass costs $597 – great value if you're travelling NZ for long.

NORTH ISLAND PASSES

InterCity also offers 13 hop-on/hop-off, fixed-itinerary North Island bus passes, ranging from short $43 runs between Rotorua and Taupo, to $249 trips from Auckland to Wellington via the big sights in between. See www.travelpass.co.nz for details.

SOUTH ISLAND PASSES

On the South Island, InterCity offers 11 hop-on/hop-off, fixed-itinerary passes, ranging from $43 trips between Christchurch and Kaikoura, to $583 loops around the whole island. See www.travelpass.co.nz for details.

Shuttle Buses

As well as InterCity and Naked Bus, regional shuttle buses fill in the gaps between the smaller towns. Operators include the following (not a finite

list), offering regular scheduled services and/or charter tours:

Abel Tasman Travel (www.abeltasmantravel.co.nz) Traverses the roads between Nelson, Motueka, Golden Bay, and Kahurangi and Abel Tasman National Parks.

Alpine Scenic Tours (www.alpinescenictours.co.nz) Runs tours around Taupo and into Tongariro National Park, plus the ski fields around Mt Ruapehu and Mt Tongariro.

Atomic Shuttles (www.atomictravel.co.nz) Has services throughout the South Island, including to Christchurch, Dunedin, Invercargill, Picton, Nelson, Greymouth/Hokitika, Te Anau and Queenstown/Wanaka.

Cook Connection (www.cookconnect.co.nz) Triangulates between Mt Cook, Twizel and Lake Tekapo.

East West Coaches (www.eastwestcoaches.co.nz) Offers a service between Christchurch and Westport via Reefton.

Hanmer Connection (www.atsnz.com) Twice-daily services between Hanmer Springs and Christchurch.

Go Kiwi Shuttles (www.go-kiwi.co.nz) Links Auckland with Whitianga on the Coromandel Peninsula daily, with extensions to Rotorua in summer.

Knightrider (www.knightrider.co.nz) Runs a nocturnal service from Christchurch to Dunedin return. David Hasselhoff nowhere to be seen...

Topline Tours (www.toplinetours.co.nz) Connects Te Anau and Queenstown.

Tracknet (www.tracknet.net) Daily track transport (Milford, Routeburn, Hollyford, Kepler etc) between Queenstown, Te Anau, Milford Sound, Invercargill, Fiordland and the West Coast.

Trek Express (☎ 027 222 1872, 0800 128 735; www.trekexpress.co.nz) 4WD shuttle services to all tramping tracks in the South Island's top half.

Waitomo Wanderer (www.travelheadfirst.com) Does a loop from Rotorua or Taupo to Waitomo.

West Coast Shuttle (www.westcoastshuttle.co.nz) Daily bus from Greymouth to Christchurch and back.

Car & Motorcycle

The best way to explore NZ in depth is to have your own wheels. It's easy to hire cars and campervans at good rates.

Automobile Associations

NZ's **Automobile Association** (AA; ☎ 0800 500 444; www.aa.co.nz/travel) provides emergency breakdown services, maps and accommodation guides (from holiday parks to motels and B&Bs).

Members of overseas automobile associations should bring their membership cards – many of these bodies have reciprocal agreements with the AA.

Drivers Licences

International visitors to NZ can use their home country drivers licence – if your licence isn't in English, it's a good idea to carry a certified translation with you. Alternatively, use an International Driving Permit (IDP), which will usually be issued on the spot (valid for 12 months) by your home country's automobile association.

Fuel

Fuel (petrol, aka gasoline) is available from service stations across NZ: unless you're cruising around in something from the '70s, you'll be filling up with 'unleaded' or LPG (gas). LPG is not always stocked by rural suppliers; if you're on gas, it's safer to have dual-fuel capability. Aside from remote locations like Milford Sound and Mt Cook, petrol prices don't vary much from place to place: per-litre costs at the time of research were around $2.40.

Hire

CAMPERVAN

Most towns of any size have a camping ground or holiday park with powered sites (where you can plug your vehicle in) for around $35 per night. You can hire campervans from dozens of companies. Prices vary with season, vehicle size and length of rental.

A small van for two people typically has a minikitchen and foldout dining table, the latter transforming into a double bed. Larger 'superior' two-berth vans include shower and toilet. Four- to six-berth campervans are the size of trucks (and similarly sluggish) and, besides the extra space, usually contain a toilet and shower.

Over summer, rates offered by the main rental firms for two-/four-/six-berth vans start at around $160/200/290 per day for a month-long rental, dropping to as low as $45/60/90 per day in winter.

Major operators include the following:

Apollo (☎ 0800 113 131, 09-889 2976; www.apollocamper.co.nz)

Britz (☎ 0800 831 900, 09-255 3910; www.britz.co.nz) Also does 'Britz Bikes' (add a mountain or city bike from $13 per day).

Kea (☎ 0800 520 052, 09-448 8800)

Maui (☎ 0800 651 080, 09-255 3910; www.maui.co.nz)

United Campervans (☎ 0800 759 919, 09-275 9919; www.unitedcampervans.co.nz)

Wilderness Motorhomes (☎ 09-255 5300; www.wilderness.co.nz)

BACKPACKER VAN RENTALS

Budget players in the campervan industry offer slick deals and funky (often gregariously spray-painted: Jimi Hendrix, *Where The Wild Things Are,* Sly Stone etc), well-kitted-out vehicles for backpackers. Rates are competitive (from $35/50 per day for a two-/four-berth van May to September; from $100/150 per day December to February). Operators include the following:

Backpacker Sleeper Vans (☎ 0800 321 939, 03-359 4731; www.sleepervans.co.nz)

Escape Campervans (☎ 0800 216 171; www.escaperentals.co.nz)

Hippie Camper (📞 0800 113 131; www.hippiecamper.co.nz)

Jucy (📞 0800 399 736, 09-374 4360; www.jucy.co.nz)

Mighty Cars & Campers (📞 0800 422 267; www.mightycampers.co.nz)

Spaceships (📞 0800 772 237, 09-526 2130; www.spaceshipsrentals.co.nz)

Wicked Campers (📞 0800 246 870, 09-634 2994; www.wickedcampers.co.nz)

CAR

Remember that if you want to travel far, you need unlimited kilometres. Some (but not all) companies require drivers to be at least 21 years old.

Most car-hire firms suggest (or insist) that you don't take their vehicles between islands on the Cook Strait ferries. Instead, you leave your car at either Wellington or Picton terminal and pick up another car once you've crossed the strait. This saves you paying to transport a vehicle on the ferries, and is a pain-free exercise.

INTERNATIONAL RENTAL COMPANIES

The big multinational companies have offices in most major cities, towns and airports. Firms sometimes offer one-way rentals (eg collect a car in Auckland, leave it in Wellington), but there are often restrictions and fees.

The major companies offer a choice of either unlimited kilometres, or 100km (or so) per day free, plus so many cents per subsequent kilometre. Daily rates in main cities typically start at around $40 per day for a compact, late-model, Japanese car, and around $75 for medium-sized cars (including GST, unlimited kilometres and insurance).

Avis (📞 0800 655 111, 09-526 2847; www.avis.co.nz)

Budget (📞 0800 283 438, 09-529 7784; www.budget.co.nz)

Europcar (📞 0800 800 115; www.europcar.co.nz)

Hertz (📞 0800 654 321, 03-358 6789; www.hertz.co.nz)

Thrifty (📞 0800 737 070, 03-359 2721; www.thrifty.co.nz)

LOCAL RENTAL COMPANIES

Local rental firms dapple the *Yellow Pages*. These are almost always cheaper than the big boys – sometimes half the price – but the cheap rates may come with serious restrictions: vehicles are often older, and with less formality sometimes comes a less protective legal structure for renters.

Rentals from local firms start at around $30 per day for the smallest option. It's obviously cheaper if you rent for a week or more, and there are often low-season and weekend discounts.

Affordable, independent operators with national networks include the following:

a2b Car Rentals (📞 0800 545 000; www.a2b-carrentals.co.nz)

Ace Rental Cars (📞 0800 502 277, 09-303 3112; www.acerentalcars.co.nz)

Apex Rentals (📞 0800 939 597, 03-379 6897; www.apexrentals.co.nz)

Go Rentals (📞 0800 467 368, 09-525 7321; www.gorentals.co.nz)

Omega Rental Cars (📞 0800 525 210, 09-377 5573; www.omegarentalcars.com)

Pegasus Rental Cars (📞 0800 803 580, 03-548 2852; www.rentalcars.co.nz)

Transfercar (📞 09-630 7533; www.transfercar.co.nz) One-way relocation specialists.

Motorcycle

Born to be wild? NZ has great terrain for motorcycle touring, despite the fickle weather in some regions. Most of the country's motorcycle-hire shops are in Auckland and Christchurch, where you can hire anything from a little 50cc moped (aka nifty-fifty) to a throbbing 750cc touring motorcycle and beyond. Recommended operators (who also run guided tours) with rates from $80 to $345 per day:

New Zealand Motorcycle Rentals & Tours (📞 09-486 2472; www.nzbike.com)

Te Waipounamu Motorcycle Tours (📞 03-377 3211; www.motorcycle-hire.co.nz)

Insurance

Rather than risk paying out wads of cash if you have an accident, you can take out your own comprehensive insurance policy, or (the usual option) pay an additional fee per day to the rental company to reduce your excess. This brings the amount you must pay in the event of an accident down from around $1500 or $2000 to around $200 or $300. Smaller operators offering cheap rates often have a compulsory insurance excess, taken as a credit-card bond, of around $900.

Most insurance agreements won't cover the cost of damage to glass (including the windscreen) or tyres, and insurance coverage is often invalidated on beaches and certain rough (4WD) unsealed roads – read the fine print. NZ's Accident Compensation Corporation (p361) insurance scheme covers fault-free personal injury.

Road Hazards

Kiwi traffic is usually pretty light, but it's easy to get stuck behind a slow-moving truck or campervan – pack plenty of patience. There are also lots of slow wiggly roads, one-way bridges and plenty of gravel roads, all of which require a more cautious driving approach. And watch out for sheep!

To check road conditions call 0800 444 449 or see www.nzta.govt.nz/traffic/current-conditions.

Road Rules

Kiwis drive on the left-hand side of the road; cars are right-hand drive. Give way to the right at intersections.

At single-lane bridges (of which there are a surprisingly large number), a smaller red arrow pointing in your direction of travel means that *you* give way.

Speed limits on the open road are generally 100km/h; in built-up areas the limit is usually 50km/h. Speed cameras and radars are used extensively.

All vehicle occupants must wear a seatbelt or risk a fine. Small children must be belted into approved safety seats.

Always carry your licence when driving. Drink-driving is a serious offence and remains a significant problem in NZ, despite widespread campaigns and severe penalties. The legal blood alcohol limit is 0.08% for drivers over 20, and 0% (zero!) for those under 20.

Local Transport

Bus, Train & Tram

NZ's larger cities have extensive bus services but, with a few honourable exceptions, they are mainly daytime, weekday operations; weekend services can be infrequent or nonexistent. Negotiating inner-city Auckland is made easier by the Link and free City Circuit buses; Hamilton also has a free city-centre loop bus; Christchurch has a free city-shuttle service and the historic tramway (now open again after the earthquake). Most main cities have late-night buses for boozy Friday and Saturday nights.

The only cities with decent train services are Auckland and Wellington, with four and five suburban routes respectively.

Taxi

The main cities have plenty of taxis and even small towns may have a local service.

Train

KiwiRail Scenic Journeys (☎ 0800 872 467, 04-495 0775; www.tranzscenic.co.nz) operates four routes, listed below; reservations can be made through KiwiRail Scenic Journeys directly, or at most train stations (notably not at Palmerston North or Hamilton), travel agents and visitor information centres:

Capital Connection Weekday commuter service between Palmerston North and Wellington.

Coastal Pacific Between Christchurch and Picton.

Northern Explorer Between Auckland and Wellington.

TranzAlpine Over the Southern Alps between Christchurch and Greymouth.

Train Passes

A KiwiRail Scenic Journeys **Scenic Journey Rail Pass** (www.kiwirailscenic.co.nz/scenic-rail-pass) allows unlimited travel on all of its rail services, including passage on the Wellington–Picton Interislander ferry. There are two types of pass, both requiring you to book your seats a minimum of 24 hours before you want to travel:

Fixed Pass Limited duration fares for one/two/three weeks, costing $599/699/799 per adult (a little bit less for kids).

Freedom Pass Affords you travel on a certain number of days over a 12-month period; a three-/seven-/nine-day pass costs $417/903/1161.

Behind the Scenes

Our Readers

Many thanks to the travellers who used the last edition and wrote to us with helpful hints, useful advice and interesting anecdotes: Andrew Flint, Erin Crampton, Hailea Aragon, Jack Maniscalco, Jenna Cock and Lisa Lü.

Author Thanks

Charles Rawlings-Way

Huge thanks to Errol Hunt for signing me up (again); and to Glenn van der Knijff, Tasmin Waby and the in-house LP staff for following through post-Errol. Humongous gratitude to my tireless, witty and professional co-authors – Sarah, Peter, Brett and Lee – who infused this book with humour and local lowdown. Most of all, thank you Meg, Ione and Remy for holding the fort while I was away.

Acknowledgments

Climate map data adapted from Peel MC, Finlayson BL & McMahon TA (2007) 'Updated World Map of the Köppen-Geiger Climate Classification', Hydrology and Earth System Sciences, 11, 163344.

Cover photographs: Front: Mitre Peak and Milford Sound, AtomicZen/Getty; Back: Jetboating on the Buller River, South Island, Matthew Williams-Ellis/Alamy.

This Book

This 3rd edition of Lonely Planet's *Discover New Zealand* guidebook was researched and written by Charles Rawlings-Way, Brett Atkinson, Sarah Bennett, Peter Dragicevich and Lee Slater, who also worked on the previous edition. We would also like to thank the following people for their contributions to this guide: Professor James Belich (History), John Huria (Maori Culture) and Vaughan Yarwood (Environment). This guidebook was commissioned in Lonely Planet's London office, and produced by the following:

Commissioning Editor Errol Hunt
Destination Editor Tasmin Waby
Coordinating Editor Gabrielle Innes
Product Editor Briohny Hooper
Senior Cartographer Diana Von Holdt
Book Designers Virginia Moreno, Wendy Wright
Senior Editor Claire Naylor
Assisting Editors Kate Evans, Jenna Myers
Assisting Cartographer James Leversha
Assisting Book Designer Wibowo Rusli
Cover Researcher Naomi Parker
Thanks to Anita Bahn, Andrea Dobbin, Ryan Evans, Larissa Frost, Jouve India, Glenn van der Knijff, Kate Mathews, Katie O'Connell, Averil Robertson, Tracy Whitmey

Index

000 Map pages

000 Map pages

How to Use This Book

These symbols give you the vital information for each listing:

☑ Telephone Numbers	☎ Wi-Fi Access	☐ Bus
☺ Opening Hours	☰ Swimming Pool	☐ Ferry
P Parking	☑ Vegetarian Selection	M Metro
⊖ Nonsmoking	☑ English-Language Menu	S Subway
✳ Air-Conditioning	⊞ Family-Friendly	☐ Tram
@ Internet Access	☒ Pet-Friendly	

All reviews are ordered in our authors' preference, starting with their most preferred option. Additionally:

Sights are arranged in the geographic order that we suggest you visit them, and within this order, by author preference.

Eating and Sleeping reviews are ordered by price range (budget, mid-range, top end) and within these ranges, by author preference.

Map Legend

Sights
- ⊙ Beach
- ⊕ Buddhist
- ⊕ Castle
- ⊕ Christian
- ⊕ Hindu
- ⊕ Islamic
- ⊕ Jewish
- ⊕ Monument
- ⊕ Museum/Gallery
- ⊕ Ruin
- ⊕ Winery/Vineyard
- ⊕ Zoo
- ⊙ Other Sight

Activities, Courses & Tours
- ⊜ Diving/Snorkelling
- ⊜ Canoeing/Kayaking
- ⊕ Skiing
- ⊕ Surfing
- ⊜ Swimming/Pool
- ⊕ Walking
- ⊕ Windsurfing
- ⊕ Other Activity/ Course/Tour

Sleeping
- ⊟ Sleeping
- ⊠ Camping

Eating
- ⊗ Eating

Drinking
- ⊕ Drinking
- ⊜ Cafe

Entertainment
- ⊕ Entertainment

Shopping
- ⊕ Shopping

Information
- ⊠ Post Office
- ⊕ Tourist Information

Transport
- ⊕ Airport
- ⊗ Border Crossing
- ⊕ Bus
- ⊕ Cable Car/ Funicular
- ⊕ Cycling
- ⊜ Ferry
- ⊕ Monorail
- P Parking
- S S-Bahn
- ⊕ Taxi
- ⊕ Train/Railway
- ⊕ Tram
- ⊖ Tube Station
- U U-Bahn
- M Underground Train Station
- • Other Transport

Routes
- Tollway
- Freeway
- Primary
- Secondary
- Tertiary
- Lane
- Unsealed Road
- Plaza/Mall
- Steps
- ⊣ ⊢ Tunnel
- Pedestrian Overpass
- Walking Tour
- Walking Tour Detour
- Path

Boundaries
- – – – International
- – – – – State/Province
- – – Disputed
- – – – Regional/Suburb
- Marine Park
- Cliff
- Wall

Population
- ⊙ Capital (National)
- ⊙ Capital (State/Province)
- ⊙ City/Large Town
- ⊙ Town/Village

Geographic
- ⊕ Hut/Shelter
- ⊕ Lighthouse
- ⊕ Lookout
- ▲ Mountain/Volcano
- ⊕ Oasis
- ⊕ Park
-)(Pass
- ⊕ Picnic Area
- ⊕ Waterfall

Hydrography
- River/Creek
- Intermittent River
- Swamp/Mangrove
- Reef
- Canal
- Water
- Dry/Salt/ Intermittent Lake
- Glacier

Areas
- Beach/Desert
- Cemetery (Christian)
- Cemetery (Other)
- Park/Forest
- Sportsground
- Sight (Building)
- Top Sight (Building)

Our Story

A beat-up old car, a few dollars in the pocket and a sense of adventure. In 1972 that's all Tony and Maureen Wheeler needed for the trip of a lifetime – across Europe and Asia overland to Australia. It took several months, and at the end – broke but inspired – they sat at their kitchen table writing and stapling together their first travel guide, *Across Asia on the Cheap*. Within a week they'd sold 1500 copies. Lonely Planet was born.

Today, Lonely Planet has offices in Franklin, London, Melbourne, Oakland, Beijing and Delhi, with more than 600 staff and writers. We share Tony's belief that 'a great guidebook should do three things: inform, educate and amuse'.

Our Writers

CHARLES RAWLINGS-WAY

Coordinating Author, Rotorua & the Centre, Wellington & Lower North Island, Best of the Rest
English by birth, Australian by chance, All Blacks fan by choice: Charles' early understanding of Aotearoa was less than comprehensive (sheep, mountains, sheep on mountains). He realised there was more to it when a wandering uncle returned with a faux-jade tiki in 1981. He wore it with pride until he saw the NZ cricket team's beige uniforms in 1982. Mt Taranaki's snowy summit, Napier's art deco deliverance and Whanganui's raffish charm have helped him forgive: he's once again smitten with the country's phantasmal landscapes, disarming locals, and determination to sculpt its own political and indigenous destiny. Charles also wrote the Plan Your Trip and Survival Guide sections.

BRETT ATKINSON

Auckland, Best of the Rest Resident in Auckland, Brett leapt at the chance to research his home town for this edition. Highlights include exploring the city's emerging restaurant scene around Wynyard Quarter, and journeying to the diverse islands of the Hauraki Gulf. Excursions further afield to Northland and Coromandel echoed family holidays in an earlier century. Brett's contributed to Lonely Planet guidebooks spanning Europe, Asia and the Pacific, and covered almost 50 countries as a food and travel writer. See www.brett-atkinson.net for his latest travels.

SARAH BENNETT & LEE SLATER

Rotorua & the Centre, Wellington & Lower North Island, Marlborough & Nelson, Christchurch & Central South, Queenstown & the South, Best of the Rest Lee and Sarah live in Wellington, but spend many months on the road each year in their small campervan, boots on board, mountain bikes on the back. Specialists in 'soft-core adventure' (tramping without crampons), they re-imagine their journeys into magazine features, and guidebooks including Lonely Planet's *Hiking & Tramping in New Zealand*, four editions of *New Zealand*, as well as *The New Zealand Tramper's Handbook* and *Let's Go Camping*. Read more at www.bennettandslater.co.nz and follow on Twitter @BennettnSlater. They also wrote the New Zealand Today chapter.

PETER DRAGICEVICH

Christchurch & Central South, Queenstown & the South After nearly a decade working for offshore publishing companies, Peter's life has come full circle, returning to his home town of Auckland. As managing editor of *Express* newspaper he spent much of the '90s writing about the local arts, club and bar scene. He has worked on four editions of the *New Zealand* guide, after dozens of Lonely Planet assignments, it remains his favourite gig.

Read more about Peter at: lonelyplanet.com/thorntree/profiles/peterdragicevich

More Writers

Published by Lonely Planet Publications Pty Ltd
ABN 36 005 607 983
3rd edition – Nov 2014
ISBN 978 1 74220 788 9
© Lonely Planet 2014   Photographs © as indicated 2014
10 9 8 7 6 5 4 3 2 1
Printed in China

CONTRIBUTING WRITERS

Professor James Belich wrote the History chapter. James is one of New Zealand's pre-eminent historians and the award-winning author of *The New Zealand Wars*, *Making Peoples* and *Paradise Reforged*. He has also worked in TV – *New Zealand Wars* was screened in New Zealand in 1998.

John Huria (Ngai Tahu, Muaupoko) wrote the Maori Culture chapter. John has an editorial, research and writing background with a focus on Maori writing and culture. He was senior editor for Maori publishing company Huia and now runs an editorial and publishing services company, Ahi Text Solutions Ltd (www.ahitextsolutions.co.nz).

Vaughan Yarwood wrote the Environment chapter. Vaughan is an Auckland-based writer whose books include *The History Makers: Adventures in New Zealand Biography*, *The Best of New Zealand: A Collection of Essays on NZ Life and Culture by Prominent Kiwis*, which he edited, and the regional history *Between Coasts: From Kaipara to Kawau*. He has written widely for NZ and international publications and is the former associate editor of *New Zealand Geographic*, for which he has also written for many years.